This comprehensive manual is design
necessary background knowledge in environmental science required
to excavate and analyse archaeological sites by rivers and on floodplains. Part I covers the techniques for studying alluvial environments, while Part II reviews the literature on the archaeology of
alluvial environments. An important theme running through the
book is the interaction between climatic and cultural forces and the
transformation of riverine environments. Bringing together information on the evolution and exploitation of floodplain and river
landscapes, it draws on examples from Britain, Europe, North
America and Australasia. *Alluvial geoarchaeology* will also interest
physical geographers, geologists and environmental scientists.

ALLUVIAL GEOARCHAEOLOGY

CAMBRIDGE MANUALS IN ARCHAEOLOGY

Cambridge Manuals in Archaeology are reference handbooks designed for an international audience of professional archaeologists and archaeological scientists in universities, museums, research laboratories, field units, and the public service. Each book includes a survey of current archaeological practice alongside essential reference material on contemporary techniques and methodology.

ALLUVIAL GEOARCHAEOLOGY

Floodplain archaeology and environmental change

A. G. Brown
University of Exeter

CAMBRIDGE
UNIVERSITY PRESS

Published by the Press Syndicate of the University of Cambridge
The Pitt Building, Trumpington Street, Cambridge CB2 1RP
40 West 20th Street, New York, NY 10011-4211, USA
10 Stamford Road, Oakleigh, Melbourne 3166, Australia

First published 1997

Printed in Great Britain at the University Press, Cambridge

A catalogue record for this book is available from the British Library

Library of Congress cataloguing in publication data

Brown, A. G.
    Alluvial geoarchaeology: floodplain archaeology and environmental
change / A. G. Brown.
      p. cm.–(Cambridge manuals in archaeology.)
    Includes bibliographical references (p.) and indexes.
    ISBN 0 521 56097 7 – ISBN 0 521 56820 X (pbk)
    1. Excavations (Archaeology)–Handbooks, manuals, etc. 2. Water-
saturated sites (Archaeology)–Handbooks, manuals, etc. 3. Soil–
Analysis–Handbooks, manuals, etc. 4. Floodplain ecology–
Methodology–Handbooks, manuals, etc. 5. Archaeological geology–
Methodology–Handbooks, manuals, etc. I. Title. II. Series.
CC77.5.B76   1997
930.1'028–dc20   96-2413 CIP

ISBN 0 521 56097 7 hardback
ISBN 0 521 56820 X paperback

To Sara and Gabriel

CONTENTS

ix

Contents   xi

ILLUSTRATIONS

Plates

Figures

TABLES

PREFACE

The origins of this book may help to explain its existence, structure and content. Having undertaken doctoral research jointly supervised by a geomorphologist and a palaeoecologist which had strong archaeological implications, I was by the mid-1980s firmly situated in a multidisciplinary and interdisciplinary approach to fluvial environments. Whilst at Leicester University my contacts grew with researchers in other departments interested in alluvial environments, most notably Zoology, Botany and Archaeology. Increasing contact with archaeologists both at Leicester University and in Leicestershire and Northamptonshire Archaeological Units stimulated my interest in geoarchaeology and the cross-fertilisation of geomorphology and archaeology. This was given a research foundation when I realised that archaeologists were regularly digging large holes in floodplains and valued stratigraphic assistance. I worked first on the Raunds Area Project, Northamptonshire, and since then have worked on many alluvial sites in the Midlands of England and elsewhere. In 1989 I took a joint appointment between Geography and Archaeology at Leicester and began to teach environmental archaeology, which included geomorphology, to archaeologists. Contact with archaeologists on a daily basis has I hope benefited this book, not least through the undermining of the simplistic and naïve tendencies concerning culture and society that are all too typically held by natural scientists.

This book stems from this history and a desire to bring together work in a variety of disciplines pertinent to the study of alluvial archaeological sites and floodplain geomorphology and palaeoecology. The book was technically conceived on a train journey back to Leicester from the Institute of Archaeology in 1985 but as this is a short journey it took some years before writing began in earnest. Its writing was given further impetus by two factors: first the very limited and generally simplistic treatment of floodplain forms and processes in most textbooks, even advanced books, and secondly a need for students and researchers to have a source of multidisciplinary information on recent and contemporary alluvial environments. There are probably no processes on floodplains which are not in reality influenced by both physics and biochemistry (in the widest sense) and in most floodplains are simultaneously artifacts of human activity. It is extremely difficult for any scientist (an archaeologist in particular given the typical archaeological training) to find an entrance into cognate disciplines which may have great importance for the understanding of processes on floodplains. The compartmentalisation of knowledge into rather arbitrary 'disciplines' which has been given renewed impetus by recent economic and academic pressures is fundamentally counterproductive in subjects such as this. Whilst the book is primarily designed for archaeologists, geomorphologists and palaeoecologists it is hoped that it will also be of interest to others, in particular engineers and ecologists, involved in current and future attempts to improve our environment by the restoration of 'natural' floodplains.

Most of all I hope that this book exemplifies a firm belief of the author's, which is that, as in science and the arts, new knowledge, at least initially, springs from the association of previously unassociated phenomena.

ACKNOWLEDGEMENTS

To acknowledge all who have influenced this book would be impossible as its conception dates back several years and it draws on all who have influenced me from an indefinable date. There are, however, several groups of individuals and institutions that have given tangible help and are acknowledged here.

Many of the ideas and case studies in the book come from discussions with my colleagues at Leicester University. In particular I must thank Rob Young, Graeme Barker and John Rice for reading and commenting on earlier drafts. My work, and this book, has greatly benefited from association with members of the former Leicestershire Field Archaeology Unit, particularly Patrick Clay, and other field archaeologists including Chris Salisbury and Ian Meadows. Many archaeologists allowed me access to unpublished or in press material for which I thank them. I have drawn on geomorphologists who have run field visits, including Martin Thorpe, Mark Macklin, Jim Rose and Jeff Vandenberghe, for which I thank them, and on the intellectual background of the British Geomorphological Research Group and the Quaternary Research Association, and also my original mentors, K. J. Gregory, K. E. Barber and C. Vita-Finzi. I must also thank members of the Institute of Archaeology, London University, for inadvertently providing the initial impetus for the book.

The production of this book could not have been possible without the superb drawing skills of Kate Moore, Ruth Pocklington and Sylvia Holyoak at Leicester and Terry Bacon at Exeter. I must also thank the Central Photographic Unit at Leicester and Andrew Teed at Exeter for excellent photographic services.

Comments made on an earlier draft by at least three anonymous referees were, I believe, extremely useful in improving the whole book. I thank all those who have allowed me to use their work, and take full responsibility for errors of interpretation and fact. The prolonged gestation of this book has been made much easier by the efficient and helpful editorial support of Jessica Kuper. Proof reading was facilitated by the kindness and generosity of the archaeologists of the Rudi-Maetonium Project, Moldova. Lastly but certainly not least I must thank Sara Mills for her attempt to force stylistic improvements and for tolerance of the whole enterprise and G. Mills-Brown for not eating all the disks.

INTRODUCTION AND THE EXAMPLE
OF THE NILE

What makes riverine or 'alluvial' environments different, both from other environments and from each other, and how does this affect the archaeological record? How can we study environmental change in alluvial environments and what impact has it had on human populations? This book aims to answer these questions. It also aims to provide an introduction to the physical and biological aspects of alluvial environments which are central to an understanding of archaeology on, under and near floodplains. Questions of preservation, transportation, burial, environment and subsistence are all intimately related to the characteristics of the landscape and are also essential components in any archaeological interpretation. Another aim of the book is to introduce archaeological aspects of alluvial history to environmental scientists and geographers because the vast majority of, if not all, contemporary floodplains have to a greater or lesser degree been altered by human activity during the last 10,000 years. Indeed some have been so altered as to make them in part artifacts and as such indicators of the impact of humans on the environment. This book is therefore about both the impact of humans on their environment, and the impact of the environment on humans. In order to illustrate this and lead the reader through the complete cycle of the inference of cultural implications from the environmental data a classic example is used: the Nile. It is all too easy for specialists, be they archaeologists or geomorphologists, to work as part of a project team on a particular area or problem and never get to see the 'big picture'. This introductory chapter and the rest of the book, whilst promoting specialist analysis of environmental data, also tries to stress the importance of a wider awareness of the potential uses and abuses of such data. It is abuse of the data which has in the past led to the twin evils of environmental relativism (i.e. the view that the environment does not have any particular role to play) and environmental determinism (i.e. the view that environment determines human behaviour).

In the last few years there has been an explosion of interest in the archaeology of wetland and alluvial environments at the research level (Coles, 1992a; Needham and Macklin, 1992). This raises the question of whether there is any such thing as the archaeology of a physical environment such as coast, floodplains or mountains. The archaeology of a particular physical environment may be distinctive for two reasons. First, because much cultural history and all prehistoric culture can only be viewed through the physical and biological

1

Table Intro.1 *The components of geoarchaeology, adapted from Hassan (1979) and Goudie (1987).*

Components	Typical methods/data
1 site location	topographic maps, thematic maps, remote sensing, geographical information systems
2 geomorphological analysis of site environs	field mapping, stratigraphy, dating
3 regional stratigraphic studies	collation of geomorphological studies, remote sensing
4 sedimentary analysis of deposit	facies identification, studies of process and provenance, e.g. mineralogy, texture, mineral magnetics
5 palaeoenvironmental analysis	facies interpretation, palaeoecology, e.g. snails, pollen, wood, phytoliths, diatoms, insects
6 modelling relationships between human activities and landscape	correlation of environmental and cultural change, resource analysis, catchment area analysis, carrying capacity and Malthusian models
7 studies of natural hazards	most of the above
8 dating	radio-isotopes, luminescence dating, acid-racemisation, palaeomagnetic dating

remains of material culture. Therefore, irrespective of more elaborate theorising, the first step is the reconstruction of the material base of societies. The conditions of burial, which control the degree and bias of preservation, are therefore of fundamental importance for all archaeologists (Clarke, 1973). Like other natural environments, alluvial systems have particular preservation (or *taphonomic*) characteristics. Indeed, floodplains, along with some other environments such as salt marshes and sand dunes, can have an excellent archaeological 'memory'. The information preserved, while providing exciting possibilities for the reconstruction of past living conditions, is controlled by a variety of physical factors; some are independent of human action, e.g. astronomically forced climatic change, and some are caused by human impact. If archaeologists are to use absence of evidence as data (which it is difficult to avoid), then all possible causes of a lack of preservation must be understood. This realisation was one factor in the rise of the research area of *geoarchaeology* (use of geological methods in archaeology) from the late 1970s onwards. Originally the result of collaboration and contact between archaeologists and geologists or geomorphologists (Davidson and Shackley, 1976; Rapp and Gifford, 1985), it has now become a recognised sub-discipline within scientific archaeology. This has occurred side by side with increased interest in other aspects of environmental and landscape archaeology and there is a large overlap between geoarchaeology and both environmental and landscape archaeology as illustrated by Hassan's (1979) 'components of geoarchaeology' (Table Intro.1).

A major objective of both geoarchaeology and broader environmental archaeology is palaeoenvironmental reconstruction, because data on changes in natural environments are of archaeological significance. It is for this reason that the first half of the book concentrates on physical and biological processes of alluvial environments which affect the formation, survival and bias of archaeological evidence from alluvial sites. While based on scientific methods, both the questions asked and the interpretation of data are as open to alternative paradigms as is the rest of archaeology (Clarke, 1972).

Alluvial environments can also be said to have their own archaeology because throughout prehistory they have, despite great variability, been distinguishable from other environments in their resources and hazards. This has led in the past to somewhat grandiose claims being made for the sociocultural effects of alluvial settlement, including the development of hierarchical social systems (Wittfogel, 1957) and the rise, and in some cases fall, of urban societies such as Mohenjo-Daro (Jacobsen and Adams, 1958; Lambrick, 1967). Later work on the settlement patterns of the Tigris–Diyala floodplain based upon field survey (Adams, 1965; 1981) has enabled a more sophisticated level of analysis balancing environmental factors. Johnson's (1972) use of central place theory showed how important water transport networks were, relative to the optimum utilisation of usable land, for the location and pattern of settlements. However, the earlier over-simplistic and deterministic ideas illustrate a potential problem faced by most, if not all, geoarchaeological or environmental work. Namely, a neo-environmental determinism derived from correlations between environmental and artifactual evidence, as is caricatured by Burgess's suggestion that the cause of the apparent increase in the deposition of bronze artifacts in rivers, lakes and springs after 1500 BC was the development of a 'water-cult' related to increased precipitation and waterlogging (Burgess, 1980 cited in Shanks and Tilley, 1987). At the other extreme, some post-processual archaeologists relegate environmental evidence to an unimportant backdrop to the myths, traditions and experiences that condition human existence. This is environmental relativism as it implies that the particular nature of the environment will have had no significant impacts on that society or culture. This book lies, along with middle range theory, somewhere in between, taking as its starting point the specification of relations between environment, subsistence, technology and social ranking. The physical and biological resources of alluvial environments are seen as offering changing, complex and integrated sets of possibilities to human groups at costs which may or may not be acceptable *when judged in their own terms*. In this sense, the book follows a possibilistic view of the relationships between human behaviour and the environment. The environment not only filters and biases our initial data but must have affected the behaviour of our subjects in varied and subtle ways, including their perception of that environment. Alluvial environments are sensitive to changing climatic conditions and the Holocene has not been climatically constant

(Kutzbach and Street-Perrott, 1985; Goudie, 1992). So the interaction between the climatic signal in alluvial stratigraphies and the cultural signal forms an underlying theme of this book. Since both the reaction of fluvial systems to external forces and human environmental modifications are spatially variable, this theme must be considered at the appropriate scales and we should be wary of making long-distance correlations or generalised statements.

Part I of the book covers the principles underlying the physical and biological processes that operate in alluvial environments and the methods used in the study of these processes. Chapter 1 introduces floodplain evolution as this is essential for studies of environmental change and its relationship to human activity. Our knowledge of how floodplains have evolved is also dependent upon dating, which is covered in chapter 2. The interpretation of floodplain sediments and soils, covered in chapter 3, is a necessary part of all alluvial archaeology. This includes a basic understanding of the processes of river flow, sediment transport, erosion and deposition. An understanding of these fundamental factors is needed for the accurate interpretation of the fluvial 'jumbling' of artifacts. Most early prehistoric artifacts, and indeed sites, are reworked and disturbed. Hand-axes are little different from the normal pebbles carried by rivers, and sites may be little more than natural zones of accumulation of these 'pebbles'. However, because archaeologists attempt to interpret both axe form and artifact or site arrangement, the role of natural processes must be understood. In describing and interpreting an early prehistoric terrace site it is impossible for the archaeologist to ignore the palaeoenvironment and this normally means integrating the archaeology with some geomorphological interpretation of the site stratigraphy. In later prehistoric contexts, the floodplain may itself be seen, in part, as an artifact of human settlement within the catchment. In order to determine the real impact of cultures on fluvial systems the natural controls on those systems must be understood, otherwise there is a very real danger that the relationships between culture and environment are obscured. Floodplain excavations can provide a wealth of environmental data and chapter 4 deals with the methods of obtaining, analysing and interpreting archaeobotanical and archaeozoological data from floodplain sites.

Part II focuses on applications of these principles and techniques to the interpretation of artifacts, sites and the relationships between human activity and the alluvial environment. Chapter 5 concentrates on those studies where the archaeology is confined to artifacts within the floodplain stratigraphy. This is most typical of Old World Palaeolithic archaeology and much of North American archaeology. One of the geoarchaeological advantages of the alluvial environment is the preservation of many sites through burial, and the study of buried sites and the history of alluviation is discussed in chapter 6. This history is related, in part, to land use, and floodplains can provide excellent information on land use history, as described in chapter 7. Indeed the floodplain is an important component of nearly all archaeological landscape

studies. The last chapter explores the peculiarities of floodplains and low terraces for human occupation, and relationships between occupation and
environmental change. This includes what T. Evans (1990) has called the asymmetry of human activities in the valley as compared with the valley sides. Can
we assume that floodplain sites are rarely, if ever, simply sites that happen to be
near rivers, i.e. how are function and environment related? Both positive and
negative factors should be evaluated in any interpretation of floodplain settlement history, even if some of these factors are archaeologically invisible, such
as perceived risk. While this book focuses on valley bottoms as blocks of landscape, they must be related to the record from the rest of the landscape. As
Evans (1990) has stated: 'What wet sites share are preservation factors and
similar environments. To divorce them from their [dry] regional cultural/
chronological context necessarily pushes their interpretation towards functional universals and environmental determinism.'

This book is segmented so that those readers requiring the scientific/environ-
mental background to alluvial environments can commence with Part I but
those only requiring floodplain archaeology *per se* can commence with Part II.
The appendices are provided as elaboration of some of the more technical
material covered in Part I, but material which is essential to practical or experimental work. An exhaustive global coverage is clearly impossible, so the aim
throughout Part II is to take some of the more important or better-documented
sites, largely from North America and Europe, and present them in the light of
the theoretical discussion in Part I. The sites are united by the fact that, in every
case, site interpretation has involved an element, sometimes large, sometimes
small, of the reconstruction of a fluvial palaeoenvironment from stratigraphic
evidence.

In order to illustrate the overall theme of the book, i.e. how geological, geomorphological and hydrological methods can be used in alluvial archaeology,
I propose to start with a classic example: the fluvial history of the Nile. The
history of the Nile in recent times as well as in the more distant past is a
complex mix of environmental, economic and legal issues (Howell and Allen,
1994), and because of its supreme importance to the Pharaonic civilisations it
has been, and continues to be, the focus of much geoarchaeological study. This
work has included a wide variety of methodologies and data sources drawn
from subjects as diverse as Egyptology, geomorphology and climatology.

An introductory example: the Nile
The high Egyptian civilisation that emerged in the late fourth millennium BC
was not only located on the Nile floodplain but was entirely dependent upon
the Nile for its survival in an environment with virtually no rain and no fresh
groundwater supplies. The classic work of Wallis Budge (1926) gives us some
insight into the importance of the Nile in Egyptian life through its mythology
and culture. Egyptians called the Nile Hapi which was also the name of the

Fig. Intro.1 Hapi the Nile God. The frog (a symbol of new birth) and the lotus plants on his head reflect the crucial role of the Nile in Egyptian agriculture as both appeared as a result of the flood. Adapted from Wallis Budge (1926).

God of the Nile. The God Hapi was depicted as a man with woman's breasts (Figure Intro.1), indicating strength, and powers of fertility and nourishment. They celebrated the God at the festivals of inundation, and because of the central role of the river in the Egyptian economy the collection of accurate hydrological records began in the First Dynasty (*c.* 3000 BC) with the engraving of maximum annual flood height on a large stone stele. The first Nilometer (fixed recording device or structure) was cut into the rocks at Samnah in the Twelfth Dynasty (*c.* 2200–2000 BC). The Nile's behaviour formed the basis of the oldest Egyptian calendar, which divided the year up into three parts, one of which (Akhet) was the main flood season. The height of the flood controlled the amount of land watered and therefore the supply and cost of bread. If the Nile reached a height of 16 cubits food supplies would normally be sufficient to supply the population for a year and this was celebrated in the 'Wafa' festival. If the flood reached 18 cubits and the middle lands were flooded the 'Neirouz' festival inaugurated the new year's day of the agricultural year, and if 20 cubits was reached the 'Saleeb' festival was held, celebrating the flooding of the high lands (Evans, 1990). Successions of 'low Niles' always produced famines such as the seven-years famine which occurred in the Third Dynasty (*c.* 3190–3100 BC). The Nile was probably just as important in pre-Dynastic and post-Dynastic times, and so its Holocene history is an essential part of the archaeology of Egypt.

The geomorphological history of the Nile has been reconstructed from studies of repeating sequences (cyclothems) of deposits in its delta (Stanley and Maldonaldo, 1979), sediments in the lower and middle valley (Butzer and Hanson, 1968; Adamson *et al.*, 1980) and deposits in the swamps of Sudan (Williams, 1966). The archaeological importance of the alluvial environment has favoured interdisciplinary approaches as typified by the surveys of Caton-Thompson and Gardner (1932) and Sandford and Arkell (1939) and later by the work of Butzer. Butzer's (1976) 'cultural ecology' approach is quintessentially geoarchaeological, including studies of valley sediments, geomorphology and ecology. The valley which Butzer describes is bounded by limestone hills to the west and cliffs to the east (Figure Intro. 2). It is floored by Pleistocene sand and gravel and there has been a long-term tendency for the river to migrate towards the eastern side of the valley. During the glacial maximum (*c.* 20,000–12,500 bp) the Nile was a highly seasonal braided river system with massive floods over four times larger than historical floods and periods of the year with no flow at all. This regime was caused by cold dry conditions in the East African Highlands and it produced a wide floodplain some 40 m above the present level between the first and second cataracts, where it corresponds with the area of the Sebilian culture. The Pleistocene period, which ended with overflow from Lake Victoria and increased rainfall in Ethiopia, was followed in the Holocene by permanent river flow and a period of extreme floods which caused incision of the river into its floodplain (Adamson *et al.*, 1980).

Up until about 5000 years ago higher rainfall than present in Ethiopia and a lack of flood storage in the slowly developing Sudd swamp resulted in centuries of high floods. These floods caused cycles of deposition and incision until Egypt and Nubia became more arid and less extreme when floods began to deposit the Arminna/Kibdi silts annually on the narrow Egyptian floodplain. Silt and sand deposition has produced natural levees and a domed cross-profile (Figure Intro. 3). Both sediments and surface features also indicate the presence of more channels in the past, some of which, such as the Bahr Yusef, still exist today. The existence of these former channels helps to explain the location of some Ptolemaic and older settlements such as Aphroditopolis and Heracleopolis. There is also documentary evidence of their existence (Strabo 17:1.4). In between these channels were large floodbasins which were flooded to a depth of about 1.5 m in a normal flood (Butzer, 1976). In its natural state the floodplain vegetation would have been evergreen forest of fig and acacia fringing the channels, and grassland or acacia-scrub savannah on the seasonally inundated flats. Palaeolithic settlements, such as those mapped by Butzer and Hanson (1968) in the Kom Ombo Plain, cluster on levees and riverbanks. This allowed easy utilisation of a variety of resources, including wildfowling in

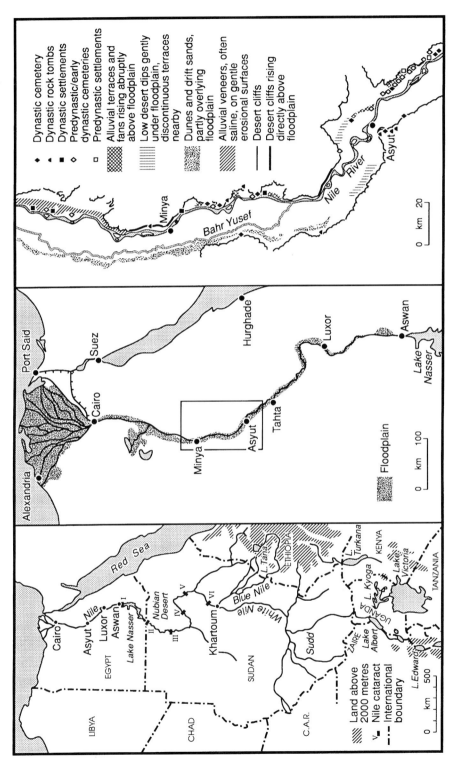

Fig. Intro.2 Map of the Nile catchment and Egyptian Nile valley showing major geomorphological features and localities mentioned in the text. Based in part on the pre-dynastic site survey by Butzer (1982) and Adamson et al. (1980).

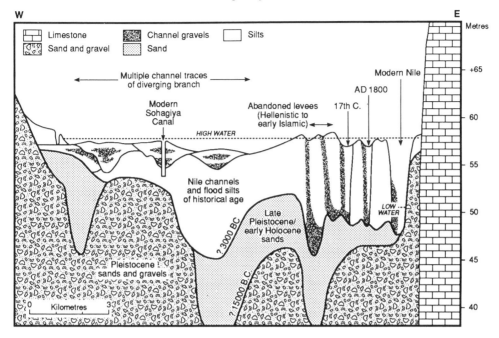

Fig. Intro.3 Simplified Nile valley cross-section near Tahta. Aapted from Butzer (1976).

the Nile and papyrus-filled cutoff meanders and backswamps and hunting big game on the open flats. Early farming communities occupied similar locations, planting crops in the wet soils after the floods and grazing animals on the alluvial flats. Artificial irrigation (which can involve as little as a few channels cut across levees) began in the late pre-Dynastic period and greatly increased the area of annual cropland and decreased the threat from poor floods. From then on, the Nile flood was managed; this included the construction of canals, dykes to confine floodwaters and facilitate transport, embankments and in upper Egypt the construction of large floodbasins. Every town and village was expected to contribute labour for this work which was supervised by the king's officials through the governors of each of the forty-two nomes or districts.

A key element in the river and flood management was recording flood heights. Undoubtedly the best-known and oldest flood records are from the Nile, and they extend back almost continuously to AD 622 with fragmentary records extending back to 3100 BC. In nearly all the dynasties some records were made of high and low floods. The Nile flood is supplied by summer monsoon rains over Ethiopia (Riehl *et al.*, 1979), while the winter flow of the river depends upon the rains near the equator. The river is therefore a barometer of two components of the climatic system and a good indicator of climatic change.

There are, however, many problems in trying to reconstruct climate from a flood series derived from this data. The completion of a full series is prevented by inconsistency between the records of different periods, with different datums being used, and even different measuring scales (Bell, 1970). The longest early fragment lasts from early in the First Dynasty (about 3050 BC) to the Fifth Dynasty (around 2500 BC). It was carved onto what is now known as the Palermo stone. Even this data set is not without problems, as Helck (1966) thinks that the largest flood value in the array may be fictitious and was invented for religious purposes. Bell (1970) has attempted a partial hydrological analysis of this data by converting it to metres. This involves assuming that two spans equals 0.524 m. Since the datum is unknown an arbitrary relation is used to compare the series with a modern series from the Nilometer at El-Roda, Cairo. The problem of the datum height is complicated by the aggradation of the river and floodplain and Bell (1970) has used a value of 1 mm yr^{-1} (derived from Butzer, 1959), to correct for this effect. Whether this is appropriate or not depends upon the measuring device that was used. The data come from the Memphis Nilometer, which if it was of the portable kind would have had a zero which moved up with the floodplain; if, however, it was of the fixed kind with a scale carved on a wharf or special well, then it would have had a fixed zero and the correction would be inappropriate. The surviving Nilometers such as that at El-Roda are Graeco-Roman and are large stilling wells often with galleries which allow water to pour in as the river level rises. Using either of the assumptions it is clear that the average flood heights decreased (from what may have been a high period) from the First to the Second Dynasty (about 3100 BC to 2800 BC), reflecting a decrease in the amount of rain from the summer monsoon over East Africa (see Figure Intro. 2). The Dynastic records show great famines caused by droughts and failure of the yearly floods in the periods 2180–2130 BC, 2000–1950 BC and around 1750 BC. Bell (1971) and Evans (1990) have argued that the First Dark Age of Egypt was brought on by a prolonged and intense drought; however, the death of Pepi II and political fragmentation were also important in the decline to anarchy that occurred at the end of the Sixth Dynasty. From the records of twenty-eight floods found in Nubia, Bell (1975) argues that during the period 1840–1770 BC there were a number of phenomenally high floods. Calculations using the stable cross-section of the second cataract with a stage 10 m higher than the average flood of the twentieth century give a discharge of 32×108 m^3 day^{-1} (22.2×105 m^3 s^{-1}). This flood was three times the magnitude of the largest floods of the last hundred years and would have been catastrophic, with a water depth on the floodplain of between 4 and 2 m above the modern flood level. Records are unavailable for the New Kingdom and the Late Dynastic period (1570–332 BC) but there are records of exceptionally high floods in the ninth to seventh centuries BC, the fifth century BC, and the first centuries AD. Flood heights increased again in the period AD 600–1000.

These records have been supplemented by excavations of Dynastic sites. The

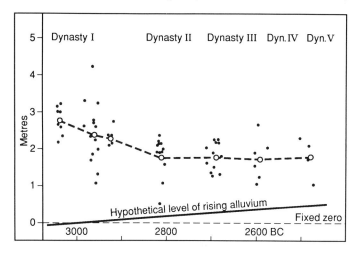

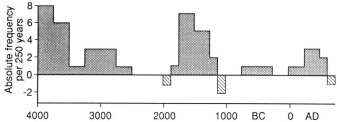

Fig. Intro.4 Height of Nile floods in metres above an arbitrary datum
(x=average) and calibrated ^{14}C for increased lake volumes in the Sahara and East
Africa since 5000 BC. Adapted from Bell (1970) and Butzer (1976).

West Bank site of Aksha in Lower Nubia showed that, at the time the temple
of Rameses II was built, average floods were a metre higher than today. The evidence for this was flood silts deposited on foundations and evidence of the
cultivation of riverside dunes without lift irrigation (Heinzelin, 1964). As
Butzer (1976) has shown, the Nile flood record agrees with the record from
East African lakes (Figure Intro.4) and from the Chad basin, but it shows
much greater short-term variability, as would be expected from the nature of
the data. The most marked trend is the desiccation after the First Dynasty
floods, and a period of at least eight centuries of a drier climate throughout
tropical Africa. The abnormally high floods around 1800 BC ushered in a
wetter period which lasted about six centuries and ended abruptly in 1150 BC.
From then to the present the Nile has fluctuated around the modern mean with
notable periods of higher and lower floods superimposed upon this trend
(Butzer, 1976). One example is the seventeenth century, when very high levels
of the yearly floods indicating heavy summer rains in Ethiopia, with low levels
at other times of the year, suggested less equatorial rain. This indicates that the
Little Ice Age regime persisted especially far south in longitudes near the

Greenwich meridian (Lamb, 1982). As early as 1925 Bliss had noted a correlation between Nile discharge and a large-scale climatic phenomenon, the Southern Oscillation.

The Nile is in one of the two principal areas on the globe affected by the Southern Oscillation, by which is meant below-normal atmospheric pressure in the central and southern Pacific at the same time as above-normal pressure across Australia, south-east Asia and the Indian Ocean. This can produce the so called El Niño events, when unusually warm water appears off the Peruvian coast and stretches into the central Pacific (called an El Niño–Southern Oscillation event). These ENSO events can cause abnormal weather conditions worldwide, and in particular affect the south-west monsoon which brings rain to the Ethiopian Highlands in July and September. Although the Nile seems particularly sensitive to these climatic phenomena, owing to the climatically marginal nature of most of its catchment, variations in the discharge of other large rivers of Africa, India, Australia and China also correlate with ENSO events (Whetton *et al.*, 1990). The Nile flood record also contains cycles associated with both the moon (18.6) and the Gleisberg solar cycle (78 years). One result of these global processes is the sequential occurrence of runs of dry and wet years, the so-called Hurst phenomena. The heavy reliance of Egyptian civilisations on the magnitude of the Nile floods and especially climatically determined sequences or 'runs' of low and high floods has been seen as being of crucial importance in the interpretation of the rise and fall of dynasties; however, other factors, such as wars and internal feuds, were involved and should not be ignored. Instead they should be considered in the light of economic stress caused by environmental change.

Although the floods and droughts certainly did cause some changes in settlement patterns and affected national and personal prosperity, the archaeological record shows that this was not always the case. For example Trigger (1970) has shown that Arminna in Nubia, which was a riverbank settlement, remained prosperous throughout a period of damagingly high floods (AD 600–1000). Studies of societies' adaptation *in situ* are probably more revealing about human environmental relations than the many studies which have 'explained' abandonment in the face of environmental stress.

We see in the geoarchaeology of the Nile an environment highly sensitive to global climatic changes, and in its cultural history great environmental awareness, illustrating that environmental change needs to be considered along with other causes of economic, cultural and social change. This consideration must, by definition, be multi- and interdisciplinary. As Figure Intro.5 illustrates, different links in the chain of culture–environment relationships require different methods of analysis ranging from sedimentology to documentary history.

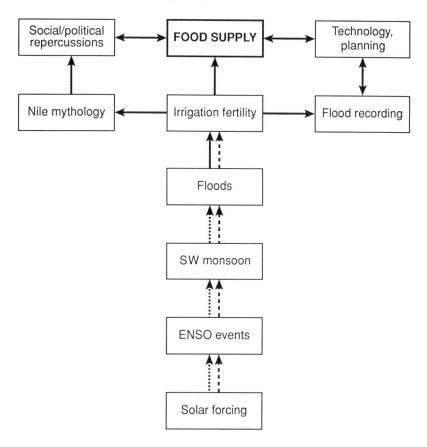

Fig. Intro.5 The climate–culture chain of the Nile valley.

PART I

PRINCIPLES

1

FLOODPLAIN EVOLUTION

Floodplains are one of the most conspicuous and widespread of all the land-forms on the earth. They are the result of both erosional and depositional processes. Over time they develop and change and so they evolve, not to any end-point but to the form that they are today or were at any point in the past. The study of the processes and history of floodplain formation is in part a historical science (i.e. geology) and has much in common with scientific archaeology in both its history and methodology. An understanding of the fundamental processes and products of floodplain evolution is essential for the interpretation of sites in alluvial contexts and can yield fascinating insights into human–environment relationships.

1.1 Floodplain evolution: an introduction

Floodplains may be simply defined as the flat areas adjacent to rivers liable to flooding. Floodplains are also complex assemblages of landforms which, as shown in Figure 1.1, include: channel features such as bedforms (ripples and dunes) and bars (e.g. point-bars), channel-edge features such as banks, benches and levées, and floodplain features such as old channels (oxbows), old levees (scroll-bars), backswamps and crevasse-splays. The formation and character of these features will be covered later in this chapter. The existence, development and arrangement of such features is a record of the past history of the river and they may also subtly constrain the current activity of the river. It is necessary to understand something of the processes of formation in order to be able to read the history of a river and its floodplain and infer any constraints or opportunities it might have conferred on past societies. Our ability to 'read' the history of a floodplain from its sediments has come from experimental studies of river sedimentation and observations of contemporary rivers in many different environments.

A basic description of the main morphological features common on flood-plains is given in Table 1.1, but they can be catagorised as bedforms (ripples, dunes, etc.), bars (point-bars, alternating bars, etc.), benches (including concave benches), floodplain landforms (levées, sloughs, etc.) and channels. These are differentiated on the basis of location (i.e. in-channel or out-of-channel), their shape (morphology) and where appropriate their composition (i.e. typical grain size of the sediments). However, none of these criteria is sufficient alone and a combination is used in the identification of alluvial facies.

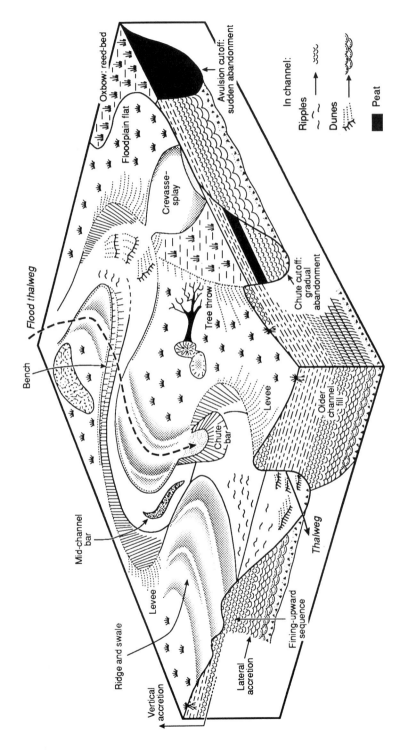

Fig. 1.1 Block diagram of landforms associated with a meandering river and its floodplain. Adapted from Allen (1965), and other sources.

For example ripples and dunes can be formed on the floodplain by overbank flows although they will generally be subsequently destroyed. The shape of benches produced by sedimentation and bank failure may be identical and overbank sediments and in-channel pool sediments may have exactly the same grain size distribution. However, a combination of stratigraphy and grain size analysis can generally identify these features from excavations or boreholes. The reason for this is that, whilst not unique, the grain size and morphology of these features reflect the processes of formation. The sedimentology of these features is discussed further in chapter 3 and details of grain size analysis can be found in appendix 2.

As early as 1906 it was realised that floodplains were not solely created by floods (Fenneman, 1906) but that deposits formed by river migration were also an important component. Although well established in the literature, the terms vertical sediments, as used to refer to overbank deposits, and lateral sediments, as used to refer to within-channel deposits, are not ideal, as within-channel deposits may have an important vertical element from deposition at the shoulder of the point-bar and on the banks (Taylor and Woodyer, 1978). Similarly, overbank sediments may not be laterally synchronous, as the location of the river may shift both over time, as may crevasse-splays which are caused by levée failures. Sediments other than those produced by floods or channel migration are also common in floodplain sequences; these include lacustrine sediments deposited in floodplain lakes, windblown sediment including loess (usually reworked, *cf.* Burrin and Scaife, 1984) and colluvium from adjacent hillslopes (Brown, 1992). In large systems such as the lower floodplains and deltas of the Rhine active windblown dunes have frequently formed during the Holocene and are recorded in sedimentary sequences (Törnqvist, 1993). In very active geomorphic regions (i.e. high slopes and/or flashy hydrometeorological regimes) another set of sediments may be present, including landslide, debris-flow and mudflow deposits. Although less common in temperate regions, throughout the Holocene, they can be important in upland areas where the result can be the destruction or burial of archaeological evidence, leaving little from which to construct the palaeoenvironment of the site.

Many sedimentology textbooks (e.g. Reineck and Singh, 1973) contain idealised floodplain cross-sections in order to illustrate the different types of floodplain sediments and their spatial relationships. However, there is no universal floodplain model because the occurrence of, and relative proportions of, each sediment type are controlled by river-type and behaviour and are therefore themselves measurable parameters of a floodplain fill. Figure 1.1 shows a segment of floodplain created by a meandering channel and Figure 1.2 shows three different but typical multiple-channel floodplains, each associated with different dominant modes of sedimentation: (a) a low-sinuosity sandy braided (unstable multiple-channel) system, (b) an intermediate sinuosity anastomosing (stable multiple-channel) system, and (c) a sinuous, avulsion-dominated

Table 1.1 *A summary of the sedimentary features and the mode of formation of the major micro-landforms found on floodplains. For more details of the sedimentology of these features and the conditions under which they are formed see chapter 3 and sedimentology texts or fieldguides such as Tucker (1982). For more details of the processes of formation consult a standard fluvial hydrology text such as Knighton (1984) or Richards (1982).*

Feature	Description	Formation
Ripples	Characteristic wave-like cross-sectional forms, either straight or crescentic in planform up to 2000 mm in length and 250 mm in height. Composed of sand.	Bedforms caused by the migration of sand under moderate water flow. Can be used to indicate current strength and flow depth. May exist on dunes (climbing ripples).
Dunes	Characteristic wave-like cross-section and planform similar to ripples but larger. Normally sand but can be composed of sand and gravel if formed by catastrophic flows.	Bedforms created by the migration of sand under slightly higher flow regimes and/or greater depths than ripples (but still lower-regime flow).
Alternating bars	D-shaped planform growing out from the banks into the channel, composed of sand and/or gravel but frequently grading from silt and sand at the edges to gravel by the bank.	Bed/channel forms caused by the deposition of sand and gravel at alternating sides of the channel associated with pool and riffle development in relatively straight reaches.
Point-bars	D-shaped planform growing out from the banks into the channel, composed of sand and/or gravel but frequently grading from silt and sand at the edges to gravel by the bank.	Bed/channel forms caused by the deposition of sand and gravel on the inner side of meanders (slip-off slopes).
Transverse-bars	Variable in planform from triangular to lenticular, across or diagonal to the flow. Either sand and/or gravel. Includes rifles.	Bed/channel forms caused by flow divergence associated with pool and riffle formation.
Mid-channel bars	Variable but typically lenticular/diamond in planform. Sand and/or gravel.	Bed/channel forms caused by flow divergence at high discharges and the development of braided river patterns. Can become part of the floodplain if stabilised by vegetation. Can also be formed by the dissection of point - or alternating bars.
Channel-junction bars	Typically triangular in planform jutting out across the mouth of one of the channels or forming a continuation of the apex of the junction. Sand and/or gravel.	Bed/channel forms which are produced by changes in flow at channel junctions and differences in the flow and/or sediment load between the main channel and tributary.

Feature	Description	Cause
Benches	Shelves or 'benches' on the bank of the channel. Generally sand, silt and clay.	Various causes from bank failure to bank sedimentation. Bank sedimentation may occur on bank failure, on channel bars or directly onto the bank often aided by vegetation.
Concave benches	Benches concave in planform formed against the upstream limb of the concave bank of tightly curving meanders and just downstream of point-bars. Often separated from the floodplain by a secondary channel on the line of the original concave bank (can form island or islets). Sand and silt/mud.	Caused by expanded flow resulting in flow separation and suspended load deposition downstream of the point-bar. Typical of rapidly migrating rivers (Nanson and Page, 1983).
Levees	Linear mounds of sand running adjacent to the edge of the channel.	Floodplain forms caused by deposition of sand at the point at which the flood waters spill out from the channel across the floodplain.
Crevasse-splays	In planform, fan-shaped lobes of sand and gravel.	Floodplain forms caused by a breach in the levees allowing bed material to be deposited on the floodplain flat.
Scroll-bars	Wave-like in cross-section and curved in planform. Composed of sand and silt.	Old levees associated with a laterally migrating channel.
Sloughs	Depressions in the floodplain surface normally curved in planform. If infilled will contain silt and clay.	Typically found between scroll-bars and either non-levee floodplain or partially infilled channels. In some cases they may also be formed or amended by flood scour.
Cutoffs/ oxbow lakes/ palaeochannels	Linear depressions in the floodplain surface, often asymmetric and either straight (ribbon lakes) or curved. If infilled may contain any sediment but typically silt, clay and peat.	Floodplain features formed by the abandonment of a former river channel by avulsion, chute or neck cutoff.
Flood channels	Floodplain features, generally straight linear depressions in the floodplain often cutting across the neck of a meander core or running at the edge of the floodplain.	Channels which only function during floods but before the river has overtopped its levees. They are generally old channels which have partially silted up but they can be caused by convergence of flow and the floodplain and scour.
Meander cores	Circular to D-shaped areas bounded by a meander. May be composed of in-channel sediments and/or overbank sediments. Commonly covered by scroll-bars.	Caused by the meander planform of the river so often the result of successive lateral levee and point-bar deposits. Can, however, be old vertically accreted floodplain or bedrock.
Floodbasins/ hams	Large areas behind the levees, very flat and featureless, underlain by silt and clay.	Caused by overbank accretion of silt and clay and protection from coarse sand deposition by levees and from meander migration.
Yazoos	Tributary channels running down the floodplain sub-parallel to the main river.	Formed where levees prevent the tributary from joining the main river. The junction may also migrate downstream owing to junction sedimentation. Named after the river Yazoo, a tributary of the Mississippi.

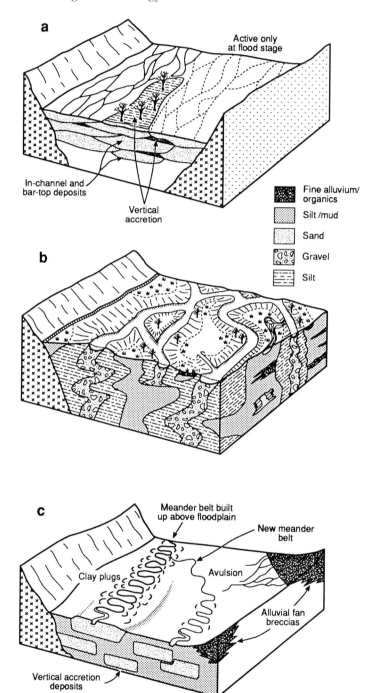

Fig. 1.2 Idealised and simplified floodplain sedimentary systems: (a) a low-sinuosity sandy-braided floodplain, (b) an intermediate sinuosity anastomosing floodplain, and (c) a sinuous avulsion-dominated floodplain. Adapted from diagrams in Smith and Smith (1980) and Allen (1965).

system. In reality these types are not always discrete, with combinations such as meandering multiple channels and intermediate types. Each of these channel-floodplain types can be seen as part of a continuum which may operate spatially, from one reach to another, or temporally, when the dominant mode of floodplain sedimentation changes as a result of changing flow, sediment calibre (size) or sediment availability. This idealised pattern is further complicated by the fact that rivers very rarely if ever start off with a 'clean slate'; some landforms inherited from a preceding regime will remain and influence contemporary processes of floodplain formation. This is the antecedence described by Croke and Nanson (1991), or inheritance, as described by Brown (1989) from the river Perry in Shropshire, England. In the Perry valley, the distribution of Holocene sediment types and rates of deposition was largely controlled by inherited downstream changes in slope which have caused relative downstream variation in stream power.

We know more about small meandering streams and their associated floodplain sediments than other channel types; this is partly due to the classic study by Wolman and Leopold (1957). They proposed a model of floodplain formation based on geomorphologic reasoning and observations of a small stream in the USA, Watts Branch Creek. In their model, overbank or flood deposits are progressively limited because as each flood layer is deposited it requires successively higher, and therefore more infrequent floods to overtop the banks, leading in time to a decrease in the rate of overbank sedimentation. They argued that this self-limiting system restricted the occurrence of overbank sediments to approximately 20% of the sedimentary fill. This argument was supported by the observation that rivers had a constant recurrence interval of bankfull discharge. However, as Kennedy (1972) has pointed out, even the data they used do, in fact, show that bankfull recurrence interval can vary by a factor of four. We now know that, within broad limits, bankfull is very variable, both reach-to-reach and within reaches, and that it can change, even over short periods of time. There are two important assumptions that underpin the Wolman and Leopold (1957) model. The first is that there is no deposition on the channel bed as this would facilitate a constant, or even increasing, rate of overbank deposition (i.e. both bed and floodplain aggradation) and the second is that the channel migrates across the entire width of the floodplain. Most channels do not do this, especially those of larger rivers; instead they oscillate across a relatively small belt or belts of the floodplain. A good example of this is the Brahmaputra in Bangladesh where the meander belt itself displays a meandering pattern (Coleman, 1969) and has migrated as a result of tectonic activity. Indeed, we can say that rivers commonly display a preferred position within floodplains, which is one possible cause of floodplain and valley cross-sectional asymmetry (Palmquist, 1975). Also, *some* rivers are remarkably stable over long periods of time despite having a meandering planform. For these reasons, exactly the opposite ratio between lateral and vertical sediments to that predicted by the Wolman and Leopold model is possible, as for example is

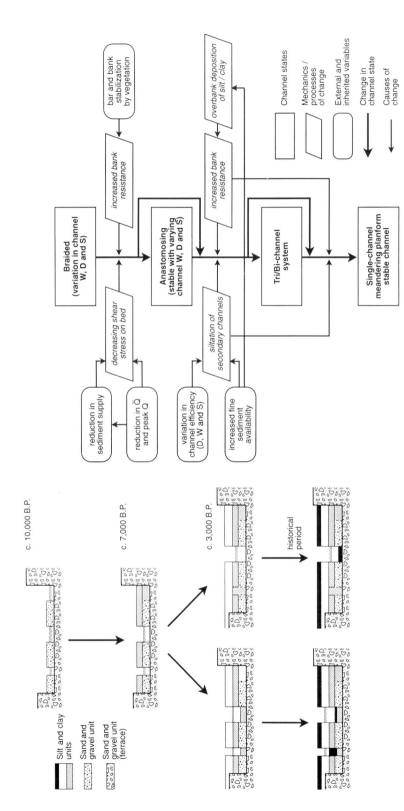

Fig. 1.3 The stable-bed aggrading-banks (SBAB) model of floodplain and channel evolution, which facilitates a continued linear rate of increase in floodplain elevation and a constant recurrence interval of overbank events due to the increase in flow passing down the primary channel as secondary channels silt up.

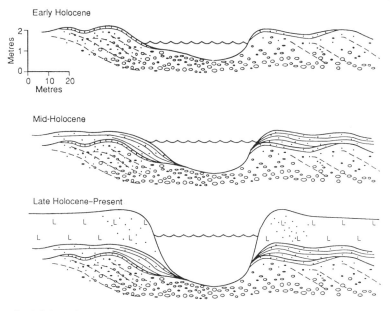

Fig. 1.3 (*cont.*)

the case with the floodplain of the Delaware river in the USA (Ritter *et al.*, 1973). The Wolman and Leopold model remains valid for the type of system they studied, which is a relatively small floodplain with a relatively high stream power. Their model also highlighted the importance of bed aggradation and degradation for the control of channel form and the mode of floodplain sedimentation.

Since overbank sedimentation is also controlled by the flood-series and sediment concentrations, there can also be continuing floodplain aggradation with no change in bed height, given increased flood magnitudes or sediment availabilities. This mechanism for floodplain evolution has been referred to as the stable-bed aggrading-banks (SBAB) model by Brown and Keough (1992a), and illustrated in Figure 1.3. The increase in bankfull capacity produced by the aggradation of the banks is one of the ways in which a constant discharge can be accommodated as the system changes from an anastomosing pattern to a single-thread meandering pattern or alternatively it may be how the river adjusts to an increase in discharge caused by climate or land use change.

1.2 River channel change and floodplains

From the preceding introduction to floodplain formation, it should be evident that channel change has important effects on floodplain sedimentation. The ability of a river to modify its planform and shape arises from a number of factors including the volume, timing and character of water and sediment supplied from upper reaches and the nature of the river's bed and banks (Church,

1992). When investigating channel change we frequently run into a methodological difficulty; this is the danger of regarding only measurable change as sedimentologically important. To avoid this problem, zero measurable change should also be regarded as one channel-change typology. The need for this approach is exemplified by Hooke's (1977) study of channel change in Devon, England. She used old maps to estimate rates of channel migration, and her results indicated that the rate of migration was very variable but could be as high as 100 m in fifty years. At this rate the entire floodplain could be reworked in well under 500 years; however, the *variability* of the rates and nature of the change complicate this picture. The mobility estimates were derived from a maximum of 40% of the basin stream length, and the other 60% showed no change at all. In addition Hooke's (1977) analysis and later work (Lewin, 1987) illustrate the frequent oscillatory nature of channel migration whereby the channel oscillates either side of a preferred path within the floodplain, leaving large areas of the floodplain untouched for hundreds, and possibly thousands of years. What these and other similar studies indicate is that even in active foothill floodplains there are reaches which are historically mobile and reaches which are not. Indeed Ferguson (1981) has drawn attention to the remarkable lack of mobility of many lowland rivers in the UK. This phenomenon, which is equally applicable to much of mainland Europe and the eastern USA is caused by generally resistant banks formed by cohesive silts, clays and peats and rather low stream power caused by non-flashy regimes and low regional slopes (Brown, 1987a). As might be expected therefore, the opposite is the case in the uplands where there are non-cohesive banks formed by sand and gravel and higher stream power caused by more flashy regimes and higher slopes. Indeed the power:resistance ratio is the most obvious control on modes and rates of channel change.

In meandering systems the most common type of channel change is meander migration. This can be classified into a number of different forms; rotation, translation, extension, enlargement and combinations of these as shown in Figure 1.4. Pattern changes may be quantified in a number of ways based upon standard morphometric measures (Figure 1.4), such as changing wavelength, amplitude or radius of curvature. However, typical river meanders are, as Carson and Lapointe (1983) have shown, often not symmetrical but asymmetrical (Figure 1.4). This asymmetry is of two kinds, down-channel delay in the inflection point and an up-valley skew of 'gooseneck' loops which look as if they have been left behind by the river. The mechanism for both, suggested by Carson and Lapointe (1983), is the down-channel persistence of helical

Fig. 1.4 River channel planform and planform changes: (a) definition of terms for meanders, (b) typical meander changes, (c) gooseneck and asymmetrical meander and cutoff evolution, (d) valley and meander belt definition. Adapted from Hooke (1977), Richards (1982) and Carson and Lapoint (1983).

a

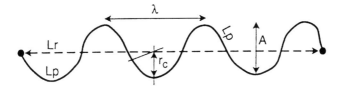

λ Meander wavelength   A   Meander amplitude
Lr Reach length r_c Radius of curvature
Lp River path length $\dfrac{Lp}{Lr}$ Sinuosity

b

Extension   Translation   Rotation   Enlargement   Lateral movement   Complex change

c

asymmetry index $z = \dfrac{100.\upsilon}{\upsilon + d}$

d

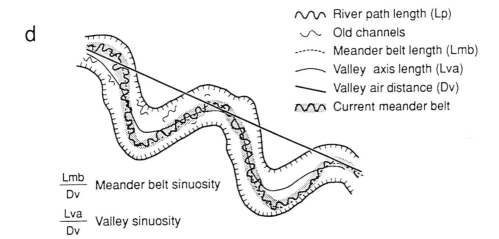

∿∿∿ River path length (Lp)
∿   Old channels
----- Meander belt length (Lmb)
─── Valley axis length (Lva)
─── Valley air distance (Dv)
∿∿∿ Current meander belt

$\dfrac{Lmb}{Dv}$ Meander belt sinuosity

$\dfrac{Lva}{Dv}$ Valley sinuosity

Plate 1.1 An aerial photograph of the junction of the rivers Trent and Soar, England, under flood conditions, highlighting floodplain topography associated with meander migration and avulsion. Flow from right to left.

circulation patterns past the meanders that formed them. These different types of bend migration will produce different sedimentary patterns, from wide arc-shaped ridge and swale topography (scroll-bars) to a chaotic pattern of super-imposed scallop-shaped ridges and linear swales (Plate 1.1). Local differences in the rate of meander migration can produce neck cutoffs; a chute cutoff is produced when a flood cuts through any part of a meander loop; where a whole segment of channel is abandoned this is called avulsion. The first two mecha-nisms form classic oxbow lakes whilst avulsion initially produces a ribbon lake, but because the meander-bend pools are the deepest part of the old channel, in time this becomes a chain of oxbow lakes as sedimentation infills the shal-lower straight parts of the channel. The different environments within the cutoff system will produce characteristically different sediments, as is illus-trated by a chute cutoff on the Murrumbidgee, Australia, described by Page *et al.* (1982) (Figure 1.5). Neck cutoffs can, in theory, be differentiated from chute cutoffs by the non-convergent directions of the two meander arms. However, in practice, they are difficult to distinguish and so an alternative is the arbitrary differentiation based entirely on the basis of the curvature angle, i.e. under or over 180°. The different styles of cutoff and varying curvatures of initial meander produces a wide variety of oxbow planforms as described by Weihaupt (1977). One of the most commonly observed processes which mod-

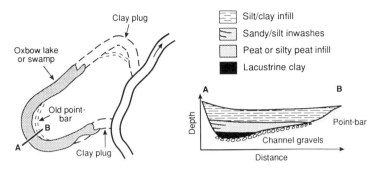

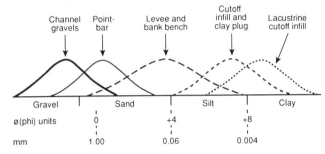

Fig. 1.5 A chute cutoff and its generalised grain size distributions from point-bar, concave-bank bench and the fill. Based on a Murrumbidgee example by Erskine *et al.* (1982) by permission of *Australian Geographer*.

ifies the planform of oxbow lakes is the deposition of a plug of sediment at the upstream end of the cutoff, often leaving the downstream end open to the river. This forms an important backwater environment in the fluvial hydrosere and a route via which flood flows spread across the floodplain in an upstream direction (Hughes, 1980).

Some rivers change their location more dramatically than by cutting off meander loops, by adopting a completely new course after a flood. The new location will generally be the lowest path on the floodplain which is not obstructed, and in systems dominated by overbank deposition this will often be at the floodplain edge or the edge of the channel belt. This dramatic change, avulsion, is essential to the development of anastomosing systems but is also common in braided and meandering systems. It is therefore of geological importance and Bridge and Leeder (1979) have modelled it in a subsiding basin context. In their model, illustrated in Figure 1.6, alluvial stratigraphy is controlled by initial floodplain geometry, a mean net deposition rate related to distance from the channel belt, compaction of the non-channel belt deposits, periodic avulsion of the belt to the lowest point on the floodplain and tectonic tilting. Avulsion is of particular importance because it produces distinctive

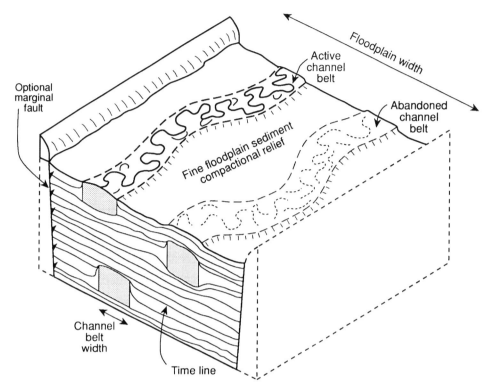

Fig. 1.6 Stratigraphy produced by the avulsion model of Bridge and Leeder (1979) for a channel belt of 600 m and 3 m deep. Vertical exaggeration is 12.5. Reproduced from *Sedimentology*, Bridge and Leeder (1979), by permission of Blackwell Science Ltd.

sedimentary sequences of alternating channel fills and overbank or lateral deposits. It can produce extremely long palaeochannels similar to ribbon lakes.

Research in more active geomorphic zones has shown that channel change can involve a dramatic change in the entire floodplain system. Nanson (1986) has described floodplains of several high-energy coastal rivers in New South Wales, Australia, which experience periodic catastrophic stripping of the floodplain surface. He has proposed a simplified model (Figure 1.7). First, overbank deposition builds a floodplain over hundreds or thousands of years; this is then stripped off to a basal lag deposit upon which fine overbank sediments again start to accumulate, until the whole process is repeated by another catastrophic event or series of events. The fundamental reason for this rather dramatic cycle is the lateral stability of the channel caused by the development of large levee banks and the high-energy, high-variability flow regime associated with tropical cyclones, but it is a possible scenario for other floodplains in climates with strong seasonal contrasts such as the Mediterranean (Plate 1.2). Likewise Erskine and Warner (1988) have shown that the periodic morpholog-

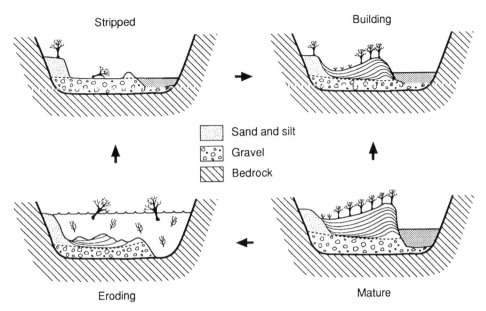

Fig. 1.7 A diagrammatic representation of the disequilibrium-stripping model of
Nanson (1986). Adapted from *Bulletin of the Geological Society of America*, by
permission of the Geological Society of America.

ical change of New South Wales coastal rivers is caused by alternating periods
of flood-dominated and drought-dominated regimes. These studies illustrate
the danger in regarding short-term climatic change as minor in comparison to
astronomically forced climatic changes which produce glacial/interglacial
cycles (Milankovitch forcing). In some regions exactly the reverse may be true.

The use of physical models to simulate floodplain formation has been far less
common than for river processes, owing to the greater complexity of the system
and size of the flume required. However, the influence of a layered floodplain
on stream morphology has been modelled by Desheng and Schumm (1986)
whose experiments produced very realistic meandering patterns with sediment
sorting on point-bars and levees. They also simulated the effects of a tectonic
bulge which resulted in a decrease in sinuosity and deposition upslope and
incision and an increase in slope downstream. Another experiment conducted
to simulate the effects of a resistant rock outcrop showed a compression of
meanders upstream which would have eventually led to neck cutoffs.

It is useful, in this context, to distinguish between internal or autogenic
channel change and externally forced or allogenic channel change. Autogenic
changes include those caused by the infilling of sediment storage sites or the
sudden channel modification associated with progressive meander-neck
erosion. Climatically induced changes in floodplain development are the most
obvious example of allogenic changes, but others include alterations in

Plate 1.2 A small floodplain from near Antequera in southern Spain showing the stripping out of much of the floodplain caused by a single rain event in November 1991. For scale note the two figures middle right.

catchment characteristics and tectonics. Many large rivers have been affected by neotectonic movements. An excellent example is the river Po in northern Italy, where a long record of extensive channel change can clearly be related to uplift caused by a buried overthrust (Braga and Gervasoni, 1989). Within Central Europe several rivers which cross the Carpathians, including the Moravia river, have also been affected by neotectonics (Havlicek, 1991). In Scandinavia, isostatic readjustment has had a major effect on the Holocene development of rivers such as the Oulanka and Oulankajoki in Finland, causing incision (Koutaniemi, 1991) and decreased gradients in the south of the country (Mansikkaniemi, 1991). Burnett and Schumm (1983) have shown how the Monroe Uplift in Louisiana has affected the channel of the Mississippi because of the appearance of a more resistant rock type, in this case a Tertiary clay. These allogenic factors, as well as autogenic factors, can cause what Schumm (1968) has termed channel metamorphosis. This indicates a complete change in channel morphology, as was the case in Schumm's (1968) classic study of the Murrumbidgee river and its palaeochannels. Since the floodplain system and channel change are intimately linked, it follows that along with channel metamorphosis we may get floodplain metamorphosis, i.e. a complete change in the surface characteristics and formational processes of floodplains (cf. Brown and Keough,1992a).

1.3 Aggradation and degradation

Whether a river erodes into its bed and eventually lowers all or part of its floodplain or raises its bed and its floodplain is fundamentally controlled by the resisting forces of bed and banks, river discharge and sediment entering the reach. These factors change the downstream slope of a river bed and thereby the long-profile, which generally, but not always, approximates to a concave semi-logarithmic form. This smooth form was traditionally taken to mean that the river was graded.

A graded river is one in which energy and load are balanced (i.e. providing competence and capacity to transport its given load, see appendix 1.2), producing gradual changes in slope in order to provide, with the available discharge and the prevailing channel characteristics, exactly the velocity needed to transport the load supplied to it (Mackin, 1948). In addition, sediment transport will vary by as much as is required to compensate for bank erosion.

An earlier conceptual model of a graded river with an equilibrium profile was used by Davis (1902) as part of his cycle of erosion, as at his 'old age' stage the river is graded along its entire length. Both Davis (1902) and Mackin (1948) accepted that graded rivers still changed (reducing their slope over time) and that different graded profiles would exist for different rivers. Breaks of slope, such as cataracts or waterfalls, were ascribed to variations in rock hardness or to a knickpoint caused by some past variation in the base-level to which the profile was graded. The lowering of base-level (e.g. the sea level or a lake level) creates a knickpoint which migrates upstream, decreasing in height as it does so and therefore ultimately producing an increased stream gradient below it (Brush and Wolman, 1960).

The assumption that river profiles have graded to former base-levels assumes that base-level change is episodic and not smooth and that knickpoints have always started at the lowest point and migrated back during a period of relative base-level stability. Observations of many knickpoints suggest that as soon as a more resistant rock is encountered the rate of upstream migration is relatively slow. An obvious example is Niagara Falls which in approximately 10,000 years has only migrated about 11 km upstream. The effect of a base-level rise is also limited, as there is little evidence that the upstream growth of a coastal sedimentary wedge will continue above the maximum point reached by the backwater curves produced by the new base-level. In the 1960s there was a re-evaluation of the traditional mechanisms and importance of grade, driven by the discovery that (a) steady state or equilibrium streams (neither aggrading nor degrading) do not necessarily have smooth profiles and (b) aggradation/degradation is determined by catchment conditions, especially slope erosion, and not by base-level control.

If we return to Mackin's (1948) definition of a graded or equilibrium channel as one 'of long-term balance between aggradation and degradation' we can still identify at least three sets of factors which can affect this balance (Richards, 1982). The first is upstream controls such as increasing sediment delivery to channels causing aggradation, or conversely, bedload entrapment by a reservoir causing degradation. The second is changes in the sediment:streamflow ratio (note that this can be accomplished by a change in streamflow only). Thirdly, there are downstream and base-level changes which may primarily be of importance in the lower reaches of rivers. As Leopold and Bull (1979) state, aggradation and degradation represent non-equilibrium situations where the power and efficiency necessary to transport the load supplied could not be provided by gradual mutual adjustment of velocity, width, roughness, pattern and channel morphology. Rivers are self-organising systems with complex (and non-linear) behaviour (Graf, 1977). There exist thresholds such as critical slopes for river patterns which, when crossed, can lead to a different rate of activity or even different dominant processes. The results can be a complex response to an external stimulus or even the passing of an internal threshold as part of steady state or dynamic equilibrium change. As outlined by Schumm (1973) the complex response of river channels can lead to the simultaneous aggradation and degradation in different parts of the floodplain system. This casts doubt on the simple and unequivocal association of entire fluvial units with a single climatic trigger.

1.4 Terraces

A change in stream behaviour from aggradation to degradation will cause incision into the old floodplain, parts of which may be left as a fluvial terrace. Terraces can be caused by any environmental factor which causes river incision, including climatic change, changes in sediment availability, changes in catchment hydrology, tectonic activity and base-level change. Irrespective of the cause, a terrace is not as easy to define as we might suppose, because, in the strict sense, it is simply a break in slope separating two relatively flat surfaces (see Figure 1.8), and if the old floodplain had a greater slope than the present floodplain, the terraces would plunge under the modern floodplain surface.

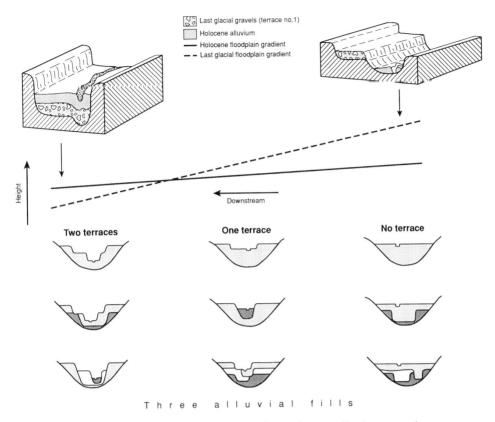

Fig. 1.8 Terrace morphology in relation to long-profile changes and combinations of terraces with alluvial fills. Lower fills in order of an increase in downstream gradient, reverse order for a decrease. Adapted from Schumm (1977) and Leopold and Miller (1954).

This is the case with many of the lower terraces of Northern Europe. Indeed, in a system that has undergone complete aggradation, terraces as such will not exist, but instead, old floodplain surfaces will be buried and form bounding-surfaces to sub-alluvial sedimentary units. A second and related problem is that very low terraces may be flooded; this is because it is the amount of incision which determines the recurrence interval of inundation under constant hydro-logical conditions. The common assumption that terraces are not flooded is not always correct, especially if there is both floodplain and channel bed aggrada-tion. If area inundated is graphed against the frequency of inundation a curvi-linear trend is normal; however, terrace inundation produces a sudden change in the gradient of the line.

In the past geomorphologists generally ascribed terrace formation to global (eustatic) sea level fluctuation (the so-called thalassostatic hypothesis) and often used terraces to estimate former sea levels as exemplified by Kidson's (1962) study of the river Exe in Devon, England. The effects of sea level change are now regarded as being largely restricted to coastal areas, and catchment, climatic or tectonic factors receive more attention, together with critical thresholds internal to the fluvial system (Schumm and Parker, 1973; Young and Nanson, 1982). However, where terraces grade into coastal beach deposits or coalesce with each other in a former coastal zone, terraces will relate to old relative sea levels and can with care be used to estimate rates of uplift (Bull and Knuepfer, 1987).

It is also important to realise that, when dealing with terrace staircases, drainage networks and catchments have not necessarily remained constant. This is particularly true where terraces are mostly fluvio-glacial and periglacial in origin. In southern non-glaciated parts of England, it was realised in the last century that the uppermost terraces (or plateau gravels as they were named by the British Geological Survey) are often rather different and vertically separated from the middle and lower terraces. Vertical terrace separation is not just a measure of climatic change, as all the major rivers of the UK significantly changed their catchment areas during the Pleistocene. This is particularly important in regions of low relief and marginal to the glaciated continental zones, including southern Canada and the northern United States. While it is the upper and middle terraces of the Old World that may contain Lower and Middle Palaeolithic artifacts, it is the lower terraces which are sources of Upper Palaeolithic and post-Palaeolithic artifacts and these generally lie close to the present river and floodplain, if not under it. However, in higher-energy environments such as the uplands in the UK (Macklin and Lewin, 1986) or many mountainous and semi-arid areas of the USA (Stene, 1980), terraces have continued to form during the Holocene and so floodplain sites may be buried, destroyed or incorporated into new terraces. In studying terrace sites, it is often the terrace edges that are of greatest interest. This is because at the edges it is often possible to see the stratigraphic relationship between the terrace, other alluvial units, and bedrock. As Figure 1.8 shows, there are many very different possible terrace and fill arrangements which have chronological implications.

A subject of particular relevance to archaeologists is the preservation of terraces and the environmental significance of terrace surfaces. Since they are the driest parts of the floodplain they have always been preferentially settled. With Holocene floodplain aggradation Pleistocene terraces frequently become gradually flooded and buried by overbank sediments producing sealed landsurfaces with remarkable preservation potential. The majority of floodplain sites are of this type and examples are described in detail in later chapters. The common preservation of palaeochannel patterns (Cheetham, 1976), old soils and habitation floors can indicate that these terrace surfaces have often undergone relatively little surface erosion. Most terrace erosion occurs by lateral meander migration which creates bluffs, and by the incision of tributaries.

A terrace, although not necessarily all of the same age, may be dated to a time window with periods of fluvial incision separating it from the rest of the staircase. Terrace gravels can be deposited remarkably quickly. In the early part of this century, each of the climatically forced terraces of the Alpine foreland were associated with one of the four glacial periods which were then believed to make up the entire cold Pleistocene record (i.e. the last two million years). Since radiometric dating and other dating methods have become available, we now know that several terraces may be formed within one cold or warm period and that, conversely, the terrestrial terrace record is also full of gaps. This is exemplified by work on the river Severn in the UK where originally Wills (1938) identified three or four terraces with the last Glacial. However, with radio-carbon dating by Shotton and Coope (1983) we now know that the Main terrace and the Worcester terrace were deposited in the window 25,000 bp to 15,000 bp and the last terrace, the Power House Terrace, was deposited between 15,000 bp and 13,000 bp. One explanation for these rapid sedimentation rates has come from the re-evaluation of terrace sedimentology which suggests significant proportions of at least one of the terraces may have been produced by a number of very large floods (Dawson, 1989).

One important result of geomorphological research on fluvial processes is that we are now forced to be more flexible in the interpretation of terrace sequences and we cannot treat them as a relatively straightforward record of environmental change. This is partly due to the destruction of evidence by erosion. If a river has occupied a valley for a considerable period of time, large events (in the broadest sense) are more likely to remove the evidence of smaller events than *vice versa*. So, paired terrace staircases can be viewed as, at best, a record of decreasingly smaller floodplains after the most geomorphologically active period in the catchment. Older deposits may be preserved under these terraces, especially in bedrock scour holes or at locations subsequently abandoned by the channel belt. These factors help to explain why it is unlikely that one river valley will have preserved terrace deposits from all the glacial/interglacial cycles known from the oceanic cores. It is important to recognise the antecedent effects caused by landscape-forming events at all scales within the fluvial system from a glacial advance to an individual flood (Anderson and Calver, 1977).

1.5 Floodplain evolution and archaeological sites

Different types of floodplain and channel system offer different opportunities and problems for floodplain utilisation in prehistory. They also vary in their typical preservation of the evidence of occupation and utilisation. The pattern of channel migration may bias the distribution of surviving floodplain sites and burial by sedimentation can reduce the archaeological visibility of sites on floodplains.

In systems that are very dynamic, such as present-day proglacial floodplains with braided channels, the stability of any location on the floodplain is very limited, generally preventing settlement. Even temporary camps or butchery sites will only survive if quickly buried rather than reworked. In more stable floodplain systems, occupation is possible and attractive, if the river and floodplain is a major source of food, or has ritual or strategic significance.

If we take a typical model of a meandering single- or multiple-channel floodplain, we can identify four environments where occupation is possible and locations where it is unlikely owing to semi-permanent high water tables (see chapter 9). Indeed, in this system there is an optimal location for settlement and that is a terrace edge, or island, at a point where a channel bluff slope is cutting into the terrace. This will generally be on the lowest morphological terrace in the valley.

Apart from site destruction by meander migration, the major risk of floodplain occupation is obviously catastrophic flooding and less obvious nuisance flooding, caused by either overbank floods or rising groundwater levels. The relative importance of overbank versus groundwater flooding is a function of the catchment and floodplain hydrology. Areas with episodic but intense precipitation will be more prone to catastrophic/destructive flooding and areas characterised by more continuous but less intense precipitation will be more prone to nuisance flooding. In addition, catchment geology either attenuates the precipitation signal or amplifies it, i.e. areas underlain by impermeable rocks and soils will produce higher and earlier flood peaks for the same rainfall than areas underlain by highly permeable rock and soils. Other factors which influence flashiness are size and slope of the catchment.

The flashiness of a catchment is described by the slope of the curve between flood height (stage) and the frequency with which that height is reached, i.e. the recurrence interval of flooding. Low terraces may be flooded depending upon the elevation relative to river height and the steepness of the flood recurrence interval curve. Both of these factors are liable to change, the former because of channel and floodplain aggradation, the latter because of climatic change, and/or hydrological change caused by humans.

It is fairly straightforward to estimate the areas inundated by floods of different magnitudes (see appendix 3), as is done for floodplain zonation planning and insurance risk assessment. It is also possible to estimate the amount of channel aggradation that would produce flooding of an area with a set frequency; however, this is complicated by any change in channel shape (i.e. assuming only bed aggradation and not equilibrium floodplain aggradation) which will alter the spill volumes of lower magnitude floods, which would in turn affect the flood series. Hydrological change is the rule rather than the exception and Howe *et al.* (1967) showed that, on the river Severn, the drainage of afforested land in the upper reaches, together with an increase in the frequency of heavy rainfall events, was responsible for the increase in the frequency of flooding in the post-1940 period, as compared with the period 1911–40. Higgs (1987) has since verified this hydrological change and shown that the increase in flood flashiness can probably be attributed to documented agricultural drainage and pasture improvements. Many studies from many

different environments have shown how most human actions such as deforestation, channel straightening (Brookes, 1988) and urbanisation (Wolman, 1967)
tend to increase flood flashiness, reduce lag times and affect sediment loads.
These studies all indicate three important points: first, that we must consider
changes in the underlying natural frequency/magnitude of rainfall upon which
catchment modifications may be superimposed. Secondly, the hydrological
effects of catchment changes will vary with catchment size, location and climate
of the area involved – it may, in some instances, need a significant proportion
of the catchment to be changed, in order to have an observable effect on catchment hydrology, especially if the areas in question are far from channels. Lastly,
any hydrological effects will vary with the return period of the event, often with
negligible consequences on large-magnitude events, although some human
actions have the opposite consequences, e.g. reservoir construction. During the
Holocene, many floodplain reaches will have experienced both hydrological
change and aggradation or degradation which may, or may not, have been
causally linked. One implication is that the recurrence interval of flooding can
never be assumed to have remained constant. This would not, however, auto-
matically necessitate a shift or abandonment of a settlement, but adaptation to
the changed local conditions. More discussion of the archaeological effects of
changes in flood frequency can be found in chapter 9.

1.6 Sites and rates of sedimentation

Sedimentation rates vary systematically with floodplain micro-environment
and non-systematically with changes in flood history and sediment availability.
This variation can have a profound effect on floodplain sites, because if the site
matrix is alluvial, the rate of sedimentation will affect the density of artifacts
in the vertical sequence (Figure 1.9). In a study of sites in the Oaxaca valley in
south Mexico, Kirby and Kirkby (1976) showed that, owing to an average rate
of alluviation of 0.25 cm yr^{-1} in 1000 years, only 0.004% of the shards from a
buried site would still be lying on the soil surface. High rates of sedimentation
tend to preserve sedimentary structures, because of a lack of bioturbation by
worms and other animals. Stein (1983) has shown how important worms can
be for the stratigraphy of a floodplain site. She found that in an archaic shell
midden in the floodplain of the Green river in Kentucky earthworms had
caused a mixing of two sediment sources (floodplain silts and lake clays),
destruction of burial pit boundaries, probable loss of seed evidence, and a
mixed chemical profile (Figure 1.10). The effects of earthworms will vary with
many factors, including species present, soil texture, nutrients and degree of
waterlogging. Both very acid (below pH 3.5) and permanently waterlogged
conditions inhibit worm activity. The exclusion of worms by waterlogging is
probably the main reason for preferential preservation of flood laminations in
backswamp locations. In general, worms also prefer mixed or loamy textures
and high organic matter input, so the most densely populated locations are
generally terrace surfaces and floodplain flats. Unfortunately, as yet, we do not

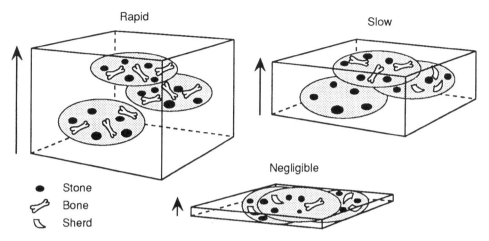

Fig. 1.9 The effects of alluvial sedimentation rate on artifact densities and spatial patterning. Adapted from Ferring (1986).

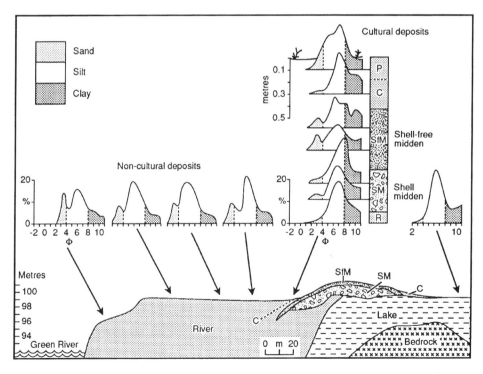

Fig. 1.10 The effects of bioturbation illustrated using grain size curves from non-cultural deposits and cultural deposits around the Carlston Annis mound, Kentucky. Adapted from Stein (1983).

know what are the maximum rates of sedimentation that worms can tolerate. However, numerous excavations of floodplain deposits show that either sediments are remarkably un-bioturbated, with good structural preservation, or the structure seems to be completely destroyed. This suggests there are threshold rates operating and combined work on both sedimentation rates and soil micromorphology (thin sectioning – see chapter 3) should be used to investigate the problem further. In other environments, the major agent of floodplain soil bioturbation will be different, such as termites in the tropics or small mammals in drylands. The ecology of these animals is also related to the nature and rate of sedimentation, often enhancing the geomorphologically determined pattern of sediment reworking and artifact disturbance.

1.7 Alluvial geoprospecting and site conservation

Because of channel change and floodplain evolution, sites are often buried, rendering them largely invisible to traditional survey techniques such as field-walking and aerial photography. The latter can, however, be extremely successful on adjacent terraces above flood level. There is also extra information which can be gained by low-level remote sensing, using either visible wavelengths, or even more valuable, thermal imaging (Allsop, 1992). For buried sites other methods can be used:

1 The inspection of natural exposures, i.e. river banks and artificial excavations including dykes, drains, etc. and gravel pits extracting sub-alluvial gravel. Working gravel pits are particularly useful, as long and deep exposures can be obtained and the working back of the face can facilitate three-dimensional reconstructions.
2 The identification of likely locations from indirect evidence, especially old channel courses and floodplain islands identified from air photographs and old maps.
3 The use of geophysical methods which have the capability to penetrate significant thicknesses of alluvium. These are seismic refraction (Coster and Gerrard, 1957) and ground resistivity/conductivity. For details of applicable seismic techniques, see Gardiner and Dackombe (1983). Seismic survey has been used to profile the base of alluvial deposits (Williams, 1968; Clark, 1989) and so can potentially identify old landsurfaces and sub-alluvial gravel 'islands'.
4 Boreholes are obviously potentially very informative, but are expensive and time consuming, depending upon the size of the area and depth of the alluvium. However, in many cases, just a few hours with an extendable hand auger can provide useful data, especially at the floodplain edges.
5 Morphometric analysis of some floodplain parameters, including width, depth and sedimentary cross-sectional area, has shown them to be statistically related to distance downstream (Brown, 1983a), basin

area and stream order (Bhowmik, 1984). In theory, this allows the use of power functions for the estimation of some sub-surface properties from map-derived data. However, these relationships will vary considerably from one system to another, owing to such factors as whether the area was glaciated, the area's lithology and climatic regime. The exponents in the equations are probably more sensitive to hydroclimatic factors, whereas the constants may reflect past geomorphological history, such as in the case of so-called misfit streams. This means that morphometric relationships can only be used as a first approximation to the depth of fill that might be expected within an alluvial valley.

Excavations of floodplain sites have shown how laterally variable the stratigraphy generally is (Needham, 1989). This variability is caused by lateral channel shifting and especially channel avulsion, producing vertical boundaries separating what Needham (1989) has called alluvial parcels. These can be of very different ages and can pose considerable problems for site correlation and reconstruction. In other locations where meander migration and aggradation have produced overlapping scroll-bars, sites may be both laterally extensive and vertically stratified, a good example being the palaeoindian sites on the Duck river in Tennessee (Brackenridge, 1984; Figure 1.11). Analysis of the stratigraphy and ^{14}C dating reveal an alternation between periods of channel stability which coincide with Early, Middle and Late Archaic artifacts and periods of aggradation by accretion on channel banks and bars. The Middle Archaic artifacts were *in situ* on a fossil floodplain surface along with the remains of hearths. Pollen evidence from the same horizon suggests a drier climate than present at this time (*c.* 4400 BC).

Negative evidence is always problematic in environmental archaeology, but particularly so in alluvial environments. This is not only because of the invisibility of sites as previously discussed, but also because sites or other evidence may be completely destroyed naturally. We know this is possible, but for obvious reasons examples are hard to find. If we take any model of floodplain formation, such as the stripping model (Nanson, 1986), we can see that a surface scatter or the remains of a hut circle would be completely destroyed with a periodicity of about every 1000–2000 years, thus severely limiting the archaeological potential of these floodplains. In summary, the archaeological potential of a floodplain and the negative evidence problem is largely dependent upon the rates and processes of floodplain evolution.

A not unrelated problem is that, in both alluvial and non-alluvial archaeology, the probability of site recovery for different periods is not independent. This is due to the greater chance of recovering reused sites (Kirby and Kirkby, 1976) and is particularly true of alluvial environments because successive occupations build up floor levels and in some cases flood protection banks, thus combating nuisance flooding and favouring continued occupation or reoccu-

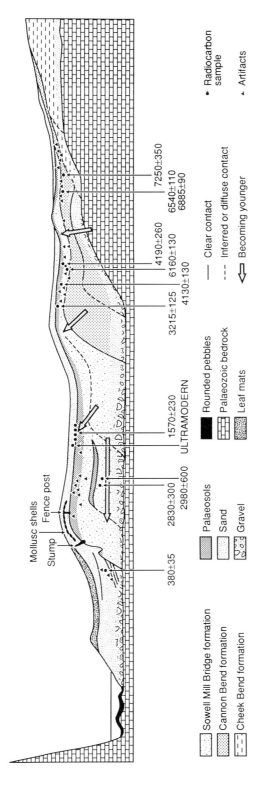

Fig. 1.11 The generalised modern stratigraphy, artifact distribution and dating of a cross-section of the Duck river floodplain, Tennessee. Adapted from Brackenridge (1984). All dates in years bp.

pation of that site. The optimal location on contemporary British floodplains is often under an existing church, because it is sited on the top of the floodplain island or on a terrace edge. A good example is the town of Tewkesbury, which lies at the confluence of the rivers Severn and Avon in England. The floodplain was in the past flooded for several days every year. The medieval town and abbey are located in the middle of the floodplain on a terrace island. The town occasionally floods; however, in the 900 years the abbey has existed, water has only ever reached half-way up the nave (in 1947).

The combined effect of these problems, e.g. site invisibility, site destruction and autocorrelation, is bound to produce a rather polarised picture with a relative lack of single-period sites and a record biased towards continually occupied sites in stable floodplain locations on the one hand, and on the other, what seem to be archaeologically barren tracts of floodplain.

Once sites have been either predicted or discovered there is the problem of excavation: is it feasible or desirable and if so should it be partial or total? Given the probable number of alluvial and other wetland sites it is impossible to excavate them all, and many would argue undesirable, given the present state of technology. It is therefore important to understand the mechanisms of preservation of organic remains in alluvial environments, if reburial or preservation is to be effective. Organic remains are preserved by the lack of microbial decomposition caused by anaerobic soil/sediment conditions. This occurs where an archaeological site lies below the watertable or in areas with high moisture levels for all or most of the year. The restoration of wetlands, including alluvial wetlands, for ecological purposes may also preserve archaeological remains if the landsurface is left intact, high watertables are maintained and deep root penetration prevented. Monitoring of water levels has been undertaken at a number of alluvial and wetland sites including the remains of the Rose Theatre by the river Thames (Orrell and Gurr, 1989) and in the Somerset Levels in south-west England (Corfield, in press). The variables which influence local groundwater levels are the stratigraphy and hydraulic conductivity of the local sediments, the slope of the floodplain watertable, flooding, rainfall and evapotranspiration from plants and the ground surface (Brown and Bradley, 1996). Largely because of variations in sediments and stratigraphy, which cause very variable local groundwater transmission rates, it is not easy to generalise about alluvial and wetland sites. However, stratigraphic investigations and monitoring of groundwater levels and soil moisture allow models to be tailored for individual archaeological sites allowing the maintenance of adequate water levels using bunds and pumping if necessary (Brown and Bradley, 1996). Water quality monitoring may also pick up warning changes in soil water chemistry caused by changing reduction–oxidation conditions allowing the rescue excavation of the site and conservation of organic artifacts using the much improved techniques available (Coles, 1990). As Coles (1995) has observed: 'wetland archaeology is likely to benefit from restoration programmes in the long run but in the short term vulnerability needs must be considered'.

2

ALLUVIAL ENVIRONMENTS OVER TIME

As the last chapter illustrated, floodplains have a history – they evolve over time. In order to be able to unravel this history and relate it to other events, be they climatic or cultural, sediments have to be sequenced and dated. Advances in dating have revolutionised not only archaeology (Renfrew and Bahn, 1991) but also recent geology (Vita-Finzi, 1973), and the development of sediment-based techniques will undoubtedly have a major impact on studies of the environmental archaeology of past societies, particularly in alluvial environments.

2.1 Dating and alluvial chronologies

The stratigraphy of a floodplain represents a time-sequence, so the development of the floodplain over time can be investigated if the stratigraphy can be dated. The dated alluvial stratigraphy or alluvial chronology can then be correlated with, or even used to date, human activity on the floodplain or in the river catchment. As with other Quaternary sediments, there are two, fundamentally different, groups of dating methods that are commonly used to date alluvial sequences. These are the *chronometric* methods that provide independent age estimates, either numerical or calibrated, but based upon some kind of physical, chemical or biological clock. Other methods are *relative*, in the sense that they operate both through stratigraphic order and through matching stratigraphic sequences to a similar sequence elsewhere which may be chronometrically dated. Some relative methods can be so well correlated to chronometrically dated or historical sequences that they can be regarded as a third category: *calibrated relative* methods. A summary of the methods and their dating ranges discussed in this chapter is given in Figure 2.1.

As in geology and archaeology the law of superposition provides the underlying principle of the sequencing of strata, with the oldest unit being at the base and the youngest at the top. However, although this forms the basis of relative dating and correlation, many geomorphic environments produce complex stratigraphies. Lateral accretion of sediment by rivers can produce vertical rather than horizontal time-lines (Figure 2.2). Floodplain stratigraphy is also complicated by processes such as partial burial, wind deflation/deposition, tree-throws and other bioturbation processes.

Relative dating and correlation
The establishment of river terrace chronologies was traditionally based on height correlation and counting back through glacial/interglacial cycles. This

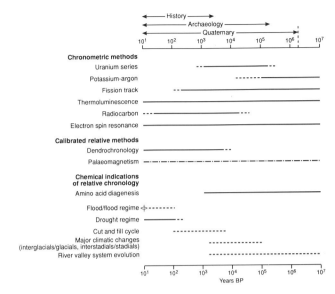

Fig. 2.1 Time spans covered by different dating methods used in alluvial
environments. Adapted from Lowe and Walker (1984). Broken lines show possible
extensions to age ranges and lines broken with dots indicate where dating is
limited to specific intervals within the age range.

is now known not to be reliable as terraces of the same height can be of different ages and we still do not have a reliable master-curve of terrestrial glacial/interglacial cycles. This is why chronometric dating is so important in allowing us to correlate the terrestrial record with the more complete record of glacial/interglacial cycles preserved in oceanic cores.

One method of relative dating, by the use of artifact typologies, provided the traditional framework for terrace chronologies of the major rivers of Europe, including the Thames in England, and the Seine in France. It has, however, long been realised that there are serious methodological and practical problems with using lithic typologies to date terraces. On the practical side, many terraces do not contain artifacts or, if they do, these are derived from older units. But the most serious problems are methodological and lie in the traditional concept of distinct tool types or industries made by distinctive human groups, which can be arranged in a chronological progression. There is considerable evidence that different cultural groups, or even different hominid species, produced and used indistinguishable tools, often separated by considerable periods of time. Largely because of the use of chronometric dating techniques and increasingly refined lithostratigraphic work, the relationship between archaeologists and geomorphologists has been reversed, i.e. it is increasingly common for the terrace to be used to give an age to the industry rather than *vice versa*. However, for post-Mesolithic alluvial units, archaeological dating can be extremely precise if fine pottery or coins are present.

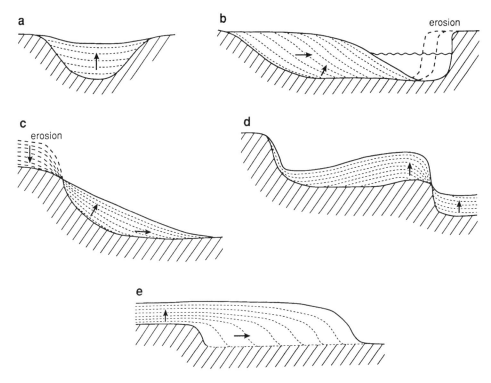

Fig. 2.2 Time-lines in different geomorphological systems. Dotted lines are isochrones (lines of equal age). (a) Lake, pond or cutoff, (b) migrating river, (c) erosion of a scarp and colluviation, (d) overbank deposition on a floodplain and in-channel deposition and (e) a prograding delta.

Another method of relative dating has been through biostratigraphic correlation using techniques such as pollen analysis. The most suitable samples are from interglacial or interstadial deposits and generally from organic palaeochannel fills below or in terraces and from lacustrine deposits interdigitating with terraces. However, vegetation change is not synchronous, and vegetation is always spatially variable, rendering the assumption of time-equivalence of similar vegetation or pollen zones problematic. Apart from the use of documented marker types (such as the rise of *Ambrosia* type pollen along with the European settlement of North America), pollen dating is entirely dependent on our existing knowledge of the history of vegetation change. Since vegetation change during the Pleistocene was highly diachronous, this is a hazardous procedure and has similar problems to those encountered with lithic industries.

In practice biostratigraphic correlation depends upon two complementary approaches. The first is the use of the fall-out of Pliocene relict species from the flora which seems to have occurred as the Pleistocene progressed, allowing dating by local or global extinctions. The second is to correlate the deposits with a type site for that interglacial. This is often not easy as full interglacial cycles are generally not preserved, and interglacial floras varied spatially owing to climatic and soil differences. The procedure is, of course, still dependent on the dating of the type site by other means. Under certain conditions it may be possible to date the site to a period or zone within an interglacial.

Iversen (1958) and Turner and West (1968) identified respectively three to four bioclimatic zones within interglacial cycles. These zones are: Protocratic, Mesocratic and Telocratic (Iversen, 1958) and Pre-/Early/Late/Post-Temperate (Turner and West, 1968). With our increasing knowledge of the complexity and asymmetry of some warm interludes (the abrupt start and slower end of inter-glacials) in the Pleistocene this approach has to be amended and used with caution (Jones and Keen, 1993). Again in practice, all possible lines of attack are used, but, in many cases, we still cannot definitively assign a deposit to a specific warm period (Barber and Brown, 1987). Furthermore, with the distinction between interstadials and interglacials being increasingly blurred and the re-evaluation of type sites, this situation is unlikely to alter. So, pollen analysis can only be an approximate form of dating and the true value of the technique in the Holocene lies in its palaeoenvironmental rather than chronological information. The problems associated with the use of fossil fauna are similar, with new dating methods changing our knowledge of local extinctions. An obvious example is the mammoth (*Mammuthus primigenius*) because although frozen carcasses from Siberia indicate it was not globally extinct until around 4000 bp it *was* believed to have become extinct in the UK around the last glacial maximum, some time between 25,000 and 18,000 bp. Recent finds have shown this not to be the case; for example, a male mammoth with two young has been recovered from a kettle-hole at Condover in Shropshire, and has been radio-carbon dated to only *c.* 12,800 bp (Coope and Lister, 1987).

2.2 Chronometric dating methods

These are methods which rely on some physico-chemical property which changes over time at a rate that can be estimated, and from an initial starting point that can be estimated (chronometric) or a seasonal event (incremental). They are often called absolute techniques (which they are not), or radiometric techniques (which only applies to some). There are four chronometric methods which are of significance for alluvial deposits – radiocarbon dating, lumines-cence, potassium-argon and uranium series – as well as dendrochronology which is an incremental method. Each will be very briefly described below with a comment on its use in the dating of alluvial deposits.

Radiocarbon dating.
This is the most important method for the construction of Lateglacial and Holocene alluvial chronologies since it covers the last 50,000 years and is the most widely used. The method is summarised in numerous publications (Lowe

and Walker, 1984; Gillespie, 1986; Aitken, 1990). The isotope ^{14}C is continually being formed from nitrogen in the upper atmosphere by high-energy cosmic radiation. This unstable isotope along with the stable isotope ^{12}C is mixed in the atmosphere and taken up by plants as CO_2 and water and so it becomes stored in various reservoirs which include not only plants but animal tissue. On the death of the organism, replacement of ^{14}C ceases and it decays back to nitrogen. As it decays it emits less beta radiation and this can be measured or counted. If the rate of decay is known, which it is, and the initial ^{14}C:^{12}C ratio is known the ratio contained in the sample can be used to determine the time that has elapsed since death. There are several assumptions and problems which will be briefly summarised. First, the original half-life measured by Libby (1955) was 5568 ± 30 years and this is the figure used for published dates; however, remeasurement has estimated it at 5730 ± 40 years. Second, the production of ^{14}C was originally thought to be constant; however, the radiocarbon dating of tree rings has shown that it is not. Variations have been caused by changes in the geomagnetic flux, changes in solar activity, fluctuations in the CO_2 uptake of the oceans, and human pollution. Human pollution has affected it in two ways: first by the burning of fossil fuels (industrial effect) which are extremely low in ^{14}C; and, since 1950, by the testing of atomic weapons which has increased the ^{14}C in the atmosphere. The result of all this, and the need to have a fixed reference point, is that uncalibrated dates are expressed in years bp with present being 1950. If calendar dates are needed the raw dates must be calibrated using the tree-ring curves (Suess, 1970). However, since these curves vary considerably from region to region (Pearson *et al.*, 1977; Pearson *et al.*, 1986), the calibration curve should be derived from the same region as the site, or the dates left uncalibrated (years BP). Significant progress has been made in the production of calibration curves, and raw radiocarbon dates are routinely converted into calendar dates using the curves of Clark (1975), Klein *et al.* (1980), Pearson and Stuiver (1986) and Stuiver and Pearson (1986). Problems have arisen owing to the wiggly nature of the calibration curves, leading to some areas where dating resolution is significantly reduced and produces artificial clustering of dates – the so-called plateau effect. One of these periods that is especially important for studies of changing alluvial environments is the Lateglacial. Some authors have used radiocarbon histograms to provide a chronology of Holocene alluvial events (Macklin and Lewin, 1993), but owing to this non-linearity of the uncalibrated radiocarbon time-scale, clusterings may occur which do not represent real-time clusterings. Stolk *et al.* (1994) have produced a computer program which corrects for this effect; it uses a 100-year moving average and shows that over 100 dates per 1000 years are required to get significant results.

In addition to the technical considerations above, there are three further sources of potential error associated with the use of ^{14}C to date alluvial environments: reworked or old organic material, pedogenic factors and rootlet contamination. The extent to which these pose problems will obviously vary with the nature of the sample and it is therefore necessary to consider the types of organics commonly found in floodplain and terrace sections that can be dated. Of most importance are wood, peat, organic mud and charcoal, especially in drier locations. Wood and charcoal produce the most reliable dates, but if not *in situ* will only give a maximum age of deposition, which in the case of charcoal could considerably pre-date deposition. Observations of the exhumation of old tree stumps by natural riverbank erosion show that the reworking, or incorporation, of old wood can occur. However, this is relatively rare for two reasons: first, wood tends to be preserved by burial in sites which are only occasionally the focus of subsequent erosion, and secondly, wood that is not buried, but exposed on the floodplain surface, decays rapidly. Good practice is to date the least abraded and degraded wood if possible. A further precaution is to identify the species (which should be done anyway) and check that it is not anomalous for the general period or the organic assemblage of the site. This reworking problem is less likely to arise with non-woody macro-fossils, but can occur with both inwashed pedogenic carbon or charcoal fragments, leading to date reversals later in the sequence (Brown and Barber, 1985).

A further problem is that many organic horizons in floodplains are palaeosols developed on buried landsurfaces. Dating the organic matter from these horizons presents the same problems as dating organic matter from other palaeosols: namely that they develop over relatively long periods of time and different fractions have different decay rates. The organic fractions can be dated separately, from the most resistant to the least resistant. This can be used to define a minimum or mean residence time for the organic matter which is related to the period over which pedogenesis operated. With mixed peaty sediment, organic muds and palaeosols, it is advisable to date separately the coarse and fine organic fraction and the humin fraction (alkali-soluble – less complex organic matter) and humic fraction (alkali-insoluble – more complex organic matter). Large, statistically significant discrepancies in these dates can indicate the mixing of organics of different provenances, a large apparent mean residence time or contamination by humic acids. For a more detailed discussion of the problems of dating palaeosols, refer to the work of Matthews (1985). A not unrelated problem is that of rootlet penetration. As overbank deposition continues on a floodplain soil, so roots will penetrate down into the older soil horizons beneath. This also contributes to the residence time of the soil organic matter. This organic overprinting can, however, be extremely useful if the roots can be excavated and separated out from the older organic matrix (Brown and Keough, 1992a, b and c). If this can be done, then a sequence of dates relating to successively higher landsurfaces may be obtained. It may even be possible to date a landsurface which has subsequently been eroded away by dating the roots that penetrated down from it.

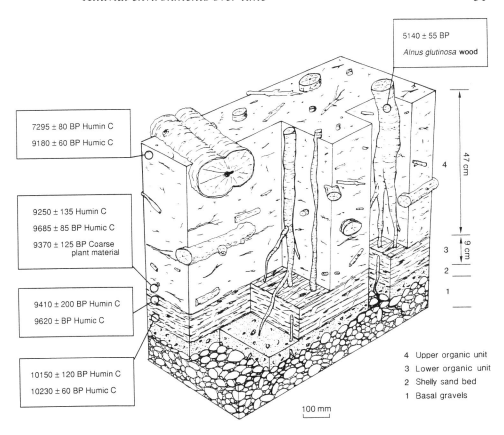

Fig. 2.3 Block diagram of radiocarbon dated infill of a palaeochannel from the floodplain of the river Soar at Cossington, England, excavated by M. Keough. Adapted from Brown and Keough (1992a). See Plate 2.1.

This approach has been followed at a palaeochannel site on the river Soar floodplain in the East Midlands, England (Brown, Keough and Rice, 1994). Here, nine dates were obtained from an excavated block 0.7 m by 0.6 m (Figure 2.3 and Plate 2.1). As can be seen, there was generally close agreement between the fraction dates of the peaty matrix, except at the top where a greater apparent mean residence time is indicated. The block accumulated probably continuously from *c.* 10,100 bp to *c.* 7300 bp but was penetrated by alder (*Alnus glutinosa*) roots from a higher landsurface around 5000 bp. Not only does the reliability and precision of radiocarbon dates for alluvial sediments vary, but so does their chronostratigraphic potential. This can be shown by reference to three different situations common in low-energy floodplain systems (Figure 2.4).

One of the ways of overcoming problems of inwashed old carbon, hard-water error and younger contamination by roots is to date small quantities of carbon of known local origin such as identified macrofossils. This has been

Plate 2.1 The excavated block from Cossington, Soar valley, England, from which radiocarbon samples were taken. See dates in Figure 2.1 (photo: M. Keough).

facilitated by the development of accelerator mass spectroscopy dating (AMS) where the ^{14}C is measured directly rather than its radioactivity. This technique, although more expensive, can date as little as 1–3 mg of carbon (Hedges, 1991) and can therefore be used for individual macrofossils whose provenance is known. It is particularly useful for sediments with complex formational histories, such as floodplain soils.

Luminescence methods
All materials that contain, or are exposed to, radioactive substances (such as uranium) are continuously bombarded by radiation. This causes ionisation and the trapping of electrons in the mineral. As radiation continues, trapped electrons build up and if they can be measured and the radiation dose rate is known, then the time elapsed since the radiation started can be calculated. This measurement is possible because if the mineral is heated it emits extra light above that normally emitted proportional to the electrons trapped – thermo-luminescence (TL). If the heating is repeated, the extra light will not be given off, as electrons will not have had enough time to build up again. In addition to measuring the light emitted, the concentration of radioactive elements can be measured by mass spectrometry.

Pottery is ideal for such dating because firing reduces the TL signal to zero (as all trapped electrons are released) if the temperature is high enough.

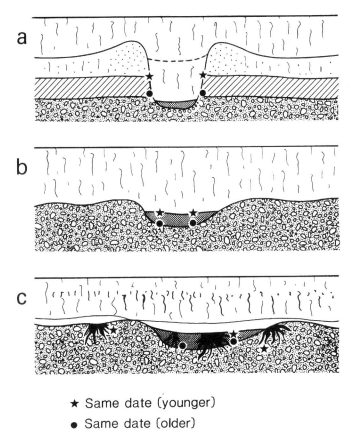

★ Same date (younger)

● Same date (older)

Fig. 2.4 Diagram illustrating the different geomorphological significance of four radiocarbon dates from three different stratigraphies of a lateral peat bed where all the dates (a) pre-date channel cutting, (b) post-date channel cutting and provide a maximum age for channel infilling and abandonment, and (c) provide the same as (b) but also the age of a landsurface formed post-channel infilling.

However, sunlight can also reduce the TL signal of sediments to zero, so loess, for example, can be dated relatively easily. Thermoluminescence has been applied to river terrace deposits outside the range of radiocarbon dating (Nanson *et al.*, 1991). It is therefore potentially of great importance for dating terrace-associated Palaeolithic artifacts and sites. When first applied to alluvial sediments, doubt was cast over whether they had been sufficiently zeroed to give the date of deposition (Berger, 1984). Owing to the dynamics of the fluvial system and the generally short period of exposure of the sediment, the thorough penetration of light for all grains cannot be assumed (Bailiff, 1992). However, Nanson and Young (1987) and Nanson *et al.* (1991) have produced TL dates from terraces of the Nepean river in New South Wales and from an alluvial sand below the floodplain of Coopers Creek in western Queensland which agree well with other dating evidence. Their conclusion is that, if the dates are from shallow sand flows deposited as sheets on floodplains, where residual TL and long-term sediment moisture contents can be accurately estimated, TL dating is reliable and can provide an excellent basis for alluvial chronologies. So far the greatest impact of TL dating in the UK has been on some classic Palaeolithic sites, including the dating of fluvial deposits at Swanscombe to around 202,000–228,000 bp which is close to previous estimates for the Hoxnian interglacial of *c.* 250,000 bp (Jones and Keen, 1993).

A similar technique, optical stimulation luminescence (OSL), probably has a wider application to alluvial deposits and requires less sophisticated equipment (Huntley *et al.*, 1985; Rhodes and Aitken, 1988; Bailiff, 1992). Visible light can be used to stimulate luminescence in quartz and infra-red radiation with feldspars. As with TL, many factors affect the accuracy of 'apparent' luminescence ages, including mineralogy, light exposure before burial-darkening (Rhodes and Pownall, 1994), overburden, erosion, and the nature of the radiation dose. This last factor is itself affected by sediment water content.

Another related chronometric method is electron spin resonance (ESR). During radioactive decay the electron bonding which is broken apart not only produces trapped electrons, but also induces altered electron energy states. The relative amount of induced electron energy states is a function of the radionuclides in the material and the time over which decay has occurred. The importance for alluvial geoarchaeology largely lies in the potential of this method for chronometric dating of flint artifacts in terrace deposits (Garrison *et al.*, 1981).

Potassium-argon series ($^{40}K/^{40}Ar$) dating

Unstable potassium decays via two pathways to either ^{40}Ca or ^{40}Ar gas. The second pathway can be used to date volcanic or metamorphic rocks rich in potassium, if the mineral structure within the rock is tight enough to prevent the 'daughter' isotope, argon gas, from escaping. The method is only of practical importance for ages over 100 Ka bp and the most commonly used rock type for Quaternary applications is volcanic ash or tephra. Tephra layers can provide excellent correlation and dating over wide areas and a wide variety of sites (Long and Morton, 1987; Dugmore, 1991). The discovery of very thin ash layers at considerable distances from their volcanic sources suggests this method may have considerable potential for dating alluvial landsurfaces where sedimentation rates are high enough and mixing is limited.

Uranium series disequilibrium dating

The isotopes ^{238}U, ^{235}U and ^{232}Th (thorium) all decay through complicated chains of intermediate isotopes to the stable lead isotopes. The uranium series method works on the basis that some of the isotopes are insoluble and others soluble in water. The insoluble ones, such as thorium, will be present in sediments and accumulate on lake beds and the sea bed. The soluble ones, such as the uraniums, may be metabolised by organisms. The former are said to be unsupported, in that they have become isolated from the rest of the decay chain, while the latter, the biogenically precipitated, are supported. The measurement of the decay products of each can yield an estimate of the age of the material (Ku, 1976). Theoretically, floodplain materials, including tufa, are suitable for this method although as yet only speleothems and corals have received much attention. A second possible material is peat which absorbs uranium from groundwater; there is the potential here for the dating of inter-glacial peaty channel infills. The major problem is the common incorporation of uranium-bearing organic detrital material in non-ombrogenous alluvial peats which are far from ideal closed systems.

2.3 Incremental and calibrated relative techniques

There are some dating methods which do not fit easily into either the relative or the chronometric category. These include dendrochronology, which, if the sample rings can be matched to one of the long tree-ring sequences continuous to the present, is effectively chronometric. If, however, they cannot, they may still be matched to a floating chronology which may be dated by other means, providing relative dating. Another technique is palaeomagnetic dating which relies fundamentally on the correlation of changes in the earth's magnetic field preserved in sediments. Because it is based upon correlation it is methodolog-ically relative; but since these changes are globally synchronous, once they have been dated by a truly chronometric method it is effectively non-relative.

Incremental techniques include all those techniques where the deposition of sediment or growth of a layer of tissue, shell or bone is a seasonal and annual event. These include annually laminated sediments in lakes (varves), and growth rings in coral and mollusca. The most useful for alluvial studies is, however, the dating of wood from tree rings – dendrochronology. Calibrated relative techniques are based upon an, ideally globally synchronous, event that is recorded in sediments and which, once dated by other means, can then be used as a datum. One example is volcanic ashes which can be preserved in sedi-ments thousands of miles away from the source and which, because all erup-tions are slightly different, may be chemically fingerprinted and related back to a radiometrically dated eruption chronology. A second calibrated relative method which has been used in alluvial environments is palaeomagnetic dating.

Dendrochronological dating
Tree-ring dating has provided detailed and accurate chronologies for several studies of floodplain development, a good example being studies of the Upper Danube and river Main in southern Germany (Becker, 1975; Becker and Schirmer, 1977; Figure 2.5). Using dendrochronological dating of fluvially

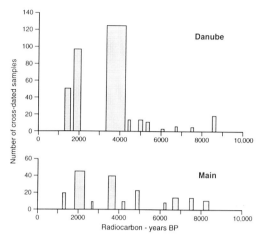

Fig. 2.5 Deposition of dated tree trunks (rannen) over time in the Main and Danube rivers. Adapted from Becker and Schirmer (1977).

deposited tree trunks (or rannen), they have shown that the Middle Ages were characterised by increased fluvial activity. In principle, tree-ring dating is relatively simple, with cross-matching of the ring widths being used to tie the alluvial wood to a fixed or floating chronology. The counting and measurement of rings has been partly automated through the use of x-ray densitometry, and curve matching can be done by computer as well as by eye. To be usable for dating, wood must be large enough to have sufficient rings and of a species for which a local curve exists. In Britain most regional curves exist for oak, although some curves do exist for other species including alder. In northern Europe and mountainous regions, including much of North America, pine species are most commonly used. However, there are several complicating factors, including standardisation for cross-dating, and false and missing rings. Details of the method and these complicating factors can be found in Fritts (1976) and Lowe and Walker (1984). Most of the complicating factors are related to the local environment and especially climatic variables which limit growth. These vary from place to place but variation in tree-ring width and wood density have been shown to correlate well with both climatic records (Fritts, 1976; Schweingruber, 1978) and streamflow records (Smith and Stockton, 1981). These relationships can be used to estimate past climate and streamflow – the sub-discipline of dendroclimatology (see chapter 8 for further discussion). The most obvious limitation of tree-ring dating is the need for tree trunks of sufficient diameter to permit dating; this biases the technique towards forested environments and sediment traps downstream of eroding banks. The most successful use of the technique in the UK has been on a reach of the river Trent near Nottingham which is discussed in detail in chapter 6.

Palaeomagnetic dating

Palaeomagnetic dating has been used for many years for fired archaeological materials, but can also be used on some natural sediments. From the remanent magnetic signature of the material an estimate is made of (a) its polarity (i.e. normal or reversed) and (b) the position of the magnetic North Pole, and these are compared with the known history of magnetic reversals and polar wandering, dated by other means. The most important characteristic of the sediment is that the natural remanent magnetism which is aligned to the ambient magnetic field must be locked into the grains at the time of formation or deposition, and in theory there are three ways this can happen.

The first is thermo-remanent magnetism which is formed as molten rock cools through the Curie point (i.e. volcanic rocks). All iron oxides demagnetise at the Curie point (675°C for haematite and 565°C for magnetite) and on cooling are realigned to the Earth's field. The second is detrital remanent magnetism, which occurs as ferromagnetic sedimentary particles settle in a column of water (e.g. lake sediments), and the third is chemical remanent magnetism acquired when ferromagnetic oxides crystallise.

Recent studies have shown that lake sediments are often subject to post-depositional remanent magnetism after sedimentation and this may well be the most important mechanism for sedimentary rocks. Using a magnetometer, the declination and inclination of the magnetic field at the time remanent magnetism was acquired can be measured. At the scale of 10^5–10^7 years polarity reverses, but during periods of fixed polarity there are shorter reversals called events; within these periods the wandering of the North Pole is also recorded. The remanent magnetism record can then be correlated with master curves from sites which have been independently dated and, because all magnetic events can be regarded as globally synchronous, the sediments can be dated quite precisely. The most suitable terrestrial sediments other than lake deposits are aeolian or loess deposits. However, recent work has suggested that a remanent magnetism may be acquired by fine alluvial deposits (Batt and Noel, 1991; Clark, 1992). Although, in principle, overbank silts could acquire a detrital remanent magnetism, the lack of water column height and constant turbulence would seem to render this unlikely and it is more probable that the signal is caused by post-depositional chemical processes. If this is commonly found to occur and is not destroyed by reducing conditions (*gleying*), it could provide a valuable addition to the methods available for the dating of non-organic alluvial deposits and the calculation of sedimentation rates. Recent studies have shown that palaeomagnetic dating seems to work in two situations, first in relatively uniform sandy silts of overbank origin which have been rapidly accreted and relatively little bioturbated, and where the natural remanent magnetism is carried by detrital magnetic grains. Such sediments have recently been dated from small river valleys north of Rome (Brown and Ellis, 1995). The second situation is where palaeochannels have been abandoned and have a silt-clay infill deposited in organic-rich stagnant anoxic conditions where the natural remanent magnetism is carried by iron sulphide minerals probably biogenically precipitated (C. Ellis and A. G. Brown, in prep.). Magnetic properties such as anisotropy of susceptibility can also yield a wealth of information on sedimentary conditions and produce estimates of palaeocurrent direction and strength from suitable sediments, generally palaeochannel infills. Palaeomagnetic dating could also be extremely useful in conjunction with mineral magnetic studies of the dating of prehistoric topsoil erosion.

Amino acid racemisation

This method is only applicable to organic matter and as yet only to bone and shell. Amino acids in proteins can survive in bone and shell long after death. The original chains of amino acids (peptide chains) break down at a relatively slow rate, if trapped in the organic structure. One of the mechanisms of this diagenesis called racemisation occurs because there are two molecular patterns of chains with identical chemical composition but reversed configuration; the so-called L-isomer and D-isomer types. On death, the L-isomers are converted to D-isomers until both are in equilibrium so the D/L ratio is 1. The rate at which this happens is thought to be partially time-dependent. However, the rate is also temperature dependent and varies for each amino acid and from species to species. Largely because of the temperature dependence, it has so far only been used to erect an amino-stratigraphy which has been calibrated by radiometric methods (in particular Uranium series dating). Its major use so far has been in the dating of interglacial raised beaches (Miller *et al.*, 1979) but the dating of non-marine shells offers the possibility of direct dating of fossiliferous terrace deposits, and it is also an important method of cross-checking other methods for Palaeolithic terrace sites. The terraces of the Avon in central England have now been dated using acid racemisation (Maddy *et al.*, 1991), allowing them to be correlated with non-alluvial deposits in the UK (Figure 2.6).

The increasing range of dating methods available applicable to alluvial sediments will reduce the bias imposed by any one sediment type or climatic regime. This is particularly true of radiocarbon as the preservation of wood and peat is not random but controlled by climate and groundwater conditions and this has probably imposed a subtle bias to alluvial chronologies from areas like the Mediterranean (see chapter 7 for more discussion of this point).

2.4 Archaeological dating: structures and pots in alluvium

Probably the best datable horizon in an alluvial unit can be a structure buried by alluvium. If floors or walls are tightly dated and sealed by alluvium they provide in theory an excellent *terminus a quo* for the overlying alluvium and *terminus ad quem* for the underlying alluvium. However, in practice this is often not the case for several reasons. One reason is that many structures discovered under alluvium are not easily dated. This is particularly true of bridge piers or causeways as they are rarely excavated and are not generally associated with datable pottery and other artifacts. Even if such a structure is dated, there can

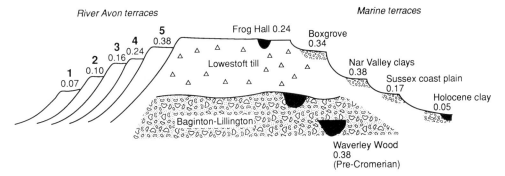

Fig. 2.6 Acid racemisation values (ratios) and a tentitive correlation of the Avon terraces, England, and marine terraces. Adapted from Maddy *et al.* (1991) and Bowen *et al.* (1989).

remain a problem in estimating the original ground level at the time of construction, as without floors and doorways it is difficult to know the depth of foundations. This means that in general the most suitable structures for dating alluvium are houses, tombs, etc. There is a subtle bias in these data as these sites will be buried in those floodplains with dense human occupation and possibly higher rates of alluviation.

Shards are frequently found in alluvial sediments. In archaeological terms they are residual (*sensu* Orton *et al.*, 1993) and there is rarely if ever any completeness in a pot or tile assemblage derived from an alluvial sedimentary unit. The literature contains rather polarised views on the efficacy of alluvial shards for dating; on the one hand diagnostic shards have frequently been used rather uncritically where no other evidence was available, on the other hand some have dismissed their use entirely on the grounds listed below:

1 They can only ever provide an *terminus a quo* for alluvial deposition, i.e. the unit must post-date the pottery, assuming, that is, that it was not in an unrecognised cut feature and part of an archaeological site.
2 Much if not most pottery and tile is undiagnostic and generally impossible to date with any accuracy.
3 Even for fine wares local chronological typologies may be approximate or non- existent.
4 Reworked shards are extremely common, as illustrated by the general occurrence of mixed assemblages, where only the youngest is of dating value.

In order to make more use of pottery and tile greater consideration needs to be given to the processes of inclusion and deposition. In general there are two inputs to floodplains, one via transport in the stream channel, the other via direct addition to the floodplain surface through manuring, rubbish disposal, accidental loss, or from a site (Figure 2.7). This produces two classes of shards, one angular and non-abraded which predominates in fine units (silts) and one

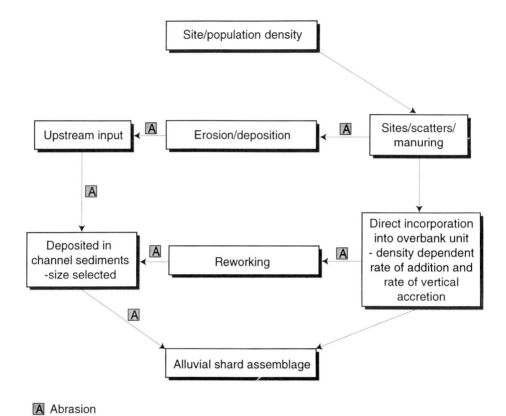

Fig. 2.7 Factors in the inclusion of pottery into alluvial sediments.

sub-angular and abraded which is more common in coarser channel units. The density of pot in fine overbank units is a function of the rate of addition to the surface divided by the rate of vertical accretion of sediment. The rate of addition will have varied owing to socioeconomic factors including site density, wealth, and agricultural extent and practices, but is probably more conservative than the rate of overbank deposition. One reason for this assertion is that rapidly deposited fine alluvial units frequently contain no pottery even in periods of known high-intensity settlement and agriculture (Brown and Ellis, 1995).

Pending further studies on the taphonomy of alluvial pot and tile it is suggested that it can at least provide a useful first-order dating control and may give some indication of the rapidity of deposition of Late Holocene units. The range of condition of pot and tile may also give some indication of the degree of reworking and direct pottery inclusion to the floodplain system.

2.5 Stability and change

Both environmental scientists and archaeologists are concerned with how and why change occurs. Change is always relative and in practice stability includes low-magnitude, undetectable and zero change. Indeed we often identify stability by looking for change, and our ability to differentiate between stability and change depends upon the sensitivity of our methods. Stability can therefore be undetectable rates of change. Both disciplines therefore share an interest in both types and rates of change.

Our ideas on the nature of change have themselves evolved over time. One of the most important theories of landscape change was based upon a decay-sequence of changes supposedly exhibited by fluvial landforms and slopes called by Davis (1902) the 'Cycle of Erosion'. After tectonic uplift catchments went through youth, mature and old-age stages (Figure 2.8). In this model of change floodplain formation was one of the characteristics of the old-age stage. Despite its many shortcomings one of the conceptual advances it contained was that it acknowledged that landform change could occur without any change in climate. This contradicted the climatic models of the late nineteenth century in which climate determined landforms and change only occurred because of climate change. Both these models were essentially concerned with long/geological time periods.

The use of systems theory from the 1960s onwards encouraged systematic identification of all the related variables in a given system, their status as dependent or independent variables and the direction of causality. The river system is an example of a process-response system which includes water and sediment transport as a response to external environmental controls. The status of variables in process-response systems varies with the time-scale of investigation (Schumm and Lichty, 1965). Davis's model operated at the geological scale. On the historic scale (the graded time-scale of Schumm and Lichty) equilibrium channel forms develop that are a response to both the amount of water and sediment supplied to the system and valley characteristics inherited from geological time, such as gradient and valley fill deposits.

The equilibrium model of river and hillslope evolution was first formulated by Gilbert (1877) and further developed by Hack (1965). The concept of dynamic equilibrium is an important one; it describes the situation when the system is in a state of balance in which every slope (including river reaches) is adjusted to every other and the overall form can remain practically constant with mass constantly moving through it, as long as the external conditions do not change. An example is a meandering river which is undergoing neither net erosion nor deposition but still migrating across its floodplain with very little change in overall form. Some of the problems associated with this model when applied to long time periods can be overcome by relating types of equilibrium to different time-scales (Figure 2.8). In the short term, river width varies owing to individual floods, but at the longer time-scale these are random perturbations about a progressive trend caused by climate change or tectonic change, i.e. the river is adjusting to remain in equilibrium with its environment. Because there are thresholds in the fluvial system, dynamic metastable equilibrium can result. So if an external change occurs the system will attempt to return to a new equilibrium state; how quickly it can do this will depend upon what is known

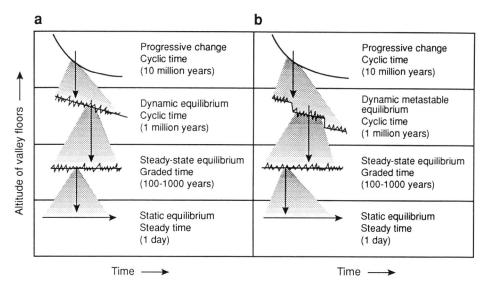

Fig. 2.8 Models of landscape change over time. (a) The Cycle of Erosion, adapted after Davis (1902), and (b) equilibrium states, from Schumm and Lichty (1965) and Chorley and Kennedy (1971).

as the recovery time of the system. In semi-arid floodplains this is a long period (30–100 years or more) and so morphology reflects the effects of the last major flood. Indeed, if the recovery time is greater than the average period between large events the system cannot achieve equilibrium. Many stratigraphic sequences, such as terraces deposited by superfloods, are now believed to be the result of this condition; here the stratigraphy represents a history of big events. Since this can also happen in temperate environments, as is exemplified by the catastrophic Lyn flood on Exmoor, Devon, in 1952 (Anderson and Calver, 1977), we need to recognise these memory effects caused by the queuing of events. One of the most important but difficult aspects of stratigraphic interpretation is the differentiation of extreme events and their repercussions from the 'normal' behaviour of the system in the face of changing external conditions, be they climatic, tectonic or human induced.

In order to be able to describe changes in any environment dating is essential, to determine rates of change as well as to place events in a geological, archaeological or historical context. While chronometric methods are preferable it is rarely possible to date all contexts or sedimentary units and so we will continue to rely upon stratigraphy and correlation at least at the site level. In order to interpret the dated stratigraphy a knowledge of the sedimentary products of earth surface processes is essential. This knowledge can be gained by observation of contemporary processes and experimentation. Geologists call this the principle of uniformitarianism which is often summarised as 'the present is the key to the past'. The next three chapters are concerned with these processes and their extrapolation to reconstructing past environmental conditions.

3

INTERPRETING FLOODPLAIN
SEDIMENTS AND SOILS

Floodplain evolution reflects the prevailing environmental conditions and changes in those conditions. This chapter illustrates how the sediments and soils which form floodplain stratigraphies can be used to reconstruct past environmental conditions.

3.1 River morphology and sedimentation

Our ability to infer past conditions from floodplain sediments comes from the analysis of contemporary rivers and their sedimentation, i.e. the present is the key to the past. It is necessary therefore to understand the general morphology (pattern and shape) of rivers and processes that operate in them. Rivers in all climatic zones vary from headwaters to outlet owing to the changing volumes of water and sediment supplied to them and the local geology and slope over which they run. In small mountainous headwaters bedrock and coarse bed material dominate the channel, resulting in steps, pools, cascades and waterfalls (Church, 1992). Alternatively in low-relief areas headwaters may be almost imperceptible wet patches (flushes), springs or field drains with cohesive peaty or clay-rich beds and banks. In larger mountain and piedmont zone rivers channel bar accumulations are important stores for bed material (Church and Jones, 1982). In these channels the pool and riffle is the major morphological feature (Figure 3.1). It is believed that the pool is created by scour during floods but under normal and low flows the velocity of water flow is faster over the shallow riffles and water is slower in the pools (Keller, 1971 and later discussion). Most riffles are composed of channel side-bars or diagonal bars (Figure 3.2; Table 1.1). If bars form in the centre of the channel or a channel side-bar is isolated from the channel bank by a flood then the channel may split into two or more channels, forming a braided pattern. In nature, channels display many planforms and there are several ways channel pattern can be classified but the most commonly used is into the categories: straight, sinuous or meandering, braided, and anabranching or anastomosing (Figure 3.3). Several studies have shown that this classification is not without problems; however, it makes intuitive sense and is widely used, while at the same time it is accepted that patterns exist and patterns can change in both time and space. Straight channels are rare in nature but, until very recently, this was the universally preferred pattern for artificial and modified channels. Even when channels appear to be straight, the line of maximum velocity and depth, the *thalweg,* alternates from side to side.

63

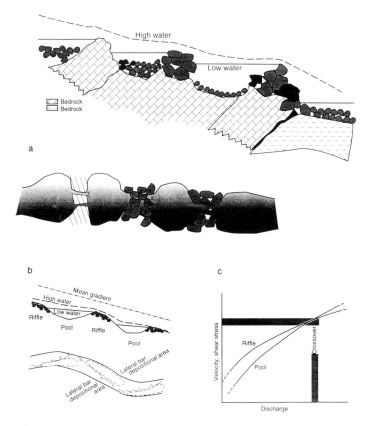

Fig. 3.1 Definition sketch of (a) a step pool channel, (b) a pool-riffle sequence, and (c) the relationship between velocity/shear stress and discharge in a riffle-pool section. In part adapted from Church and Jones (1982).

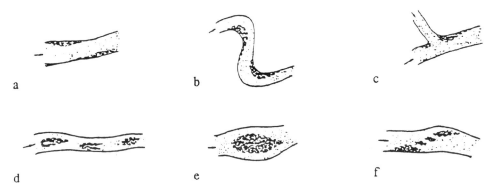

Fig. 3.2 Morphological classification of channel bars: (a) channel side-bars, (b) point-bars, (c) channel junction bars, (d) mid-channel bars, (e) diamond bars and (f) diagonal bars. Adapted from Kellerhals and Church (1989).

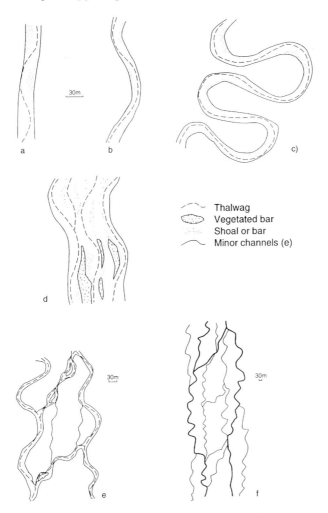

Fig. 3.3 Channel pattern types: (a) straight, (b) sinuous, (c) meandering, (d) braided, (e) anastomosing and (f) anabranching.

Therefore, a straight channel can be regarded as a proto-sinuous or meandering channel. The degree of meandering or sinuosity is calculated relatively easily (see Figure 1.4) and is a useful parameter as it describes the complexity of the channel pattern and is a measure of the travel-path of water and sediment. Braided rivers (Plate 3.1) have a relatively wide channel in which there are mobile bars or low islands splitting up the thalweg. These bars are inundated by high flows which need not inundate the floodplain. In the sense that these bars are part of the channel system the braided pattern can be distinguished from discrete multiple channel or anastomosing patterns where individual channels bisect the floodplain surface. Both anastomosing and anabranching channels have many cross-connected channels of a sinuous, meandering or even

Plate 3.1 A braided, wandering gravel-bedded river in north-eastern England.

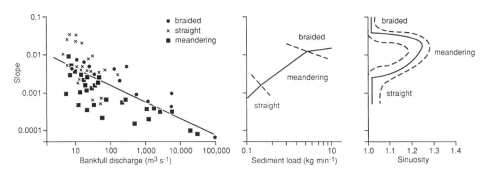

Fig. 3.4 Leopold and Wolman (1957) discrimination between straight, meandering and braided channels (*left*); Schumm and Khan (1972) discrimination (*right*).

braided type and are really floodplain/channel classifications rather than channel types. In most cases the existence of features like levées and the type and maturity of soils and vegetation also distinguish anastomosing from braided systems. Much research has gone into explaining what is in reality a continuum of river forms using flow, physiographic and other variables.

In a classic study of river channel patterns Leopold and Wolman (1957) showed that braided channels occur at higher slopes and discharges than meandering channels (Figure 3.4a), and Schumm and Khan (1972) have shown that there are thresholds of increasing sediment load between straight, meandering and braided patterns (Figure 3.4b). Although slope, discharge and load are of paramount importance, other factors such as the nature of the banks also affect channel pattern. Lewin and Brindle (1977) have shown that free meandering is prevented by obstacles such as railway embankments or other artificial structures or by bedrock and this can cause a square-wave type meandering pattern. Channel pattern is dynamic in both space and time because it is controlled fundamentally by the distribution of erosive forces and resisting forces along channel boundaries (the so-called force:resistance balance).

In alluvial channels generally with a meandering planform the distribution of energy in relation to bed material produces the pool riffle sequence. Riffles, which are normally spaced about 5 to 7 channel widths apart, are high points in the river long-profile, with pools the low points spaced in-between. The riffles are generally composed of coarser sediment, e.g. pebbles, and have always been a focus of human activity as they are the easiest points to ford rivers. The bed sediment in pools is finer although this may be underlain by sediments just as coarse as in the riffles. The change from pool to riffle is the product of flow variation as at low flow, flow over the riffles is shallow with a steep gradient whereas in the pools flow is slower, deeper and with a gentler water surface gradient. The result is a higher velocity on the riffle which washes out fine sediment into the pool where it is deposited. But, as observed by Keller (1971) and confirmed using flow modelling (Keller and Florsheim, 1993), at high flows the situation is reversed: flow is faster across the pools and slower across the riffles. Shear stress is also reversed at high flow (Lisle, 1979) and sediment sorting occurs as coarse sediment is scoured from the pools at high flows and deposited on a riffle, but as flow declines the scour surface will be buried by finer sediment.

Open channel flow is characterised by the development of secondary circulation systems which vary from pool to riffle, around a meander bend (Figure 3.5), in response to irregularities in the bank (Plate 3.2) and at junctions with backwaters (Plate 3.3). From the helicoidal flow theory it was proposed that there exist two spiral currents or cells in straight and moderately wide channels, which are replaced by a single spiral cell at bends that erodes the outer bank and deposits on the inner bank. However, direct observations have shown that two cells can exist at meander bends (Hey and Thorne, 1975). They converge at the water surface around the bend at the pool and show surface flow divergence at inflection points where riffles occur. In reality, complex and irregular river channels commonly have several cells at different flows which results in a complex distribution of erosion and deposition that is not easy to predict. Examples include deposition on steep banks, on the outer bends of meanders and erosion of inner banks. In pools, flow is convergent at the surface and plunges, while on riffles surface flow is divergent. It is the development of cell asymmetry at the outside of the meander bend that is responsible for bank erosion and channel

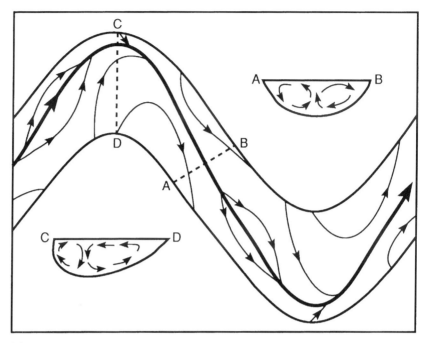

Fig. 3.5 Flow circulation around a meander bend. Adapted from Hey and Thorne (1975).

Plate 3.2 Secondary flow circulation caused by bank irregularities and picked out by foam, on the river Liffey, Ireland.

Plate 3.3 Dead water with a secondary flow vortex picked out by foam at the junction of a backwater and a main channel, from the river Ae, Dumfriesshire, Scotland.

migration (Hey and Thorne, 1975). Keller (1972) has proposed a useful five-stage conceptual model to explain the development of alluvial stream channels based upon the creation of pools and riffles from asymmetrical shoals (see Figure 3.6). In stage 1 there are no pools or riffles and the dominant bedforms are assymetrical shoals. In stage 2 incipient pools and riffles are spaced about every three to five channel widths and the dominant bedforms are still asymmetrical shoals. In stage 3 the pools and riffles are well developed with a spacing of five to seven channel widths and the dominant bedforms are pools and riffles with asymmetrical shoals which are now incipient point-bars. In stages 4 and 5 the pools lengthen relative to the riffles and point-bars develop. Stages 3 and 4 are crucial in this model as this is when characteristic meander planforms are initiated. In braided systems, pool–riffle sequences are associated with each thalweg or channel thread, so that there are multiple flow cells, the number and location of which change as bars are created and destroyed. With anastomosing channels, on the other hand, each channel operates as a separate meandering channel and channel change operates through migration or more commonly the sudden adoption of a new channel through avulsion: this can occur with or without the complete abandonment of the old channel. In general, channels reoccupy old abandoned channels, since these are often the lowest part of the floodplain. This makes avulsion a quasi-predictable process.

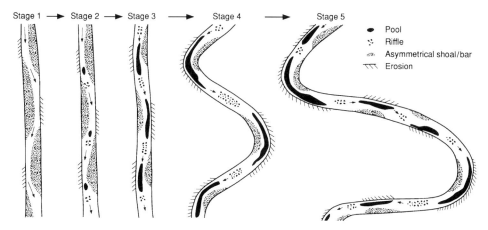

Fig. 3.6 The Keller five-stage model of meander development. Reproduced from the *Bulletin of the Geological Society of America*, Keller (1972), by permission of the Geological Society of America.

The hydraulics of flow in pools and riffles has direct consequences for the sorting and burial of artifacts and other archaeological materials such as bones, as will be shown later in this chapter. The location of former pools and riffles can therefore be of great importance for archaeological 'site' interpretation.

3.2 Floodplain sediments

The deposition of sediments on riffles, on mid-channel bars either longitudinal or transverse, and on channel inner bends as point-bars produces characteristic channel sediments which are one component of floodplain or terrace deposits. From excavations into these deposits the following sedimentary characteristics can be recorded: grain sizes (texture), the arrangement of grain size variation (fabric), preferential orientation of particles (imbrication, Plate 3.4), small boundary-defining structures within units or beds, and the stacking and order of these units or beds (architecture). The fabric, structures and architecture all relate to the conditions of deposition. Figure 3.7 illustrates the relationship between fabric, structure and architecture. Fundamentally the procedures are the same as those used in the basin analysis of geological fluvial sediments, a good general outline of which can be found in Miall (1983).

The main depositional unit of meandering streams is the point-bar (Figure 3.8; Plate 3.5). The point-bar consists of two components, a basal platform of gravel only moved in floods and continuous with the riffles, and a supra-platform component controlled by the distribution of stream power around the bend during the falling stage. Sediment size declines from the scour-pool up the bar surface, because bed velocity and shear stress decrease up the point-bar surface. This means finer particles migrate further up the point-bar, and since

Plate 3.4 A section through the drained bed of the river Perry, Shropshire, England, showing a variation in clast size from cobbles to fines, stratification, variation in fabric and slight imbrication. The tape case is 15 cm in diameter.

the bedforms which produce sedimentary structures are controlled by stream power and particle size, they have a characteristic relationship to their location on the point-bar. Lower down, however, where stream power is higher, dunes may develop whereas higher up ripples develop. For more detail on the many forms of ripples and dunes see a standard sedimentology text such as Leeder (1982). Ripples and dunes are associated with lower regime flow. This is indicated by the Froude number which is a measure of the ability of a gravity wave to travel upstream (see appendix 1). When flow is critical (Froude number in excess of one) a gravity wave cannot travel against the flow, so if a pebble is thrown into the river ripples will not radiate upstream. For those requiring a more detailed introduction to the basis of river flow see appendix 1 for an introduction to hydraulics and sediment transport theory. For lower regime flow the Froude number is well below one (a gravity wave can travel upstream), and flow is referred to as sub-critical, dunes and flat beds form under the transitional regime (Froude number 0.3–0.8) and antidunes formed by standing waves under upper regimeflow. Flow regime as used here describes the hydraulics of the flow as explained more fully in appendix 1. Very slow flow is laminar with water travelling like sliding sheets, but most flow is turbulent and may be critical at high discharges.

The migration of ripples and dunes creates diagnostic cross-bedding which can be preserved in-channel and sometimes even in overbank sediments.

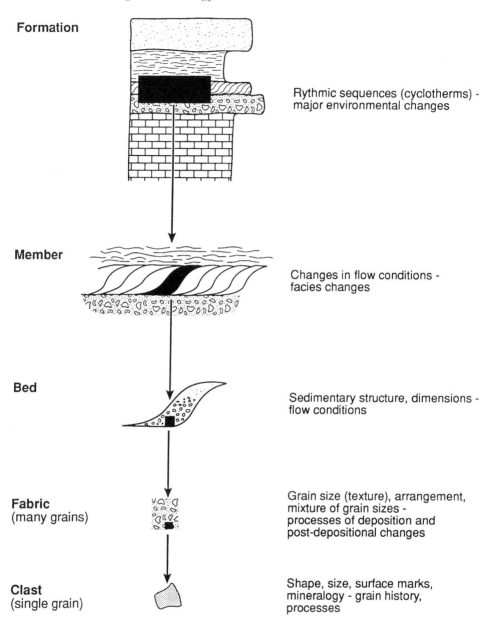

Formation

Rythmic sequences (cyclotherms) -
major environmental changes

Member

Changes in flow conditions -
facies changes

Bed

Sedimentary structure, dimensions -
flow conditions

Fabric
(many grains)

Grain size (texture), arrangement,
mixture of grain sizes -
processes of deposition and
post-depositional changes

Clast
(single grain)

Shape, size, surface marks,
mineralogy - grain history,
processes

Fig. 3.7 Sediment fabric, structure and architecture.

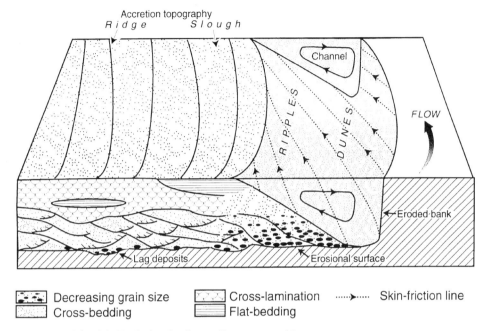

Fig. 3.8 Typical point-bar sedimentary architecture.

Particle size sorting and bedform development also produce the characteristic point-bar stratigraphy (Figure 3.8); a fining upward sequence (Allen, 1965; 1977) with, from base to top: an erosional surface, channel lag deposits, coarse sand with large-scale cross-stratification, progressively finer sands with ripple cross-laminae and, at the top, silty-clay deposits formed by overbank flow. This idealised sequence can only develop where flow velocity and bed material are in equilibrium; variations in gravel:sand supply ratios will cause departures from this model as will post-depositional disturbance caused by soil processes or ploughing. Large floods may reverse this sequence, producing a unit with reversed grading, i.e. coarsening up from silts to sand or gravel. The recognition of these reverse graded units is helpful in identifying periods of hydrological change and in particular slack-water deposits – palaeoflood indicators *sensu* Baker (1974a); Kochel and Baker (1982) and Baker *et al.* (1983).

High-energy braided streams which are constantly eroding and depositing material within the channel zone, can develop at a variety of spatial scales and for limited periods of time (Passmore *et al.*, 1993). The principal channel processes involved in braiding are: longitudinal bar formation which produces bedded gravels, bedform generation which produces cross-bedded sands and gravels, and channel scour-and-fill which produces erosional surfaces. Low-water accretion can also produce laminated fines and mud-drapes (Miall, 1977). Miall has identified ten lithofacies (sediment assemblages characteristic of certain depositional processes) for braided environments as listed below:

Plate 3.5 Point-bars developing from alternating bars on a river in eastern Spain.
This river reach resembles stage three in the Keller model.

massively bedded gravel Gm
trough cross-bedded gravel: Gt
planar cross-bedded gravel: Gp
trough cross-bedded sands: St
planar cross-bedded sands: Sp
ripple cross-bedded sands: Sr
horizontally bedded sands: Sh
scour-fill sands: Ss
laminated sand-silt-mud: Fl
mud and silt drapes: Fm

The processes responsible for depositing these facies types are longitudinal bar
formation and accretion (Gm), bedform generation and migration (Gp, St, Sp,
Sh), channel scour and fill (Gt, Ss), low-water accretion (Sr, Sh, Fl, Fm) and
overbank sedimentation (Fl). Miall (1973) used Markov chain analysis (which
identifies repeated pattern in sequences) to reveal preferred successions, two
examples of which are:

Plate 3.6 Mudballs on the floodplain of the river Turon in southern Spain after a flood in November 1989.

> modern gravelly braided stream: Gm → Sh → Sr → Fm
> modern sandy braided stream: St → Sp → Sp,Sh,Sr or St → Fm →
>   Sp → Ps,Sh,Sr

The differentiation of ancient meandering and braided environments is, however, not a simple task. It cannot be assumed that all course-bedded sand and gravel deposits such as characterise most fluvial terraces were deposited in a braided environment.

So far we have only considered deposits of the channel zone. However, alluvial sequences commonly contain non-channel sediments which also relate to channel type, pattern and rate of migration. These include: crevasse-splay deposits, fine overbank deposits, channel fill deposits, lacustrine deposits, organic deposits and colluvium, as introduced in chapter 1. Crevasse-splay deposits are formed by a break in river levées allowing bed material, traction and suspended load to splay-out onto the floodplain surface in the form of a ribbon or fan. This is one of the ways in which bedload, including brick, tiles and mudballs (Plate 3.6) may be incorporated into overbank sediments. Floods transfer momentum and carry suspended material onto the floodplain. As velocities decline both in time and away from the channel, suspended sediment may settle out by size/density and produce coarse–medium sand lobes on levées (Plate 3.7) and, where velocities are lower, flood couplets. These couplets are formed because fine sand and coarse silt settle out quickly and are then covered

Plate 3.7 Levee sediments formed by a single flood of the river Soar, England. Note the confined lobe-like form and the way in which the sand has migrated from the channel by avalanching as indicated by the slip face (on which the lens cap sits). The feature is composed of well-sorted uni-modal medium to coarse sand.

by a layer of fine silt and clay which is probably deposited in the form of micro-aggregates. These couplets if not bioturbated may form laminated sediments (Plate 3.8). Deposition will depend not only on sediment characteristics and concentrations, but also on flow velocities and current patterns, which in turn are affected by floodplain topography, roughness and wind. A few studies have managed to monitor flood inundation or map trash (Plate 3.9) and sediments immediately post-flood and they have shown how complex velocity patterns are, how spatially variable sedimentation is and how important floodplain vegetation is as a roughness component (Popov and Gavrin, 1970; Lewin, 1978; Brown, 1983b). It should be remembered that, if flood water does not completely infiltrate or evaporate but flows back into the channel as stage falls (return flow), then potentially a large amount of the suspended sediment may be transported back into the channel, reducing deposition, and eroding the flood deposits (Plate 3.10). Net erosion can even occur and the scour of flood-deposited silt by returning flow is commonly seen on floodplains with relatively high gradients and high sediment loads (Plate 3.11). Some attempts have been made to model flood deposition, particularly grain size variation, modelling turbulence and convection as diffusion processes (James, 1985; Pizzuto, 1987). Marriott (1992) has used textural analysis of a flood of the river Severn in order

Plate 3.8 Laminated overbank sediments from the Lower Severn, England.

Plate 3.9 A trash line at the crest of a levée of the river Soar, England.

Plate 3.10 Erosion of overbank deposits from a flood of the river Turon in southern Spain, November 1989. Note pen for scale.

Plate 3.11 Erosion of the floodplain soil after a flood on the river Ae, Dumfriesshire, Scotland. Note the turf roll at the base of the ranging pole.

to test James's (1985) model and found it satisfactory in relative terms. However, these models ignore the effects of vegetation, by regarding it as constant, and in practice are probably only applicable to grassed floodplains. The deposition of silt and clay is complex and controlled by several factors including aggregation (both in the water column and on plant leaves), impact-sedimentation and possibly electrochemical forces, and it is not sufficiently understood for deterministic modelling. A feasible short-term alternative is to define a trap efficiency for different types of vegetation which could be spatially distributed in a floodplain model. However, more studies are required of flood sedimentation in different land uses. An alternative is the determination of typical sedimentation rates for different land uses from caesium-137 (^{137}Cs) cores (Walling *et al.*, 1992; see below).

In many parts of the world permanent or semi-permanent water bodies exist on floodplains, especially in large systems like the Amazon. These are often quite complex, with channels connecting them to the main river system which experience reversed flow during some parts of the year. While floodplain lakes are rare in the temperate zone (largely owing to artificial drainage) they were common in the past, as is attested to by lacustrine (lake) sediments in floodplain sequences (Brown, 1987b; 1989). These lakes were generally shallow and base-rich and they deposited marl, laminated silts and clays. The smaller oxbow lake or abandoned channel can also produce pockets of lake sediments normally with the addition of overbank sedimentation.

Overbank sedimentation rates vary considerably, as shown by radiocarbon-dated units in the floodplain of the river Severn (Figure 3.9). Another method of determining recent overbank accumulation rates is by the measurement of the concentration of ^{137}Cs in the sediments and the use of the known fallout rates since the start of atomic tests in the 1950s (Walling *et al.*, 1992). This method has yielded rates of approximately 0–7 mm yr^{-1} on the floodplain of the river Culm in Devon, with the highest rates being close to the channel on the levée. Rates for a large area of floodplain at the junction of the Severn and Avon rivers in Worcestershire vary from 0 to 10 mm yr^{-1} but with the highest rates on the Avon levee, probably owing to its greater suspended sediment load (Brown *et al.*, 1987). Within oxbows, sedimentation rates can also be surprisingly high. In general, however, rates are highest nearest to the active channel (Lewis and Lewin, 1983). The nature of the sediments will vary depending on whether the oxbow is still a routeway for some flow from a tributary or if it is still used as a flood-channel. Organics are often associated with oxbows or palaeochannels and will be discussed in detail in chapter 4. Here however, we will, distinguish between autochthonous organics which have accumulated on the floodplain surface or in the channel and allochthonous organics which are not *in situ* and have been transported prior to deposition.

Autochthonous organics can be volumetrically significant floodplain sediments such as wood or reed peat and can be several metres thick in large floodplains. These peats and organic soil horizons in vertical floodplain

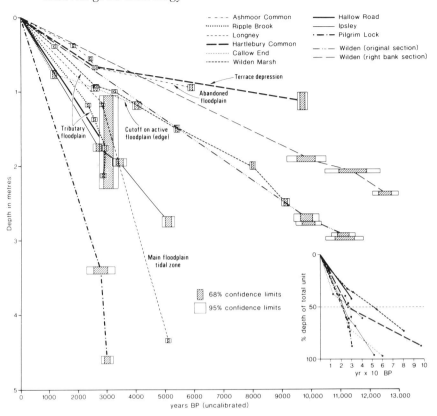

Fig. 3.9 Accumulation rates from radiocarbon dated units from the floodplain of the river Severn, England. Adapted from Brown (1987b).

sequences are often regarded as recording a standstill phase in inorganic overbank sedimentation. A better way of conceptualising this is to say that, other things being equal, organic content is inversely related to the relative rate of inorganic overbank deposition. In reality, most autochthonous floodplain organic-rich sediments, with the important exception of raised bogs (which are ombrotrophic – fed by rainfall and domed), can be placed on a mineral/organic continuum which is controlled by protection from inorganic sedimentation and groundwater conditions which control preservation.

The identification of fluvial facies has frequently been attempted by determining the quantity of different grain sizes such as cobbles, pebbles, sand, silt and clay (for details of the method, see appendix 2). The use of simple grain size statistics (e.g. d^{50} which is the median grain size by weight) or cumulative frequency curves can be indicative of broad transport mechanisms and can be used to estimate past critical shear stresses and velocities for the bedload fraction, as is described later in section 3.3 of this chapter (see also appendix 1).

However, owing to several factors including the grain sizes available for transport and the similarity in fluid forces that can occur in different environments there is no single fluvial environment that has a *unique* grain size distribution. However, along with sedimentary structures and other evidence such as fossils, grain size can indicate the hydraulic conditions of deposition and thus the sedimentary environment.

A semi-empirical method of distinguishing between transport modes is the CM diagram as originally proposed by Passega (1957). A plot is made of the d^{50} (M) against the smallest particle size in the coarsest one percentile (C) of the grain size distribution. It is therefore a plot of sorting and flow competence. Passega identifies five transport fractions: rolling (R), bottom suspension (BS), graded suspension (GS), uniform suspension (US) and pelagic suspension (PS) (Figure 3.10). Although there are theoretical problems with this approach, as we cannot identify these fractions satisfactorily on the basis of transport dynamics and indeed we know that their grain size would vary with changing flow conditions, Passega (1964) has shown that the method does differentiate between different floodplain environments in the Mississippi valley. Brown (1985a) has used it in combination with multivariate methods and the texture triangle to describe a generalised floodplain sequence from a backswamp location (Figure 3.10). Facies identification is at its easiest and safest when several characteristics can be used, including the geometry of the deposits, sedimentary structures, grain size, organic content and any fossils present (including trace fossils).

Floodplains are by definition bounded by steeper slopes which can contribute sediment to the floodplain surface. In geomorphically active environments this may be obvious, i.e. fans or cones, but even in temperate or humid environments a considerable proportion of floodplain sediments may be colluvial or of slope origin (Lattman, 1960; Brown, 1992). In so-called dry valleys, which are common in, but not restricted to, porous lithologies, the entire valley-fill may be colluvial in origin, and be rich in archaeological remains (Bell, 1983). The term colluvium covers slope deposits moved by shallow surface flow (i.e. non-channelled or slope-wash) or by mass movement (slow creep or landsliding). Observations in eroding fields reveal that, in fact, much colluvium is moved by channel flow in small rills before being deposited as a sheet downslope (Plate 3.12). The relative proportions of these different deposits, and their architecture, are controlled by the history of channel change and floodplain evolution.

3.3 Palaeohydrology

Under rather restricted circumstances it may be possible to estimate past river dimensions and discharge both from channel sediments and from preserved channel forms. This has formed the basis of the sub-discipline of palaeohydrology. Palaeohydrology has been defined as 'the science of the waters of the

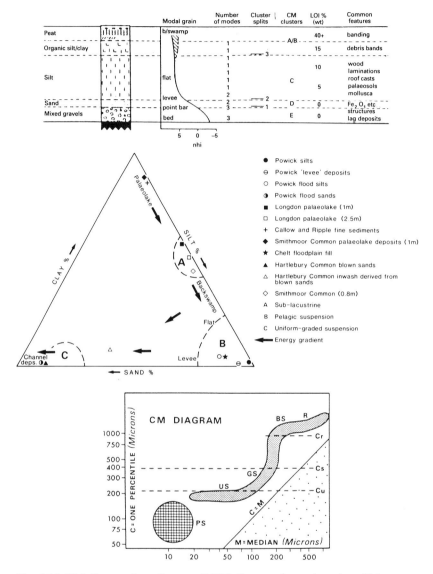

Fig. 3.10 CM diagram from Passega (1957). See text for explanation. CM diagram, texture triangle and a typical backswamp sequence from the river Severn, England. Adapted from Brown (1985a).

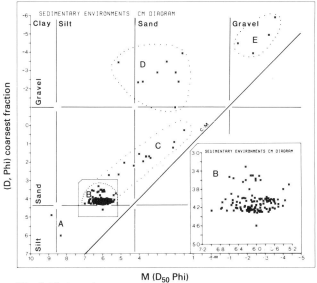

Fig. 3.10 (*cont.*)

Plate 3.12 Rills, erosion and colluvial deposits at the edge of the floodplain and slope base, caused by a single storm, Leicestershire, England. Note trash line produced by overbank peak flow prior to the deposition of the colluvial deposits.

Earth, their composition, distribution, and movement on ancient landscapes from the occurrence of the first rainfall to the beginning of hydrological records' (Schumm, 1977). Or to put it more succinctly 'the study of fluvial processes in the past and their hydrological implications' (Cheetham, 1976). This section covers the methods used which are essentially refinements of stratigraphic analysis (palaeoflood and discharge reconstruction) and the application of sediment transport theory (palaeohydraulics). The wider application of palaeohydrology to archaeology and environmental change is discussed in chapter 8. Under some circumstances, it may be possible to estimate past river dimensions and discharges from both fluvial deposits and preserved channel forms and these two methods are introduced in the following two sections.

Flow reconstruction from palaeoflood deposits

Two types of deposits have been used: fine overbank deposits left in rock-gorges by floods, and bed material moved by floods. In addition, if preserved, palaeochannel dimension can be used to predict former discharges. The general approach of extending flood frequency analysis by using Holocene stratigraphy was suggested by Costa (1978). He showed the way in which you could use several types of deposit, some of which are listed below:

1 tree-ring analysis of trees uprooted or scarred by floods
2 radiocarbon dating of sediments eroded by a flood
3 radiocarbon dating of flood deposits
4 radiocarbon dating of fine lenses of sediment buried by coarse flood deposits
5 radiocarbon dating of soils or organics in slack-water deposits
6 cumulative soil properties in flood deposited or eroded sediments.

The method of reconstructing palaeofloods from 'slack-water' deposits in gorges was described by Kotchel and Baker (1982), Baker (1983) and Baker *et al.* (1985). These studies have used radiocarbon dating to provide a chronology and frequency for the deposits, most of which have been laid down on rock ledges or terraces, such as in the Katherine Gorge, Northern Territory, Australia. It must be remembered that the method will give a partial series, because only floods that are high enough to top the previous flood deposits will be recorded, although they may be smaller than the last flood, as is illustrated in Figure 3.11. Baker *et al.* (1985) found that the discharge of the 1957 flood calculated from the height of the deposits (4000–4500 m^3s^{-1}) was very close to the nearest recorded discharge for the flood. More recent work (Baker, 1989) has enabled a complete flood frequency curve to be established for the Salt river in Arizona. An important constraint on this method is that the cross-section must have been stable, so bedrock gorges are ideal; however, other sites can be used if this stability can be demonstrated. An archaeological application of the method has been provided by Chatters and Hoover (1986), from a site on the Upper Columbia river in Washington for the period AD 120 to 1948. They sur-

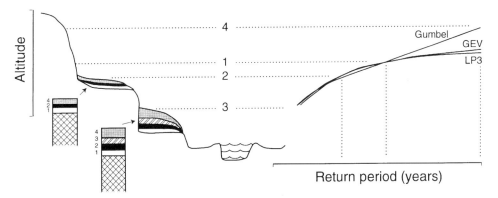

Fig. 3.11 Flood deposits illustrating the relationship between event and stratigraphy at two different heights and a flood frequency curve from the Salt river in Arizona, produced using records extended by flood sediments. Adapted from Baker (1989).

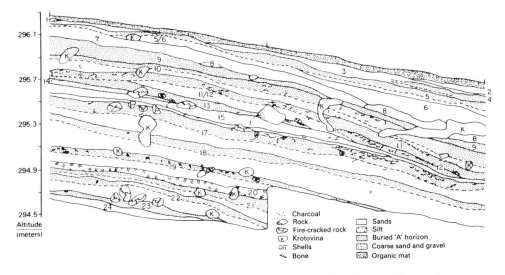

Fig. 3.12 The flood stratigraphy of the Columbia river site, Washington State. Adapted from *Quaternary Research* (Chatters and Hoover, 1986), by permission of the University of Washington.

veyed the river and floodplain cross-section and used standard flow equations such as Manning's to compute discharges. The site was located on a 15 m wide terrace at approximately the same height as the highest recorded flood stage, which was in 1948. The stratigraphy revealed a sequence of interstratified overbank sediments with artifacts. In all there were twenty-seven distinct strata, mostly graded to massive poorly sorted sand and silt (Figure 3.12). The sediments were dated by radiocarbon and artifact typology. The heights of the strata were used to compute palaeodischarges using breaks in the accumulation rate curve to define periods during which the number of floods which occurred between the maximum and minimum discharges (set by the strata

Table 3.1 *Computed discharges for the Washington river for AD 120 to 1948 (from Chatters and Hoover, 1986). The mean frequency is calculated as the time elapsed divided by the number of sediment deposition events.*

Time (yrs AD)	Minimum estimated discharge (m^3 sec^{-1})	Maximum estimated discharge (m^3 sec^{-1})	Mean frequency (yrs)
120–1020	16,100	17,200	84
1020–1390	17,200	17,600	30
1390–1948	17,600	18,100	142

height) could be expressed. This produces a frequency of floods for three periods as shown in Table 3.1. As the table shows, the frequency of flooding was much greater in the period AD 1020–1390 than in AD 120–1020 or since 1390. Chatters and Hoover were also able to assign a recurrence interval to the largest recorded flood in 1948, which is approximately 1 in 140 years for the last 600 years; before then it would have been 3 to 4 times more common. This reveals an important point: all recurrence intervals of events are relative to the period over which relative climatic stability can be defined (Brown, 1991). So for this and other analyses the recurrence interval should be quoted with its relevant 'period'.

A more frequently used palaeohydrological method has been the estimation of past formative discharges from channel geometry and from sediments deposited by the flood. The use of channel geometry will be discussed in the next section. The velocities and shear stresses of formative flows can be estimated using tractive force theory. There are several methods by which this can be done (see Table 3.2 and appendix 1.3). The idea is to estimate the competence of past flows from the largest particle that was moved in the flood and from this to estimate the velocity and in some cases the depth of the flow. An early attempt to do this was by Dobbie and Wolfe (1953) who estimated the discharge of the tragic Lynmouth flood in the UK in 1952, which deposited boulders on the floodplain weighing up to 7500 kg. In an important study of Quaternary terraces in Colorado, Baker (1974b) estimated past flows from the largest particle size using Shield's equation as modified by Novak (1973). The simplified expression used (for clear water) was: DS/1.65d = 0.06, where D is depth of flow, S is energy slope (approximately equal to water surface slope) and d is the intermediate particle diameter. He also used a bedload equation to estimate channel capacity with the aim of estimating the minimum stage at which the sediment could have been transported. The velocity from competence, the stage from capacity and the width and slope from the sediment body of the braided channel deposits were then used to calculate discharge using Manning's equation. One of the problems with the use of the non-dimensional

Table 3.2 *Commonly used formulae for the computation of palaeodischarges (adapted from Maizels and Aitken, 1991).*
See also appendix 1.

Calculated parameter and method	Equation and reference(s)	Notation	Data requirements and references
Critical flow depth: du Boys/Shield	$d_c = T_c/\gamma S$ Andrews 1983	T_c critical shear stress $= 0.0834(D_i/D_{50})^{-0.872}$ $(\gamma_s - \gamma)D$ (see Andrews, 1983) γ specific weight of water γ_s specific weight of sediment S hydraulic gradient $D(D_i, D_{50})$ intermediate clast diameter	River hydraulic gradient (slope), transported grain sizes
Resistance models: Manning's n	Manning–Strickler $n_s = 0.039\, D^{0.16}$ Manning–Limeriros $n_l = \dfrac{0.113 d^{0.16}}{1.16 + 2.0\log(d/D)}$ Jarrett $n_j = 0.32 S^{0.38}\, d^{-0.16}$	d flow depth	Flow depth and clast size data
Darcy–Weisbach–Hey resistance model:	$\dfrac{1}{f_{HEY}} = \dfrac{2.3}{k\sqrt{8}} \log\left(\dfrac{ad}{3.5 D_{84}}\right)$	f Darcy–Weisbach friction factor k von Karman's coefficient a a channel shape factor where $a = 11.1\,(R/d_{max})^{-0.314}$ where R is the hydraulic radius	Hyraulic radius, flow depth and sediment calibre Thorne and Zevebergen (1985)
Henderson model:	$f_{HEN} = 0.113\,(d/D)^{0.33}$	d_{max} maximum flow depth f_{HEN} Henderson friction factor	Henderson (1966)
Mean velocity models: Manning	$V_c = d^{0.67}\, S^{0.5}/n$	V_{wmin} minimum velocity V_{wmax} maximum velocity	Flow depth slope and friction factor
Colebrook-White	$V_c = \dfrac{8gdS}{\sqrt{f}}$		Costa (1983)
Costa Williams envelope curve	$V_{co} = 0.18(D.10^3)^{0.487}$ $V_{wmin} = 2.05\, D0.5$ $V_{wmax} = 14.53 D^{0.5}$		Williams (1984)

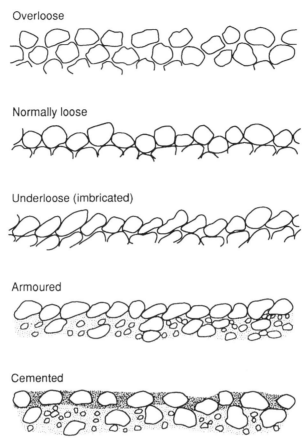

Fig. 3.13 Overloose, normally loose, armoured and cemented channel beds. Adapted from Church (1978).

Shield's equation has been the effect of underloose and overloose channel beds, as illustrated in Figure 3.13. This will produce underestimates of the critical tractive force for underloose beds and the opposite for overloose beds; however, corrections can be made for this. Palaeohydraulic methodologies are generally based upon either the Chezy, Manning or Darcy-Weisbach flow equations with input parameters calculated using critical tractive force theory (Table 3.2). Variants can be used for clear water and normal boundaries and sediment laden water with underloose boundaries. Which method is appropriate will depend upon the size distribution and sorting of the sediments. However, in all cases variation between methods is at least 100% (Church, 1978). Dawson (1989) has estimated past discharges from flood deposits in the Main Terrace of the Severn valley, and shown a range of errors associated with the input variables which can be as much as one order of magnitude. When compounded, larger errors can result. The sources of the overall error include both assumptions made in the method (e.g. steady uniform flow) and these input variables errors. Some of the variables, specifically energy slope and channel width, are difficult to measure when defined channels are not present. The good preservation of channels can greatly increase accuracy.

Palaeohydrology from former channel dimensions
Many excavations have revealed palaeochannels which, in theory, should provide as accurate estimates of past discharges as present channels. There are two ways in which this can be done, using empirical relationships between planform dimensions, such as meander wavelength and discharge, and through estimation of channel capacity and the direct use of standard flow equations with an estimated velocity. The former method relies on relationships of the form: $\lambda = kQ^z$ where λ is meander wavelength (or channel width), k is a constant, Q is discharge and z is an exponent. Typical values of k and z can be found in Dury (1965), Carlston (1965) and Richards (1982). With rather ill-defined limits, similar power functions can be used to define a most probable causal discharge (e.g. $Q_{1.58}$) from a variety of morphometric variables for different environments. The direct use of palaeochannel capacity and flow equations such as Chezy, Manning's or Darcy-Weisbach (preferable on theoretical grounds) should be relatively straightforward. However, there are a number of problems, some of which are listed below:

1 Channel system: was it a uni-channel floodplain or were there other channels taking flow at the same time?
2 Capacity: is the full channel height preserved?
3 Capacity: is the trench perpendicular to the flow? If not a correction must be made.
4 Recurrence interval of bankfull: some figure has to be used, e.g. $Q_{1.58}$.
5 Slope: can bed, banks or floodplain be used?
6 Roughness: it must be estimated or calculated from form and bed material.

Although all of these will cause significant variation in the final estimate, the first is particularly serious, as it will produce major underestimates since it is known that multiple-channel patterns were more common in the past than they are now over much of North-West Europe (Brown, 1987a). This technique has been used with most success in Eastern Europe, where meandering rivers with relatively undisturbed floodplains have preserved many generations of palaeochannels which can be radiocarbon dated. Rotnicki (1983) has used both meander geometry and channel capacity to estimate past flows of the Prosna river in Poland (Figure 3.14). He has also used both geometry and palaeohydraulic methods to estimate discharge of the river for the last 12,000 years (Rotnicki, 1991). Some of the short-term fluctuation is probably due to variation in the flow frequency of channel-forming discharges, disequilibrium and errors, but the overall trend agrees broadly with other Holocene palaeoclimatic reconstructions.

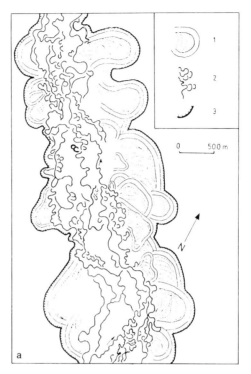

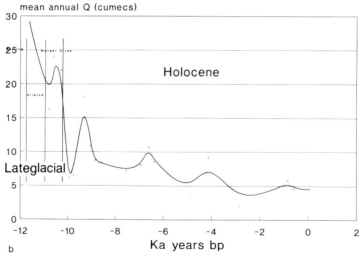

Fig. 3.14 (a) The planform and morphology of meanders of the Posna river used for palaeohydrological reconstruction. Adapted from Rotnicki (1983). (b) A histogram of the estimated discharge variation of the Posna river for the last 12,000 years. Constructed from data in Rotnicki (1991).

3.4 The fluvial transport of archaeological materials

The processes and analytical methods described here have direct relevance to the location and interpretation of archaeological finds and site excavations. As in other branches of the subject, an attempt to specify the causative processes can lead to new interpretations of the data. Artifacts including tools, pottery, building materials and bones can be regarded as particles and subjected to the same methods of analysis as natural particles. Many artifacts have been transported by water before burial or retrieval. Two areas of taphonomic research have emerged: one is the effect of this transportation on artifact shape and size, where the aim is to use this information to recognise fluvial transport and possibly predict rank order and distances of transport, and the other is the identification and elimination of any bias in preservation caused by fluvial transport processes. The inspiration for this research has undoubtedly come from Palaeolithic archaeology where these problems are most acute and in particular where the need to recognise derived material has been understood.

Geomorphologists have studied the attrition or abrasion of particles of all sizes in both laboratory and field conditions using a variety of methods. They have found that while attrition partly depends on the lithology, larger particles are abraded much faster than small ones and the rate of abrasion varies considerably in response to the energy in the system. In many cases, the identification of abrasion is the prime evidence that a cache of Palaeolithic tools is not *in situ* and it is therefore not a site in the restricted sense (primary site). The abrasion rate of a fresh and sharp flint artifact is proportional to the hardness of the flint, the velocity of the current, the shape of the implement and the other materials present in the system. If we regard the shape as constant (i.e. typologies defined by shape), and other materials constant, then we can see that the rate still depends on both hardness and stream energy. Shackley (1974) illustrated how measurements of abrasion can indicate different environments, i.e. edge rounding by sand and smaller particles and percussion craters formed by impacts with larger pebbles. This is both directly and indirectly the result of stream energy. Several experiments have been conducted with modern facsimile artifacts. Harding *et al.* (1987) placed sixty hand-axes (from lanceolates to refined cordiforms and ovates) into the river Ystwyth in Mid Wales. They were weighed and measured prior to emplacement, and after a flood twenty-seven were found, reweighed and remeasured. The experiment went some way to verifying several predictable if inconvenient hypotheses, one being that the distance moved varied greatly depending upon where the axes had been placed; those placed on gravel bars had moved furthest. These studies reveal that hand-axes behave like normal bed material, in that they move episodically, spend considerable periods in channel storage, and abrade and develop surface polish relatively quickly. It should also be remembered that these experiments have generally simulated short periods of relatively quiescent conditions which may not be appropriate for Palaeolithic hand-axes which in North America and Europe may have undergone reworking under periglacial conditions.

The transport and abrasion of bones can be approached in the same manner. However, bones are more irregular in shape and have a lower density of around 1.7–2.0 g cm^{-3} when fresh (Weast, 1976), falling to well below 1 g cm^{-3} after partial dissolution and water loss. In terms of shape bones can be characterised as either rod-like, e.g. leg or rib bones; blade-like, e.g. scapula; or spherical, e.g. human skull. Not only may different bones be selectively transported or deposited but their entry into the fluvial system may be already biased as has been shown by studies of bone movement on slopes (Frostick and Reid, 1983). This is in addition to all the non-geomorphological sources of bias such as predation, butchery practices and decay. In a detailed attempt to model the fluvial taphonomic processes, Hanson (1980) identified different classes of assemblage:

Type 1:   Not transported by running water, least transportable elements completely or preferentially retained. Subtypes: (a) never exposed to running water (e.g. cave or pond); (b) exposed to running water, transportable elements potentially removed or depleted (e.g. residual accumulations on a floodplain).

Type 2:   Transported by moving water, least transportable elements left upstream. Subtypes: (a) transported into a very low-energy environment, easily transported elements preferentially represented. (e.g. flood accumulation); (b) exposed to moving water after fluvial transport from initial site; transportable elements potentially removed or depleted (e.g. channel bed or point-bar).

The existence of these assemblages is dependent upon the assumption that bones travel independently, i.e. skeletons are disarticulated, and non-fluvial biases which may even occur in the river system, e.g. scavenging by carnivorous fish, are of little importance. Hanson (1980) calculated the force per unit area produced by the stream velocity profile on a rod-shaped bone (bovid phalanx) resting on the channel bed where the bone was about 30 x the size of the bed roughness elements (Figure 3.15). As the fluid force or shear stress increases, the bone moves by either sliding or rolling. Sliding will occur when the shear stress exceeds resistance due to friction between bone and bed which is proportional to the normal force (submerged weight of bone on a horizontal bed and without lift). If movement is by rolling the moment of force will balance around the fulcrum.

The mathematical descriptions of these processes as given by Hanson (1980) only hold under rather limited conditions but are useful approximations and outline the methodology. The bone is just as amenable as any other irregular particle to the analytical approaches described in Table 3.2. By substitution of different bone shapes and sizes, or different flow conditions, relative transport-

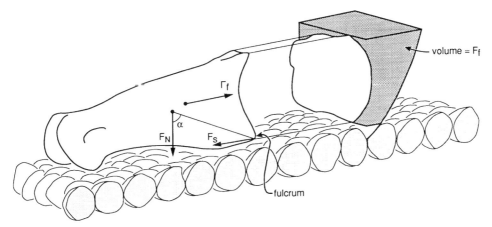

Fig. 3.15 Forces acting on a submerged bone. Fluid force (F_f) whose quantity is approximated by the volume of the shaded area, must exceed the frictional resistance force (F_s) to initiate sliding. For rolling, the moment (force times length) of fluid force about the fulcrum must exceed the moment of normal force (F_N) which can be assumed to be equal to the submerged weight. Adapted from Hanson (1980).

ability can be estimated and therefore potential bias. This approach has been tested both in the laboratory flume and in the field. Within the constraints imposed by uniform flow assumptions, those bones theoretically more transportable do travel farther and an expression can be defined virtually independently of flow and bed conditions. This is because the critical factors are: cross-sectional area, submerged weight of the bone, and bone-shape because it affects the drag coefficient. The larger the cross-sectional area, the more likely it is to move but this is balanced by the submerged weight, i.e. the heavier it is the greater shear stress is required. The relative transportabilities of bones shown in Figure 3.16 can be calculated using Hanson's equations from data given by Behrensmeyer and Hill (1980).

These experiments have also shed some light on the downstream loss of material, although it seems as if destruction is, at most, weakly correlated with transport distance. This is because it is largely 'random accidents of exposure' to destructive agents which cause bone destruction. It is therefore doubtful if decay constants or decay-type curves (cf. radioactive isotope half-lives) are of much value, except as a statistical description of the overall probability of destruction.

An alternative and more pragmatic approach is to concentrate entirely on the conditions of deposition and the location of artifacts or bones with respect to the morphology of the system. Frison (1976) attributed clusters of mammoth bones at the Colby site from the North-West Plains of North America to deliberate piling or stacking after butchery and processing.

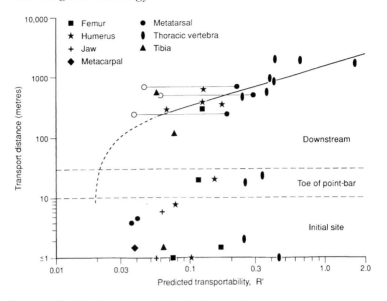

Fig. 3.16 Predicted transportability (using standard transport theory) against observed transport distance for selected bones after one season in the East Fork river, Texas. Adapted from Hanson (1980).

Shipman (1981) has pointed out that the bone clusters occur at either a bend or a pool in the ancient arroyo, where, she suggests, mammoth carcasses would probably be deposited naturally by the flow (Figure 3.17). There are several ways in which these two hypotheses could be tested: by analysis of the arrangement of the skeletal elements in each pile and by detailed micro-stratigraphic work to investigate the relationship between the bones and water-transported clasts (pebbles and mud balls) in and on the scatter or pile. Detailed drawings of the piles (Frison, 1976) do suggest the clusters originated from articulated parts of the animals (Figure 3.17) and the location of one of the piles was on the sloping bank of the arroyo with some of the bones scattered onto the arroyo bottom. In conclusion, the stacking of some of the bones on top of each other, the lack of a clear pool location and the presence of tools in each pile (though not many) suggests that they were the result of human action and not lag deposits. However, this site still exemplifies many typical problems; for example, how were the piles buried by alluvium without being disturbed? The consideration earlier in this chapter of channel form and sediment deposition is the starting point for the estimation of the trap efficiency of the various microenvironments of the fluvial system. Pools act as traps for artifacts of many types, from golf balls to wood, which once it is fully saturated will move as bed material.

Another approach to the identification of fluvially dumped flint assemblages is the recognition of scatters characteristic of the flint flaking process.

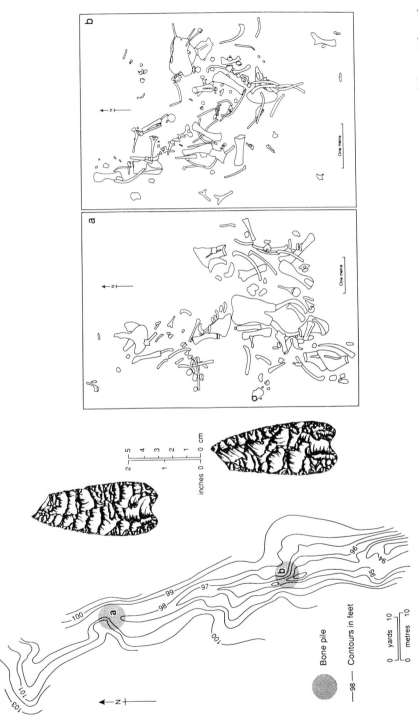

Fig. 3.17 The two piles of mammoth bones in the arroyo at Colby, Kansas (a), and (b) and detailed drawings of them. Adapted from Frison (1978).

Newcomer and Sieveking (1980) have, by using an experimental approach, shown how the most important factor in affecting the size and shape of flake scatter patterns is the knapper's sitting position. None of the patterns they show display typical spatial characteristics that could be associated with fluvial deposition, i.e. there is no preferred flake orientation and very little scatter asymmetry in sorting.

Our power to predict the distance travelled by an artifact will always be limited by our imperfect knowledge of hydraulic processes, the variability of the materials and the complexity of the system. However, the examination of the condition and microstratigraphy of a complete hoard *in situ* does allow the application of the principles and theories outlined in this chapter; these can take us well beyond the 'fluvial jumbling' level of explanation.

3.5 Floodplain soils

Floodplain soils are the product of a combination of sedimentary, hydrological and ecological processes (Gerrard, 1987). Their distribution reflects patterns of past alluvial deposition, water regime and vegetation distribution. Alluvial soils fall into two catagories: those without horizons which are undeveloped or unripened (lithosols in the UK, see Table 3.3 and entisols in the USA) and those with horizons altered or changed by soil-forming processes to a greater or lesser extent. As can be seen in the table, the principal diagnostic character-istics in the UK system are horizonation, calcareous/non-calcareous nature, and hydromorphism (mottling reflecting gleying). In the USA soil taxonomy system flood plain soils vary from entisols (fluvents) which are weakly devel-oped to various types of inceptisol (e.g. Ochrepts) which are moderately devel-oped soils with no spodic, argillic, natric or oxic horizons but which may have cambic or histic horizons. In the FAO/UNESCO system most alluvial soils belong to the group fluvisols. Of great importance is the quality of the river sediment, as it determines the initial conditions from which soil development occurs. The suspended load may have high levels of secondary clay minerals, adsorbed minerals and organic matter, especially if it derived from the erosion of topsoils. The total nitrogen content of alluvial mud can be high (Jenny, 1962) as can the concentration of phosphorus adsorbed onto mineral particles. The value of flooding alluvial soils in order to maintain their high nutrient status has been known and exploited for centuries (see chapter 6).

The characteristics of cumulative soils on floodplains are a product of both sedimentologial and pedological processes and specifically the accumulation rate and depth of pedological alteration (Walker and Coventry, 1976). The pattern of alluviation causes the superficial similarity between alluvial soil maps from very different climatic zones (cf. Holmes and Western, 1969; Blake and Ollier, 1971). The channel zone is associated with lithosols which may be gravelly or unripened fine sediment, often laminated with inherited micro-aggregates and organic matter. Towards the edge of this zone, a weak soil

Table 3.3 *The classification of alluvial soils in the UK system (from Avery, 1980).*

UK: major soil group	Soil group	Soil subgroup
3. *Lithomorphic A/C soils* Shallow with a distinct, humose or peaty topsoil but no subsurface horizons more than 5 cm thick.	3.3 *Ranker-like alluvial soils* In non-calcareous recent alluvium 3.7 *Rendzina-like alluvial soils* In little-altered calcareous alluvium, at least 30 cm thick	3.31 *Typical ranker-like alluvial soils* (unmottled) 3.32 *Gleyic ranker-like alluvial soils* (faintly mottled)
5. *Brown soils* With dominantly brownish or reddish subsoil and no prominent mottling or greyish (gleying) colours above 40 cm depth.	5.3 *Brown calcareous alluvial soils* In recent calcareous alluvium more than 30 cm thick 5.6 *Brown alluvial soils* In non calcareous loamy or clayey alluvium more than 30 cm thick	5.31 *Typical brown calcareous alluvial soils* (unmottled) 5.32 *Gleyic brown calcareous alluvial soils* (faintly mottled with permeable subsoil) 5.33 *Pelogleyic brown calcareous alluvial soils* (faintly mottled and clayey with slowly permeable subsoil) 5.61 *Typical brown alluvial soil* (unmottled) 5.62 *Gleyic brown alluvial soil* (faintly mottled with permeable subsoil) 5.63 *Pelogleyic brown alluvial soils* (faintly mottled and clayey with slowly permeable subsoil)
8. *Groundwater gley soils* Seasonally waterlogged soils affected by a shallow fluctuating groundwater table.	8.1 *Alluvial gley soils* With distinct topsoil, in loamy or clayey recent alluvium more than 30 cm thick 8.5 *Humic-alluvial gley soils* With a humose or peaty topsoil in loamy or clayey recent alluvium not more than 30 cm thick	8.11 *Typical alluvial gley soils* (loamy with non-calcareous subsoil) 8.12 *Calcareous alluvial gley soils* (loamy with calcareous subsoil) 8.13 *Pelo-alluvial gley soils* (clayey with non-calcareous subsoil) 8.14 *Pelo-calcareous alluvial gley soils* (clayey with calcareous subsoil) 8.15 *Sulphuric alluvial gley soils* (extremely acid subsoil within 80 cm) 8.51 *Typical humic-alluvial gley soil* (with non-calcareous subsoil) 8.52 *Calcareous humic-alluvial gley soil* (with calcareous subsoil)

Table 3.3 (*cont.*)

UK: major soil group	Soil group	Soil subgroup
		8.53 *Sulphuric humic-alluvial gley soil* (with extremely acid subsoil within 80 cm)
10. *Peat soils* With more than 40 cm of organic material in the upper 80 cm or with more than 30 cm over gravel NB Most peat soils are non-alluvial in origin but may grade into alluvial soils in large floodplain basins and around lakes. Also found in backswamps and palaeochannels isolated from inorganic sedimentation.	10.1 *Raw peat soils* In undrained organic material that has remained wet to within 20 cm of the surface 10.2 *Earthy peat soils* Normally drained	10.11 *Raw oligo-fibrous peat* (fibrous with pH less than 4.0) 10.12 *Raw eu-fibrous peat soils* (fibrous with pH above 4.0) 10.13 *Raw oligo-amorphous peat* (humified pH below 4.0) 10.14 *Raw euto-amorphous peat soils* (humified with pH above 4.0) 10.21 *Earthy oligo-fibrous peat* 10.22 *Earthy eu-fibrous peat* 10.23 *Earthy oligo-amorphous peat* 10.24 *Earthy eutro-amorphous peat* 10.25 *Earthy sulphuric peat soils*

structure may develop. In the levée zone, soils are often sandy in texture, are free-draining, and exhibit moderate soil structure. There is a gradation into floodplain flat soils which generally become finer and increase in organic matter away from the channel and towards groundwater gley soils which occur in the backswamps (Schmudde, 1963). In floodplains where flooding has been controlled, warp soils are created (Bridges, 1973). The texture of floodplain soils, although primarily of sedimentary origin, is also affected by pedological processes. This can include clay translocation producing clay coatings on peds in the B horizon (Brammer, 1971). Although the processes producing these clay coatings (cutans) are not fully understood three factors seem to be impor-tant. First, summer cracking in clay-rich soils, secondly, post-flood draw-down of water, and thirdly, flood and rainfall induced pore-water pressures. The depth to the watertable and REDOX (reduction/oxidation) boundary is important, as above this, leaching and decalcification are dominant, and soil structure will develop due to oxidation and biological activity. Indeed, the depth of blocky ped development is a useful indication of the depth of soil development which is normally closely related to relative height on the flood-plain.

    In arid and semi-arid soils where potential evapotranspiration exceeds pre-cipitation salt accumulation can ocurr (Varallyay, 1968) and this can adversely

Table 3.4 *Some common minerals formed in floodplain sediments.*

Mineral	Chemical formula	Environment of formation
gibbsite	$Al(OH)_3$	wet tropical
limonite	$Fe_2O_3.H_2O$	temperate
jarosite	$KFe_3(SO_4)_2(OH)_6$	temperate–estuarine
viviantite	Fe_2PO_4	temperate
calcite	$CaCO_3$	semi-arid and arid
halite	$NaCl$	semi-arid

affect the agricultural potential of floodplains; archaeological examples of this are discussed in chapter 8. The mineralogy of alluvial soils reflects climate and lithology of the catchment as well as the weathering environment (Demumbrum and Bruce, 1960). In wet tropical catchments, quartz is by far the most important mineral (Edelman and Van der Voorde, 1963) along with the formation of gibbsite ($AL(OH)_3$) (Herath and Grimshaw, 1971). In the dry tropical zone, kaolinite and montmorillonite are more common along with the accumulation of carbonates (Razzaq and Herbillon, 1979). Temperate flood-plains can contain a variety of minerals of detrital origin and some of sec-ondary origin. Quartz is again nearly always dominant but with varying amounts of feldspars, clay minerals, oxides, hydroxides, carbonates and heavy minerals. The mineralogy, especially the heavy mineral assemblage, is often of use in indicating sediment provenance and changes in the principal sources of river sediments. Several studies have shown how both historic and prehistoric metal mining may be identified from fine floodplain sediments using heavy mineral analysis (Macklin and Lewin, 1989). However, some alteration does occur in temperate floodplains including the formation of new minerals (Table 3.4). Limonite ($Fe_2O_3.H_2O$) and jarosite ($KFe_3(SO_4)_2(OH)_6$) can be formed by the reaction of sulphuric acid (H_2SO_4) with feldspars. The sulphuric acid is the result of oxidation of pyrite which is a common constituent of some estuarine, saltmarsh and lacustrine sediments. Iron and manganese mottling, concre-tions, and even cementation occur in alluvial soils, with distribution and type closely associated with REDOX conditions (Vepraskas and Bouma, 1976). As many temperate floodplain soils are hydromorphic (formed under waterlogged conditions), new minerals are formed by reduction. Sulphate will be reduced to sulphides, including ferrous sulphide by the bacteria of the genus *Desulphovibrio*. The blue colour observed in many alluvial soils is caused by the formation of vivianite (ferrous phosphate). Even a very disturbed floodplain like that of the river Severn can still show soil variations which are related to the pattern of floodplain evolution. The finest soils are the oldest, and the coarsest soils are the youngest formed on ridges accordant with the present channel (Hayward and Fenwick, 1983). Because floodplains have a high

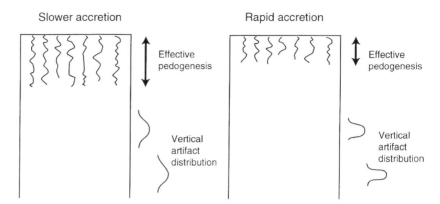

Fig. 3.18 The mean residence time of soil in the pedogenic zone of an alluvial sequence (time equivalence of depth of effective pedogenesis) and its probable effect on the vertical distribution of artifacts.

preservation potential soils are commonly preserved in floodplain depositional sequences as palaeosols the study of which is palaeopedology.

3.6 Archaeology and floodplain palaeosols

Alluvial palaeosols are extremely common in the geological record; in the Lower Old Red Sandstone in Britain alone between 400 and 600 are exposed. The standard geological model of alluvial palaeosol formation consists of phases of soil development and a variable deposition rate (Figure 3.18). Most alluvial palaeosols are polygenetic, having been subjected to more than one phase of soil development. This is dependent upon the pedogenetic residence time which is the period during which the soil is in the zone of alteration or pedogenesis. Using average accumulation rates and a 2 m depth of pedogenesis this will be of the order of 2000 years. Palaeosols integrate climatic factors such as fluctuations in the water table, and these effects can be strong enough to survive burial or subsequent pedogenesis in a non-alluvial context such as a terrace surface. This subsequent pedogenesis can be useful as in several environments sequences of soils have been related to the age of the terrace or surface (Table 3.5). The concentration of dithionite extractable iron (Fe_d) and illuvial clay in the B horizon, reddening (rubefaction) and the loss of soluble salts and oxides have all been shown to be so closely related to soil age that they can be used as proxy dating methods. However, climate change complicates most sequences and should be taken into account (Johnson *et al.*, 1990). Although originally a method applied to Pleistocene terrace soils (Harden, 1982), quantitative indices of soil formation have been successfully used to differentiate Holocene terrace soils in upland Britain (Robertson-Rintoul, 1986). The principal soil characteristics used were: total depth, depth of B horizon, organic carbon content, pH and iron content. Soil stratigraphic

Table 3.5 *Studies of soil chronosequences on alluvial landsurfaces.*

Location	Climate	Gains with age	Losses with age or decrease	Source
Cowlitz R., Washington,	cool temperate	Fe_d, clay, depth, reddening (rubification), horizonation	CaO, Na_2O, pH	Dethier, 1988
Kennet valley, UK	cool temperate, lowland	reddening (rubification) clay, heavy minerals (atmospheric input)	—	Chartres 1980
Glen Feshie, Scotland	cool temperate, mountainous	depth, depth of B horizon, reddening, Fe_d in B, Fe_d B/C, increasing podzolisation	Fe_d A/B (iron bleached from developing E horizon)	Robertson-Rintoul 1986
Truckee R., Nevada	sub-humid	Fe_d (ratio to Fe_o used)	Fe_o	Alexander, 1974
Savannah R., South Carolina	humid	clay, depth, clay, coatings, structure, Fe, Mg	pH	Foss and Segovia (1983)

units from terraces in Glen Feshie in the western Cairngorm mountains of Scotland suggest five phases of terrace formation at 13,000, 10,000, 3600, 1000 and 80 bp with incision in the intervening periods (Robertson-Rintoul, 1986).

The rate of soil development on floodplains is inversely proportional to the rate of overbank deposition, so when alluviation decreases or stops, then organic rich A horizons can develop. These can be preserved under structures and are especially useful for the determination of past floodplain conditions. Unusually clear alluvial palaeosols have been described from the floodplain of the river Perry, Shropshire (Brown, 1989). Two organic palaeosols were preserved in a vertically accreted silty clay. Both were ^{14}C dated, one to 7480 ± 50 bp and the other to 6820 ± 50 bp (Figure 3.19 and Plate 3.13). Neither had suffered significant erosion or much post-depositional mixing probably owing to rapid burial. Pollen analysis indicated that both had developed under a woodland cover.

One of the most useful techniques for investigating the history of floodplain soils and their archaeology is soil micromorphology. This involves the collection of undisturbed samples, impregnation with a resin, cutting and grinding them to thin sections and examination under a microscope. The terminology of micromorphology is complex and the reader is referred to several texts and handbooks (Brewer 1976; Fitzpatrick, 1984; Bullock *et al.*, 1985; Kemp, 1985b

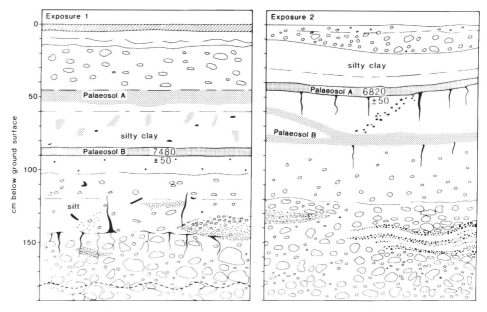

Fig. 3.19 An exposure of the palaeosols in the floodplain sediments of the river Perry, Shropshire, England. Reprinted from *Journal of Quaternary Science*, Brown (1989), by permission of John Wiley and Sons Ltd.

and Courty *et al.*, 1989) but the major characteristics that are investigated are listed below:

void spaces:	distribution, size and shape of soil pores
S-matrix:	the matrix type from matrix to clast supported
organic components:	organic residues, root material, micro-fauna
coatings:	composition, thickness, distribution, e.g. cutans
pedofeatures:	concretions, depletions, crystal growth.

Soil micromorphology has been particularly valuable in the investigation of soil disturbance and history in relation to agriculture (French, 1990). Micromorphological features that can give valuable indications of human activity on floodplains include: agricutans often containing charcoal caused by agriculture and organic-rich argillans which can be caused by clearance.

French (1988; 1990) has used micromorphology to examine the nature of pre-Neolithic soils in the lower Welland valley in eastern England. The present floodplain soils are decalcified brown earths, but the pre-Neolithic are argillic (clay rich in the B horizon) brown earths overlain by alluvium and peat. The argillic nature of these buried soils reflects their formation under free-draining stable, probably wooded, conditions. Some sites, associated with structures, show micromorphological evidence of early (probably Neolithic) soil dis-

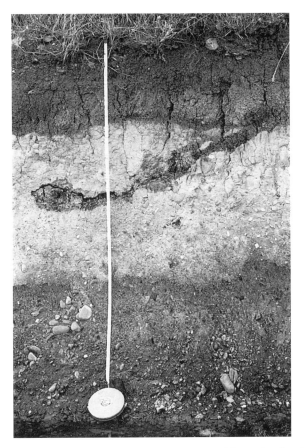

Plate 3.13 A section of the upper palaeosol from the river Perry, Shropshire, England, revealing a *c.* 6800 year old burrow. See Figure 3.19 and text for more details.

turbance and at one site, the floodplain 'island' of Maxey, this was great enough to have caused soil movement by windblow. This, and other work on the Thames floodplain (Limbrey and Robinson, 1988), illustrates the as yet largely unrealised potential of micromorphology in the investigation of human activity on floodplains.

The examination of both floodplain sediments and soils in the field and laboratory can provide detailed information on the local palaeoenvironment which may have implications for the regional palaeoenvironment. Post-depositional processes are also important, especially for the interpretation of palaeosols. Thus the history of a floodplain and to a large extent its catchment can be reconstructed and related to the pattern of human impact and climate change. Floodplains are biologically rich and diverse environments dependent upon both sedimentological and atmospheric inputs, and it is this subject that forms the basis of the next chapter.

4

FLOODPLAIN ECOLOGY, ARCHAEOBOTANY AND ARCHAEOZOOLOGY

This chapter examines the ecological characteristics of floodplains, how these are related to environmental parameters and how past environmental conditions can be reconstructed from organic materials preserved within floodplain sediments. The implications for past cultures lie in the resources that these ecologies provide at different times and in different places.

4.1 Floodplain productivity

Floodplains are more productive than the land that surrounds them owing to the greater availability of water and nutrients. However, their productivity still varies with latitude and local climatic factors. The net above-ground primary productivity of a forested fen in Minnesota has been measured as $746 \, g \, m^2 \, yr^{-1}$ while that of a Louisiana bottomland hardwood forest is $1374 \, g \, m^2 \, yr^{-1}$ (Mitsch and Gosselink, 1993). Net productivity and the difference between floodplain productivity and that of surrounding land is controlled by water supply. In the humid tropics where there is abundant year-round water this difference is minimised and the floodplain margin may not be an obvious ecological feature (Figure 4.1). As seasonal contrasts increase and rainfall decreases in the subtropical climates, the difference is at its maximum because of the greater supply and storage of water in floodplains. In Cool Temperate zones the contrast is smaller and differences in soil type and agricultural potential become more important. In the Boreal zone disturbance of vegetation by highly active rivers complicates the situation. The difference between floodplain net primary productivity and dryland net primary productivity structures the rest of the ecosystem, increasing both animal and plant resources. Climatic variation in this productivity difference, along with variation in the size of the resource, needs to be appreciated if we are interested in both differences in the settlement history of different regions and human actions designed to modify floodplain productivity.

4.2 Hydrological controls on floodplain vegetation

Temperate and Boreal floodplains commonly contain several nested wetland systems which can be classified according to their position on a hydrodynamic energy gradient (Gosselink and Turner, 1978). They vary in hydrological regime and in their water–plant–sediment interactions. The single most important regulator in alluvial wetlands is usually hydroperiod which is the

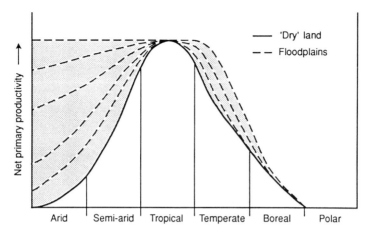

Fig. 4.1 Theoretical floodplain and non-floodplain annual productivity and the differential productivity with climate.

duration, frequency, depth and season of flooding and the depth of the water-table (Lugo, Brinson and Brown, 1990). Floodplains are therefore especially sensitive to changes in catchment conditions, including land use; so, even if they are unmanaged, their ecology will be affected by human activity. They are also more changeable over time than most other terrestrial ecosystems owing to both autogenic and allogenic factors. Under certain circumstances floodplains may record their own ecological and hydrological history in organic and mineral sediments and this provides us with an invaluable tool in the reconstruction of past environments, hydrological conditions and resources.

The primary controls on floodplain ecology are the water regime and the stability of each patch of floodplain surface. Secondary controls include soil type and fertility. All of these factors are intrinsically related to the pattern and processes of floodplain formation. The water regime of floodplain soils varies from free-draining droughty soils on levees to permanently waterlogged hydro-morphic soils in backswamps. Soils also vary in texture from sands and gravels in high-energy zones to silts and clays in low-energy zones with organic matter content ranging from medium to very high levels (over 60% in some back-swamps). The water regime of floodplain soils is a function of the water regime of the river, adjacent slope inputs and the hydrological properties of the flood-plain soils and sediments (Bradley and Brown, 1992). The most obvious example of the effect of the sediments themselves is the existence of perched aquifers. These are common in many temperate floodplains and are formed by impermeable layers in depressions sealing them off from the strata below, so that when the regional watertable falls the site remains waterlogged. The most common case is a cutoff with clays deposited in the oxbow lake, prior to channel incision and a fall in the floodplain watertable. Using a general model of the hydrological characteristics of floodplain soils we can generate a

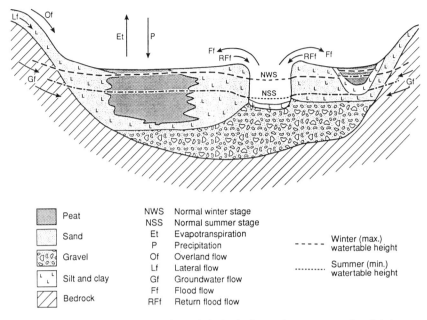

Fig. 4.2 A simplified representation of the hydrology of a temperate floodplain.

simplified model of floodplain hydrology (Figure 4.2). Inputs are from rainfall, throughflow and channel flow. All three are capable of producing flooding independently of the others especially in larger catchments, as follows:

1 A flood produced entirely by the river from precipitation and/or snowmelt in the uplands but no contribution from precipitation in the lowlands – only common in large catchments.
2 Very heavy rainfall on the floodplain/lowlands exceeding the infiltration capacity and/or storage capacity of the floodplain soils and producing puddles which coalesce to form nuisance flooding.
3 A combination of river flood and 2 – most common.
4 A lowland tributary produced flood – rare except in combination with 3.

These flood types may be the result of particular synoptic patterns (i.e. the occurrence of westerly depressions, etc.) and so their relative frequency is affected by climate change. They also have different hydrological characteristics in terms of the shape of the hydrograph and sediment sources. Type 1 or a 'dry flood' is of particular human significance as in large basins with mountains there may be little or no indication that a flood is about to occur in the lowland zone. This is particularly common in semi-arid regions. In temperate regions groundwater conditions on the floodplain are often important, both exacerbating floods and giving some flood warning.

The floodplain watertable will reflect the hydraulic conductivity of floodplain sediments. For a given hydraulic gradient the watertable will follow the ground

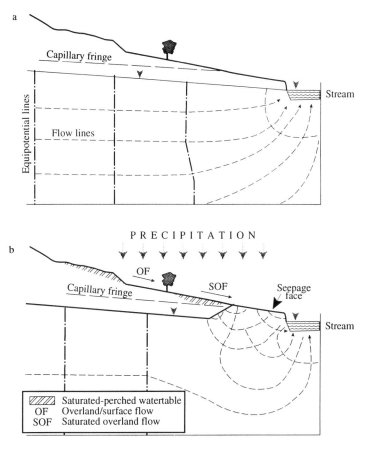

Fig. 4.3 Floodplain watertable rise and the capillary fringe (a) prior to rainfall and (b) after rainfall. Adapted from Gilham (1984) and Abdul and Gilham (1984).

topography more closely in soils with low hydraulic conductivity (e.g. silts and clays) and less closely in sediments with higher hydraulic conductivities (e.g. sands and gravels). This means that it may be quite irregular across the flood-plain, reflecting the different rates of lateral and vertical water transmission. Floodplain watertables may also respond rapidly and disproportionately to a precipitation event (Figure 4.3). This has been observed in several field and lab-oratory experiments (Sklash and Farvolden, 1979; Gilham, 1984; Abdul and Gilham, 1984) and it is caused by the existence of a capillary fringe which is the zone above the watertable which remains saturated at negative pressure. This zone may extend for just a few centimetres to several meters above the watertable. The addition of a small amount of rainfall may cause this water to move to positive pressure conditions thus causing a sudden increase in the watertable height. This process is an important cause of the rapid addition of old water to stream hydrographs prior to the input of storm water to the channel.

Floodplains form extensive aquifers the use of which is essential in most environments for water supply. In arid and semi-arid environments shallow wells and boreholes allow farming and subsistence in otherwise unfavourable locations. These aquifers are, however, sensitive to climate change and drawdown owing to over-exploitation. Natural recharge by rainfall can be increased by the creation of structures which concentrate storm waters and exploitation can be made easier by the construction of cisterns. These aspects of floodplain hydrology and resources are discussed further in chapters 8, 9 and 10. The hydrology of floodplains also provides the natural template for floodplain ecology as described further in the rest of this chapter.

4.3 Vegetation and sedimentary environments

The patchwork of soils with different water regimes, stabilities and nutrient contents allows plants with different adaptive strategies to coexist on floodplains. For temperate floodplains, it is possible to divide floodplain environments into three broad categories in addition to the river itself: (a) relatively free-draining and coarse-textured soil environments, (b) levées and intermediate floodplain flats, and (c) backswamps and floodplain hydroseres. An additional vegetation-dominated environment described below is that of the organic-debris dams and associated channels.

Sand and gravel environments

These are not only free draining, but frequently disturbed, and have undergone little or no weathering *in situ*; they thus have little soil development and low levels of nutrients especially nitrogen. Most nutrients must be derived either from allochthonous mud and particulate organic matter or directly from the river water. This niche is occupied by plants which have relatively short lifecycles, expend a relatively high proportion of energy on reproduction, are tolerant of disturbance and frequent inundation and are shade intolerant. The life-form of these plants tends to be herbaceous or shrubby. Using the C-S-R system (competitor-stress-tolerator ruderal) of comparative plant ecology (Grime *et al.*, 1979), these plants are typically stress-tolerant ruderals (S-R) and in reproductive terms they tend to be r-selected species characterised by high growth rates and a large proportion of their energy expenditure going into reproduction (Odum, 1975). Typical sedimentary environments include: pointbars, braid-bars (Plate 4.1), mid-channel bars and crevasse-splays. Where the bars are the result of lobes of bed material migrating out from the channel during floods an abrupt change in vegetation may occur at the scarp face of the lobe (Plate 4.2). This is common in active and aggrading reaches of braided channels.

Levée and intermediate flat environments

Natural levées, which tend to be most pronounced in mixed load systems where there is sufficient sand, frequently carry rather different vegetation from the rest of the floodplain. Natural levée vegetation does, however, grade into the floodplain flat community. The lack of natural floodplains in North-West

Plate 4.1 The Ae in Dumfriesshire, Scotland, has reaches that are meandering, stable, braided and anastomosing. The photo shows a wide gravel bar with vegetation on older parts of the bar surface in the distance.

Plate 4.2 Lobes of bedload gravel splaying out from the channel and deposited on an older bar surface on the river Ae, Dumfriesshire, Scotland. Note the abrupt change in vegetation at the scarp face of the lobe.

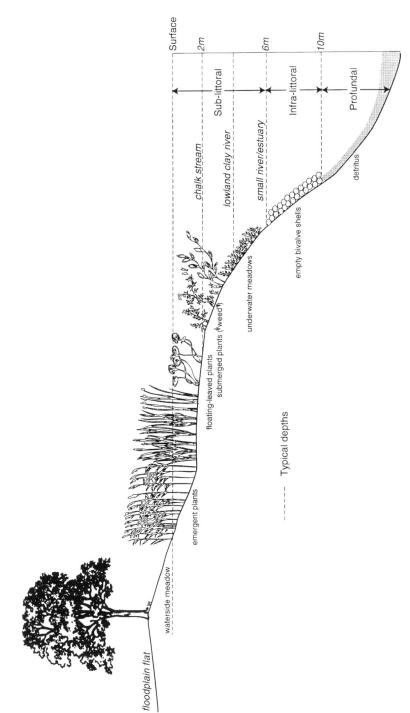

Fig. 4.4 Channel-edge ecotones and the vegetation gradient. Adapted from Naiman *et al.* (1989).

Table 4.1 *The general relationship between vegetation associations and floodplain topography for bottomland hardwood forests in south-eastern USA (extracted from Wharton et al., 1982).*

Floodplain zone	Vegetation association
river channel – edge	submergent/emergent aquatics, black willow, cottonwood
natural levee	sycamore, sweetgum, American elm
backswamp or first terrace flat	sugarberry, American elm, green ash or overcup oak, water hickory
low first terrace ridge	sweetgum, willow oak
high first terrace ridge	upland forest: white oak, blackgum, white ash, hickories, winged elm, loblolly pine
oxbow	bald cypress, tupelo
second terrace flats	sweetgum, willow oak
low second terrace ridge	swamp chestnut, cherrybark oak
high second terrace ridge	upland forest
upland	upland forest

Europe and much of North America has meant that most studies have come from subtropical and tropical environments or Boreal environments and very little is known about the natural levée communities in temperate floodplain systems. The levée and channel edge, including the intermediate zone (Petts, 1987), is in reality a micro-gradient composed of a series of zones which include the water's edge, the bank edge, the levée summit and a slope grading into the floodplain flat (Figure 4.4). The ecology in each of these zones typically varies from emergent aquatics such as bulrushes (*Typha latifolia*) to dryland herbs. It is also not clear to what extent this variation has changed since the removal of floodplain forest. An excellent example of the relationship between vegetation associations and floodplain microtopography is given in studies by Wharton *et al.* (1982) of a bottomland hardwood forest in south-eastern USA (Table 4.1). The micro-relief and the vegetation do not show a smooth change from one zone to the next and communities vary owing to fluctuations in the elevation of any geomorphological feature. Soils tend to be sandy and relatively free draining. There is some evidence that plants play an important role in ameliorating this by trapping fine sediments and thus increasing the nutrient content of levée soils (Brown and Brookes, in prep.). Many of the species typical of this environment such as the common stinging nettle (*Urtica dioica*) are indicators of disturbed ground and have high growth rates when nutrients are added to relatively poor substrates (Bannister, 1976).

Backswamp environments
More is known about the ecology of these environments in temperate floodplains because they were the last areas to be cleared and have in some locations

survived to the present day. The high organic matter content of backswamp soils is caused by a lack of free oxygen (anaerobic conditions) due to water-logging which results in low decomposition rates. Plants in this environment face two principal problems; first, a lack of available nitrogen due to the rate and pathway of decomposition, and secondly, a lack of oxygen, producing reducing conditions. These conditions favour many of the monocotyledon species (rushes, reeds and grasses) and some of tree species, especially those able to fix nitrogen directly, such as the alders. The chemistry of backswamps will depend upon the geology of the basin, with most being either alkaline or circumneutral in pH. However, in catchments on acidic bedrock backswamps can be acidic and have a pH as low as 3. Although the chemistry will alter the flora of backswamps many species, both monocotyledons and some dicotyledons (including trees such as alder and birches), are remarkably tolerant and can be found associated with a wide range of pH values.

In addition to these environments the land-water ecotones are extremely important in floodplain systems as they are characterised by higher biological diversity than adjacent patches and can occur in practically all floodplain environments (Naiman *et al.*, 1989).

Organic debris, dams and associated channels
Vegetation can also create hydrological and sedimentary environments. The cleared and tamed floodplains of North America and North-West Europe are far removed from the largely forested floodplains from which they evolved. Along with ecological change, some important channel environments have largely disappeared. Fortunately, studies in some of the few remaining forests large enough to have natural floodplains have illustrated the potential role of these processes.

In forested floodplains, trees fall into and across rivers; there is also a high input of organic material of all sizes from trunks to the microscopic. McDonald *et al.* (1982) have shown that in the Redwoods of northern California, this organic debris can be the fundamental control on channel pattern and channel change. Obviously, the Redwoods are rather an extreme case, but studies in other ecosystems have shown similar processes operating, if not so dramatically. Even in small floodplains (with small trees), such as in the New Forest in Hampshire, England, organic debris forms small dams (Plate 4.3). These retain fine sediment and, when they burst, send small flood-waves down the channel (Gurnell and Gregory, 1984). Studies of a small multiple-channel (anastomosing) river in south-western Ireland have shown how organic-debris dams are one of the causes of channel diversion and the maintenance of an intricate and diverse fluvial system (Harwood and Brown, 1993). Dammed channels become dead-water zones with a decrease in water depth and more open canopy (owing to the tree fall responsible for the dam) which results in increased growth of aquatic plants and invasion by emergent aquat-

Plate 4.3 A small debris dam from the New Forest, England.

ics. This can result in the terrestrialisation of channels (Brown *et al.*, 1995). In Boreal environments trees much smaller than the channel widths are still important because they can from a nucleus for bar formation (Nanson, 1981) as illustrated in Plate 4.4. Even in arid and semi-arid environments organic debris can be important. The lower Murray in Australia is now completely blocked by river red gums which used to be regularly cleared out for the paddlesteamer traffic.

When considering the importance of organic debris on past channels in cleared landscapes, there are two points worth remembering. First, that trees of the wildwoods were not of the same shape and size as those of the same species we see today; for example, both birch and alder are commonly thought of as rather short almost scrubby trees, but this need not be the case as both can grow to over 20 m with straight single trunks and form a canopy crown. This obviously makes a considerable difference in terms of their potential hydrological effects. Secondly, in some regions, mammals such as the beaver can have a remarkable effect on fluvial processes. The European beaver (*Castor fiber*) can have a considerable impact upon forest growth, local groundwater tables and river conditions. A mature European beaver is about 1 m long and weighs 15–30 kg. It will fell just about any tree species, up to a diameter of about 1 m, for food and shelter, although it prefers poplar, willow and maple. The lodges it constructs across streams can be up to 3 m high and will be constantly repaired (Plate 4.5). The trees within them will also sprout. The effect

Plate 4.4 Mid-channel bar ridges formed behind fallen and transported trees on the river Ae, Dumfriesshire, Scotland.

Plate 4.5 A beaver dam and lodge from a small Polish river (photo: A. Witt).

of beavers can be extremely important because they will attempt to dam all the watercourses in an area, often the only limit being set by the density of exist- ing dams. The rise in the local watertables kills trees by paludification, and once dead the trees are easily blown down by wind. It is not known how long the dams and lodges generally last, but some are known to have existed for over 1000 years (Coles, 1992a). The result will be a stepped stream profile with very effective sediment traps and the accumulation of lake-like sediments in small steep stream valleys, a phenomenon hard to explain without some local control on base-levels. Coles (1992a) has suggested beavers may have been a major cause of Late Mesolithic and Early Neolithic clearance in the UK, through the paludification of river- and stream-side forest. The European beaver became extinct in Britain sometime early in the medieval period and was subsequently eradicated from mainland Europe until the only native populations left were in Poland, south-eastern France and eastern Europe. The North American beaver, which is fundamentally the same species (*Castor canadiensis*/*Castor fiber*), still has a major impact on Canadian fluvial systems, especially in pro- tected areas such as the Algonquin National Park.

The pattern of these environments, including those caused by beavers, is fundamentally controlled by the geomorphic system, including the size, slope and regime of the river, its sediment load and its history of channel movement. The species composition of these environments is also the result of adaptive evolution and adjustment to climate change, including the return-migration of species in areas glaciated in the Pleistocene. These ecological factors operate through colonisation and succession.

4.4 Colonisation and succession

Newly created landsurfaces on floodplains can be colonised by plants whose seeds can arrive by wind, animal vectors or water. Water is also an effective means of vegetative colonisation through the transport of living gametes along with organic debris. The colonisation of surfaces is rapid because of these different mechanisms and the proximity of seed sources. However, seedling mortality is often very high. Floodplains are not simple hydroseres (if simple hydroseres exist at all), but do have strong components of hydroseral succes- sion within their pattern of vegetation change. Whereas strongly determin- istic patterns can be shown in the vegetation change of cutoffs (open water species → floating aquatics → attached aquatics → reed-beds → willow or alder scrub), this is just one component of floodplain vegetation and all these successional stages can occur in close proximity at all times. Neither is the floodplain just a simple patchwork of parcels of different successional stages, as events such as floods, channel change and changes in the sedimentation rate will affect all parcels to some extent, and these are normal components of the system. Because the pattern of vegetation colonisation is so closely tied to floodplain development, Everitt (1968) was able to construct maps of the age

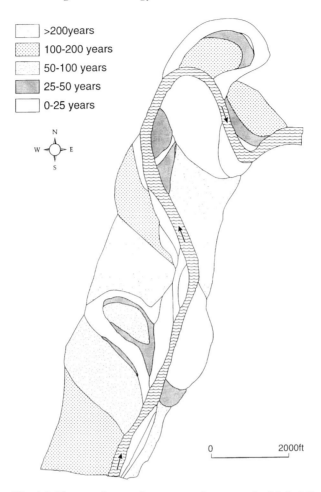

>200years

100-200 years

50-100 years

25-50 years

0-25 years

0   2000ft

Fig. 4.5 The age classes of cottonwood trees on the Little Missouri floodplain, Wyoming. Adapted from Everitt (1968).

of the floodplain of the Little Missouri river in North Dakota, from coring and ring-counts of cottonwood trees (*Populus sargentii*). The floodplain forest is composed of a series of even-aged stands which exhibit a progression in age up-valley and away from the channel, providing a complete record of the historical migration of the channel (Figure 4.5). This allowed Everitt to calculate floodplain deposition and erosion rates. He also noted how flood-training of saplings could occur whereby a sapling bent parallel with the flow is buried and shoots produce linear clumps of trees as a result.

Our ideas concerning succession have been profoundly changed by studies of wetlands. The classical view of hydroseral succession where waterbodies are terrestrialised by the build-up of inorganic and organic material cannot fully explain either the pattern of communities on floodplains or observations of floodplain vegetation change. The end-point of dry land is highly unlikely without hydrological change. Walker (1970) found from pollen and bog stratigraphy that successional sequences in northern peatlands were variable, with reversals and skipped stages, and these were influenced by the dominant species first reaching a site. A bog rather than terrestrial forest was the most typical end point. Wetlands may also exist virtually unchanged for 1000 years or more, while some, particularly raised (ombrogenous) mires, may respond to decade to decade shifts in the precipitation evapotranspiration ratio (Barber, 1976; Barber *et al.*, 1994). All alluvial wetland successions are influenced by allogenic factors, including flooding, groundwater changes, climatic change, subsidence and vegetation disturbance. Van der Valk (1981) has therefore replaced the classical autogenic succession model by a Gleasonian model in which the presence and abundance of each species depends upon its life-history and its adaptation to the environment of a site. The environmental factors make up the 'environmental sieve' in this model and, as the environment changes, so does the sieve and hence the species present. This may help to explain why raised bogs developed on some floodplains during the Holocene and not on others. Given a suitable hydrology (near-surface saturation) it seems most probable that it was the immigration of particular moss species such as *Paludella squarrosa* and a fall in the calcium content of groundwater that facilitated the growth and eventual dominance of the bog (*Sphagnum*) mosses which build raised bogs (Bohncke and Vandenberghe, 1984; Aalbersberg, 1994). This is an example of how, in reality, both autogenic and allogenic forces act to change alluvial vegetation.

4.5 The floodplain and river continuum
In the continuum model of river ecology, river and riparian vegetation zonation describes an environmental gradient to which individual species are responding. The reason why zonation is so sharp in many river/floodplains is that environmental gradients are ecologically steep and groups of species have similar tolerances and so tend to group on these gradients. The principal gradients are those already identified: hydroperiod, watertable depth and soil fertility. The systematic and progressive nature and pattern of floodplain sedimentation creates environments along these gradients, so creating chronosequences of vegetation. These chronological or developmental patterns of floodplain vegetation are therefore the result of both autogenic and allogenic forces.

The river/floodplain ecosystem can be regarded as a continuum from headwaters to the sea. Organic matter is the linking and driving component of the river continuum model of fluvial ecology, as proposed by Vannote *et al.* (1980). The model, which is analogous to the model of downstream physical energy expenditure devised by geomorphologists (Langbein and Leopold, 1966), proposes that energy input and organic-matter transport, storage and use by macroinvertebrate functional feeding groups (e.g. shredders, grazers, collectors and predators) is largely regulated by fluvial geomorphological processes

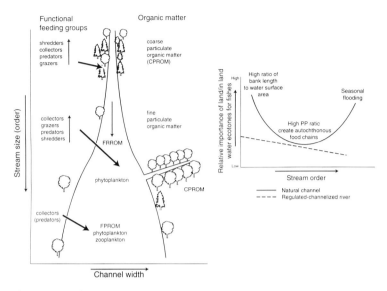

Fig. 4.6 The river continuum model and the relative importance of functional feeding groups and land-water ecotones. Adapted from Vannote *et al.* (1980) and Naiman *et al.* (1989).

(Vannote *et al.*, 1980). This is shown diagrammatically in Figure 4.6 which also shows how the relative importance of land-water ecotones changes along the river continuum. Although coarse organic matter is an important input in headwaters it may also be added downstream by tributaries and bank erosion. Coarse organic matter which becomes buried can be regarded as a net output from the system. The continuum model provides a standard against which changes in organic matter inputs can be compared both for present and, theoretically, for past hydrological systems. However, it is not a universally applicable model and it is biased towards those processes that predominate in forested landscapes.

4.6 Ecological studies of floodplains in different environments

Most of the studies of floodplain ecology (of which there have been remarkably few) have tried to link the functioning of the different floodplain environments with spatial patterns in vegetation. A comprehensive review of the ecology, hydrology and distribution of alluvial forests is given by Brinson (1990). The studies briefly described here have been chosen to cover different climatic zones and floodplain types.

The Boreal Zone
The Tanana river floodplain in Alaska has been studied extensively by ecologists over several years (Walker and Chapin, 1986). The vegetation pattern of

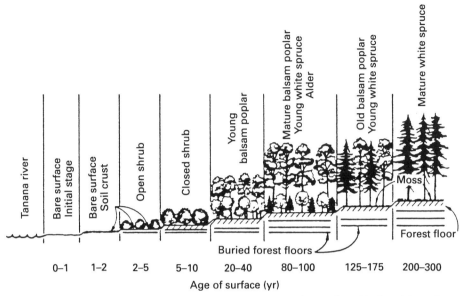

Fig. 4.7 A vegetation transect across the Tanana river valley, Alaska. Adapted from Van Cleve and Viereck (1981), by permission of Springer-Verlag.

the floodplain is composed of eight ecological zones as shown in Figure 4.7. These zones represent a chronosequence away from the channel with changing vegetation and soil conditions. Van Cleve and Viereck (1981) point out that there are physical controls, such as the frequency of flooding, that are super-imposed over the entire successional sequence. Studies of the seed rain onto silty-bars by Walker *et al.* (1986) showed that some seeds of all species arrived in all successional stages but were most frequent in the successional stage dominated by that species; they also showed that buried seeds were not important. Flooding produced substantial seedling mortality in early successional stages. In mid-successional stages willow was out-competed by alder owing to its shorter life-span, grazing by hares and shade intolerance. Walker and Chapin (1986) have shown that competitive interactions are more important in succession with alder (*Alnus tenuifolia*), fixing nitrogen which enhanced the growth of both willow (*Salix alaxensis*) and poplar (*Populus balsamifera*). However, alder also inhibited seedling growth by both root competition and shading. Walker and Chapin (1986) also showed the importance of the growth rate for controlling the dominance of species in different successional stages. Early successional species such as willow and poplar grew faster than alder, which grew faster than spruce, which was the only species which continued to establish itself in later successional stages. These studies have shown that the vegetation pattern of the Tanana floodplain is a 'result of complex interactions of life history, facilitative, competitive and stochastic processes' (Walker and Chapin,

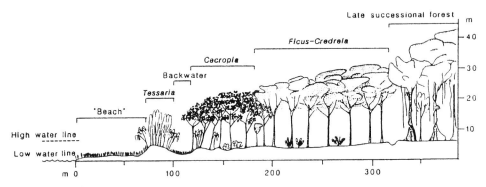

Fig. 4.8 A vegetation transect across the Lower Amazon floodplain. Reprinted from *Nature,* Salo *et al.* (1986), Macmillan Magazines Limited.

1986) but that facilitative interactions between species are not of primary importance, or indeed essential.

The Humid Tropical Zone

Tropical floodplains are probably the richest ecosystems in the world (Colinvaux, 1987). The high diversity and high productivity of tropical systems results from high and constant mean annual temperatures, high precipitation and inundation. The pattern and periodicity of inundation is extremely important for the interchange of organic matter from soils and vegetation to surface waters. In the Amazon system over 1300 species of fish are known and the estimated total is probably over 2000, whereas the whole of Europe has 192 species (Sioli, 1975). This richness is also due to the long history of the ecosystem and the wide variety of habitats, especially seasonally variable land/water boundary ecotones. Important habitats include forest creeks, floodplain lakes, floating meadows of grasses and other macrophytes, mouth bays and Igapo forests. Igapo forests are seasonally flooded forests associated with so-called blackwaters which are acidic and do not produce large amounts of autochthonous phytoplankton. Figure 4.8 shows a schematic cross-section of the Amazon valley and some of its environments, including the Igapo forest, gallery forest and the backwater side-arms or parana. However, the floodplain rainforest is highly dynamic and large-scale forest disturbance is caused by lateral erosion and channel changes; indeed, as much as 26% of the western Amazon lowland forest is identifiable as of recent successional origin (Salo *et al.*, 1986). This large-scale disturbance may be one of the mechanisms involved in maintaining high between-habitat diversity, which contributes to the high diversity of the whole system. Another cause of disturbance is catastrophic drainage of floodplain lakes caused by the bursting of debris dams. Large organic debris plays an important part in the dynamics of the system and especially of tributary streams. Although inundation is a primary control on the system, other factors involved include organic matter decomposition rates which are closely related to patterns of soil saturation caused by variable source areas (Nortcliffe and Thornes, 1988).

The Semi-Arid Zone
The spatial pattern created by groundwater is more obvious in semi-arid environments than any other. This is because productivity and biomass in this moisture-stressed environment are directly related to groundwater flow and soil moisture regime. A well-documented and well-known example is the bottom-lands of the Gila river in Arizona (Gatewood *et al.*, 1950). The land subject to flooding is 1.5 km in width and covered by low-lying phreatophytes with the most common species being cottonwood, willow, baccharis (*Baccharis* spp.), mesquite (*Prosopis velutina*) and saltcedar (*Tamarix gallica*) which was introduced from the Mediterranean. Along the Rio Grande, between El Paso, Texas and Albuquerque, New Mexico, Campbell and Dick-Peddie (1964) recognised five alluvial vegetation classes forming a continuum from south (the most xeric) to north (Figure 4.9).

In the Mediterranean basin natural floodplain vegetation is very rare and even in the Mediterranean zone of North America only 10% survives (Warner, 1984). Part of the floodplain in the Sacramento valley which has survived shows a gradient of species and canopy height away from the river. Forest only develops in areas not frequently flooded or affected by lateral erosion, giving much of the floodplain an open aspect (Figure 4.10). Some of the floodplains of central and northern Australia which have been relatively untouched by agricultural development show how closely contemporary vegetation is related to fluvial history. There are three generations of channels that cross the Riverine Plain in New South Wales (Schumm, 1968): prior channels which are straight and have been dated to *c.* 100,000 BP, ancestral stream channels which are more sinuous and date to *c.* 40,000 BP and the Holocene channel network (Page *et al.*, 1991; see chapter 5 and Plate 5.1). The prior channels support isolated strips of open gum woodland, while the ancestral streams are preserved as large oxbows (or billabongs) within or at the edge of the present floodplain which supports red gum forest (Plate 5.2). A more thorough discussion of the Riverine Plain palaeochannels can be found in chapter 5. In arid and semi-arid areas the creation of groundwater sources by ancient river systems may have permanent effects on the distribution of vegetation, plant and animal resources.

The Temperate Zone
It is doubtful if there are any large floodplains in the Temperate Zone which have not been disturbed to a significant extent by human activity during the Holocene. It is therefore difficult to find 'natural' floodplain systems as most have been deforested and drained, leaving only isolated pockets of wet wood-

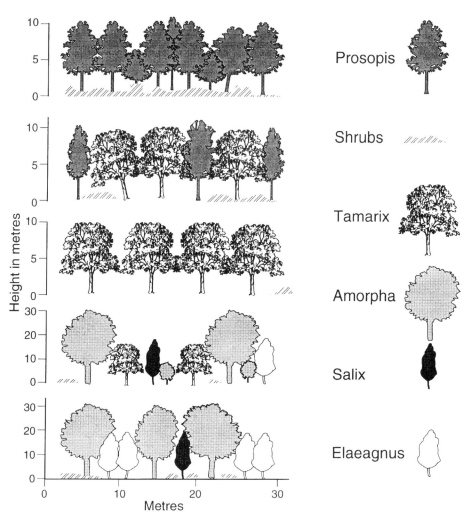

Fig. 4.9 Vegetation classes from the Rio Grande floodplain. Adapted from Campbell and Dick-Peddie (1964).

land, bog and swamp, as well as the refugia of the riparian zone. Research on some of the less disturbed segments of floodplains in Europe does, however, provide some useful information on non-managed floodplain ecology. An example is work by the World Wildlife Fund/Auen Institute for Floodplain Ecology on the Rhine near Vienna (WWF, 1985) and the floodplain forest of the Offendorf Nature Reserve on the French side of the Rhine floodplain near Strasbourg (Klein *et al.*, 1995). In these forests the varying flood durations, which depend upon elevation, cause characteristic patterns in the distribution of plants and animals. White willows, which are inundated on average 190 days yr^{-1}, characterise the lowest zone, whereas higher zones with fewer days of

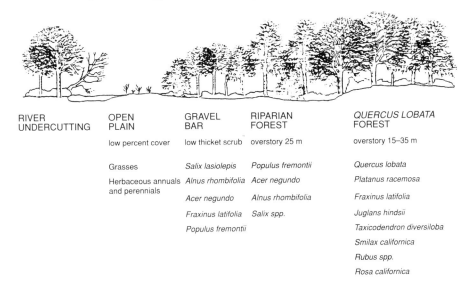

RIVER UNDERCUTTING	OPEN PLAIN	GRAVEL BAR	RIPARIAN FOREST	*QUERCUS LOBATA* FOREST
	low percent cover	low thicket scrub	overstory 25 m	overstory 15–35 m
	Grasses	*Salix lasiolepis*	*Populus fremontii*	*Quercus lobata*
	Herbaceous annuals and perennials	*Alnus rhombifolia*	*Acer negundo*	*Platanus racemosa*
		Acer negundo	*Alnus rhombifolia*	*Fraxinus latifolia*
		Fraxinus latifolia	*Salix spp.*	*Juglans hindsii*
		Populus fremontii		*Taxicodendron diversiloba*
				Smilax californica
				Rubus spp.
				Rosa californica

Fig. 4.10 A vegetation transect across the Sacremento valley in California. Adapted from Brinson (1990).

inundation are covered by oak (*Quercus robur*), elms (*Ulmus minor* and *Ulmus laevis*) and ash (*Fraxinus excelsior*), which together form the bottomland hardwoods.

Detailed studies of floodplain ecology have been carried out in the floodplain forests of southern Moravia in Czechoslovakia by Penka *et al.* (1985). This work has been centred upon the International Biological Programme Floodplain Forest research station near Lednice on the floodplain of the river Dyje. Using the Braun-Blanquet phytosociological system of classification they have grouped the forests into associations: willow–alder (*Saliceto–Alnetum*), elm–ash (*Ulmeto–Fraxinetum*), oak–ash (*Queceto–Fraxinetum*) and elm–ash–hornbeam (*Ulmeto–Fraxinetum–Carpineum*) with relèves of sedges (*Carex* spp.), yellow flag (*Iris pseudacorus*) and other herbaceous species. A distinction is made between those communities which can tolerate long periods of inundation and saturated soil conditions (hygrophilous) and those which cannot. The most important control on species composition is moisture regime which changes not only the composition of the herb layer but also the classification of forest types (Figure 4.11). These studies have also shown how changes in the forest ecology are closely linked to changes in the river's hydrological and sedimentary regime. Silting of one of the Dyje river channels and raising of a weir induced a succession of species dependent on recurrent waterlogging, including an increase in the lesser pond sedge (*Carex acutiformis*), yellow flag and creeping jenny (*Lysimachia nummularia*) within the *Ulmeto–Fraxinetum–Carpineum* woodland. The forests of the Dyje have been preserved in a relatively natural condition, because of their role in the

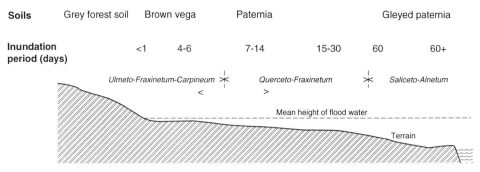

Fig. 4.11 Vegetation associations across the river Dyje floodplain in Czechoslovakia. Adapted from Penka *et al.* (1985).

protection of the state border and also skilled management of forest and game during the Middle Ages when they were used for hunting by the nobility.

One of the most interesting sites in Europe is the unique floodplain forest on the river Lee near Macroom, County Cork, in the Republic of Ireland (Brown *et al.*, 1995). It is called the Gearagh ('wooded river' in Gaelic) and consists of a maze of anastomosing channels running through dense woodland with an unusual and rich tree and ground flora, which was studied by many eminent botanists including Praeger, Tuxen, Braun-Blanquet and Tansley (O'Reilly, 1955; White, 1985). It was believed that the entire woodland had been destroyed by a reservoir created in 1954. However, owing partly to a study by a local schoolboy, Tom Hickey, it was discovered that about 100 ha still persists in a relatively undisturbed state at the upstream end (White, 1985, and see Plates 4.6 and 4.7). The higher islands and islets are relatively dry, although still inundated by high flows, and these provide rooting sites for oak (*Quercus robur*), ash (*Fraxinus excelsior*), birch (*Betula pubescens*), hazel (*Corylus avellana*) and hawthorn (*Crataegus monogyna*). Alder and grey willow (*Salix atrocinerea*) occur on the lower wetter islands and margins of the channels. The rich ground flora includes wild garlic (*Allium ursinum*), marsh marigold (*Caltha palustris*), bugle (*Ajuga reptans*), enchanter's nightshade (*Circaea lutetiana*), Irish spurge (*Euphorbia hybernia*) and meadowsweet (*Filipendula ulmaria*). In addition to over 100 other species of flowering plants, there are thirteen recorded ferns, one of the most common being the royal fern (*Osmunda regalis*), and a large number of mosses, liverworts and lichens. Many of the channels are entirely shaded by trees, but where they are not, a rich aquatic flora exists. The islands and islets are stabilised by vegetation and the channels vary in width and depth with scour holes at confluences, pools and shallows. There are many backwater areas which contain slack-water even at moderately high flows (Harwood and Brown, 1993). Organic debris of all sizes is abundant and channel morphology is considerably affected by roots, fallen trees, branches and debris dams. Unfortunately, relatively little is known about these forested anastomosing systems with their great cross-sectional and reach

Plate 4.6 The Gearagh, Co. Cork, Ireland: islands inundated in a flood.

variation in hydraulic geometry, flow velocity, flow direction and bank/bed resistance. The Gearagh does, however, provide probably the best analogy that exists in North-West Europe today for the Cool Temperate Mid-Holocene alluvial forests.

While studies of semi-natural systems are of great value in providing models of the functioning of past floodplain ecosystems, the contemporary ecology of most temperate floodplains is the result of both indirect impacts and management within the constraints of the floodplain system. A good example of this is the floodplain of the river Itchen in southern England (Tubbs, 1978). The Itchen is a chalk stream with a high baseflow contribution and a very non-flashy regime. It is also nutrient rich, with high concentrations of phosphorus and nitrogen. The vegetation was surveyed in 1976 and classified into four major types. One type was fen which included both woodland dominated by alder and/or willows and also oak, ash, hawthorn and sloe (*Prunus spinosa*) in drier areas. The fen in wet areas was dominated by tall grasses and herbs, especially the common sedge (*Phragmites communis*) and reed-like plants, includ-

Plate 4.7 The Gearagh, Co. Cork, Ireland: discharge across an islet (towards the viewer) into a slow mud-bed channel.

ing the reed grass (*Phalaris arundinacea*), branched bur-reed (*Sparganium erectum*) and bulrushes (*Typha latifolia*). The other types include wet meadows which supported over 50 species m², unimproved but poor grassland derived from herb-rich meadows by constant heavy grazing and drainage, and improved grassland. In addition, the Itchen has a particularly rich aquatic flora in the channel and riparian zone, and it also supports the cultivation of watercress (*Rorippa nasturtium-aquaticum*). The floodplain is also important for riverine, meadow and fen bird species. The present ecology of the Itchen floodplain is the result of a complex land use history which probably began as early as the Bronze Age with clearance of the wet alder woodland, followed by drainage and the manipulation of watercourses for mills, navigation and floodmeadows. The Itchen floodplain is largely cleared, as is common with most temperate floodplains, and this limits their potential as analogues of past, more wooded, but still managed, floodplains. One partially wooded, managed floodplain system that has survived is Litovelské Pomoraví near Olomouc in southern Moravia, Czech Republic (Plate 4.8). The area, which is a mosaic of deciduous forest, channels, oxbows and grasslands, was declared an Ecological Reserve in 1990. The channelisation and control of a natural anastomosing river by the use of weirs and bank protection has created a stable multiple-channel system with high vegetation diversity and many rarities including 250 red data book species. The waterbodies vary from oxbows through deep slow-water channels behind weirs to steep gravel-bedded channels. However, the system is highly vulnerable to changes in groundwater levels and water quality caused by abstraction and agriculture (Kostkan, 1992).

Plate 4.8 Channels within the Litovelské Pomoraví wooded floodplain, Czech Republic: a deadwater channel, a slow–medium channel with partial debris dam and a fast gravel-bedded channel with bank erosion and mid-channel bars forming around tree trunks.

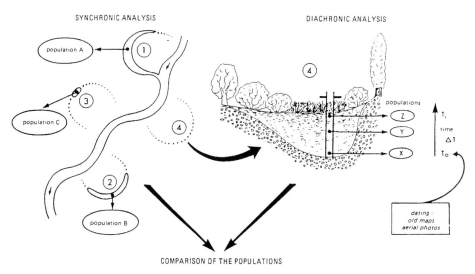

Fig. 4.12 Synchronic and diachronic analysis. Reproduced from *Regulated Rivers*, Amoros *et al.* (1989), by permission of John Wiley & Sons Ltd.

Climate change (both in the past and in the future) will alter the global distribution of these environments, with the most profound and immediate effects being felt in marginal zones, and floodplain management has taken place concurrently with natural change which may or may not have been in a complementary direction. Archaeological evidence of floodplain management and environmental change is discussed in chapters 6 to 9.

4.7 Floodplain palaeoecology

Floodplains of large rivers generally offer a range of potential sites that can yield palaeoecological data. These range from floodplain lakes, through much smaller dead-water bodies to lateral peat deposits and even in some areas raised bogs (i.e. ombrogenous or rain-fed bogs). Many palaeoecological studies on floodplains have made implicit use of the fact that floodplains present a variety of different successional habitats in different stages of development at any one time and also that some of these habitats preserve a record of past ecological changes. This has been made more explicit in the model of synchronic and diachronic analysis used by Amoros *et al.*(1987) and illustrated in Figure 4.12. Most of the techniques used in the diachronic analysis of floodplain palaeoecology have been adapted from lake and peat bog studies. Despite many practical and interpretive disadvantages, floodplains do have one great advantage for palaeoecological work and that is their frequency. Even in areas barren of lakes, they permit palaeoecology to be studied from the uplands and glaciated regions to the lowland plains. Floodplains do have several disadvantages, one of which is frequent disturbance that may produce hiatuses in the record.

Another can be (depending upon the aims of the study) the isolation of the floodplain sites from the surrounding non-floodplain vegetation by the flood-plain corridor vegetation. The ability to infer ecological conditions outside this zone is a function of the palaeoecological method or data source and the size and location of the site.

The preservation of organic remains is vary variable in floodplain environments and largely determined by the water regime. Chemical conditions are of secondary importance and, as long as decay is slowed down or inhibited by waterlogging, organic remains, including non-woody tissue and pollen, can survive in both acidic and alkaline environments. This means that, for *in situ* macroscopic remains, there is a bias towards the wetter floodplain environments. Permanent waterlogging can occur in non-organic and coarse deposits; therefore, if wood and other organic materials are deposited contemporaneously with gravels and they remain waterlogged, they will be preserved. Beyond these general taphonomic statements, more specific constraints have to be examined organism by organism.

In practice, no method really provides a comprehensive picture of past ecological conditions, only a fragmentary picture of some parts of the ecosystem from which the rest is inferred. Often, it is only a part of the system that is under investigation, such as water chemistry or forest resources. The choice of palaeoecological method is inevitably a compromise between the questions most in need of being answered, and the opportunities offered by the environment. The questions asked of palaeoecological data vary from those requiring relatively little inference from the data to those requiring far too much. Figure 4.13 summarises some of the inferential stages involved in palaeoecological reasoning. There are problems at each point apart from taphonomy. The death assemblage may not mirror the living assemblage in, for example, age structure. Many animals do not expire in random locations but tend to die in 'cemetery' locations. Living assemblages are themselves not always easy to describe and classify, as witnessed by the vast literature on the subject, since the result largely depends upon the method used, e.g. life-form versus floristic classification in plants. We also have to assume that the ecophysiology of the species has not changed in the time period being studied. While this is true for the last 10,000 years and probably the last 1–2 million years for many species, it is patently not true for many other species, especially those with relatively short life cycles which are genetically plastic and therefore ecologically adaptable. Darwin's theory of evolution was after all partly based on the observations of small, but ecologically very important, adaptations of birds caused by isolation of populations in the Galapagos Islands. So, while trees seem relatively slow to adapt, other species are not, including herbaceous weeds, small mammals, birds, insects and viruses. With some of these organisms, it may be that palaeo-ecology is the only way to identify their adaptive history, i.e. from their past ecological niches. An example of the practical problems this poses is given by

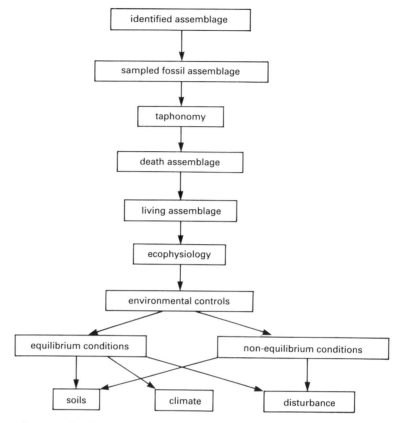

Fig. 4.13 The chain of inference in palaeoecology.

beetles (Coleoptera): they are excellent indicators of past temperatures until the late Holocene, when human activity, producing new habitats and internal climates, complicates the method.

The second way in which ecological change is important is through disequilibrium change. This is ecological change when there is no environmental change; it occurs because not all populations are in equilibrium with their environment, especially climate, and because of the lags produced by the processes of colonisation and succession. Since life on the Earth is structured in trophic levels, with each level dependent upon the level below, there will be a lagged response to any change although this lag will generally decrease with increasing trophic status. This problem is at its most acute in glaciated latitudes of the Old World and North America, where vast areas have been in climatic disequilibrium for a significant part of the Pleistocene. Last of all, if we wish to use palaeoecology to reconstruct past environmental controls, then we must be able to isolate and quantify these environmental controls. This is not easy, as is shown by the volume of modern ecophysiological studies. In particular, problems have arisen because it is now clear that the law of limiting factors (Leibig's Law) as originally proposed is inadequate as it is not necessarily the one factor which is in least supply in relation to demand (e.g. water, light, nitrogen and other nutrients) that controls productivity, but complex interactions between factors involving inhibition, facilitation and blocking.

From this brief discussion, it might seem a hopeless task to reconstruct past ecologies, let alone past palaeoenvironments. However, this is not the case, for three principal reasons:

1   Uniformitarianism works far better for processes than for forms. This is because there are certain rules set by the physics of this planet which organisms must obey in order to survive, e.g. the laws of thermodynamics dictate that organisms must balance their heat budget.

2   Mutation is limited in its effects and takes time, i.e. it is the small but significant changes to a species which eventually cause speciation and diversity. Whether or not evolution has occurred in bursts or as a gradualistic process on the geological time-scale is irrelevant at the human time-scale where it is relatively slow and dependent upon either the generation time of the organism or its acceleration by humans (selective breeding).

3   For many organisms it does appear that one or two environmental factors have, within certain limits, an overriding control on survival, reproductive success or the growth rate, so much so in some cases that statistically significant relationships can be established. For example, the diatom flora of a lake can be used to predict the average lake pH with remarkable accuracy (Batterbee and Charles, 1986; Birks *et al.*, 1990).

The first stage in all alluvial palaeoecological work is the description and sampling of sediments, ideally from exposures but otherwise from cores. Organic sediments are generally described using the Troels-Smith system (Troels-Smith, 1955) or a modified version (Barber, 1976; Aaby and Berglund, 1986), as outlined in Figure 4.14. It involves a categorisation of organic remains, which requires a relatively low level of operator expertise, into herbaceous material, moss, wood and inorganic material and an assessment as to whether it is *in situ* or detrital. The occurrence of some of these types such as *Turfa lignosa* (wood peat) has obvious palaeoecological implications, but, in addition, other sediment descriptors used, such as the degree of humification, can also have palaeoenvironmental significance.

Plant macrofossils

Plant macrofossils, which are plant remains visible to the naked eye, are both common and varied in alluvial deposits in the temperate zone. They are variable in both type and provenance, the latter being a matter of interpretation from the depositional setting and evidence of transport. Wood and woody tissue can preserve well in waterlogged conditions with the internal structure or wood anatomy allowing identification to the genus and often species level.

Physical properties

Nigror (nig):	darkness, white-black
stratificatio (strf):	degree of stratification
elasticitas (elas):	degree of elasticity, 0 = plastic
siccitas (sicc):	degree of dryness

Boundaries

Lim (L):   0 = more than 10 mm, 4 = less than 0.5 mm

Humicity (visible degree of decomposition)
humo 0:   plant structure fresh, water squeezes out
humo 4:   no visible plant structure, whole matrix squeezes out

Components

Substantia humosa (Sh):	disintegrated humous substance, no structure
Turfa bryophytica (Tb):	moss peat
Turfa lignosa (Tl):	wood peat
Turfa herbacea (Th):	herbaceous and rootlet peat
Detritus lignosus (Dl):	wood fragments over 2 mm
Detritus herbosus (Dh):	fragments of herbs over 2 mm
Detritus granosus (Dg):	fragments of wood, herbs and animals 0.1-2.0 mm
Limus detrituosus(Ld):	homogenous mud of micro-organisms (e.g. algae)
Limus humosus (Lh):	humified elastic mud sedimented in water
Limus siliceus organogenes (Lso):	diatomite
Limus calcareus (Lc):	marl (CaCO3 of organic or inorganic origin)
Argilla (A):	clay and colloids, grains not visible (<0.002 mm)
Argilla granosa (Ag):	fine silt (0.002 mm-)
Grana arenosa (Ga):	coarse silt (-0.6 mm)
Grana saburralia:	sand (0.6 mm-2.0 mm)
Grana glareosa:	gravel (2-20 mm)

example:
nig4,srf0,elas3,sicc1;lim.sup.1;humo4,Ld4,Dh1,Ag+,Ga+ = blackish-fine detritus mud

The above are simplified and exclude larger grain size descriptors. For more detail see Troels-Smith (1955), Aaby and Berglund (1986) or Barber (1976)

Fig. 4.14 A simplified outline of the Troels-Smith method of recording organic sediments. The above are simplified and exclude larger grain size descriptions. For more details see Troels-Smith (1955), Aaby and Berglund (1986) or Barber (1976).

As there are now many specialist books on wood identification, including roots (Jane, 1956; Schweingruber, 1978; Cutler *et al.*, 1987) and computer identification keys (Wheeler, 1986), only a brief outline will be given here. The internal structure or wood anatomy depicted in Figure 4.15 is composed of rings formed by variations in the growth rate during the year. The size, shape and number of vessels are used to identify species: hardwoods are either ring-porous with larger spring vessels than summer vessels (e.g. oak), or diffuse-porous with more uniform vessels (e.g. beech). Some conifers have resin canals, others do not. The state of preservation of the vessels and rays can yield valuable information on the history of the material. In addition examination of the wood can reveal if the bark has been removed and if the ends have been snapped, decayed, cut or shaped. Although few experiments have been done to confirm this, observation suggests that bark removal is caused by fluvial transport and exposure, so no bark removal at all suggests very little transport and limited exposure prior to burial. Whether the wood is allochthonous or autochthonous is not easy to prove except where it is in its life-position. An example of life-position is where the tree bole is sitting upright or near upright with the roots penetrating the underlying gravel strata.

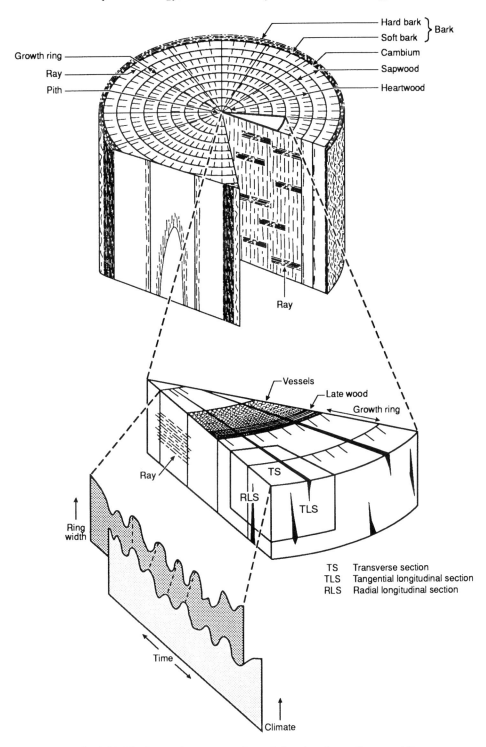

Fig. 4.15 The internal structure of wood showing the sections used for identification and a tree-ring curve.

Non-woody macrofossils can be divided into stems, leaves, fruit, seeds, stamens and buds. They are common in fine alluvial deposits, organic muds and floodplain peats and can be extracted relatively easily by gently breaking up the sediment, using a disaggregating agent (such as NaOH) and wet sieving (Wasylikova, 1986; Grosse-Bruckmann, 1986). On archaeological sites plant macrofossils, including carbonised fruit and seeds, may be recovered by flotation. Identification is based on a reference collection and, to a lesser extent than microfossils, on dichotomous (i.e. branching) identification keys. Fragments may be identified and counted from a set volume to derive a concentration or, more often, will be visually assessed on a semi-quantitative scale (e.g. as present, rare, occasional, frequent or abundant), or a grid may be used to estimate the percentage coverage of a petri-dish. Which method will be used depends on the aims of the study (and the amount of money available) and in most cases only presence/absence is required for a taxa list. However, semi-quantitative diagrams can be valuable especially where conditions are slowly changing. Macrofossils are most revealing about the local vegetation and especially hydroseral succession. Indeed, Walker (1970), in a classic paper, was able to challenge the traditional deterministic view of hydroseral succession in North-West Europe using macrofossil data. By identifying the most common successions of communities from the peat stratigraphies, he was able to demonstrate that the most preferred pathway in western Britain led to sphagnum bog, rather than oak woodland.

Cutoffs often contain *in situ* plant macrofossils which reflect the seral stages of cutoff infilling. There may also be an allochthonous input by wind, tributary streams or floods. For example, alder catkins are commonly found some distance from alder trees and in accumulations of flood debris. There are many pathways by which macrofossils may be incorporated into the floodplain fill, as well as problems associated with differential production and differential preservation (Watts, 1978). It is possible for very resistant macrofossils to be reworked into later deposits, which may produce anomalous radiocarbon dates as mentioned in chapter 2. At least in glaciated regions, this problem is generally limited to Holocene materials, and will not influence estimates of the antiquity of the earliest occurrence of any particular species in the palaeoecological history of a floodplain. In practice, detailed stratigraphic work, attention to the condition of the macrofossil fractions and the identification of any anomalous components will minimise the risks of dating reworked macrofossils.

Plant microfossils: pollen, spores and diatoms
Pollen analysis and macrofossil analysis are complementary techniques. Pollen analysis can provide a picture of the non-site as well as site vegetation, but it is often taxonomically less precise. Although in general macrofossil-rich sediments contain pollen this is not always the case, as demonstrated by two examples, one obvious, the other not; first, in coarse deposits, trees and organic debris may be deposited in 'natural traps', but pollen will not. Secondly, many

of the chalk valleys of southern England contain substantial thicknesses of reed-peat but sometimes contain little or no pollen. In this case, the most likely cause is the watertable which fluctuates relatively little but is slightly higher during the autumn and winter, allowing the preservation of dead plant material, but falls during the late spring and summer, causing enough oxidation and microbial activity to destroy the pollen but not the macrofossils (Barber, pers. comm.). Pollen may also be preserved in non-organic deposits such as loess and alluvial silts and clays.

Details of the methods of pollen extraction and analysis are described in a number of texts (Moore *et al.*, 1991; Faegri and Iversen, 1990), but extraction methods fall essentially into two types:

1   Standard chemical methods based on the oxidation of organic matter (hydrolysis) and digestion/dissolution of inorganic matter by strong acids such as hydrofluoric acid. These can be adapted to cope with the generally high inorganic content of alluvial samples by repeated or extended digestion or even digestion under pressure. In practice, pollen concentrations down to about $3x10^5gr^{-1}$ cm^{-3} can be analysed using these methods.

2   Physical methods based on the differential settling velocity of pollen from other fractions using liquids of different specific gravities (such as sugar solutions) and the use of very fine sieves. When perfected, these methods may greatly reduce the preparation time for pollen analysis and lower its cost.

As with many micropalaeontological techniques, there is a compromise between taxonomic detail and time or sample size. However, as a result of improved keys and a large number of modern pollen floras (Erdtman *et al.*, 1961; Punt, 1976–), taxonomic detail has increased steadily over the years. Identification may be aided in the near future by automated image analysis which has already been shown to be possible using scanning electron micrographs of pollen surface textures (Langford *et al.*, 1986). However, it must be remembered that pollen analysis is a statistical procedure based upon sampling and so confidence limits are dependent on the number of grains counted (Maher, 1972).

Pollen has been traditionally used for palaeoclimatic reconstruction with the aid of assemblage–climate associations, indicator species (Iversen, 1944a) or regression equations (Webb, 1980), and via climostratigraphy or biostratigraphy for dating. Its most obvious and most fundamental use is for vegetation reconstruction and it is this that is most relevant to studies of floodplain evolution and the palaeoenvironments associated with alluvial archaeology. Many pollen studies of alluvial sediments have been reported as just lists of types and percentage occurrence; however, from suitable sites (the most waterlogged), coherent pollen diagrams can be constructed (Brown, 1982). There are several floodplain facies from which percentage diagrams have been

Table 4.2 *The condition of pollen grains (pollen preservation categories modified from Cushing, 1967).*

Category of deterioration	Features	Process	Floodplain environments
corrosion	exine pitted/etched	oxidation	peats/soils
broken	ruptured/split/fragmentary	abrasion/oxidation	coarse deposits/soils
crumpled	folded/twisted	disturbance	soils
degraded	surface texture fused/opaque	reworking	soils/oxidised peat

produced, including: cutoff infills, buried lateral peat beds, terrace depressions (if they are perched aquifers) and backswamp peats. If the site has no, or few, hiatuses and a reasonably smooth accumulation curve, it is possible to construct an influx diagram (using concentration x accumulation rate, in grains cm^{-2} yr^{-1}). Influx diagrams are known to be superior when bare ground is an important feature of the surrounding area, such as is the case in the Lateglacial and after severe human disturbance. In these cases, species replacement is not reflected in the inter-relatedness of percentages. Influx diagrams allow ecological processes such as succession and competition to be investigated using pollen analysis (Bennett, 1983; Brown, 1988).

The interpretation of floodplain and terrace depression pollen diagrams faces the same problems as other environments, along with some others. The universal problems which are well known and discussed in many texts can be summarised by the three differentials: differential preservation, differential productivity and differential transport/contributing area. Differential plant pollen productivity is not known to be different in alluvial as compared with non-alluvial sites. There is, however, evidence that pollen preservation varies with environment and that some alluvial environments may have biased spectra as a result. From the work of Sangster and Dale (1961) we know that some pollen types, such as poplar and bulrush, are more likely to be destroyed in ponds, which are rather similar to cutoffs, than in lakes or bogs. Many alluvial diagrams have parts of the spectra where concentrations are very low and the number of types is reduced to those known to be more resistant, such as ferns (*Filicales*), other spores and *Compositae liguliflorae* type (daisy family) (Lewis and Wiltshire, 1992). In addition, typically more degraded and damaged pollen is found in alluvial contexts owing to abrasion by inorganic particles and partial oxidation (see Table 4.2 for more details). Some floodplain environments are not permanently waterlogged and exposure to continued evaporation is one of the most important causes of pollen degradation (Holloway, 1981); so the interpretation of pollen from these sites must pay due attention to differential degradation as well as to the mechanisms of transport. Indeed, one of the most significant complicating factors in alluvial sites is the transport/contributing source area differential. Much work has been done on the

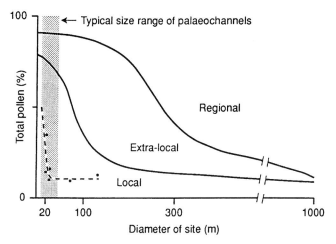

Fig. 4.16 The Jacobsen and Bradshaw model of pollen recruitment. Adapted from Jacobsen and Bradshaw (1980).

windblown component and Tauber's (1965) model is applicable to floodplain sites such as oxbow lakes. The atmospheric pollen input can be divided into the rain-out component (largely long-distance), canopy component, the trunk-space component and the local component from plants growing on the site. The relative proportions of these components will vary with oxbow size. Several other workers have looked at the decrease in windblown pollen away from a vegetation boundary (Salmi, 1962) and found an exponential rate where the b term was affected by the prevailing wind direction and pollen grain size. Dispersal equations similar to those used for smoke plumes have been used to model this process (Prentice, 1985). The most widely quoted model, produced by Jacobsen and Bradshaw (1981), would suggest that from an oxbow lake of about 30 m in diameter (ignoring any shape effects) approximately 8% of the pollen would be of regional origin, 13% extra-local and 79% local (Figure 4.16). Their model does not have any site input, but cutoffs will have an important site input as they easily become choked with vegetation as succession proceeds. Figure 4.17 takes the Tauber model and adapts it for a typical cutoff which also carries some inflow from a minor tributary. A lateral peat bed, which has accumulated as peat under a canopy of wet woodland, can be viewed as similar to a woodland soil with site size varying from zero (i.e. no canopy break) to the dimensions of a small forest hollow or clearing. In both cases, the main source areas are relatively small and this is why, in pre-deforestation floodplain sites, pollen diagrams generally reflect the local and extra-local zones. This is an advantage rather than a disadvantage if the floodplain vegetation is the focus of interest. However, in many investigations it is not and there are two approaches to 'seeing through the floodplain corridor vegetation to the surrounding landscape'. One approach is to assume, preferably on the basis of macrofossil analysis, that all the inputs of certain pollen types are exclusively

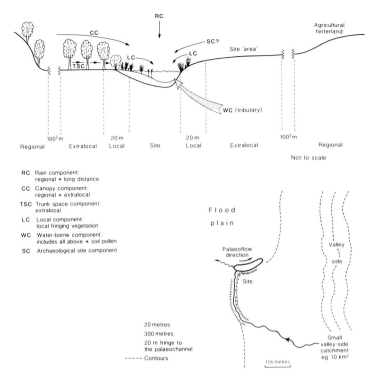

Fig. 4.17 A modified version of the Tauber (1965) model for a small oxbow lake with a small stream input.

floodplain in origin and remove them from the sum (Janssen, 1959). Apart from the vast number of grains which may have to be counted to obtain a reasonable pollen sum, there are two other problems with this approach. First, as succession occurs local vegetation will change and so therefore should the sum, making the resultant diagram very difficult to interpret. Secondly, the assumption that all the pollen of a species such as alder comes from the floodplain will effectively render it invisible in the rest of the landscape where it could be an important component. For these reasons, and to ease the comparison of diagrams, most workers have moved to a total land pollen sum which commonly only excludes aquatics, spores and sometimes Cyperaceae (sedges). The second approach is the comparison of floodplain and non-floodplain sites from the same region.

One reason why alluvial deposits were avoided in the past, even when they were adjacent to archaeological sites, was the fear that pollen would be selectively transported by water either into or out of the site. The ecological coherence of floodplain diagrams suggests this is not an insurmountable problem. This is supported by some laboratory experiments by Brush and Brush (1972) which suggest that differential settling out of flood waters is unlikely, owing to the constant turbulence (including thermally induced) and low specific gravity

Table 4.3 *The typical size, specific gravity and terminal velocity of selected pollen grains (data from Pohl, 1937, Dyakowska, 1937, Erdtman, 1969 and other sources).*

Pollen type	Typical size m	Specific gravity gr cm^{-3}	Terminal velocity m s^{-1}
Pinus sylvestris	80×40	0.39	2.5
Corylus avellana	43	1.00	2.5
Fagus sylvatica	41	0.71	5.5
Salix caprea	26×21	1.43	2.16
Ulmus glabra	29×36	1.42	3.24
Lycopodium spp.	35−50	1.17	1.76−2.14
Polytrichum spp.	10−15	1.53	0.23

(Table 4.3); either all types will be suspended or all will settle out, whereas a substantial component of differential settling may occur with wind. So, while flood waters often contain high concentrations of pollen (Brown, 1985b), flood deposits often contain very little. Indeed Brown (1985b) has recorded concentrations as high as 230 grains ml^{-1} during a flood on the Highland Water in the New Forest, England, whereas a silt flood layer sampled after the event, but before it had dried out, had a very low concentration of under 10 grains cm^{-3}. As has been shown by studies of the pollen budgets of small lakes, most of this waterborne pollen enters lakes and ponds (Peck, 1973; Crowder and Cuddy, 1973). It should also be noted from these studies that the waterborne pollen spectra probably reflect the vegetation of the basin more accurately than the windblown component.

Pollen diagrams from floodplains and lakes are one of the prime data sources for studying the processes of floodplain colonisation, competition, succession, natural disturbance and anthropogenic influence. Anthropogenic activity has received far more attention than the other factors mentioned, but Bennett (1983) has calculated the doubling times of the Early Holocene rise in tree taxa around Hockham Mere, in eastern England, from an influx diagram. We now know that vegetation response was significantly lagged behind climate change in the Early Holocene and the composition of the flora varied owing to the distance of refuges, differential migration rates, successional processes and local soil variations. This is indicated by significant differences between pollen diagrams from adjacent areas, such as the delayed appearance and rise of taxa, or even reversals in the order of dominance. Palaeovegetation maps have been produced in Europe (Huntley and Birks, 1983) and in the United States, using pollen analysis (Delcourt and Delcourt, 1981), and Bennett (1989) has attempted to map the forest types present in the United Kingdom at 5000 BP. At this scale, floodplains are invisible except for large low-lying areas such as

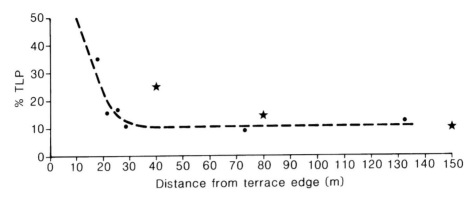

Fig. 4.18 The decline in lime pollen across a floodplain using data collected by Brown (solid dots) and Waller (stars). Reproduced from *New Phytologist*, Brown (1988), by permission of the New Phytologist Trust.

the East Anglian Fens or Somerset Levels. At the regional scale, the role of floodplains becomes more evident, especially for wetland taxa. In this context the debate as to the processes involved in the immigration, rise and eventual dominance of alder in southern Britain is particularly interesting and is discussed further in chapter 7.

Because very different soils can lie adjacent to each other on floodplains, it is possible to add a spatial aspect to the pollen diagram interpretation taking into account the ecophysiology of the taxa. For example, Brown (1988) has shown that the very high level of lime pollen found in some floodplain sites comes from lime forest on adjacent terraces. This is confirmed by a decline in the values of pollen away from the terrace edge (Figure 4.18). Other factors such as natural vegetation disturbance on floodplains due to windthrow and floods are difficult to isolate from anthropogenic activity. Janssen (1972) has compared pollen diagrams from a small floodplain surrounded by sandy acidic uplands, the Dommel valley, in north Brabant in the Netherlands, with extensive raised bogs 30–40 km to the east. This revealed that in the Sub-Boreal the uplands were covered by grassland, heath and oak–birch woods, whilst the valley was covered by alder and reed swamp. In order to evaluate the role of local effects, Janssen (1986) has proposed the use of contrast diagrams where the curves for selected taxa of different ecological affinities are superimposed for sites in the river valley and adjacent uplands.

Pollen analysis (and other techniques discussed in this chapter) can be used in one of two ways: first, in a forensic science manner to give a detailed description of the local impacts of human activity and, secondly, as part of a wider palaeoenvironmental reconstruction which sets human actions in an environmental context. Obviously, the two are closely related as detailed studies of single sites may be aggregated with non-site studies to give the regional picture. This chapter concentrates on the broader approach as the on-site analysis should ideally be part of standard archaeological practice and the techniques are essentially the same. It is important to have some idea of the archaeological questions being asked about the area. The sites and methods used in environmental reconstruction should depend upon these questions and the scale of archaeological investigation. If it is a broad regional scale then pollen analysis from large sites will be suitable; if, however, it is the sub-regional landscape archaeology that is of interest, then a range of smaller sites and different methods will be more appropriate. A network of smaller sites with overlapping age-ranges is necessary for the determination of past vegetation pattern at this scale. For this to be achieved, the independent dating of sites is essential. An alternative for smaller areas is three-dimensional pollen analysis if a suitable site exists (Smith and Cloutman, 1988). With this technique, spatial pattern is identified by the pollen trends revealed by the different directional axes. Traditionally, palaeoecologists have attempted to infer the spatial pattern by ecophysiological reasoning, in a similar manner to the identification of floodplain and non-floodplain components of a spectrum. This is often reinforced by a knowledge of the local flora from macrofossil analysis. This procedure is ultimately unsatisfactory, as it assumes that the soil and water characteristics (of the soils) on different lithologies were similar to those today. There is here an important role for palaeosol pollen analysis in the determination of local soil/vegetation conditions. In some locations, such as near the floodplain/ dryland boundary, the assumption of soil/vegetation differences is possible, but in others, such as around most dryland archaeological sites, it is far more problematic. Indeed, the traditional association of chalk with light woodland (easy to clear) and claylands with dense woodlands (difficult to clear) is highly questionable and should not be over-emphasised.

Temporal resolution is also a problem in the archaeological use of palaeoecology, as it depends upon the rate of organic sedimentation, and this is very variable in floodplains. Cutoffs, for example, often infill very rapidly and therefore, while offering good temporal resolution, often fail to demarcate the occupation phases of the adjacent site. The extremely high resolution of some bog and lake sites (Waton, 1982; Simola, 1977), which can be down to a few years or even months, is the exception rather than the rule, and more commonly, a series of snapshots will have to be pieced together. In the last twenty years, palaeoecological methods have become far more useful to archaeologists owing to: (a) quantitative reconstruction of past vegetation histories and environmental controls, (b) emphasis on small sites with source areas which relate to human site catchment areas, and (c) the realisation of the potential of non-traditional sites such as cutoffs, forest hollows and soils. Indeed, it must surely be time to move this material from the appendix to the body of the archaeological report.

There is, however, one serious problem that has arisen, which is a form of reinforcement syndrome. Because palaeoecologists often cannot, from their data, identify the cause of a change, such as a sudden fall in trees and rise in herbs and shrubs, they have used archaeological data to aid interpretation of the feature, as, for example, a clearing created by Neolithic people. Subsequently, archaeologists have used the work by the palaeoecologists uncritically and taken it to support a subsistence base founded upon forest clearance for agriculture. In other words, both disciplines shore each other up on the back of human vegetation disturbance. A classic, but more complicated example of this is the elm decline seen in most of the pollen diagrams from North-West Europe around 5300 bp, which was successively interpreted as a climatic event (Iversen, 1944b), as a selective defoliation for cattle fodder on the basis of an Eastern European ethnographic parallel (Troels-Smith, 1960), as just the most visible expression of widespread deforestation (Smith, 1981) and most recently, on independent palaeoecological grounds, as due to disease, probably facilitated by clearance (Girling and Greig, 1985; Girling, 1988). The only way to avoid this is to evaluate the different lines of evidence separately, to remember the inferential limits of the data and not to strive for a coherent and non-contradictory account at all costs. This is equally, if not more, applicable to the other microfossils described in this chapter.

In the course of identifying pollen and common spores, other far less well known microfossils are frequently encountered. These have been extensively studied by Van Geel (1986) and are mostly fungal spores. Despite the problems of identification some have been shown to have quite specific ecological affinities. Two that are common on floodplains include *Gaumanomyces* spores from a parasitic fungus which grows on Cyperaceae (sedges) and another is the ascospore *Mougeotia* which is only found in pools and puddles which dry out in summer. It is generally assumed that these non-pollen microfossils do not travel far and so may add extra information to the pollen analysis of local conditions.

Diatoms are unicellular algae which may be preserved in sediments because of a strong exoskeleton or frustule made of biogenic silica. They have a variety of life-forms and can be found in a variety of habitats including large rivers, cutoffs, marshes and soils. They are relatively easy to extract (Batterbee, 1986) and can be identified below species level. Work on their ecology by Hustedt and others has led to a series of environmental spectra into which species may be allocated. These include a salt-tolerance spectrum (the Halobian system), a nutrient status spectrum (several methods including the Araphidineae:Centrales ratio), a pH spectrum (Hustedt, 1937–9) and a thermal spectrum. These systems all have considerable problems in their accuracy and applicability, although salinity and pH are the most reliable (Batterbee, 1986). Diatoms have as yet been used relatively little in the reconstruction of floodplain environments, despite occurring in high concentration in some backswamp deposits (especially epipelic and epiphytic species). Occasionally, bands of pure white diatomite can be found in these

Table 4.4 *The ecological groups of freshwater snails (after Sparks, 1961).*

Group	Preferred habitat	Representative species
slum	poor water quality, small water bodies subject to drying out, stagnation and temperature variation	*Lymnaea truncatula* *Planorbis leucostoma*
catholic	wide range of habitats except worst slums	*Lymnea palustris* *Planorbis cristata*
ditch	clean slow-moving water (e.g. ditches) with abundant growth of aquatic plants	*Vavata cristata* *Planorbis planorbis*
moving water	streams and larger ponds with some flow or currents	*Valvata piscinalis* *Bithynia* spp.

sediments (Brown, 1983a). One reason for their neglect is that less is known about the environmental controls of attached species in comparison to planktonic species, although work has been done in rivers in the United Kingdom (Swale, 1969), the United States (Patrick and Reimer, 1966) and elsewhere (Foged, 1947–8). They may also be derived from a variety of environments upstream. However, Brown and Barber (1985) have shown how they can indicate a change in floodplain hydrological conditions, even prior to this being reflected in the sedimentary record. Diatom analysis has been applied to samples from the medieval town of Svendborg in Denmark (Foged, 1978), illustrating the poor water quality of many of the town ditches, dykes and moats, and the proximity of saline water from the coast. Similar work has been undertaken on other waterfront sites, and in London diatom work has been undertaken in order to test the hypothesis that the Roman Thames might have been freshwater whereas the present river is tidal (supposedly owing to tectonic subsidence). The diatom evidence from Roman waterfronts in the City of London clearly shows that the river was as tidal then as it is now (Batterbee, 1988).

Animal remains: snails and insects
Freshwater, and to a lesser extent, dryland mollusca are extremely common in alluvial deposits, especially the basal units of palaeochannel infills. They can even make up a significant proportion of the sediment. They are relatively easily extracted, although with clay-rich sediments disaggregation may be difficult without crushing the shells. In the United Kingdom, there are only some fifty native species and so identification to species level is not tremendously difficult. They have been extensively used in both interglacial and glacial contexts as palaeoclimatic indicators. In the late Holocene, the climatic linkage is largely replaced by a habitat linkage associated with human activity. The percentage of species from dry ground can be highly significant, indicating direct soil input from valley sides (Shotton, 1978), and the freshwater species may be allocated to one of four environmental groups following Sparks (1961; see Table 4.4).

Work by Evans *et al.* (1992) has shown that variations in wet-ground taxa can reflect changes in floodplain vegetation, although there are several problems caused by taphonomic mixing, behavioural mixing and the lack of modern comparative data. Evans *et al.* (1992) recommend the use of autochthonous deposits, such as fine-grained overbank deposits which lack river species or fine-grained river deposits which lack land species, in order to define past 'taxocenes'. Mollusca can also give sedimentological information, as death assemblages of freshwater mollusca can indicate dead channel areas or even extensive flood events. Brown (1983b) reported that after a flood of the river Stour in Dorset, UK, the floodplain was covered with mollusca and sediment flushed from the channel bed. The most common mollusca were the swan mussel (*Anodonta cygnea*) and duck mussel (*Anodonta anatina*); these species can also occasionally be found in life-positions in lower point-bar sediments.

In general, insects have several advantages for palaeoenvironmental work. These include: the vast number of species that exist, their penetration into almost all ecological niches, their strong relationships to environmental conditions and their high mobility. Of all the insects, beetles (Coleoptera) are particularly useful, because their strong exoskeletons are preserved in a wide variety of sedimentary environments and because there is a long record of taxonomic work. Samples can be collected from exposures, disaggregated, sieved and Coleoptera separated from other organic remains by paraffin flotation. While some species clearly indicate changes in climate (Coope, 1986; Atkinson *et al.*, 1986), others can indicate the presence of grazing animals (e.g. dung beetles), the presence of different types of water-bodies, from still to fast-flowing, and human activity including crops and buildings. In a study of the contemporary floodplain of the river Soar in England three different habitats were differentiated: riparian damp grassland, fen (including cutoffs) and fen/carr (willow with seasonally standing water) (Greenwood, pers. comm.). It was also noted in this and another study (Shotton and Osborne, 1986) that flood refuse typically contained species derived from all alluvial environments, but not species adapted to fast flow, who successfully held on! The ability of Coleoptera to indicate specific past conditions has been used by Osborne (1974; 1988) to show that during the Bronze Age the river Avon in Worcestershire had a clean stony bed without the covering of mud and silt that is seen today. This is inferred from the large numbers of beetles from the family Elmidae in the sample. The beetles also showed that the floodplain was already cleared of trees by this time and covered with open grassland maintained by large grazing animals, presumably domestic cattle. There seems little doubt that the full potential of Coleoptera for palaeoenvironmental analysis of floodplains has yet to be realised.

The insect remains most commonly recovered from alluvial contexts, other than Coleoptera, are water fleas or Cladocera (Frey, 1986) and to a lesser extent water midges or chironomids (Hoffmann, 1986). Cladocera are relatively easily extracted by methods similar to those used for pollen analysis, but without the use of acetylation which can damage the chitin exuvia (Frey, 1986). Over ninety species occur in European inland waters (Amoros and Van Urk, 1989), but the most useful for palaeoenvironmental inference are found in still waters, including oxbow lakes, pools, marshes and backwaters. Cladoceran analysis of a core from a cutoff on the Upper Rhone in France has provided evidence of succession caused by the embankment of the river in the 1880s (Roux *et al.*, 1989).

Chironomids, or in practice the head capsules, can be preserved in large numbers and have been shown to be good indicators of past ecological conditions (Amoros and Van Urk, 1989). These distinctive head capsules allow identification although not always to species level: details of the methods of sampling and analysis can be found in Walker and Paterson (1985) and Hoffmann (1986). Several workers have identified characteristic habitats which include: mobile sand, snag habitats produced by branches and trees in the river, the hyporheic zone (interstitial water-flow through gravels) and eroding clay banks (Barton and Smith, 1984). Klink (1989) has shown that chironomids characteristic of shifting sand habitats were common in the Lower Rhine prior to the eighteenth century and their decline is probably due to channel constriction and deforestation of the floodplain. This study seems to show that past river entomology can be reconstructed accurately from vertically accreted alluvial sediments, allowing the possibility of extending the use of biological pollution indicators back into the past.

There are many other fossils that can occur in floodplain sediments and which can yield significant palaeoenvironmental information. These include mammals (especially small mammals), fish remains (Casteel, 1976) and rhizopods (Tolonen, 1986). However, most are rare, although some are more common on archaeological sites themselves. A possible exception to this are ostracods which are small arthropods (0.15–15 mm long), with a carapace composed of two chitinous or calcareous valves. They occupy nearly all marine and freshwater environments, and much is known about their rather restricted ecological preferences. Details of extraction and identification can be found in Brasier (1980). Although they have generally been used in the study of ocean cores and coastal environmental sequences as they are excellent indicators of salinity, they have also been used in lacustrine (Frey, 1964) and alluvial environments where leaching has not occurred. In a study of alluvial peats from the rivers Avon (Worcestershire) and Thames, Siddiqui (1971) identified nineteen species. All the species are still living in North-West Europe and their ecology suggested that the Avon peat was deposited in a pool of standing water whilst the Thames peat accumulated in a channel or pool with slow-flowing water and abundant macrophyte growth.

4.8 Dendroclimatology
As mentioned earlier in this chapter, the width of annual tree rings is related to the climatic conditions during the growing season. It is therefore possible to

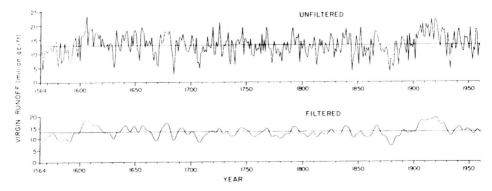

Fig. 4.19 Dendrohydrological reconstruction of streamflow from northern Arizona back to 1580. From Smith and Stockton (1981) by permission of *Water Resources Bulletin*.

reconstruct past climate from tree-ring width given certain constraints. This technique is called dendroclimatology, or dendrohydrology if it is stream flow that is estimated (Bradley, 1985). These constraints include, the removal of age-related systematic ring width variation, species sensitivity and the stability of the contemporary ring width–climate relationship. The particularly useful aspect of this technique is that the chronology can also be given by the rings; indeed it was the matching of tree rings for dendrochronology that led to the realisation that the data could provide a climatic record. Briffa *et al.* (1983) have used tree-ring widths from thirteen sites in the UK to construct a regression model predicting temperature and rainfall. When tested against independent data the correlation coefficients are highly statistically significant and stability of the relationship is high over the period 1830 to 1970. Jones *et al.* (1984) have used ring width of oak trees to reconstruct riverflow from three catchments in southern England from 1850 to the present. Interestingly the reconstructions seem to be more reliable for low flow, and this could be very useful as our ability to quantify past droughts is generally inferior to our ability to quantify past floods. There is little doubt that this technique may eventually be able to provide an accurate climatic record for the majority of the Holocene. The technique has been used in Arizona to reconstruct stream flow back to 1580 (Smith and Stockton, 1981; see Figure 4.19). Again the potential is there to use ponderosa pine or other sensitive, long-lived species to extend the record back to the Early Holocene. One importance of this work is that it has shown that the period of our instrumentation, upon which we have based our long-term 'norms', has not been typical of even the last 500 years, let alone the last millennium or longer. This has direct implications in the design of dams, spill ways, flood schemes etc., as discussed further in chapter 10 in conjunction with the non-biological methods described in the previous chapter.

PART II

APPLICATION

5

ARTIFACTS FROM FLOODPLAINS AND RIVERS

This chapter is concerned with the palaeoenvironmental and archaeological record that has been derived from terrace gravels and associated sediments. In these contexts archaeological sites are generally either accumulations of derived artifacts or concentrations of discarded tools associated with temporary camps. The cultures responsible are predominantly non-agricultural and although they undoubtedly had impacts on the environment, floodplains were essentially natural. The combination of geology, geomorphology and archaeology needed to study these sites is typical of the sub-discipline of geoarchaeology and alluvial geoarchaeological studies from both North America and Australia are described here as the clearest examples of this type of archaeology. The multi-disciplinary approach is exemplified by the Thames, England; however, the palaeoenvironmental data have been accumulated over many years, leading, unsurprisingly, to variations in coverage and quality which make unrealistic a definitive Pleistocene and archaeological history of this and other rivers. Instead, the discovery and excavation of new sites will lead to the revision (or abandonment) of current models (Gibbard, 1994; Bridgland, 1994) just as they revised models before them (King and Oakley, 1936).

5.1 Palaeolithic terrace sites and floodplain use

Artifacts and bones from river gravels form some of the earliest evidence of the peopling of North America and Australasia. The archaeology of the Palaeolithic in Europe is also predominantly derived from terrace gravels, caves and rock fissures. As Wymer (1976) has pointed out, 'artifacts in river gravels constitute 95% of the evidence for Lower Palaeolithic human activity in Britain and over most of the Northern hemisphere'. As discussed in chapter 1, this presents particular problems as can be encapsulated by three questions posed by Wymer (1976): (a) is the archaeological evidence in a primary context, (b) is it derived from a primary source, or (c) is it derived from a secondary source? To these can be added a fourth question: (d) do the different elements of the assemblage, even if they are derived, have a functional link or is it a fortuitous combination? Depending upon the answers to these questions the archaeological implications are radically different. This is especially important if the whole river valley or basin has no primary context sites, as is probably the case with the Upper Thames (Briggs *et al.*, 1985). These problems have led Wymer (1976) to caution that, 'unless there is evidence to the contrary, such artifacts should be regarded as derived'. The site, as such, therefore, rarely has functional meaning; however, using environmental techniques we can build up an environmental framework within which Palaeolithic women and men lived, and in this sense the environmental evidence is a major component of the archaeology.

The stratigraphic and spatial distribution of artifact recovery is undoubtedly a function of gravel exploration and archaeological activity as well as the patchy nature of artifact density. Any attempt to assign palaeoenvironmental significance to find distribution must allow for this bias in the record. Therefore, while many authors have stated that major river valleys, terraces, levées, and wide tributary junctions, were highly attractive locations for Palaeolithic activity this is fundamentally an inductive belief and, though reasonable enough, difficult to quantify because of the nature of the record we have. One way forward is through the modelling of distribution data using weightings based on some measure of the intensity of gravel exploitation and archaeological activity in an area.

5.2 Geoarchaeological studies of terrace gravels in southern England

Despite its modest size the Thames is probably the most intensively studied valley in the world and, because it was largely beyond the glacial limit, provides a long Pleistocene sequence that can be correlated with the ocean record (Bridgland, 1994). Geoarchaeological studies of the pre-Holocene Thames valley fluvial deposits have contributed to our knowledge of Palaeolithic archaeology in two ways. One is through a better understanding of the relationship between the causes and processes of terrace aggradation, incision and the archaeological record; the second is through the changing geography of Palaeolithic landscapes. Based upon new sites and the reinterpretation of old studies, Green and McGregor (1980) proposed a schema of terrace development in the Thames which is not dissimilar to that proposed by Wymer (1968). The schema (Figure 5.1) commences with an interglacial floodplain composed of channel-deposits, overbank silts and organic sediments. They suggest that under conditions which promote neither net aggradation nor net erosion, the floodplain depth would be equal to the difference between maximum channel scour and the levée top, which in the case of the Thames would be about 4–6 m. This bears many similarities to models proposed for floodplain evolution during the first 4000 years of the present interglacial (Brown *et al.*, 1994). Also, as McGregor and Green (1983) have shown, terraces on chalk, as most of the Thames terraces are, will suffer severe structural rearrangement by subsidence, caused by solution, during temperate periods. The change from interglacial to periglacial conditions causes a metamorphosis into a braided system, resulting in erosion of the pre-existing interglacial alluvium and floodplain widening by lateral erosion, which in places creates a rock bench. In this schema full glaciation brings falling base-levels, causing downcutting which produces terraces. It

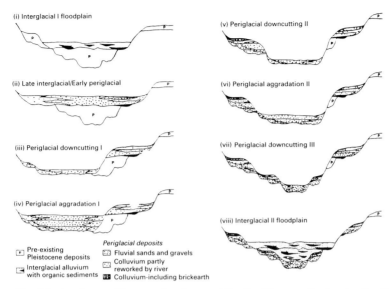

(i) Interglacial I floodplain

(ii) Late interglacial/Early periglacial

(iii) Periglacial downcutting I

(iv) Periglacial aggradation I

(v) Periglacial downcutting II

(vi) Periglacial aggradation II

(vii) Periglacial downcutting III

(viii) Interglacial II floodplain

Pre-existing Pleistocene deposits

Interglacial alluvium with organic sediments

Periglacial deposits

Fluvial sands and gravels

Colluvium partly reworked by river

Colluvium-including brickearth

Fig. 5.1 A schema of terrace development for the Thames, England, after Green and McGregor (1980).

is, however, more plausible to assign a direct climatic cause: seasonally high flows and erosion caused by snow and the melting of ground ice. In simple terms terraces are generally deposited at the beginning and end of cold periods when sediment supply exceeds discharge, and downcutting occurs when discharge exceeds sediment supply. Downcutting or rejuvenation as it is also termed is limited by base-levels set in most basins by sea level. The width of the valley and number of benches reflect the rate and continuity of downcutting. In this model interglacials (temperate stages) are characterised by less powerful rivers which oscillate between net erosion and net deposition reworking small areas of the floodplain, producing, as they do so, channel fills and limited overbank sediments. This model implies the complexity of terrace deposition, the importance of thresholds and the multiplicity of conditions under which both aggradation and incision may occur. Another implication is that the form of terraces may be relatively simple but the depositional chronology may not be; for example, older terraces may occur both above and below younger terraces in a staircase and it is even more common for a terrace to comprise two units of different ages. The work on the Thames highlights two general and closely related problems: one is that we have little idea of the relationship between the length and severity of a climatic episode and the degradational or aggradational response. Secondly, we rarely have much information on the rates of gravel deposition. However, based upon contemporary geomorphological studies and reinterpretations of some terrace units, it seems likely that we have generally underestimated the episodic or pulse-like nature of valley alluviation during the Pleistocene. This is relevant to the interpretation of Palaeolithic artifacts, i.e. long periods of relative fluvial inactivity when flints would be manufactured and scattered, and shorter periods of intense activity reworking and concentrating them in gravel units.

The studies of the Thames have also shown how different the geography of a region is from one interglacial to another (Gibbard, 1994; Bridgland, 1994). If we suppose that floodplain locations, especially tributary junctions, were favoured by human groups, then the archaeological record will follow the changing pattern of river systems. The identification of this from the archaeological record is dependent upon the adequate dating of artifacts from non-derived contexts.

When we look at Palaeolithic sites on a regional scale, such as in the Thames basin, several general problems become apparent. The first is correlation and chronology. By their very nature, terrace fragments may not be unequivocally traceable down a river system. Ideally a combination of surveying, stratigraphic description and lithological analysis is required in order to correlate fragments with key sites where more than one formation is present. None of these methods alone can be relied upon; for example, the same lithological content does not necessarily imply time equivalence, especially where rivers are reworking previous gravel terraces. The use of chronometric dating methods, especially luminescence and amino acid, is invaluable in supplementing biostratigraphic and lithostratigraphic methods of correlating floating chronologies to the oxygen isotope chronology (Bridgland, 1994). The Thames shows how the future understanding of industries, in both temporal and regional terms, is fundamentally dependent upon the unravelling of the Pleistocene chronostratigraphy of terrace deposits in North-West Europe. Refinement of the chronology may lead to further questioning of the true significance of tool typology, especially in the Lower and Middle Palaeolithic, and the relationship of typologies to cultural change. A second and not unrelated problem is that of the reworking of artifacts. The vast majority of the sites to be mentioned in this chapter contain older reworked artifacts. This is because the major source of gravel within the Thames basin is the terrace deposits and it is from cold/cool-stage gravel accumulations that the majority of artifacts have been recorded. Those from interglacial channel-fills and overbank sediments are less likely to be derived and may provide a less contaminated data set for the investigation of typological change.

The four succeeding sections discuss in a little more detail the geo-archaeological record of the pre-Holocene Thames in order to illustrate the methods and concepts employed in this type of geoarchaeology and give a catchment framework to the history of occupation and environmental change. Discussion of Palaeolithic sites in Britain will here be confined to this one area as it has a large number of fluvial sites, whilst the majority of important Palaeolithic sites elsewhere in the British Isles are from caves and rock shelters

(Gamble, 1986). More specifically the Thames basin has been chosen for two reasons; first, work on the terrace gravels has been continuous since the nineteenth century and more sites are known from this catchment than any other. Secondly, because the valley lies, at least partially, outside the maximum extent of ice during the Pleistocene, it therefore represents a more complete record of fluvial deposition and, although it has changed its lower course during the Pleistocene, the changes in the valley and catchment boundary have been less than those for the other major British rivers such as the Severn and Trent (Bridgland, 1994). Indeed, throughout the Middle and Late Pleistocene there has always been a Thames in *approximately* the same area and flowing in approximately the same direction as it does today. Whilst it is unlikely that there will ever be a totally satisfactory chronology for the whole of the basin, a concentration of work in the area has provided an improved framework which can be related to evidence of human occupation and the global record of climate change.

From an archaeological to a geological chronology

Until the 1950s the archaeology dated the geology, but it is now increasingly the other way around. From the nineteenth century onwards the traditional chronology of Northern European Pleistocene terraces was based on a combination of hand-axe typology, stratigraphy and counting climatic episodes back in time or from the top of the sequence down. This methodology was based on the belief that axe typology followed a clear progression from what we perceive as crude or simple, to elegant or complex, and that this happened at roughly the same rate in different places. This was allied to the belief that a typology was representative of a 'culture'.

This chronology and methodology has been questioned for a variety of reasons (Green and McGregor, 1980). First, the traditional chronology was at odds with revised Pleistocene chronologies from ocean cores and from new terrestrial sites in North-West Europe which showed an extremely complex picture of glacial, interglacial, stadial and interstadial stages. The ocean cores, for example, show at least thirty warm/cold cycles and the terrestrial record has improved through the discovery of more sites and also through new chronometric dating techniques (Lowe and Walker, 1984: Jones and Keen, 1993). However, the terrestrial record in Britain still shows major discontinuities in comparison with the ocean record and the much more detailed chronologies from the Netherlands and Germany. A chronology is given in Table 5.1, but it must be noted that there is considerable debate and uncertainty about not only the position of major British stratigraphic units, but also the number of pre-Pastonian and post-Hoxnian–pre-Ipswichian climatic cycles present in the British record (Jones and Keen, 1993).

The undoubted improvement in our chronological knowledge of the Pleistocene deposits in North-West Europe has allowed some re-evaluation of

Table 5.1 *A simplified Pleistocene chronology for southern England with climate and, where possible, estimates of sea level. Note that there is still considerable uncertainty, especially in the Lower Pleistocene (before the Pre-Pastonian) and between the Hoxnian and Ipswichian stages. Correlations with the European and North American sequences are also especially problematic for these stages and so only the later stages are included. (From Bowen, 1978, Jones and Keen 1993, and Wymer 1985.)*

Stage (UK/Europe/USA)	Climate (central-southern England)	Oxygen isotope stage	Sea level
Flandrian/Holocene	temperate	1	high 0 m
Devensian/Weichselian/ Wisconsinian	cold, glacial, with evidence of at least 3 interstadials: *c.* 11,500 bp, 43,000 bp and 85,000 bp	2–4/5a–d	low, −60 m
Ipswichian/Eemian/ Sangamon	temperate	5e	high 6–8 m
Wolstonian 3/ Late Saalian/ Illinoian	cold, periglacial–glacial	6	low
Ifordian	temperate	7	high 15 m
Wolstonian 2/ Mid Saalian	cold, periglacial	8	low
Wolstonian 1/2	temperate–cool	9	—
Wolstonian 1/ Early Saalian	cold, not periglacial	10	—
Hoxnian/Holsteinian	temperate	11	high 20 m
Anglian	cold, glacial (maximum extent)	12	low
Cromerian	temperate	13	high
Beestonian	cold, periglacial–glacial		low
Pastonian	temperate		high
Pre-Pastonian	cold non-glacial, park–tundra		low
Bramertonian	temperate		high
Baventian	cold, periglacial–glacial		low
Antian	temperate		high
Thurnian	cold non-glacial		low
Ludhamian/Eburonian	temperate		high
Pre-Ludhamian	cool–temperate		—

the lithic record. This has increased our knowledge in three areas: (a) The relative time-span of industries, including overlap; (b) the identification of regional differences in industries; (c) the association of industries with climatic change, known from independent sources. Of course there may be no such thing as an industry in the chronological sense but instead types of tools manufactured at the same or different times in different places. In their study of the Upper Thames, Briggs *et al.* (1985) suggest there is no obvious typological sequence correlated with the depositional sequence: 'implements of relatively refined technology occur in some of the older deposits (e.g. the Wolvercote

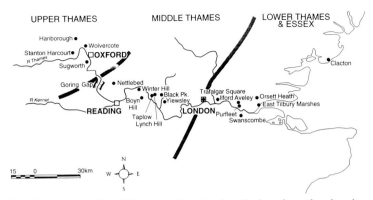

Fig. 5.2 A map of the Thames valley showing the location of major sites mentioned in the text. Adapted from Bridgland (1994).

Channel) while less refined artifacts can be found in some of the younger terrace gravels'. While this may be partially due to reworking, it may also reflect a lack of typological progression in the traditional sense: the balance between the two is difficult to resolve without artifacts in securely dated contexts and primary position.

For the purposes of this chapter, the Upper Thames is defined as upstream of the Goring Gap, near Wallingford (Figure 5.2), and the Lower Thames as downstream of the City of London, with the Middle Thames in between. Whilst the river catchment has changed during the Pleistocene its relative relief has remained at about 325 m and it is therefore a low-relief, low-slope catchment. The river valley is flanked on the west by the Jurassic Oolite of the Cotswold hills, on the north by the chalk of the Chiltern hills and on the south by the chalk of the North Downs. Underlying much of the valley are impermeable marine deposits including the Jurassic Oxford and Tertiary London Clays. The Thames, which flows along the approximate mid-line of a syncline (i.e. it is a strike river), has migrated in a southerly direction owing to the influence of ice and concurrent with the geology (synclinal shifting *sensu* Bridgland, 1985). This has led to the preservation of the most complete terrace sequence on the northerly dip-slope (Bridgland, 1994). The subsidence of the North Sea basin may have had a minor effect during periods of high sea level but does not seem to have been a major control (Bridgland, 1994). Within this physiographic framework the river network has contracted, expanded and shifted during the last two million years.

Studies in the Upper Thames valley
Throughout the valley the majority of artifacts, including hand-axes, were discovered in the nineteenth century as a result of hand digging and grading of gravels. Although attempts to develop a regional chronostratigraphy for the Thames date from this period, the major seminal works were written during the

Table 5.2 *The Thames terrace and channel members from various sources including Briggs (1985), Bridgland (1994), and Gibbard (1985) as modified by Bridgland (1994). There is considerable controversy over the status of the two stages between the traditional Wolstonian (E. Wolstonian/E. Saalian here) and the Ipswichian (5e), and previous Upper Thames schemes put the Hanborough Terrace gravel as Early Wolstonian and the Sugworth channel as Hoxnian rather than Cromerian. Bridgland (1994) places major rejuvenation events (downcutting) in the L. Devensian (probably stage 4), stage 6, stage 8, stage 10 and stage 12.*

Stage	Upper Thames	Middle Thames	Lower Thames	^{18}O
Flandrian	*alluvium*	*Staines alluvium*	*Tilbury alluvium*	1
L. Devensian	Northmoor/Floodplain gravels	Shepperton gravel Langley silt complex	Shepperton gravel/ submerged	2–4
M Devensian interstadials		Kempton Park deposits	submerged	5a/5c
E. Devensian	Summertown-Radley upper gravel		East Tilbury Marshes gravel	5d–2
Ipswichian	Eynsham gravel	Reading Town gravel Trafalgar Square deposits Crayford silts and sands	submerged	5e
Unnamed (cold)/ L. Wolstonian/L. Saalian	Stanton Harcourt gravels	Taplow gravel	East Tilbury Marshes gravel	6
Marsworth/Intra Saalian temperate episodes	Stanton Harcourt channel	Redlands Pit, Reading	Aveley/Ilford/W. Thurrock	7
M. Wolstonian/ M. Saalian	Wolvercote terrace gravel chalky boulder clay	Lynch Hill gravel	Sandy Lane sand Basal Mucking gravel Corbets Tey gravel	8
E. Wolstonian/ intra Saalian temperate episode	Wolvercote channel deposits	Basal Lynch Hill gravel?	Ilford, Purfleet	9
E. Wolstonian/E. Saalian	Hanborough gravel	Boyn Hill gravel	Basal Orsett Heath gravel	10
Hoxnian	reworked mammalian fauna		Swanscombe deposits Dartford Heath gravels	11
Anglian	Basal Hanborough terrace gravel Freeland formation Moreton Drift?	Basal Boyn Hill gravel Winter Hill/Westmill gravel	Basal gravel at Swanscombe	12
Cromerian	Sugworth channel deposits	Pre-diversion members	No Thames valley	13
E. Pleistocene	Combe formation	Pre-diversion gravels		13

Notes:
Italics=Temperate (interglacial or interstadial) stages

first half of this century. Since the 1970s, there has been the discovery and excavation of new sites, and along with this a re-examination of the traditional chronology using new dating techniques.

In the Upper Thames the seminal work on the terraces was by Sandford (1924) who established a sequence with five members. This has been reinterpreted and added to by Briggs *et al.* (1985) and Bridgland (1994). As can be seen from Table 5.2, terrace and channel members have been named dating from as early as the Cromerian interglacial complex, taken to be equivalent to oxygen isotope stages 13–21. Any attempt to date and correlate the terraces of the Thames is problematic partly because, although limited help is given by the periodic injection of outwash from the Chalky Boulder Clay of the Midlands, the Midland chronology is just as problematic as that of the Thames. Irrespective of the detailed correlation of the deposits, Briggs *et al.* (1985) point out that three main geomorphological situations have existed. These are: (a) river terrace gravels which have mostly aggraded in cold-stage braided river environments; (b) channel-fill deposits generally associated with warm-stage meandering rivers; and (c) phases of downcutting which have left the terraces exposed as a staircase. Lower Palaeolithic artifacts, common in the Thames gravels, are of two types or 'industries' – hand-axes, collectively called Acheulian, and cores and flakes assigned to a 'Clactonian' type industry. Both hand-axes and flake/core industries show more advanced features higher in the sequence, using more sophisticated knapping known as the Levallois technique (Bridgland, 1994). Figure 5.3 gives a summary of the relationships between Palaeolithic artifacts and the terrace and channel infill deposits, and as Briggs *et al.* (1985) point out, most artifacts are found concentrated towards the base of the depositional units and no obvious typological sequence correlates with the sequence. Both these factors are undoubtedly related to the mode of transport (bed load) and deposition (as lag deposits) of the artifacts and reworking of the older gravel units. One of the earliest artifacts recovered from the terraces is an Acheulian hand-axe from near the base of the Hanborough terrace. Although not securely dated, this terrace is probably Anglian in age, although this is dependent upon the date of the Wolvercote channel infill (Table 5.2). It is also likely that the hand-axe was reworked along with faunal remains from deposits belonging to the previous interglacial. The Wolvercote channel itself contains some of the best evidence of human occupation with eighty-three hand-axes and about a hundred flakes of Late Acheulian type. The most likely source for the raw flint, which was worked at the Wolvercote site, is the Chiltern foothills about 20 km to the south-east (Roe, 1976). Unfortunately the original site is inaccessible and more recent exposures near-by have not contained artifacts.

The artifacts from the Stanton Harcourt gravels, generally, display Middle Acheulian affinities but are undoubtedly a mixed assemblage containing older reworked artifacts, many recorded from lag deposits. The Eynsham gravels

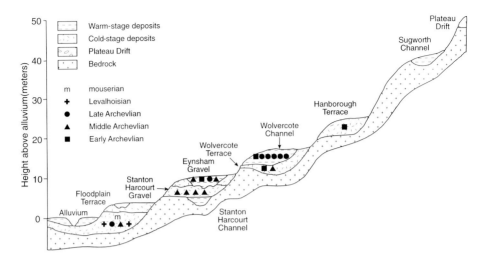

Fig. 5.3 A diagrammatic summary of the artifact-bearing units in the Upper Thames. From Briggs *et al.* (1985), by permission of the authors.

have also yielded a mixed collection of Middle and Late Acheulian tools from a number of sites. The lack of refinement of these tools is regarded by Briggs *et al.* (1985) as probably due to a lack of available stone, although this implies some factor preventing the importation of better-quality stone from further afield; something which had occurred in the Lower Pleistocene. The floodplain terrace, which is relatively securely dated to the late part of the Middle Devensian Interstadial, contains both Acheulian (Middle and Late) and Levalloisian artifacts and it seems likely that, while the Acheulian are reworked, the Levalloisian artifacts may reflect a contemporary industry in the area. The problems faced by any interpretation of the Palaeolithic in the Upper Thames all ultimately derive from a lack of primary sites. This is exacerbated by many of the classic finds not being accompanied by detailed stratigraphic sections which can help define the sedimentary context.

Studies in the Middle Thames valley
The Middle Thames has been studied for longer and more intensively than the Upper Thames: the classic studies are by Whitaker (1889), Hare (1947), Sealy and Sealy (1964), Wooldridge (1938) and Gibbard (1985). Indeed, it has provided a focus for classic works on Palaeolithic archaeology and river deposits, for example by Zeuner (1945), Wooldridge (1957), and Wymer (1968). A summary of early work is given by Gibbard (1985) and it is his summary of the chronostratigraphic evidence that will be used here as a framework for the discussion of individual sites. It is the Middle and Lower Thames that has

changed its course most during the Pleistocene. Prior to the Anglian, the Thames flowed to the north-east through the vale of St Albans to either the Wash or the Essex coast near Colchester. A major diversion occurred when a first Anglian ice advance diverted the Thames south down the valley of the river Lea and then east to the southern Essex coast. A second Anglian ice advance may have pushed the Thames further south to a line approximately along the present valley axis (Figure 5.4; Baker and Jones, 1980; Bridgland, 1988). Previous interpretations assigned these diversions to separate glaciations, for example the double-drainage hypothesis proposed by Wooldridge (1938).

There are two units in the Middle Thames regarded as pre-Anglian (probably Cromerian complex). These are the Nettlebed gravels and the Nettlebed interglacial deposits which are pre-diversion gravels (Table 5.2). After these deposits, but before the Anglian, four cycles of downcutting and deposition have been recorded. The high content of quartz pebbles in these deposits indicates some drainage input from the Midlands to the north. The Winter Hill gravel is regarded as being Early Anglian, although largely on the basis of its erratic content. This gravel marks the termination of the Midlands input. The proximity of ice during the Anglian is also responsible for the creation of several small proglacial lakes; it also, as previously mentioned, shifted the Thames to a new more southerly course through a spillway system, as is recorded by the distribution of the Black Park gravel. There is relatively little deposition of Hoxnian interglacial sediment recorded from the Middle Thames, but, as will be discussed later, there is important evidence of both human activity and environmental conditions from the Clacton channel deposits in Essex and the Upper Barnfield Pit units at Swanscombe on the Lower Thames estuary. There are, however, the Slade Oak Lane deposits (an infilled doline, Gibbard, Bryant and Hall, 1986) and the fossiliferous Hatfield organic deposits in the vale of St Albans which are Hoxnian stages I–IIb (Gibbard and Cheshire, 1983). The next aggradational unit after the Hoxnian in the Middle Thames is the Boyn Hill gravel which follows closely the modern trend of the Thames, through Reading. It accumulated under periglacial conditions and is artifact poor. The succeeding Lynch Hill gravel contains abundant Acheulian artifacts but it has been regarded as, at least in part, a derived assemblage, possibly from some unknown intervening interglacial, indicating erosion of Clactonian and Acheulian material from Swanscombe age deposits.

The best evidence of Palaeolithic occupation in the Middle Thames comes from sites at Yiewsley which consist of gravel pits in the Lynch Hill terrace. Artifacts have been recovered from the area since 1885 and it was partially re-excavated and examined in the 1960s and environmental studies conducted. The Yiewsley site includes both the Stoke Park and Lynch Hill terraces. The Stoke Park terrace is underlain by what is locally known as the Gouldsgreen

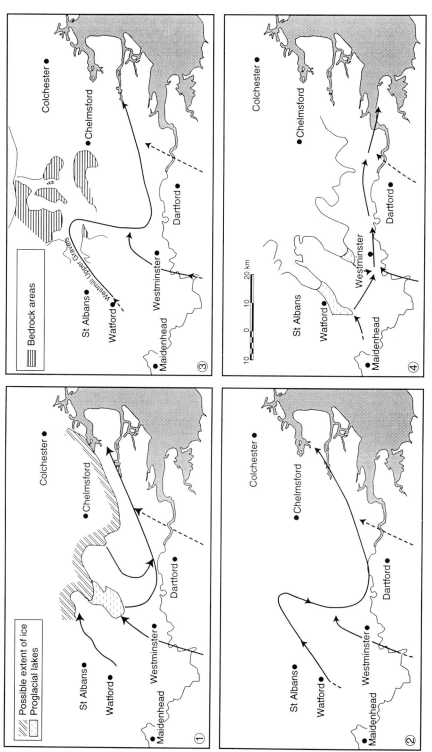

Fig. 5.4 The diverted Anglian course of the Middle Thames. Adapted from Baker and Jones (1980).

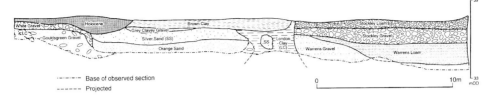

Fig. 5.5 Detail of part of the east face of Warrens Lake Pit, Yiewsley, Thames valley, illustrating a locally complex stratigraphy. Note the ridge of London clay dividing the sequence, the transported, or possibly rafted, London clay in the Gouldsgreen gravel and the silver sand incorporated into the London clay. The most probable cause of this is intense periglacial activity. Adapted from Collins (1978).

gravel and loam, whereas the lower Lynch Hill terrace is underlain by the Warrens gravel and loam, and the Stockley gravel and loam (Figure 5.5). Unfortunately, the exact location of all the early artifact finds is unknown, but the majority came from pits in the Warren and lower Lynch Hill units. From one pit, the Eastwood pit, over 1300 artifacts were recovered. The soliflucted gravel seems to have been the main Levallois level, while the Warren gravel is the main Acheulian level, and the Gouldsgreen gravel is the major Clactonian level. Owing to the site's richness, Collins (1978) suggests it represents prolonged occupation, although not necessarily continuously. Pollen analysis of the four major stratigraphic units shows that the Gouldsgreen gravel was cold/cool temperate with pine, birch and oak being the most common taxa. The Warrens loam, overlying the Warrens gravel, also contained a cool temperate flora which was increasingly warm towards the top and the base of the Stockley gravels. Unfortunately, the preservation of the pollen is poor and concentrations low. The spectra are also not very diagnostic apart from indicating that the sediments are Middle to Late Pleistocene in age. They are also open to two interpretations, an open riverine facies of an interglacial or a fragmented record from a temperate period, or periods, within a glacial episode. Two gravel units succeed the artifact-rich lower Lynch Hill gravels; the upper Lynch Hill gravels and the Taplow gravels. They were regarded as late Wolstonian by Gibbard (1985), but considering the evidence for two interglacials between the Hoxnian and Ipswichian, from the sites at Marsworth and Wolvercote, both probably represent Mid to Late Saalian glacial periods equivalent to oxygen isotope stages 8 and 6.

The Ipswichian (Eemian/Sangamon) in the Middle to Lower Thames is recorded from the classic site at Trafalgar Square (Franks, 1960). The environment was one of shallow floodplain channels and cutoffs containing aquatic vegetation and surrounded by grass and herb-dominated vegetation. The floral records, which include Southern European types such as water chestnut (*Trapa natans*) and Montpelier maple (*Acer monspessulanum*), are from IpII which is the warmest zone and corresponds to oxygen isotope stage 5e. The fauna includes hippopotamus and other herbivores which may have been important in maintaining the openness of the floodplain environment that is otherwise difficult to explain. Several other sites show very similar conditions in the Lower Thames, including Ilford and Aveley. Another site at Crayford is particularly interesting as its faunal assemblage of mammoth, woolly rhinoceros (*Coelodonta antiquitatis*), musk ox (*Ovibos moschatus*), giant ox (aurochs, *Bos primigenius*), red deer (*Cervus elaphus*), horse (*Equus ferus*), wolf (*Canis lupus*) and lemming (*Lemmus lemmus*) demonstrates that the environment was also a cold steppe sometime in the Ipswichian. The site has Levallois artifacts associated with it, indicating that Levallois occupation continued into this cold interlude. The complexity of the Late Ipswichian is also attested at Aveley where there is a stratigraphic boundary with elephant below and mammoth above, which Stuart (1976) regards as representing successive phases of the Ipswichian.

The Early Devensian is recorded in the area by the Reading Town gravels, which contain heavily rolled Acheulian type hand-axes, probably derived from the Lynch Hill gravels; these may themselves have been derived from an earlier interglacial. The Middle Devensian, as recorded by the Kempton Park gravel, and the Late Devensian Shepperton gravels are archaeologically barren because of the inhospitable tundra conditions preventing occupation by humans.

Gibbard (1985) has attempted to relate the hand-axe typology of Wymer (1968) to stratigraphic units in the Middle Thames. He used principal components analysis to determine groups of samples or sites which contained typologically similar artifact assemblages. What is most obvious from this analysis is the similarity of most of the assemblages, although there are two discernible groups: (a) Levallois technique dominated assemblages, and (b) assemblages containing both Acheulian and Clactonian type material. In addition Acheulian type material occurred in all the five gravel units included in the study. These findings illustrate the very limited value of artifacts for relative dating and are indicative of the problems of typological overlap and reworking.

Studies in the Lower Thames valley
The Pleistocene history of the Lower Thames has recently been re-evaluated by Gibbard (1994). The terrace record in the Lower Thames commences during the Anglian with the Dartford Heath gravel. Stratigraphically above this lies an extremely important complex of deposits. These are the Swanscombe deposits, named after one of the most important Lower Palaeolithic sites in Britain, at Swanscombe in Kent. This site has been the subject of several studies of both environmental and chronological significance and will be described in some detail.

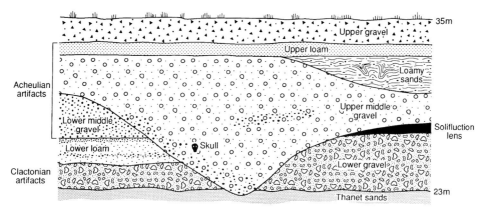

Fig. 5.6 Generalised stratigraphy from Swanscombe, Thames valley. Adapted from Gladfelter (1975).

The site is important for several reasons, including the quantity and quality of the artifacts, the clear stratigraphic separation of the Acheulian above the Clactonian industries, and the Swanscombe skull fragments found in 1935. The skull is intermediate between *Homo erectus* and *Homo sapiens Neanderthalensis* (Bridgland, 1994). The site also has a working floor and there is some evidence for the hominid use of fire. It is not therefore hard to see why it is one of the most intensively studied Palaeolithic fluvial sites in North-West Europe. The 13 m of deposits sit in a bedrock channel carved from Eocene Thanet sands, and are composed of five stratigraphic units. These are listed below and illustrated in Figure 5.6.

Top	Barnfield Upper gravel
	Barnfield Upper loam
	Barnfield Lower Middle and Upper Middle gravel
	Barnfield Lower loam
Bottom	Barnfield Lower gravel

Although there is a lot of local variability, associated with lateral facies changes seen in different pits, the generalised stratigraphy, as revealed by the 1968 excavation (Conway, 1968) and exposures studied in 1982, is relatively simple. The basal unit, the Barnfield Lower gravel, is a horizontally bedded, cold-climate deposit at the base but becomes temperate at the top. At the very bottom of this unit is a coarse gravel with striated flints that, it has been suggested, is partly of solifluction origin (Marston, 1937). This suggestion is supported by a poorly sorted sandy-clay with pebbles described in the 1968 excavation in trench A. This unit passes up into a fine buff-coloured lenticularly bedded loam which is probably a marsh or overbank deposit. It contains a distinctively interglacial fauna with elephant and rhinoceros. At the top of this unit, Kemp (1985a) has recognised a palaeosol. Both these lower units contain the Clactonian industry. Above the palaeosol, the Barnfield Lower Middle and Upper Middle gravel displays frost structures at its top and has a cold-climate fauna which includes lemmings (*Lemnus lemnus*). The Barnfield Upper loam may be either a loessic deposit or more likely a freshwater deposit, perhaps incorporating a reworked loessic component. Unfortunately, it contains no fauna or pollen. The Barnfield Upper gravel is also interpreted as a solifluction deposit on grounds of clast angularity, texture and structure. Molluscan analysis by Kerney (1971) has added important detail to this overall environmental history of changing conditions. There are four main pulses of land mollusca. During deposition of the Barnfield Lower gravel and early Lower loam the mollusca indicate open, hazel-dominated, woodland with reedswamp and fen (Phase I). In the upper half of the Barnfield Lower loam, there is a period of deforestation when dry grassland species make up to 80% of the sample (Phase II) but by the time of deposition of the Lower Middle gravel, dense woodland cover had returned (Phase III). In the Upper Middle gravel, the mollusca indicate damp, open, grassland and there is an influx of open-country rodents (Phase IV). It is obvious from this outline that the sequence represents changing environmental conditions, such as those that occur during the transition from an interglacial to a glacial period with associated short-lived climatic oscillations. There has, of course, been intense interest in the age of the deposits. Of chronostratigraphic significance is the appearance in Phase II of an assemblage of southerly species of mollusca – the Rhenish suite – so-called because of its similarity to the Great Interglacial (Hoxnian) deposits of the Rhine. This has been taken to indicate a physical link between the two river systems during the Hoxnian (Bridgland, 1994). On the basis of the mollusca and the relation of the deposits to the Boyn Hill terrace gravels and indications of an overall shift from interglacial to glacial conditions, the traditional interpretation has been that the sequence spans the period from Hoxnian zone HIIb or c, through the Mid and Late Hoxnian, to the Early Wolstonian (Early Saalian, Table 5.2), possibly including an early Wolstonian/Saalian interstadial (as represented by the Upper Loam). There have been attempts to date the deposits, radiometrically using uranium series dating (Szabo and Collins, 1975). The date of 326+99–54 Ka bp corresponds to oxygen isotope stage 9 which is about 80 Ka years earlier than the traditional correlation with the Hoxnian stage 11. A Hoxnian correlation remains probable, in view of the molluscan evidence, and if Marsworth and other sites such as Ilford and Purfleet represent a pre-Ipswichian post-Hoxnian interglacial correlative of oxygen isotope stages 9 and 7.

The deposits at Swanscombe are of particular geoarchaeological importance because they show the potential wealth of gravel-dominated fluvial sequences as revealed by sedimentological and palaeobiological studies. The site also illustrates some typical problems, including the existence of hiatuses and the variability of the preservation of palaeoecological data.

Another important and rather similar site is the channel deposits at Clacton-on-Sea, type site of the Clactonian industry. Its importance lies in its location on the south-east Essex coast, marking a pre-Anglian northerly course of the Thames and providing a link between the Thames terraces and the glacial stratigraphy of East Anglia (Bridgland, 1994). Several sequences have been logged and excavated at Clacton. Of most interest are the cross-sections of a large palaeochannel (Oakley and Leakey, 1937) and narrow marginal channels (Singer *et al.*, 1973), all of which cross the present coastline (Bridgland, 1994). The sections show a shallow gravel-filled channel system up to 80 m wide, banked against London Clay on the south side and interdigitating with shelly sands on the north side. The channel close to the London Clay bank was filled with marl, covered, as was the rest of the section, by alluvial clay. Frozen-ground phenomena, including involutions, were commonly observed in the gravels. The majority of the archaeology was discovered in the top of the gravels, under the marl. In the absence of clustering related to human activity, such as produced by flint knapping, it was concluded that the flints and bones were not *in situ* but had been transported. However, while some were abraded, others were in mint condition and may have been derived from the adjacent clay bank. From excavations in the 1930s Oakley and Leakey (1937) recovered 190 artifacts in unabraided condition suggesting the proximity of a working floor. The evidence available in the 1970s suggested several possible explanations for the distribution and condition of the flints and bone (Singer *et al.*, 1973):

1   They were thrown from the nearby bank.
2   They were reworked from earlier deposits or surfaces at the time of gravel deposition.
3   They were discarded on the gravel bed when the water level was low.
4   They were derived from erosion of the channel into its outer bank.
5   They were moved by colluvial processes from the adjacent slope.

Considering the differential preservation of the lithics, it seems highly likely that more than one of these processes produced the assemblage. Wymer (1985) suggested that the abraded flint which was evenly distributed throughout the gravels represented an earlier occupation pre-dating gravel deposition (i.e. reworked) and that the mint-condition artifacts, which even retained micro-wear evidence of use, that were found at the top of the deposit had been incorporated into the gravels by trampling on a wet floodplain working surface. In 1987 a flint flake was found *in situ* at the very top of the channel/floodplain deposits. Since it is now clear that hand-axes were manufactured before the deposition of the Clacton channel deposits (e.g. at Boxgrove, a Cromerian complex site: Roberts, 1986) the lack of hand-axes in the 'Clactonian assemblage' is not of chronological significance (Bridgland, 1994). Rather it may be due to the existence of a cultural border between an Eastern European–Asian flake-core industries province and a Western and Southern European hand-axe province (Roe, 1981; Bridgland, 1994).

Clacton has also provided a large amount of palaeontological data. The mammalian remains include straight-tusked elephant (*Palaeoloxodon antiquus*), two species of extinct rhinoceros (*Dicerorhinus hemitoechus* and *Dicerorhinus kirchbergensis*), giant beaver and a sub-species of fallow deer (*Dama dama clactonia*) larger than that found today (Lister, 1986). The molluscan fauna, as at Swanscombe, contains elements of the Rhenish fauna and both estuarine and freshwater species. Although Clacton is generally correlated with the lower units at Swanscombe, uranium series dating has given an age of 245+35–25 Ka bp (oxygen isotope stage 7c) rather than an expected age for the Hoxnian of *c.* 400–470 Ka bp (oxygen isotope stage 11). More recent work using amino acid dating has suggested greater ages comparable to the ages derived from Swanscombe which is also correlated with oxygen isotope stage 11 (Bowen *et al.*, 1989). It now seems fairly certain on geochronological and biostratigraphic grounds that the Clacton channels do represent parts of the immediately post-diversion (post-Anglian) Thames–Medway river with Swanscombe upstream and some link to the Rhine downstream.

The next stratigraphic unit, after the Barnfield units, which contains substantial quantities of Palaeolithic artifacts in the Lower Thames is the Corbets Tey gravel which is the downstream equivalent of the Lynch Hill gravel and which is now assigned to a post-Hoxnian pre-Ipswichian glacial–interglacial cycle correlated with oxygen isotope stages 10–8 (Bridgland, 1994). A complex stratigraphy has been re-examined at Purfleet (Bridgland, 1994). The site has a Clactonian type industry which is stratigraphically succeeded by an assemblage which includes flakes manufactured using the Levallois technique – currently its first appearance in the Thames valley if, as Bridgland suggests, it belongs to oxygen isotope stage 9. The number and complexity of sites discovered or re-excavated in the last twenty years have posed a considerable chronostrati-graphic problem with two possible solutions: either these deposits related to the existence of as yet unnamed warm interludes as previously mentioned, or they are the result of the complexity of the Ipswichian stage and the natural variety of depositional environments in the Thames valley. The problems arose partly because several sites showed similar pollen assemblages but different mammal assemblages. Most notably, a site at Aveley was originally correlated with the Ipswichian (oxygen isotope stage 5e) on pollen grounds but its large mammal fauna did not correlate with nearby classic Ipswichian deposits (i.e. Trafalgar Square). Amino acid dating and lithostratigraphy suggest it and another site at Ilford (Uphall Pit) belong to a late post-Hoxnian pre-Ipswichian temperate stage correlated with oxygen isotope stage 7. Other than the classic Middle–Lower Ipswichian interglacial site at Trafalgar Square, which is rather inaccessible to re-investigation, there is now a lack of securely dated Ipswichian deposits in the Lower Thames. This is probably a real phenomenon caused by the submergence of the Essex coast and Lower Thames by the high interglacial sea level.

The East Tilbury Marshes gravel in the Lower Thames, which is equated with the Middle Devensian Kempton Park gravels in the Middle Thames, contains Mousterian type axes. The Late Devensian in the Lower Thames is represented by a continuation of the Shepperton Gravels and Langley Silt complex which has been given a thermoluminescence date of *c.* 17,000 bp (Gibbard, Switsur and Wintle, 1986).

When it is considered that at the global scale the Thames is a small river, the complexity revealed by the sedimentary sequence seems astonishing. There are, however, several reasons for this. The area has received intensive work over a century or more which included hand excavation for sand and gravel, and urbanisation of the valley has also produced thousands of sections and exposures. Moreover, the basin lies sub-parallel to the maximum limit of one glaciation and within the proximal zone of at least four other glacial advances, and Pleistocene climate change was both complex and rapid. The sequence today and the history of its evolution and interpretation also illustrate several general points concerning fluvial geoarchaeology. For example, it is rarely, if ever, possible to correlate fluvial deposits confidently on any single criterion, particularly the pollen record but also other biostratigraphic elements and lithostratigraphy. Also, geochronological methods such as amino acid and luminescence are invaluable tools for the erection or testing of a chronology and can allow the artifact record to be evaluated by archaeologists independently of any assumed typological progression. Geoarchaeological methods applied to long fluvial sequences therefore have the potential to free Palaeolithic archaeology from the shackles of chronology, allowing important new questions to be asked concerning regional distributions and technological change.

5.3 North American alluvial geoarchaeology

The environmental context
Geoarchaeology, as a sub-discipline, is particularly associated with New World archaeology. There are several reasons for this, among them the rather different educational background of some archaeologists/anthropologists in North America which is more scientific and less based upon classical studies, as well as the nature of New World sites. Most sites are prehistoric, tend to be multi-period or poorly dated, and have often been excavated as part of a regional programme. Indeed, in many New World sites, the stone artifacts and geoarchaeological evidence is the sum total of the site; so it is not surprising that many archaeological studies have taken an explicitly geoarchaeological approach. The aim of this section is to examine a selection of these studies, highlighting methods and the contribution of the geology or geomorphology to the archaeological conclusions. Since it would be impossible to cover the entire New World, examples are drawn exclusively from North America. The

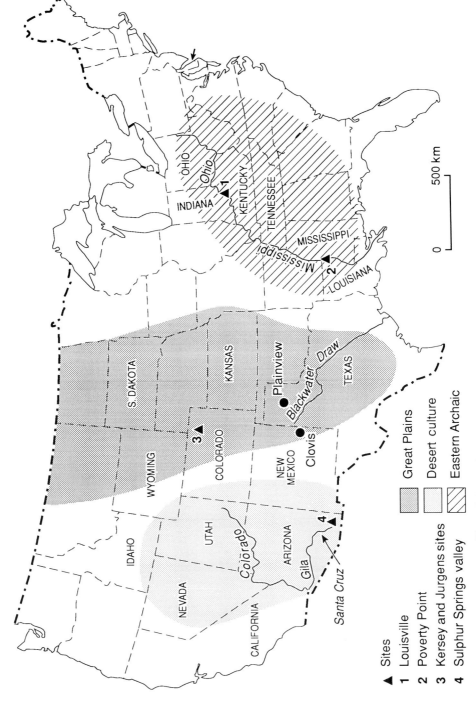

Fig. 5.7 Map of North America with regions and sites mentioned in the text.

▲ Sites
1 Louisville
2 Poverty Point
3 Kersey and Jurgens sites
4 Sulphur Springs valley

Great Plains
Desert culture
Eastern Archaic

archaeological background to the New World and its population can be found in texts such as Fiedel (1987), and New World chronology is covered by the volume edited by Taylor and Meighan (1978). The studies discussed here, which are taken from three physiographic and archaeological regions in North America – the Great Plains, the arid Southwest and the Mississippi basin (Figure 5.7) – correspond approximately to the Great Plains culture, Desert Culture, and Eastern Archaic and Mississippian cultures and their precursors. Before discussing these areas the initial environmental and archaeological context requires some comment.

The Quaternary history of North America differs from that of Eurasia in many important aspects. The continental ice sheets of North America had spreading points in eastern/central Canada from which glaciers moved both northwards and southwards, and there was another spreading point from the Canadian Rockies. This led to a western ice sheet (Cordilleran) and an eastern ice sheet (Laurentide). At its maximum extent, some 18,000 bp, ice covered all of Canada, the Great Lakes Basin as far south as northern Indiana (with the exception of a driftless area in Wisconsin) and the eastern seaboard as far south as New Hampshire. Since the classic volume by Wright and Frey (1963), the deglaciation chronology of North America has been refined and it is now accepted that the ice sheets had not retreated fully until about 6000 bp (Wright, 1971; Porter, 1983). There is little evidence of the Lateglacial climatic oscillations recorded in North-West Europe, except possibly in Canada. This suggests that they were related to changes in the Gulf Stream and the North Atlantic polar front initiated by the melting of the Laurentide ice sheet.

Turning to the archaeological context, on the basis of genetic and anatomical evidence, especially osteodontological, the first certain inhabitants of the New World came from north China. A sinodontal dental pattern has been recorded from many skeletons dating from between 11,000 and 10,000 bp found in North America, including Sulphur Springs woman (Turner, 1983; Waters, 1986a). The peopling of America can be viewed as a combination of the right people in the right place at the right time, i.e. modern *Homo sapiens sapiens* having reached Siberia from northern China could cross to North America via the large ice-free land bridge called Beringia, which existed between Siberia and Alaska during the Late Pleistocene. Although this combination may have existed as early as 35,000 bp onwards, the lack of a traversable ice-free corridor between the Cordilleran and Laurentide ice sheets may have prevented colonisation of most of the Americas prior to about 15,000 bp. According to Martin (1973) the population front took about 500 years to reach Mexico from the ice-free corridor; however, the simple wave-like model proposed by Martin is contradicted by several reliable finds and it is likely that the pattern and timing of colonisation was much more complicated (Meltzer, 1989; Lynch, 1990). Whatever the earliest date of entry there is excellent evidence from sites in New Mexico, such as Folsom, of the use of Clovis-type points to hunt bison (*Bison antiquus*) and other components of the extinct North American megafauna. Since evidence of pre-Clovis or so-called pre-projectile occupation of the New World is a matter of some controversy, the geoarchaeology of what may well not be archaeological sites at all is obviously problematic, largely because the evidence of human activity must ultimately be derived from either artifacts or bones (see the discussion of Australasian geoarchaeology, pp. 184–9 for a further discussion of this point). Studies showing that the pre-projectile lithics could be natural cannot entirely resolve the problem.

The Great Plains
If early humans did enter America via Beringia and the ice-free corridor along the Mackenzie river valley, they would have crossed the Northern Great Plains to the Central and Southern Great Plains. There are several Plains sites (including Clovis Lake Beds, Blackwater Draw and Domebo) that have yielded Clovis-type projectile points taken as indicating occupation by the Llano culture. The sites described in this chapter cover the late palaeoindian period (*sensu* Haynes, 1971) to the Early Woodland period, and are located in the states of Oklahoma, Colorado and Wyoming. The sites with some of the earliest records are from the Middle South Platte river, the geoarchaeology of which has been studied by Holliday (1985). This area has many well-known palaeoindian sites (Klein site, Powers site and others) which have been studied with two aims in mind: first, to set these sites in their palaeoenvironmental contexts, and secondly, to establish a regional geoarchaeological chronology. A particularly important site is Dent, Weld County, where Clovis-type points were found along with mammoth (*Mammuthus primigenius*) remains, although the bones may have been redeposited. Other important sites include Jurgens and Frazier sites, both of which have yielded evidence of butchery of bison (*Bison antiquus*) and lithic artifacts including projectile points (Figure 5.8). These sites are located in the Colorado Piedmont structural basin which contains a sequence of sediments, topographic terraces and floodplain or fill terraces and aeolian deposits. The highest and oldest terrace, the Kersey terrace, consists of bedded sands and gravel 10 m above the South Platte floodplain on the south bank. On the north side of the valley, a terrace named the Pleasant valley terrace is regarded as being coeval with the Kersey terrace (Scott, 1963; Holliday, 1987). The discovery of Clovis-type points within the terrace and radiocarbon dates at a site post-dating terrace formation indicate that the terrace was forming at 11,000 bp but had ceased formation by 10,000 bp. The Kuner terrace, which lies 5–6 m above the floodplain, contains artifacts belonging to the Duncan and McKean cultural complexes and so may date to the Middle Archaic, somewhere between 5000 and 3000 bp. The lowest terrace, the Ranch terrace, which is only 1–2 m above the floodplain, has weakly developed soils and is probably less than 1000 years old. The aeolian dunes are Holocene in age and probably

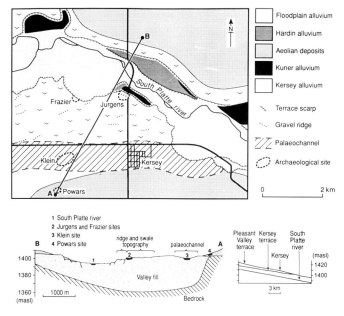

Fig. 5.8 Kersey site, Dent County, and the Kersey terraces, Colorado. Adapted from Holliday (1987).

recent, as suggested by the weak soil formation. The location of the archaeological sites, which are mostly campsites and butchery/processing sites, is notable as they occur on the edges of the ridge and swale surface at either terrace–terrace boundaries or bedrock–terrace boundaries, with one exception which occurs in a relict palaeochannel.

This work has important geomorphological implications, suggesting aggradation of the South Platte river during the Late Pleistocene, Early Holocene incision of at least 5 m, Mid-Holocene aggradation and, finally, incision and increased aeolian activity probably due to increased aridity.

To the north, in Wyoming, Reider and Karlstrom (1987) have described an Archaic site at Laddie Creek which drains to the Big Horn basin. The valley contained both alluvial and colluvial units. These included alluvial sands and gravels on the valley floor and colluvium on a terrace (Figure 5.9). This pattern continued with fine-grained alluvium being deposited in the valley until possibly as late as 3000 bp, when the rate of deposition seems to have declined, accompanied by some stream incision and lateral channel change. The authors looked in detail at soil formation and noted the development of cumulative soils with over-thickened A horizons formed during the Mid-Holocene or so-called altithermal (*c.* 7500–4000 bp). These soils indicate continued groundwater flow from springs during the dry altithermal. The climate of the Great Plains during the altithermal is generally regarded as having been significantly drier and hotter than today (Street-Perrott *et al.*, 1989). Reider and Karlstrom

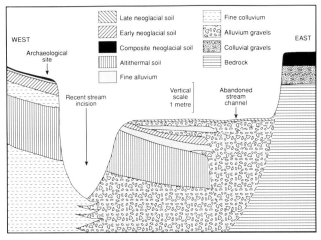

Fig. 5.9 Laddie Creek stratigraphy, Wyoming. Adapted from Reider and Karlstrom (1987).

(1987) have used pollen and opal phytoliths to show that the vegetation surrounding the site was a foothills-scrub community while the valleys supported lush grass growth. This study shows that even during dry periods when caliche was forming over much of Wyoming (Leopold and Miller, 1954; Huckleberry, 1985) the existence of foothills springs allowed continuous occupation by palaeoindians. The study also highlights the value of analysing cumulative soil profiles in order to provide palaeoenvironmental evidence of a local nature in dry environments.

To the south, in western Oklahoma, Ferring and Peter (1987) have described the geoarchaeology of the Dyer site on Bushy Creek, a tributary of the Arkansas river system. The authors emphasise the role of the fluvial environment in site formation, in particular the concentration and distribution of artifacts. The Early Holocene regional archaeology is generally characterised by the occupation of large mound-dominated settlements in the Arkansas and Red River valleys reflecting an increased sedentism. The Dyer site sits on the boundary between an upper and a lower terrace. Four stratigraphic units have been identified with *in situ* Late Archaic/Woodland artifacts in the upper part of the higher terrace (unit Qa_2) and Late Prehistoric artifacts in unit Qa_3 (Figure 5.10). In both cases the deposits were fine-grained overbank alluvium. From volumetric sampling Ferring and Peter (1987) discovered that the concentration of artifacts was much higher in unit Qa_2 (Late Archaic/ Woodland) and the lowest unit than in unit Qa_3 (Late Prehistoric); but radiocarbon dating revealed that this was largely a function of the accumulation rate. The spatial clustering of quartzite debitage in unit Qa_2 can be explained by bioturbation (windthrow), animals and pedoturbation. Rapid burial and inhibited turbation is recorded from unit Qa_3. Ferring and Peter (1987) suggest that the

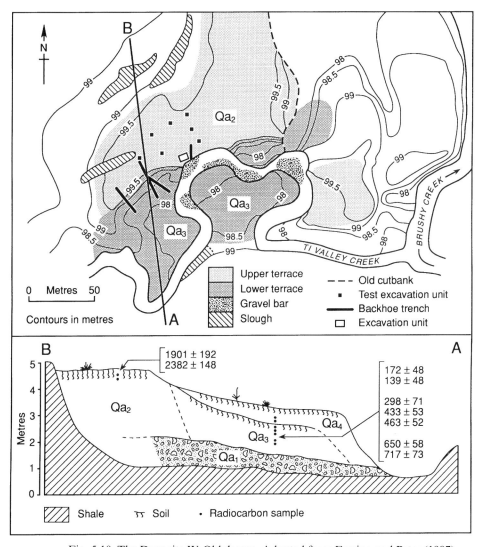

Fig. 5.10 The Dyer site W. Oklahoma. Adapted from Ferring and Peter (1987).

evidence supports the hypothesis of infrequent intensive occupation in the Late Archaic/Early Woodland (2400–1900 bp) and more frequent but less intensive occupation in the Late Prehistoric (700–300 bp). This probably reflects a shift in regional settlement patterns: from a widely dispersed pattern dominated by long-term hunting camps to logistical sites associated with permanent settlements located in river valleys possibly associated with horticulture. What is of particular interest at the Dyer site is the movement of occupation downslope from the upper terrace surface to the lower terrace and its continued use for some 400 years despite frequent flooding.

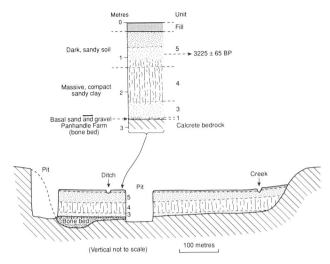

Fig. 5.11 The stratigraphy at Plainview, Texas, adapted and simplified from Holliday (1985).

The most southerly sites from the Great Plains considered here are from the Southern Plains of Texas and New Mexico which have been worked on by Haynes (1971) and Holliday (1985). Two particularly important sites are Clovis and Plainview. The Clovis site, known as Blackwater Draw, was discovered during gravel extraction and the stratigraphy consists of a spring basin about 6 m deep, infilled with spring and lacustrine sediments. The palaeoenvironmental interpretation is: erosion in the basin before 11,000 bp, the deposition of spring sediments during the Clovis cultural period, the existence of a highly productive lake, some erosion around 10,000 bp, then continued lacustrine sedimentation until 8500 bp when soil erosion and extensive fluvial erosion began which has continued episodically to the present. The Plainview site, Hale County, Texas, was discovered by caliche quarrying operations and consists of a bed of the bones of the extinct bison (*Bison antiquus*) and lithic artifacts including the 'Plainview point'. The stratigraphy of the site is particularly interesting, revealing a shallow floodplain fill about 600 m wide with a lower gravel unit cut into the caliche, which has a bone bed on its surface covered by sandy clay (Figure 5.11). The stratigraphy reportedly indicates that the kill took place in an abandoned meander and the bones were quickly covered by sandy alluvium. Holliday (1985) excavated new sections at both sites and conducted detailed textural, mineralogical and pedological (including soil micromorphology) analyses of the sediments, largely with the aim of defining regional palaeoclimatic variation. He has concluded that, although there are differences in the sedimentary sequences at Clovis and Plainview between 12,000 and 8500 bp, this was probably caused by the different pattern of spring activity at each site in the face of aridification. The sites have also produced evidence of two episodes of severe drought between 6000 and 4500 bp, but since then the climate has remained essentially similar to today's, i.e. semi-desert, although there have been several shifts towards aridification during the last 1000 years. These sites and the nearby site at Lubbock Lake suggest, contrary to earlier published work, that the vegetation of the Southern High Plains has been open grassland with some non-coniferous trees from at least the Late Pleistocene right up to the present. These excavations have given studies of palaeoindian cultures in the Southern High Plains a more accurate and detailed picture of changing environmental conditions and changes, allowing the effects of social and cultural factors to be related to environmental factors. The importance of environmental conditions on the Clovis, Plainview and Folsom hunters is exemplified by their use of natural traps to kill, or help kill, big game. These traps included dry river beds (arroyos), small cliffs and even sand dunes (Fiedel, 1987). Additionally, most of the important multi-function sites, especially the Folsom sites, were located close to playas, now dry but then water-filled.

The arid and semi-arid Southwest

A similar, if not more varied, palaeoenvironmental context for prehistoric studies exists in the Southwest, in the states of California, Nevada, Arizona and New Mexico. The association between prehistoric occupation and climatic change has always been a major theme for this area, as exemplified by the studies of the Pueblo Indians by Bryan (1954), the work of Antevs (see Haynes, 1990) on the Cochise culture and Hack's (1942) study of the changing physical environment of the Hopi Indians of Arizona. Indeed one could argue that the links between geomorphology, prehistory and palaeoclimate have traditionally been closer here than any other region of the New World. The Southwest is also one of the earliest homes of dendrochronological studies at the Laboratory of Tree Ring Studies at the University of Arizona. One area that has received particular attention is Whitewater Draw in the Sulphur Springs valley, southern Arizona (Waters, 1985). From the alluvial deposits at this site has come one of the earliest burials in North America, dating from between 8200 and 11,000 bp (Waters, 1986b). Earlier this century, artifacts were discovered, along with the remains of mammoth (*Mammuthus*), horse (*Equus*), camel (*Camelops*) and bison (*Bison*). The artifacts, which included milling stones, are generally recognised as coming from the Cochise culture (12,500–11,000 bp) but on other grounds it had been suggested that the site was a specialised plant-processing site associated with the Clovis culture. Geoarchaeological research has been undertaken by Waters (1985) to try and resolve this problem. As can be seen from Figure 5.12, Whitewater Draw consists of a series of cut and fill units about 7 m deep, including a basal gravel which dates to 15,000–10,000 bp and then a series of alluvial units of sand which show a considerable lateral diachrony and phases of downcutting as well as aggradation. The artifacts and hearthstones

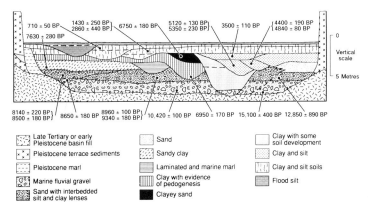

Fig. 5.12 A generalised cross-section of the alluvial stratigraphy of Whitewater Draw, Arizona, redrawn from *Quaternary Research,* Waters (1986b) by permission of the University of Washington.

which were found in unit Da (basal gravels) along with large lumps of charcoal are taken as evidence that the eroded campsite was not far upstream. Sulphur Springs stage artifacts have also been found in unit Db (sand above basal gravels) and both artifacts and articulated burials have been recovered from unit Dc (upper sand – right edge of fill). Waters (1986a) suggests that the campsite was located very close by, probably on a crevasse-splay or levée adjacent to the stream. The dates on these units and from another site at Labuser (Haynes, 1982) place the Sulphur Springs stage between 10,000 and 8000 bp and therefore post-dating the Clovis culture. The major problem that these sites present is that extinct megafaunal remains are found in units Da, Db and Dc, when extinction is normally ascribed to the Clovis stage. Two explanations have been discussed by Whalen (1971): first, that the remains come from a relict population which survived in a fortuitous location; and secondly, that the bones are derived from older deposits. It is suggested that at this site and others, the bones if derived, would not be articulated, or show evidence of butchery. There are several problems here: (a) evidence of butchery does not *ipso facto* discount a derived origin, especially as in this case Clovis cultural remains are found in the region (Hester, 1972); (b) contemporary bones may be disarticulated, completely or partially by a number of processes which do not involve fluvial deposition; and (c) dating control on its own should not be used to argue in favour of a derived origin, on the grounds that the remains are anomalously late, as this may obscure the real date of extinctions. From the discussion in chapter 3 it is clear that what is needed is further information in four areas: (a) the spatial pattern of bones in order to unravel the death history of the animal; (b) evidence on the wear of all the bones and fractures that might be associated with fluvial transport; (c) very close examination of any diagen-etic features that might be associated with the previous burial; and (d) examination of the microstratigraphy around the bones and the relationship of them to any sedimentary structures such as imbrication.

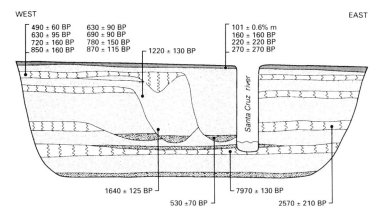

WEST

490 ± 60 BP
630 ± 95 BP
720 ± 160 BP
850 ± 160 BP

630 ± 90 BP
690 ± 90 BP
780 ± 150 BP
870 ± 115 BP

1220 ± 130 BP

EAST

101 ± 0.6% m
160 ± 160 BP
220 ± 220 BP
270 ± 270 BP

Santa Cruz river

1640 ± 125 BP
530 ±70 BP
7970 ± 130 BP
2570 ± 210 BP

Fig. 5.13 Generalised stratigraphy from the northern section of the San Xavier reach of the Santa Cruz river, Arizona. Adapted from Waters (1988).

Partly because of these problems of interpretation and the ambiguity of the evidence from Sulphur Springs stage sites, Waters (1986b) acknowledges that 'evidence for a Sulphur Springs Pleistocene fauna overlap during the terminal Pleistocene is possible'. This debate shows how critical the association of artifacts and bones in alluvial deposits can be. In this case, the question as to whether the shift in emphasis from hunting to collecting began before or after the extinction of the megafauna partially rests upon it. Waters (1985) has interpreted the whole Whitewater Draw stratigraphy in terms of several degradational and aggradational events; the major ones, such as the onset of degradation around 8000 bp, were caused by climatic changes. Other events which seem to occur in relatively stable climatic periods and do not correlate well from valley to valley (Haynes, 1981) are believed to be caused by intrinsic geomorphic thresholds peculiar to each basin (Waters, 1985). This, of course, urges caution against regional correlation of fluvial episodes without independent dating controls.

A similar environmental pattern is revealed by studies of the San Xavier reach of the Santa Cruz river, also in southern Arizona (Waters, 1988). The Holocene sequence shows aggradation of sand, gravel and clay probably deposited by a braided stream, followed by channel erosion and widening between 8000 and 5500 bp. This was followed by vertical aggradation and five periods of channel cutting (Figure 5.13). Waters (1988), following Haynes and Huckell (1986), suggests that a combination of instability associated with rapid aggradation and water level fluctuations may be responsible for the phases of downcutting during the last 2500 years. The trigger may have been Late Holocene flooding, possibly associated with El Niño episodes. Waters (1988) even suggests that Hohokam agricultural drainage ditches could have acted as loci for erosion, as has happened in the historical period. The alluvial development of the San Xavier reach has several important implications for the archaeological record and its recoverability. The alluvial sequences of aggradation, stability and degradation will create gaps and variable vertical density of finds; this will vary spatially, thus also affecting the spatial pattern of artifacts and sites. In particular, Waters (1988) argues that in zones IV and V palaeoindian and Early Archaic remains are absent as a result of erosion, but this cannot be easily differentiated from a lack of occupation. This study does, however, illustrate the potential of reach analysis, by showing how both the environment and Hohokam settlement patterns changed from about 1500 to 500 bp (see Figure 5.14). Waters (1988) clearly believes that these environmental changes were directly responsible for most of the change in settlement pattern during the Hohokam ceramic period. Of particular note is the importance of the distribution and growth of spring marshes (cienegas) and the indications that even over relatively short time periods the distribution of floodplain resources can shift significantly, especially in semi-arid environments. However, although the mechanisms of environmental change are relatively well known in this case, the mechanisms of the cultural change remain hidden. It is not known how the pattern changed, whether it was by mass migration, slow migration (gravitation) associated with changing site dominance, the role of population change or outside factors.

The Mississippi basin
A climatically contrasting region which also provides a wealth of studies of the relationships between floodplain development and cultural change is the Mississippi basin or Eastern Archaic region. Within the Mississippian basin, there is no certain evidence of human occupation preceding the appearance of fluted-point cultures around 10,000 years ago (Griffin, 1978). Pollen analysis has provided a regional picture of Holocene vegetation change (Delcourt and Delcourt, 1981). As can be seen from Figure 5.15, the valley was then covered by cypress–gum (*Taxodium–Nyssa*) surrounded by mixed hardwoods and in the south oak–hickory–pine (*Quercus–Carya–Pinus*). The maps also show how vegetation boundaries and belts have been closely related to the valley throughout the Holocene. The earliest cultural complex in the Upper Mississippi is the Durst and the earliest complexes in the Lower Mississippi are at Jones Creek and San Patrice. Study of the alluvial valley and its sediments has played an important part in the development of the geoarchaeological chronology of the eastern United States, notably through the pioneering work of Fisk (1944), although much of his model of Late Pleistocene and Holocene Mississippi valley development has subsequently been revised (Saucier, 1974; 1981). During the Late Wisconsin glaciation, the Central Mississippi valley was occupied by a braided system but by about 9000 bp the system was changing to a meandering planform (earlier than suggested by Fisk) producing meander belt one. Saucier (1974) has shown that during the hypsithermal (dry) period, from 8700 to 6500 bp, the river created a sequence of meanders indicating a reduced discharge. By 6000 bp, the river was flowing in meander belt three but shifted

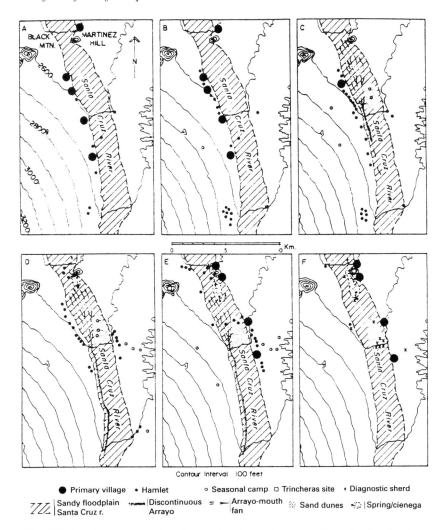

Fig. 5.14 Landscape reconstruction and settlement patterns from the San Xavier reach of the Santa Cruz river, Arizona. (a) Rillito phase (1150–1000 bp), (b) early Rincon sub-phase (1000–950 bp), (c) middle Rincon sub-phase (950–850 bp), (d) late Rincon sub-phase (850–800 bp), (e) Tanque Verde phase (800–650 bp), (f) Tucson phase (650–500 bp). Adapted from Waters (1988).

to meander belt four about 4800 bp. Around 3000 bp, the river shifted for the last time to its present meander belt (five, see Figure 5.16).

Gray (1984) has investigated the relationships between alluvial sediments and artifacts for the Ohio river in Kentucky which is a major Mississippi tributary. The Ohio river valley displays numerous linear ridges sub-parallel to the river, upon which palaeoindian settlement sites were known to exist (Figure 5.17). As one would expect, in general, they get younger towards the river, and in this reach also in a downstream direction. These ridges are not the

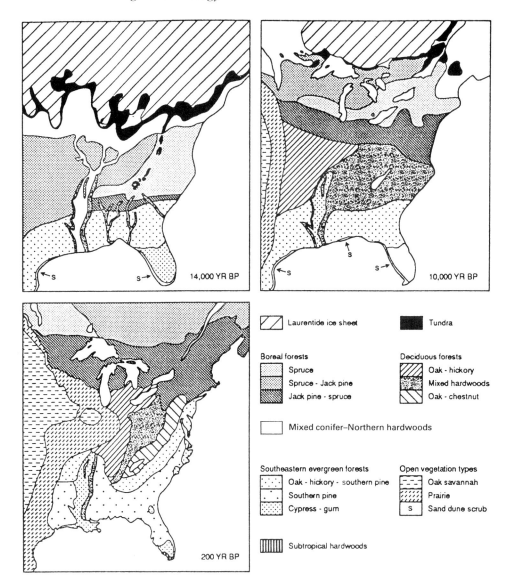

Fig. 5.15 Palaeovegetation maps for eastern North America, 14,000, 10,000 and 200 bp. By 5000 bp substantially the same map existed as at 200 bp. Redrawn from *Geobotany II*, Delcourt and Delcourt (1981), by permission of Plenum Press.

remains of old channel levées but are interpreted as a form of crevasse-splay, formed by currents flowing down the floodplain, with coarser ridge sediments deposited as prograding cusps and finer sediments settling into the swales. The origin of the spacing and location of these ridges is not clear. There has been limited reworking of Pleistocene sand and gravel and a lack of development of free meanders, probably as a result of the superimposition of drainage across a

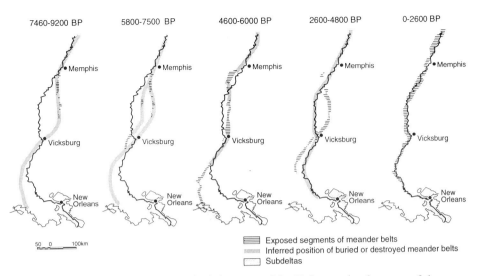

Fig. 5.16 The five meander belt stages of the Holocene development of the Central Mississippi, from Saucier (1974).

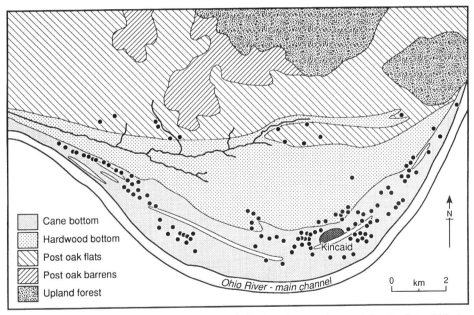

Fig. 5.17 The distribution of Mississippian sites on the north bank of the Ohio in Black Bottom, Ohio. Adapted from Muller (1978).

rock ledge. The sediments covering the ridges and infilling the swales are silts, silty fine sand and fine sand. These deposits contain chipped flint and small fire-cracked stones of cultural origin. The occurrence of bimodal grain size curves for some of the sedimentary units is taken by Gray (1984) to indicate mixing by human activity, although it could also have been formed by the addition of two log-normal components from the overbank sedimentation, i.e. the saltation and fine suspension components. Non-anthropogenic mixing agents such as worms and tree-throw may also mix sediments of two different grain size distributions. The association of mixing with a concentration of artifacts nevertheless adds weight to the cultural site interpretation. The three Holocene sets of ridges in the investigated reach, although different in altitude, do represent a historical sequence that has been constructed laterally as the river has shifted its course.

The prehistoric occupation of the floodplain is closely associated with the development of these bars. All four archaeological sites in the reach, Spadie, Rosenberger, Villier and Longworth-Gick, occur within 400 m of the easterly bank of the river. The Longworth-Gick site has nine undisturbed cultural horizons extending from Early Archaic to the Archaic–Woodland transition (*c.* 2500 bp). The Villier site is Late Archaic–Early Woodland transition, as is the Spadie site. All three sites show only seasonal occupation; the fourth, Rosenberger, is a year-round habitation (village) site of a Late Archaic to Early Woodland and is also a burial ground. This site is higher than the others and has received little overbank sedimentation since its early occupation. Studies at this site have several interesting implications. First, the site illustrates how autocorrelated site occupation on floodplains is and how, despite flooding, sites will be reused even by different cultures. Secondly, it shows unequivocally that this channel of the Ohio has not significantly shifted laterally in an easterly direction; but, as it has shifted slowly to the west, new sites have been established on new levees. A second channel probably existed to the east some time between 15,000 and 12,000 bp. Indeed, only a small percentage of the floodplain in this reach has been reworked by the channel during the last 10,000 years, thus producing a positive archaeological bias in the region.

The Mississippi valley is also associated with the emergence of complex social organisation, as reflected by the building of burial mounds and earthworks. The earliest example of this in the east is from Poverty Point in Louisiana (Muller, 1978). This site, which dates from 3200 bp, consists of several mounds, some very large (21 m high and 183 m across). The site is believed to have been the capital of a chiefdom and implies a large available labour force able to supply around 3 million person-hours (Fiedel, 1987). The mounds and concentric embankments lie adjacent to the river. The early date of mound construction at Poverty Point has been used to support the case for diffusion of mound construction from Mexico, but Fiedel (1987) argues that the early flowering of the Poverty Point culture is more likely to be the result of its 'location in proximity to diverse and abundant riverine resources'. Also, mound building makes particular sense on floodplains and need not necessarily be seen as an imported habit. By this time, although the vegetation of the floodplain had not altered, it was surrounded by a southern pine community.

The Mississippi is also the home of the Mississippian culture which has been characterised as the 'river corridor culture'. It began around 1300 bp (AD 700) within the meander-belt zone in the lower alluvial valley and expanded along the floodplains within, and eventually outside, the Mississippi drainage basin. One area of interest from the centre of the basin is the Kincaid site at the confluence of the Ohio, Cumberland and Tennessee rivers, in an area known as Black Bottom (Muller, 1978). The site lies on a large point-bar complex of the Ohio in an area which is known from geomorphological work to have relatively slow sedimentation rates and considerable channel stability. Alexander and Prior (1971) showed differential rates of overbank deposition on levées, ridges and swales, with more rapid deposition on levées which was compensated for by channel erosion (i.e. preventing the abandonment of the floodplain). They suggest that long-term dynamic stability of the river in this reach is the result of periods of limited bank erosion and bank deposition, the net effect providing a stable site for human occupation. The Kincaid site is large, with 20 ha enclosed by its palisade, which is surrounded by over 100 other smaller sites (Figure 5.17). The sites are almost exclusively restricted to the southern cane biome. This biome was also heavily settled 130 km upstream in south-western Indiana during the Yankeetown (AD 800–1000), Angel (AD 1000–1300) and Caborn-Welborn (AD 1300–1800) phases. Muller (1978) show that the vast majority of sites of the Angel and Caborn-Welborn phases are located on the floodplain terraces with only a few small hamlets elsewhere. However, there are major differences between the settlement patterns and hierarchies of these two phases which are undoubtedly socially controlled, possibly by warfare. This recognition of a social, non-subsistence control over settlement pattern within an alluvial context is important as the correlation of Mississippian sites with alluvial soils has been the basis of a strong functionalist argument.

Lewis (1974), Butzer (1976) and others have argued that, because the alluvial soils are more productive with less labour input, the 'least cost' solution is therefore to settle the alluvial lands. This does not explain why other non-alluvial but equally workable and fertile soils, such as loess, seem relatively unsettled. As Muller (1978) point out, other factors (including the ease of clearance of the cane, grazing and gathering resources, transport and communications) may be equally as important as 'soil fertility'. Even these constraints leave room for the actual settlement pattern to be socially mediated and this calls into question a simple functionalist explanation of settlement patterns in alluvial valleys.

In an integrated study of multi-period settlement around Big Lake in the Lower Mississippi valley, Guccioni *et al.* (1988) have shown how in the Middle

Holocene floodplain conditions became suitable for settlement as a meandering channel replaced part of the braided channel system. Flooding of the terrace formed a levée, eventually reducing flooding and allowing soil to develop which was fertile and suited to agricultural exploitation. The diversity of resources increased with the development of backswamps and, in the Late Holocene, the establishment of bottomland forest. This environment was intensively exploited for over 3000 years despite occasional flooding, a trade-off of the kind which is examined further in chapter 9.

5.4 Australasian alluvial geoarchaeology

Both the Late Quaternary environmental history of Australasia and its archaeology have received disproportionately little attention in comparison with Europe and North America. The continent, which is the largest landmass in the southern hemisphere, has a crucial role in the investigation of climate change, its timing and nature in relation to northern hemisphere changes and astronomic forcing. Its very different human history, now believed to extend back over 50,000 years (Roberts *et al.*, 1990), makes it a constructive contrast in the study of the relationships between humans and their environment. Australasia is for these reasons now receiving more attention in both general Quaternary accounts (Williams *et al.*, 1993) and studies of fluvial environments (Warner, 1988).

One region of particular interest is the vast flat plain known as the Riverine Plain through which run the Murray, Murrumbidgee, Darling and Lachlan rivers. The gradients of these sinuous rivers are extremely low. The travel time for water from the headwaters of the Murray to Wentworth (Figure 5.18) is three months, and the Lachlan river disappears at Oxley into a maze of distributary channels in the Great Cumbung Swamp, only connecting with the Murrumbidgee in times of flood. The Anabranch river to the west of the Riverine Plain divides into so many tortuous channels that it has given its name to that particular channel pattern. The Riverine Plain is also criss-crossed by a remarkable pattern of palaeochannels. Three generations of channels exist on the plain: the contemporary channels which are highly sinuous, suspended-load type and two generations of palaeochannels (Schumm, 1968; Bowler, 1978). The younger generation of palaeochannels, which have been referred to as prior streams, resemble the present channels, but are about twice the size and preserved as oxbow lakes or billabongs (Plate 5.1). The older generation, referred to as ancestral streams, are much less sinuous, anastomosing and shallower, but about three times wider than the present channel. Today they are only visible as ribbons of gum trees along small generally dry creeks (Plate 5.2). The channels are filled with medium to coarse sand, reflecting bedload transport through the ancestral system. These palaeochannels imply climate change, from a drier environment when the highlands were less protected by vegetation – allowing floods to transport large quantities of sand into the river system –

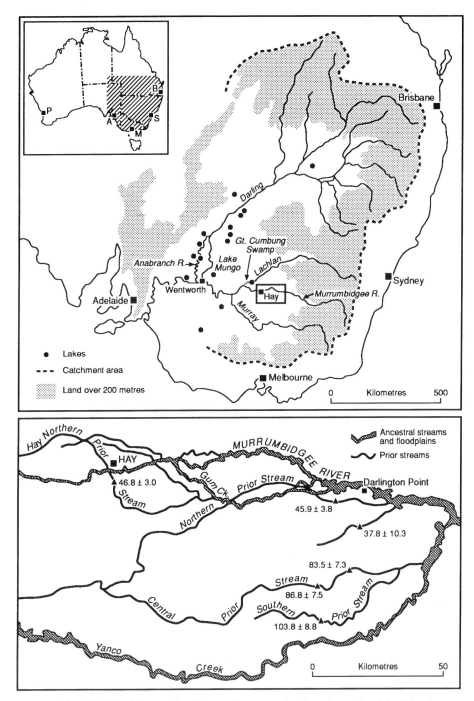

Fig. 5.18 The Murray–Darling catchment and palaeochannels of the Riverine Plain around Hay, New South Wales. Adapted from Page *et al.* (1991).

Plate 5.1 Palaeochannels on the Riverine Plain, south-eastern Australia. A cutoff or billabong from an ancestral channel of the Murrumbidgee.

Plate 5.2 Palaeochannels on the Riverine Plain, south-eastern Australia. Gum Creek – a prior stream channel of the Murrumbidgee.

to the prior channels reflecting a period of greater vegetation cover when slopes were protected, despite higher rainfall under humid conditions. Thermoluminescence dates suggest that the metamorphosis from the anastomosing ancestral system to the meandering prior rivers was between 80,0000 and 50,000 bp (Page *et al.*, 1991). The development of the large meandering pattern correlates well with high lake level in south Australia. Tectonism and other local influences complicate the picture, but the metamorphosis was an important change in the environment and resources of the Riverine Plain. The abandoned ancestral channels provide important linear aquifers and springs which were attractive locations for Aboriginal activity, as indicated by the discovery of Aboriginal skeletons buried in ancestral stream infills near Hay.

A similar metamorphosis of stream channels has been documented from northern Australia (Nanson *et al.*, 1991). Using thermoluminescence dated river, lake and dune sediments, Nanson *et al.* (1992) have suggested that the wetting and drying of the continent approximately parallels northern hemisphere fluctuations, with fluvial conditions dominant in the last two interglacials (oxygen isotope stages 5 and 7), aridity in the last glacial period, interrupted by a pluvial phase *c.* 55,000–35,000 years ago and possibly in the Early Holocene. The most likely mechanisms for this alternation of wet and dry periods is southward shifting of the tropical monsoon. An excellent example of the integrated palaeoenvironmental reconstruction and archaeology in this region is provided in the Kakadu Project (Northern Territories) (Jones, 1985). Seven sites were excavated, including two rock shelters famous for their art (Anbangbang I and Nauwalabila I also known as Lindner) in the catchment area of the South Alligator river. Work on this river has shown how the environment has changed dramatically from 30,000 bp through to the millennium prior to European arrival. The changing distribution of lagoonal watercourses or billabongs, the expanding sandsheets and then the development of wetlands and swamps was driven by climate and the associated postglacial eustatic rise in sea level (Figure 5.19). Geomorphological studies of the Magela Creek in the adjacent East Alligator river catchment have revealed a palaeochannel system underlying the present floodplain which started to fill by vertical accumulation about 8000 years ago (Nanson *et al.*, 1993). The accelerating rate of channel filling was the result of a decrease in the competence of flows associated with drier conditions in the Holocene and the backwater effects of sea level rise. As with the South Alligator system, this caused an expansion of swamp lands, alluvially dammed tributary lakes and deferred tributary–main stream junctions (where the tributary runs down the floodplain adjacent to the main river for some distance before joining it, i.e. a yazoo). The resultant strips of levée land make attractive occupation- or campsites. The changing environment provided a changing spectrum of natural resources. Before the formation of the freshwater swamps, the population density was low, but it increased subsequently and especially around 1400 bp, when extensive

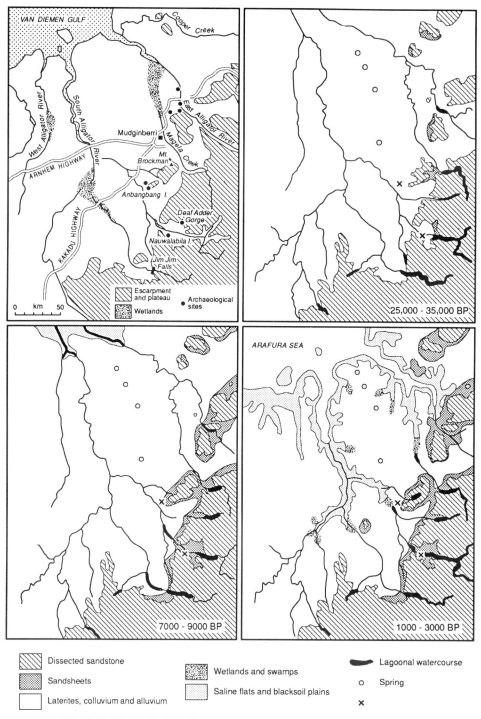

Fig. 5.19 The evolution of the environment of the Kakadu region, Northern Territories, Australia. Adapted from Jones (1985).

alluvial peats began to form and there was a great increase in the range of available resources in the area. Large camps were established on the swamp edges to exploit the mosaic of resources. Organic remains from Anbangbang I reveal a broad-spectrum economy with over fifty animals and a wide variety of plants. Swamp resources included freshwater turtles, mussels and crocodile eggs, as well as dryland species such as little red flying fox, short-nosed bandicoot, kangaroo and wallaby.

We are just beginning to realise how closely the cultural history of Australia is related to these environmental changes, challenging the traditional view of continuity relative to the glaciated latitudes. The wet phase *c.* 55,000–35,000 bp which filled Lake Mungo and attracted some of the first peoples in Australia was replaced by desiccation in the glacial maximum rendering it unsuitable for human habitation. The environmental changes of the Riverine Plain changed the available resources and altered the human carrying capacity of the land. An interesting contrast with North America is that the European colonisation of the last two hundred years caused very little in the way of catastrophic erosion and sedimentation. The reasons for this are both cultural and environmental. On the cultural side, the colonisation was slower, involving a less dramatic change in vegetation, with sheep grazing being much more important than ranching and arable. On the environmental side, the landscape responded differently. It is a very old landscape; denudation rates are low compared to more tectonically active or glaciated environments (Young, 1983) and its palaeoclimatic history is different from that of the northern hemisphere continents. The result is that fluvial systems are supply limited and rivers are frequently not in a simple equilibrium, but instead are prone to sudden pulse-like changes (Nanson and Erskine, 1988). This stream behaviour is also related to the bimodal nature of climate change with alternations at a variety of temporal scales between drought-dominated and flood-dominated regimes. This must be taken into account when trying to understand the aboriginal land relationships in the past and the likely responses of the landscape to future climate change, coupled with a large predicted increase in the Australian population.

The old view of Australia as a continent peopled for a short time and with a static cultural history must now be abandoned; its cultural history has probably been no less varied than its environmental history. The links between the two, which may be particularly close in Australasia partly as a result of isolation, provide great stimulus for further geoarchaeological research.

5.5 Geoarchaeological studies and archaeological inference

The studies described here, although nominally all concerned with geoarchaeology and alluvial sites, do tend to fall into two categories. These can be characterised as locational studies and palaeoenvironmental studies. The locational studies are mostly concerned with identifying the characteristics of the alluvial system which seem to have some explanatory power over site location, while the palaeoenvironmental seek to supplement and explain site history, function and type, via changes in the natural environment. These categories are not, and should not, be mutually exclusive, but they differ in emphasis. While the former studies may have more elegance, allowing the proposition of statistically significant models of location, they have serious shortcomings. These include an inability to cope with change that might not be environmentally forced, a danger of compounding site preservation and site location, and a tendency towards archaeological banality of the 'most fishing villages are located by water' kind. Indeed, some of these studies are essentially environmentally determinist and leave little space for social factors. Those studies where site location is not the main object of study are less likely to succumb to these pitfalls. For example, the detailed analysis of changing environmental conditions around one or a few sites may reveal little, or no, locational adaptation to changing conditions; likewise, profound social change during a period of environmental stability may be seen as a cause of settlement change. These integrated studies are essentially possibilistic and probabilistic, but can still illustrate how, in the broadest sense, the simultaneous study of alluvial environments as well as of material remains is a necessary part of the explanation of social and cultural changes in Eurasian, North American and Australasian prehistory.

The studies discussed so far in this chapter have been based on either artifacts recovered in the course of quarrying for aggregate or archaeological surveys and excavations. Another source of artifacts is from the dredging of rivers and canals. This is particularly important in areas with a long history of river engineering for navigation purposes. These finds do, however, present particular problems of interpretation.

5.6 Interpreting artifacts from rivers

Most archaeological museums contain many artifacts which have been dredged from river beds. Unlike the rare discovery of a ceramic crayfish trap (probably sixteenth or seventeenth century) dredged from the river Waveney, eastern England, in 1951 (Jennings, 1992) most of these artifacts are completely out of context. They can be spectacular objects, such as the Battersea or Witham shields, or more mundane artifacts, such as coins, pottery and bone. The interpretation of most river objects faces two problems. First, the only means of dating for most objects is typology, and second, it is difficult to know where, how and why these objects ended up in the river. There are three possible ways that such objects may enter the river: (a) erosion of riverbank sites, (b) loss from boats, at fords, etc. or (c) thrown in as votive offerings or as part of burial ritual (a known Celtic practice). Since these finds come from dredging, the distribution at the reach or sub-catchment scale largely reflects the distribution of channelisation and drainage schemes. The result is that maps of artifacts of different types and ages will inevitably display similar patterns. Ehrenberg's

(1977) study of Bronze Age spearheads from the Thames valley illustrates the subtlety of this process. Most of the spearheads come from dredging by the Thames Conservancy, most dredging has been done in downstream reaches and the location of finds was only recorded to the nearest town, bridge or lock. So it is not surprising that the distribution maps show clustering at downstream locks and bridges. This data cannot therefore be used to prove early occupation of contemporary bridging points, likely though this may be. Of more use are the differing patterns of different ages or types of artifacts in relation to their non-riverine occurrence and the relationship between riverine and non-riverine hordes of weaponry.

Large-scale drainage of the river Witham in Lincolnshire has produced spectacular metal objects. These have included many Bronze Age and Iron Age swords (including the Fiskerton sword) and scabbards, an Iron Age trumpet (or carnyx), Roman skillets, Anglo-Saxon hanging bowls and Viking weaponry and equestrian equipment (White, 1979). Various aspects of these finds and others like them have led archaeologists to suggest that many may not have been deposited in the river through loss or erosion. First, there is a preponderance of valuable weaponry, nearly always in excellent condition. Secondly, swords and shields often occur in multiples and a comparison can be made with a few sites where ritual emplacement is almost certain, such as the Bronze Age site at Froslunda in Sweden, where fourteen shields were deposited in shallow water at exactly the same location and on a single occasion (Hagberg, 1988). The votive interpretation of Bronze and Iron Age river metalwork has been reviewed by Bradley (1990) who presents convincing evidence that, in North-West Europe, the practice of making such votive offerings declined during the Early Iron Age, possibly owing to a shortage of metal, but was revived in the later Iron Age, as is illustrated by the classic site of La Tène in Switzerland. Bradley also suggests that the wooden structure at La Tène, previously interpreted as a bridge, could have been specially designed for the emplacement of offerings in deep water, and this may have been the case with the causeway running out into the river Witham at Fiskerton. Bradley goes on to suggest that the practice became more diverse in terms of the types of offerings and more institutionalised in the Late Iron Age.

The study of river artifacts, while offering us a tantalising glimpse of prehistoric ritual behaviour, also illustrates how alert we must be to the physical and cultural processes that affect distribution patterns in the alluvial archaeological record and how these may be overcome by comparing riverine and non-riverine assemblages.

6

THE RISE AND FALL OF FORESTED FLOODPLAINS IN NORTH-WEST EUROPE

Floodplain environments in North-West Europe changed profoundly at the end of the last glaciation and have continued to change, although less dramatically, during the Holocene. Climate change affected the hydrology, sedimentology and vegetation of floodplains. As the rivers and vegetation changed so did floodplain resources. From at the latest the Neolithic (*c.* 6000 bp) vegetation was also influenced by human activity. Thus floodplain history is the result of spatially variable interactions between people and natural factors such as climate change, ecological dynamics and soil development. This chapter uses selected examples of northern and central European rivers to outline changing floodplain environments from the Lateglacial to the Mid-Holocene. These environments include Lateglacial floodplains, the Early Holocene floodplain environments of Mesolithic gatherers-fishers-hunters (hereafter referred to as g-f-hs), and the land use changes of floodplains into the Neolithic and Bronze Ages. It would be impossible to cover comprehensively the whole of North-West Europe, or to provide a uniform temporal coverage, if only for reasons imposed by the pattern of Holocene floodplain evolution itself and because of the patchy distribution of research. Therefore, the approach has been to select some of the most informative studies, largely from the British Isles, which have a direct bearing on the archaeology of floodplains and their sites.

Floodplains in the Temperate and Boreal zones have changed dramatically since the glacial maximum *c.* 18,000 years ago. In a broad sense, we can identify three different geological contexts within which these changes have taken place. These three contexts are a modified version of Starkel's (1991a) ten types of European river system evolution.

1 River systems recently developed on areas covered by ice during the last glaciation and affected by tectonic movements, e.g. Scandinavian (or Canadian) rivers.

2 River systems of the former periglacial zone, partly influenced by ice sheets and glacio-fluvial and fluvio-periglacial processes. The lower sections of these rivers may have been affected by eustatic changes, e.g. the rivers of southern England.

3 River systems of the former cold-steppe and forest-steppe zone, usually deeply influenced by neotectonic movements, e.g. most of the rivers of Central and Eastern Europe.

These river types have been subject to different internal (endogenic) controls on Holocene floodplain evolution through inherited factors like initial slopes, bedrock topography, and local sediment type. All these river types have also been subject to changing external (exogenous) controls, the major ones being (a) continuous climatic change, (b) relative sea level change in coastal zones and (c) changes in the availability of sediment. This last variable, sediment supply, is controlled partly by climate but also by ecological factors, such as vegetation migration, colonisation, disease and anthropogenic disturbance. The evolution of North-West European river systems is the product of both endogenic and exogenic factors; this means that the history of each floodplain will always differ to some extent but there will be regional similarities caused by common factors.

At the inter-regional level the main causes of variation in sediment histories may be climatic, geological and anthropogenic; intra-regional variations are more likely to be due to land use changes within catchments. Scale is therefore very important in the interpretation of alluvial chronologies. In addition, conditions are not uniform down the river valley and so, at any one time, the sedimentary regime may vary from reach to reach, making it important to investigate the alluvial long-profile. This chapter uses some examples of Northern and Central European rivers to outline changing floodplain environments from the Lateglacial to the Mid-Holocene.

6.1 Lateglacial fluvial change and the Upper Palaeolithic

The climatic change at the end of the last glaciation had the most profound effects on river valleys in both North America and Northern Europe. This fluvial transition involved a complex metamorphosis of rivers and their floodplains. The severe climatic oscillations of the Lateglacial probably had the most profound hydrological effects in more northerly latitudes, e.g. Britain, southern Scandinavia and upland regions, where we can expect to find major changes in discharge, discharge regime and sediment availability. Dramatic change in fluvial regime occurred at this time. We now know that these changes were extremely abrupt, indeed the 7° C warming at the end of the Younger Dryas may have occurred in as little as fifty years (Dansgaard *et al.*, 1989), a rate well in excess of the possible adjustment of either ecology or fluvial landforms.

Several sites on the river Nene in eastern England (Figure 6.1) have revealed channel change in the Lateglacial. At Raunds a channel was cut into gravels of Lateglacial stage Ic (presumed Bølling) and subsequently filled with organic sediments during the Lateglacial interstadial (Allerød equivalent). Eight hundred metres upstream a palaeochannel with an organic infill has yielded a basal radiocarbon date of *c.* 11,400 bp (uncalibrated) and a date of *c.* 9400 bp (uncalibrated) at the top of the organic infill (Plate 6.1). The relatively common occurrence of cross-bedded sands and gravels of equivalent age suggests channel migration, probably by meandering channels, during the Lateglacial

Fig. 6.1 Location of sites in the East Midlands, England, mentioned in the text.

interstadial. Basal dates from palaeochannels have been recorded in the Netherlands (Vandenberghe, 1987; Bohncke and Vanbenberghe, 1991) and Poland (Kozarski, 1991). Evidence from a site only 4 km upstream of Raunds indicates even greater fluvial activity in the Lateglacial. At Ditchford (Figure 6.2) the entire sub-alluvial gravel suite (first terrace *sensu* Castleden, 1976) was deposited between *c.* 11,200 bp and 10,200 bp. Other sites in the Nene valley also suggest greater reworking of the Pleistocene gravels in the upper part of the middle valley than in the lower valley. This is probably due to the reduction of slope caused by Lateglacial floodplain erosion by meltwater discharges, with relatively little upstream gravel supply, resulting in downstream aggradation. However, this model does not apply universally and not even to all of central England. Evidence from Mountsorrel on the Soar valley, and only 60 km to the northwest of Ditchford, indicates that initial deposition of the sub-alluvial gravels commenced just before 28,000 BP and deposition could have continued until as late as 10,200 BP. A similar sequence has also been found in the eastern

Plate 6.1 Lateglacial peat lens from an eroded channel fill from the Raunds reach of the Nene floodplain, Northamptonshire, England.

Netherlands (Van Huissteden *et al.*, 1986; Vandenberghe and Van Huissteden, 1989). While there are hard-water problems with the majority of the radio-carbon dates from the Mountsorrel site, a reliable date was obtained from twigs within a shallow palaeochannel which is cut into the basal gravels (Figure 6.2). This and another date at Syston (Bell *et al.*, 1972) confirm that the basal gravel unit in the middle Soar was mostly deposited during the Pleniglacial. The Soar floodplain gravels seem to have undergone only minor reworking in the Lateglacial whereas at least some reaches of the Nene exhibit a major incision and aggradation cycle. The two basins are in most ways very similar with the exception that the Upper and Middle Nene is orientated generally West–East while the smaller Soar valley is orientated South–North. Although this may have had effects on the snowmelt and permafrost regime in this area the reasons for the differences in fluvial history are not known.

A site on the Lower Stour (Staffordshire) near its junction with the river Severn has provided another Lateglacial fluvial record for central England (Shotton and Coope, 1983). Radiocarbon dating of organics overlying gravels indicates that the deposition of the lowest terrace of the Severn valley, the Power House terrace which is sub-alluvial below this locality, must have taken place before 13,000 BP Indeed all the three lowest terraces, Power House, Worcester and Main, must have been deposited during the Pleniglacial between 25,000 BP and the Lateglacial interstadial. It may be relevant that this site lies

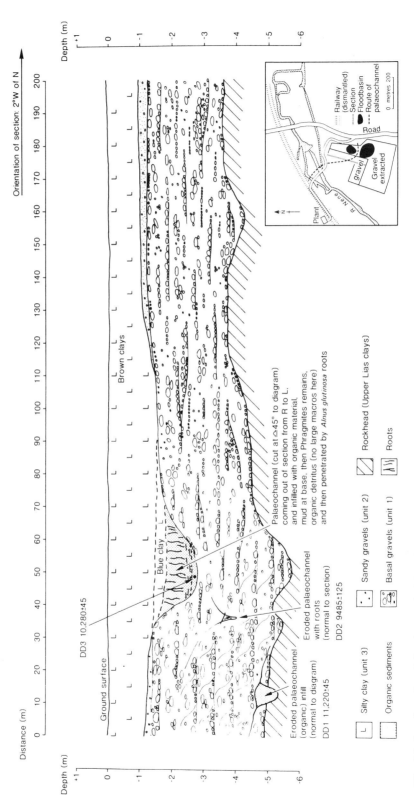

Orientation of section: 2°W of N

Depth (m)

Distance (m)

Ground surface

Brown clays

DD3 10,280±45

Blue clay

Palaeochannel (cut at ≃45° to diagram)
coming out of section from R to L,
and infilled with organic material,
mud at base, then Phragmites remans,
organic detritus (no large macros here)
and then penetrated by Alnus glutinosa roots

Eroded palaeochannel
with roots
(normal to section)

DD2 9485±125

Eroded palaeochannel
(organic) infill
(normal to diagram)

DD1 11,220±45

Silty clay (unit 3)

Organic sediments

Sandy gravels (unit 2)

Basal gravels (unit 1)

Rockhead (Upper Lias clays)

Roots

Depth (m)

Railway (dismantled)
Section
Floodbasin
Route of palaeochannel

0 metres 200

Road

Gravel
Gravel
extracted

R. Nene

Plant

N

Fig. 6.2 Stratigraphy of the site at Ditchford in the Nene valley, England.

towards the upper end of the Lower Severn where the Holocene floodplain is incised into the terrace gravels. The floodplain stratigraphy of the river Gipping in East Anglia studied by Rose *et al.* (1980) shows considerably more reworking and aggradation of the floodplain during the Lateglacial. Meandering during the Lateglacial interstadial is replaced by braiding in the Younger Dryas which is succeeded by a fixed channel and deposition of fine overbank sediments in the Holocene.

A major feature of the Lateglacial stadial (Younger Dryas) and Early Holocene is an increase in channel abandonments, as revealed by a dramatic increase in the gradient of the cumulative number of radiocarbon datings for peat at palaeochannel bases in the Soar and Nene valleys. Palaeochannels invariably had organic sediments at or just above their beds.

Despite the large amount of work on the Lateglacial of North-West Europe and the recognition of a Lateglacial fluvial unit in the fills of most European river valleys, very few studies have been able to relate river behaviour to climatic change at the valley scale. One notable exception to this is Rose *et al.*'s (1980) study near Sproughton of the channel changes of the river Gipping over the last 13,000 years. During the early and middle Lateglacial interstadial, the channel was relatively stable but changed to an unstable condition during the Lateglacial interstadial and throughout the Younger Dryas stadial. This can be seen in Figure 6.3, where the Younger Dryas deposits are cut into the interstadial fluvial and lacustrine deposits. The changes from discontinuous gully development prior to the interstadial, to stable meandering (as indicated by large-scale cross-sets), to braiding (as indicated by small-scale cross-sets), are attributed to changes in regime associated with snow-melt and changing sediment supply from hillslopes. What makes Sproughton particularly interesting is the incorporated archaeological material which includes Late Palaeolithic points and blades (Wymer *et al.*, 1975). The lowest barbed point seems to have been incorporated into the bedload deposits during late zone III (Younger Dryas) and the upper barbed point during zone IV (Pre-Boreal). The upper point may have been deposited onto the palaeosol developed on the floodplain-bar, which was subsequently submerged by Holocene backswamp peat deposits. The peat base is diachronous with peat development on the highest parts of the old floodplain not initiated until the Atlantic (*c.* 5000 bp). This is the result of the rising watertables associated with sediment accumulation in the valley and possibly a general rise in groundwater tables in the Mid-Holocene.

Evidence of human occupation in the Lateglacial in Northern Europe is largely restricted to cave or rock shelter sites, good examples being Kent's Cavern in south-west England, Cresswell Crags in midland England and La Cotte de St Brelade in the Channel Islands. A few open sites indicate hunting activity during the Lateglacial as far north as northern England. At Poulton-le-Fylde in Lancashire an elk/moose (*Alces alces*) skeleton was discovered associated with barbed bone points, which have been dated to zone II (the Lateglacial

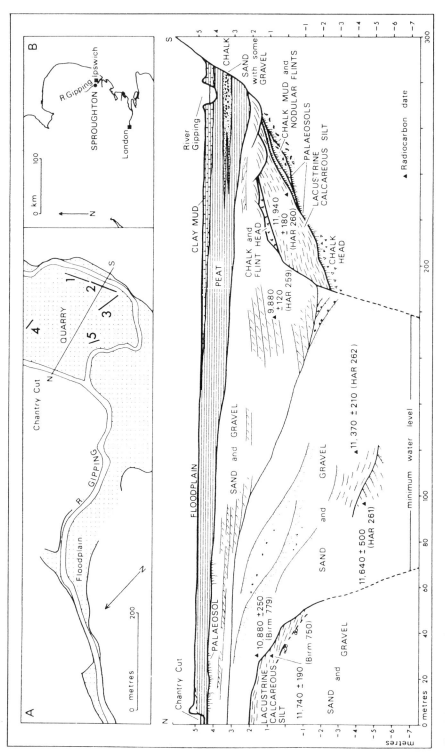

Fig. 6.3 A representation of the general stratigraphy at Sproughton on the river Gipping, England, and location of the barbed points. Reproduced from Rose et al. (1980) and Wymer et al. (1975) by permission of J. Wiley and Sons. Ltd.

interstadial). There is also evidence that human occupation persisted right through the Lateglacial stadial (Younger Dryas, zone III), although it may well have been seasonal in nature as may have been the case at Sproughton. Its long-blade industry which differs significantly from the Cresswellian industry can be regarded as transitional to the Mesolithic.

Excavations in and around the Colne valley, a north bank tributary of the river Thames, have over many years revealed glimpses of associated sedi-mentary, vegetational and archaeological changes at the Lateglacial/Early Holocene boundary (Lewis and Wiltshire, 1992). Excavations at Three Ways Wharf have used micromorphology and pollen analysis to reconstruct the environment of a Lateglacial flint scatter (zone III, *c.* 10,300–10,000 bp) and Early Holocene flint scatters (*c.* 8000 bp). The scatters were the result of food processing employing fire on a gravel bar or island. The vegetation surround-ing the gravel bar was initially sedge swamp, with an open floodplain and regional pine woodland on dryland. By the Early Holocene/Mesolithic the sedges had largely disappeared, and the floodplain which may have supported some hazel (*Corylus*) and later alder (*Alnus*) was surrounded by an increasingly temperate woodland with the immigration of oak (*Quercus*) and ash (*Fraxinus*). The site was abandoned in the Late Boreal as the watertable rose and peats accumulated. Again the widespread formation of peats in valley bottoms in the Late Boreal–Early Atlantic may have had an effect on both site pattern and subsistence strategies, at least causing some element of resource substitution (Lewis and Wiltshire, 1992).

6.2 Early Holocene fluvial environments and the Mesolithic

Although not as dramatic as the Lateglacial the Holocene has seen significant climate change and associated changes in fluvial environments. The Blytt-Sernander scheme of Postglacial climatic zonation was originally proposed for Scandinavia but has subsequently come to be used as a sub-division of the Holocene throughout Europe. Radiocarbon dating of the period boundaries (Smith and Pilcher, 1973) and climatic discontinuities (Wendland and Bryson, 1974) along with work on sensitive environments such as lakes and bogs have validated it in terms of the general climatic trends but added considerable and important detail.

While the concept of Pre-Boreal and Boreal dryness still seems to hold, an equally important consideration is the migration of vegetation across Europe, its dynamics and the associated changes in biochemical weathering and soil development which alter basin hydrological response. During the recolonisa-tion of northern Europe, a new vegetation pattern emerged. This is well illus-trated by Van Leeuwaarden and Janssen's (1987) analysis of the pollen record from oxbow lakes and upland pingo melt-holes in North Brabant, Netherlands, during the Lateglacial and early Postglacial. They showed that the successional pathway varied between the two environments between 12,000 bp and 7300 bp, not so much in the order of appearance of the river-forest trees, but in the time of appearance due to edaphic differences between the more fertile and wetter soils in the valleys and the nutrient-poor upland soils (Figure 6.4). These can be described by the following successional notation:

$$\text{valley } B \Rightarrow B_{PO} \Rightarrow B_P \Rightarrow P_{BC} \Rightarrow P_C \Rightarrow A_T$$
$$\text{upland } B \Rightarrow B_C \Rightarrow \quad C_Q \Rightarrow C_{QU}$$

where B = *Betula*, PO = *Populus*, P = *Pinus*, A = *Alnus*, T = *Tilia*, C = *Corylus*, Q = *Quercus* and U = *Ulmus*

Brown (1988) has also illustrated the emergence of the ecotone between the floodplain and terrace slope environments during the Early to Mid-Holocene in the West Midlands of Britain. The early rise in alder (*Alnus*) in some valleys, which still, however, occurred well after it first arrived in the region (assuming it had not survived through the Devensian) may well be due to out-competition of willow (*Salix*) which had itself out-competed birch (*Betula*), owing to changing floodplain conditions and soil development. There are therefore complex reciprocal linkages between vegetation and sedimentation on Holocene floodplains. Irrespective of whether a native inoculum may have persisted through the Devensian, the most probable agencies of the spread and then the expansion of alder are dispersal by birds and disturbance by beavers and human activity (Chambers and Elliott, 1989).

An important secondary consideration in the Early Holocene is the strong role of inheritance in fluvial systems. This includes the filling of natural stores and changes in the drainage network and channel pattern which can produce changes in sediment conveyance and output with no change in climate or catchment controls (Brown, 1987b). By the Atlantic, floodplains had evolved to be highly interrelated biophysical forest systems upon which Neolithic and later peoples were to have a tremendous impact.

The majority of excavated Early Mesolithic sites in Britain still come from southern and eastern England and many were located by lakes, although, as the work previously discussed implies, there is undoubtedly an under-representation of alluvial sites owing to later burial. The distribution can be seen as a fragment of the European distribution stretching from France and the Low Countries across the North Sea basin. One of the most important European sites, Star Carr in Yorkshire, has provided a large amount of evidence on Mesolithic palaeoeconomy and especially the utilisation of the native fauna, including the importance of a spectrum of ungulates, such as red deer (*Cervus elaphus*), aurochs (*Bos primigenius*), elk/moose (*Alces alces*) and roe deer (*Capreolus capreolus*). The site at Star Carr was at the edge of palaeolake Pickering, which filled with calcareous muds and then organic sediments, produced by natural hydroseral succession from open water to reedswamp to fen carr. Detailed stratigraphic work by Cloutman (1988) has also shown that, at the Boreal–Atlantic transition, there was retrogressive succession, caused by a rise in the water table; the site was drained by the evolving river Hertford at

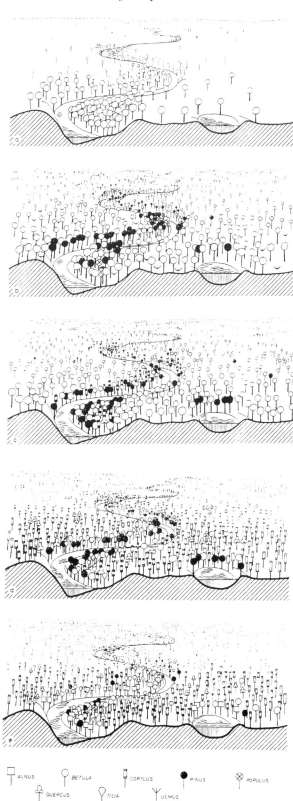

Fig. 6.4 Time correlations of the assemblage zones from the valley cores (EVM and KLD) and the upland pingo cores (KHV/SRV) in the southern Netherlands. Adapted from *Boreas,* Van Leeuwarden and Janssen (1987), by permission of Elsevier Science.

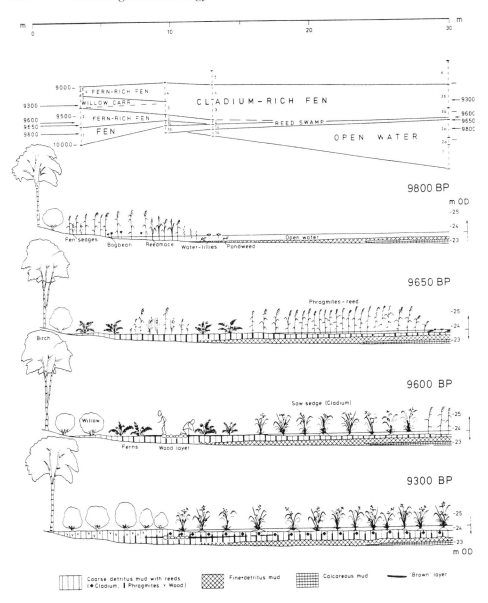

Fig. 6.5 An interpretive reconstruction of the depositional sequence at Star Carr, Yorkshire, England, redrawn from Cloutman and Smith (1988). Reproduced by permission of The Prehistoric Society.

some time in the Atlantic period. From detailed borings and computer mapping, Cloutman and Smith (1988) have shown that the occupation site was located at the mouth of a shallow gully or valley on a hillock which extended into the lake basin and ended in a spit. Using stratigraphic, macrofossil and pollen evidence, they have reconstructed the sequence of local vegetation development (Figure 6.5). The sequence shows that within 500 years there were significant changes in the local environment. During the period of occupation, the site was dominated by ferns, with sedge fen (*Cladium*) dominating the inshore environment: a classic ecotone location. Interestingly, at this and several other northern lake and river sites there is little evidence of fishing. One problem here is that many excavations, including Starr Carr, did not involve sieving for fish bones; however, it is also possible in the light of studies of fish migration that at this time there were relatively few freshwater fish, owing to the slow rate of natural dispersal north from catchments draining the south-east of England. Fishing and sea-shore gathering were important parts of the economy for later Mesolithic coastal sites such as Morton Tayport in Fife, Scotland. During the Boreal, human occupation seems to have spread to the northern uplands and much of our evidence of Mesolithic seasonal occupation camps and their ecological environment comes from the Pennines (Jacobi *et al.*, 1976) and North York Moors (Simmons *et al.*, 1981). There is, in North-West Europe, a distinct lack of well-documented Mesolithic sites located in alluvial contexts; but before going on to discuss possible reasons for this, some exceptions must be noted.

Two examples from southern England are Thatcham in the Thames valley and Shippea Hill, a multi-period site on the river Little Ouse in the East Anglian Fenland. The earliest horizons at both are Late Mesolithic. The site at Shippea Hill consisted of an Early Bronze Age henge on a sand bank by a deep channel which formed a roddon. Roddons are upstanding but low linear mounds which traverse the Fenland of East Anglia, and which have been formed as a result of the infilling of palaeochannels by silt, clay and tufa. They are surrounded by peaty floodplains which have been lowered subsequently by drainage and peat wastage. At the base of the site is a lower peat of Boreal age which contained Mesolithic flint. Excavations in the vicinity were started in 1931 by the Fenland Research Committee. The first were at Plantation Farm (Figure 6.6), followed by excavations at Peacock's Farm in 1934, re-excavated in 1960 (Clark and Godwin, 1962) and resampled with additional stratigraphic investigations in 1984 by Smith *et al.* (1989). Older sediments were proved by borings made in 1937 at the Old Decoy site. All these sites are associated with the old course of the river Little Ouse, close to the Fen margin. Both Plantation Farm and Peacock's Farm are located on sand ridges on opposite sides of the roddon marking the old course of the river. The borings at the Old Decoy site proved that the channel had been abandoned by the river prior to the Pre-Boreal, probably in the Lateglacial. From this site, a pollen diagram was produced covering the Pre-Boreal to the Atlantic. The oldest archaeological level at Peacock's Farm, the black sand within the lower peat, dates from between 8500 and 6800 bp (Boreal). It seems that Mesolithic occupation of the sand bank occurred during the first half of this period and, in more recent rein-vestigations, a number of test pits on the mound edges revealed a sandy fill with charcoal and flints interpreted as hearths. The size (generally 20–60 cm in depth) and the asymmetric bowl-shape of several of them are also suggestive

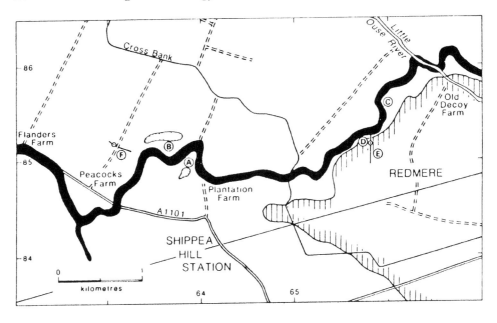

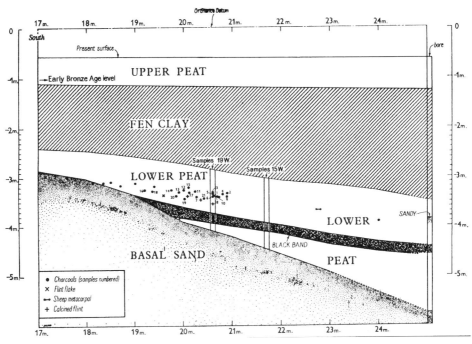

Fig. 6.6 Map of the Shippea Hill sites with an outline of the stratigraphy at Plantation Farm, Cambridgeshire, England. Reproduced from Waller (1994) and from Clarke and Godwin (1962), by permission of *East Anglian Archaeology* and *Antiquity*.

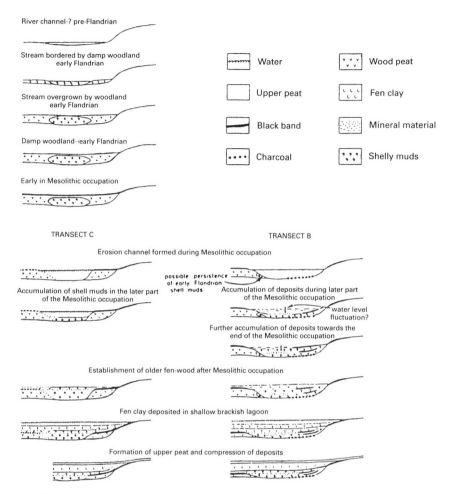

Fig. 6.7 A reconstruction of the fen edge environment from the channel at Peacock's Farm, Cambridgeshire, England. Redrawn from Smith *et al.* (1989).

of a primary origin as tree-throw pits. Through the stratigraphy and palaeoenvironmental analysis, including macrofossils, foraminifera and pollen, Smith *et al.* (1989) have proposed a detailed history of the site, including the channel, stretching from the Lateglacial to the post-Mesolithic deposits of the Fen Clay (Figure 6.7). One reason why these sites are so important for European prehistory is that, being located in an alluvial basin, continuous deposition predominantly of organic sediments allows the production of complete pollen diagrams from very close to the site of occupation.

The first pollen diagram at Shippea was produced in the 1930s (Godwin, 1940); new diagrams which reflect the increasing technical refinement of the method were produced in the 1960s and in 1989 (Smith *et al.*, 1989). From this last diagram, Smith *et al.* have interpreted the decline in trees at the Mesolithic level and evidence of burning as the result of human activity, although they also mention some evidence of dryness during this period. It might be pointed out that the relative reduction in tree pollen (by a maximum of 30%, of a tree pollen sum) could also be caused by tree-throw and burning, and artifacts could be interpreted as the result of opportunistic occupation and preservation of a natural clearing. In this context, three-dimensional pollen diagrams for the site might prove particularly informative. The Neolithic 'A' level at Peacock's Farm (approximately 6000 bp) is succeeded by the freshwater Fen Clay (freshwater here but associated with a transgression towards the coast) which fills in the Neolithic channel. The Early Bronze Age level sits above the Fen Clay in the base of the 'Upper Peat' and the silt infill of the roddon associated with the Romano-British transgression contains Romano-British to ninth-century arti- facts. The whole area represents a palimpsest of changing conditions in this flu- vially dominated environment which was exploited repeatedly by prehistoric peoples.

The complex changing river network of the area has been investigated in tandem with the archaeological work (Sealy, 1979) to give an unusually precise picture of landscape change, which could form the basis of a resource-based spatial model. Shippea Hill illustrates the advantage in terms of environmental evidence that an alluvial site has. In many ways, the excavation at Peacock's Farm was a landmark in environmental archaeology, as Godwin (1978) has commented: it 'convincingly demonstrated . . . the enormous potentialities of a stratigraphic approach in sites that have been selected for their Quaternary geological setting: it heralded a widespread change in manner of approach to the problems of British Prehistoric archaeology'.

From the alluvial fill of the river Kennett, a tributary of the Thames, excava- tions at Thatcham revealed a Maglemosian site (Wymer, 1962; Churchill, 1962). During the Mesolithic, pollen zones IV–VII, the site was located on the edge of a floodplain lake. Although some authors have attributed the existence of the lake to beaver activity, floodplain lakes were a common feature of small to medium-sized river valleys during the Early Holocene in Britain; they were fundamentally the result of Lateglacial fluvial deposition which created shallow water-filled depressions with a relatively short active life (Brown, 1987b). The stratigraphy of the Thatcham site is illustrated in Figure 6.8 and the sequence of deposition would seem to be as follows. The earliest sedi- mentary event is algal marl deposition along the edge of the terrace gravel start- ing during the Pre-Boreal (*c.* 10,000 bp). The flint artifacts are incorporated into Boreal horizons of the marl indicating Mesolithic activity on the gravel terrace. This occupation must have ceased by zone VIIa in the Atlantic, as the hearth site was buried by silt and peat accumulation had begun. Later, with a drying out of the peat, flooding may have eroded some of the marl and redistributed some of it along with artifacts, on top of the sediments on the

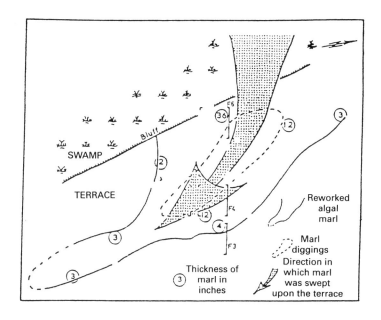

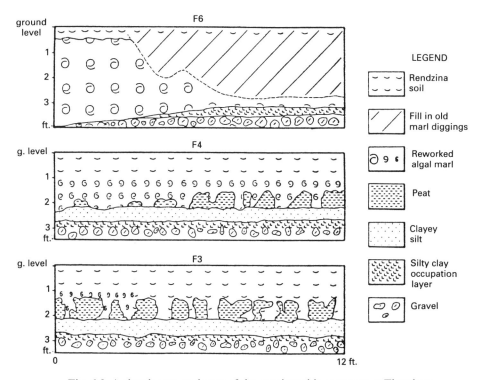

Fig. 6.8 A sketch map and part of the stratigraphic sequence at Thatcham, Berkshire, England. Adapted from Churchill (1962).

terrace. Finally, a rendzina soil profile developed on the reworked algal marl. If this is the correct sequence, and this cannot be certain, then it clearly indicates a major phase of quite damaging floods sometime during the Late Holocene.

An important and remarkably rich alluvial site has been excavated at Noyen-sur-Seine, northern France (Mordant and Mordant, 1992). The Mesolithic of the Paris basin is relatively well known but most of the sites have come from gravel 'islands', and organic channel and valley bottom sites are rare. The excavation of several over the last few years suggests this is due to factors controlling discovery (e.g. lowered watertables), rather than avoidance of valley bottoms by Mesolithic people. During the Pre-Boreal, the Seine valley at Noyen contained wide shallow channels which filled with gravel and organic silts. During the Boreal, there is evidence of additional small channels which changed rapidly and filled with gravel and organic debris. It is in association with these channels that Mesolithic fish-traps were found, suggesting that they had been placed in small, shallow channels independent of the main river in a system that was probably transitional between braiding and anastomosing. As is discussed in chapter 8 in connection with medieval fish-traps, this is the ideal environment for this type of fishing, which it seems has been in intermittent use in Europe for the last 8000 years. During the Atlantic, the area reverted to grassy marshland and the channel was confined to approximately its present position in the Early Bronze Age. The finds, which include bones, flints (no microliths), bone tools, fish-traps, a basket and a dug-out canoe, lie in the bottom of the swampy channel, having fallen down from the settlement which was on the gravelly channel bank. The dug-out canoe (pine hollowed by burning) found with organic debris was probably washed away in a flood. Fishing was mainly for eel (*Anguilla anguilla*) and pike (*Esox lucius*) and occurred throughout the year but especially in summer. The eels were caught in the traps and smoked and the pike caught using straight hooks. The abundant mammal bones show that the site was a base camp, with the animals butchered at killing sites and brought back to be cooked. People exploited the river by hunting beaver (*Castor fiber*), otter (*Lutra lutra*) and the European pond tortoise (*Emys orbicularis*), the forest edge and floodplain grassland for wolf (*Canis lupus*), aurochs (*Bos primigenius*) and roe deer (*Capreolus capreolus*), and most of all the forest itself which provided red deer (*Cervus elaphus*), wild pig (*Sus scrofa*) and lynx (*Felix lynx*). There are subtle changes in site use from the Middle to Late Mesolithic when the site was occupied for a shorter season. The site has also provided a high-resolution pollen diagram covering 4000 years which, interestingly, shows no evidence of Mesolithic clearance in a landscape clearly heavily utilised by humans (Leroyer, 1989, cited in Mordant and Mordant, 1992). The first evidence of clearance and fire is from the Late Neolithic. The diagram does, however, reflect the variety of vegetation types in the valley: gravelly islands covered with grass and bushes, swamps and river channels bordered with alder (*Alnus*), woodland and loessic terraces support-

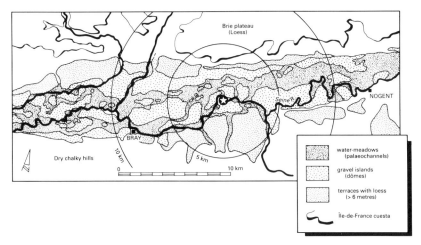

Fig. 6.9 Reconstruction of the environment around the Mesolithic site of Noyen-sur-Seine, Paris basin, France. Adapted from Mordant and Mordant (1992).

ing hazel (*Corylus*), oak (*Quercus*) and elm (*Fraxinus*) forest (Figure 6.9). Both the excellent preservation of artifacts, such as the traps and basket, and the high resolution of the environmental evidence are the result of the alluvial environment and its powers of preservation. Not only has the site revealed much about the exploitation of floodplain resources, but also the valley sides and plateau where the winter camp was located probably less than 5 km away.

Many Mesolithic sites in North-West Europe such as these classically occupy locations providing excellent access to a variety of habitats including riverine/lacustrine, grassland, forest edge and forest. This implies a wide subsistence base within a small area: an important risk-minimising strategy. However, the record is heavily patterned by factors of discovery and excavation methodology. So, although the British mainland sites do not reveal large amounts of fish bone, and the reasons for this are far from clear, sites in Ireland, such as on the Bann river, have done so, the fish being predominantly salmon and eels (Woodman, 1978). It has been suggested that this is a variation in the subsistence base caused by the impoverished nature of the native Irish fauna (Roberts, 1989); however, the continental data suggest that it may be the British record that is unusual here, owing either to excavation techniques or to the history of fish migration. The sites described here and most other alluvial Mesolithic sites in Europe come from either lake margins or relatively large alluvial floodplains. It is tempting to see here a site selection in favour of multiple resources and optimal foraging/hunting strategy, but there may also be a bias against sites in smaller river valleys which do not have sand and gravel quarries or industrial development. With the present density of well-excavated sites, it is not realistic to discuss variations in Mesolithic population density or differential valley occupation; however, the increasing rate of discovery of valley sites renders this a possibility in the near future for some regions.

6.3 Mid-Holocene floodplain forests and human impact

The Late Boreal and Early Atlantic saw profound changes in the floodplain environments of many North-West European river valleys. There is evidence from predominantly non-alluvial sites of a rise in watertables and from alluvial sites of either a lack of sedimentation or the initiation of cut and fill cycles (Robinson and Lambrick, 1984; Brown and Keough, 1992a). This and the changes that occurred in floodplain vegetation have been attributed to greater precipitation caused by increased oceanicity of the climate associated with the Holocene sea level rise. Rivers may well have had more equable river regimes with higher summer flow and clear-water floods, although the increase in precipitation may have, to some extent, been offset by the higher evapotranspiration and interception losses associated with a forest cover (Lockwood, 1979). This regional climatic change and evidence of a rise in watertables in coastal areas may have been particularly marked in Britain because of its isolation as an island by the re-entry of the sea to the Straits of Dover *c.* 8200 bp and recurrent transgressions before sea level reached approximately its present height around 3500 bp. This event also had an important effect on the British and Irish flora and fauna. Although there is abundant evidence that alder (*Alnus glutinosa*) was present in northern France and Britain before 10,000 bp, it was around 2000 years before it became a major forest component. The expansion of alder, although rather abrupt at most sites, was diachronous in Britain by at least 2300 years. These characteristics are consistent with a model of alder migration, probably with two or more European foci, with expansion being controlled by local factors including competition. It was not a simple response to climate change but probably related to the increase in fine and organic-rich fine soils covering and developing on coarser gravelly bars and banks (Brown, 1988). It is also possible that the spread of alder was facilitated by vegetation disturbance by beavers (*Castor fiber*) and Mesolithic g-f-hs (Smith, 1984). Once alder had invaded North-West European floodplains, it was not easily removed and had profound effects on channel processes and floodplain ecology. In particular, the dense alder woodlands inhibited channel change and were probably responsible for the maintenance of anastomosing channel systems into the Atlantic, for which there is evidence from the Thames (Needham, 1992), East Midland valleys (Brown and Keough, 1992c) and the Gipping (Rose *et al.*, 1980). A similar co-evolution of vegetation and channel pattern seems to have occurred in northern Germany (Hagedorn, pers. comm.) and can be inferred in north-western France (Morzadec-Kerfourn, 1974).

Neolithic alluvial sites are far more common than Mesolithic alluvial sites for many reasons, the most obvious probably being increasing population density. However, the difference still remains problematic, partly because it is more extreme in river valley bottoms than it is in the rest of the landscape.

Archaeologists have tended to favour general explanations based on the number and behaviour of Mesolithic peoples, i.e. low population density, and seasonal exploitation of river valleys, upland environments, lakes and coasts. An alternative, or at least additional, explanation can be sought in the fluvial environment itself. Many studies of floodplain alluviation in Britain have shown considerable thicknesses of Lateglacial and Post-Boreal sediments, but frequently relatively few sediments from the Early to Mid-Holocene (Boreal and Early Atlantic). This is illustrated by Macklin and Lewin's (1993) survey of dated alluvial units in lowland and upland Britain (Needham and Macklin, 1992) and longitudinal work on valleys in southern Britain (Burrin and Scaife, 1984; Scaife and Burrin, 1992). Additionally, in the cases where several palaeochannels have been dated from one reach, there is often a conspicuous lack of evidence of channel abandonment during the period 9000–5000 BP. There are two possible causes. First, floodplain erosion with incision and a net loss of sediments from the reach which may have removed the evidence. However, in many lowland river valleys there is little evidence of significant Early Holocene erosion, unlike the uplands where Early Holocene terraces can be found (Macklin and Lewin, 1986). An alternative explanation is channel stability, relatively little channel change and low rates of, or no, overbank deposition across much of the morphological floodplain. This is in agreement with the vegetation evidence previously discussed derived from floodplain peats. The floodplain soils developed on Glacial and Lateglacial gravels were also in some cases stripped off or truncated by overbank floods in the Mid- to Late Holocene (Brown and Keough, 1992a).

In the larger and more active lowland and piedmont rivers of central Europe which have a continental regime, we see more evidence of aggradation and incision cycles in the Early Holocene. Studies on the Wisloka and other rivers in Poland (Starkel, 1981; Mamakowa and Starkel, 1974) and in the Czech Republic (Rybnicek and Rybnickova, 1987) have shown that Boreal–Atlantic are characterised by fluvial incision and the erosion of floodplain peats. Not surprisingly, the lower reaches of many large continental European rivers display a tendency towards aggradation by fine rather than coarse sediments and peat growth (Vandenberghe and de Smedt, 1979).

Neolithic landsurfaces have been excavated from most of the major river valleys of Europe. Particularly well-documented evidence of Neolithic valley settlement comes from Pleszow in the Vistula valley, Poland. Godłowska *et al.* (1987) have examined the impact on the valley vegetation from pollen cores from oxbow lakes close to the Neolithic settlements on a loess terrace (Figure 6.10). The palaeochannels date from the Late Mesolithic (before 6300 bp). Clearances are associated with each of the seven settlement phases from the Musik phase (around 4200 BC) through to the Funnel Beaker culture (2800 BC). It is important to note the great variation in vegetation impact and other changes in the natural environment between the phases (Figure 6.11). An

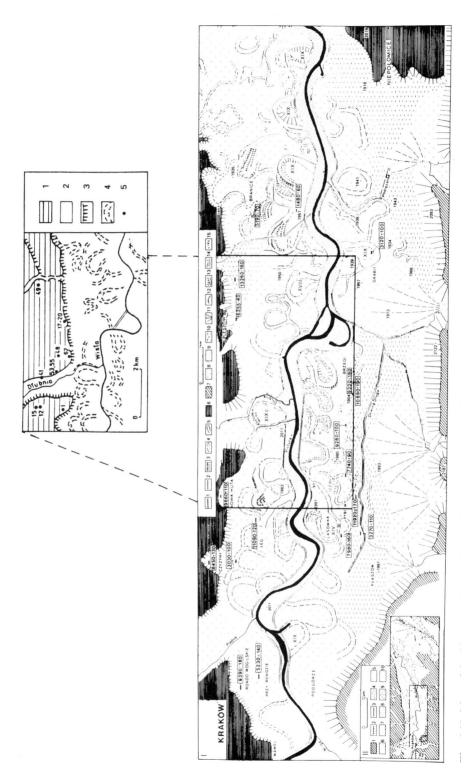

Fig. 6.10 Map of the Pleszow settlement in the Vistula valley, Poland. Key: 1 loess terrace, 2 Holocene alluvial plain, 3 edge of loess terrace, 4 palaeochannel of Holocene age, 5 archaeological sites. Adapted from Godłowska *et al.* (1987).

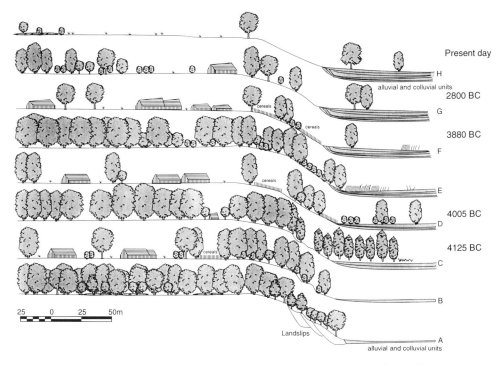

Present day

alluvial and colluvial units

2800 BC

3880 BC

4005 BC

4125 BC

cereals

cereals

cereals

cereals

25   0   25   50m

Landslips

alluvial and colluvial units

H
G
F
E
D
C
B
A

Fig. 6.11 A visualisation of the settlement phases at Pleszow, adapted from Godłowska *et al.* (1987).

example of this is the evidence of valley-side landsliding in the first phase. The environment into which the first Neolithic population moved, probably from the north-west, was almost entirely wooded: the valley floor with willow (*Salix*), poplar (*Populus*) and alder forest; the upland and terrace slopes with mixed elm (*Ulmus*), ash (*Fraxinus*), oak (*Quercus*) and lime (*Tilia*) forest. The oscillations of tree pollen, hazel (*Corylus*) pollen and some charcoal are relatively minor in magnitude; however, there remains the possibility that they may be natural in origin, caused by fire, wind-throw and landsliding (Godłowska *et al.*, 1987). By phase two, cereal cultivation is present and the clearance evidence in pollen diagrams much more pronounced. Phase three records abandonment of the Linear Pottery culture at Pleszow and regeneration of the woodland, although cereal cultivation on a small scale continued at a greater distance from the abandoned channels. Phase four is correlated with a growth of a new settlement on the terrace, of the Zeliezovce cultural phase. Rather complex changes in the floodplain environment occured during this phase, as the valley floor became drier with a decline in water plants and an increase in dryland plants. This may have restricted the growth of alder and promoted cereal cultivation on the lower terrace slopes. The relative importance of hydrological change and anthropogenic activity in the decline of alder at this time is unknown; however, alder recovered towards the end of the phase, when there was a period of flooding as recorded by a thin flood silt. The flooding forced abandonment of the lower fields and encouraged reed growth. Between cultural phases two and three, there was a hiatus in settlement and a decrease in human exploitation of the floodplain environment, with the establishment of the Lengyel culture at Pleszow. The pollen diagram shows a far greater degree of deforestation than had occurred before and it is tempting to suggest that an important landscape threshold had been crossed: that is, from frag-mented clearances set in a 'matrix' of woodland to large interconnected cleared areas with woodlands isolated in the landscape. This deforestation seems to have been largely associated with arable cultivation, meadows and willow scrub in the Funnel Beaker cultural phase. This expansion of culti-vated land was probably responsible for the slope wash which, after 2800 BC, seals off the palaeochannels and ends the organic record. As well as giving us one of the most complete histories of settlement and landscape history from the Neolithic, this study highlights an interesting problem, hidden in many other studies. This is the extent to which the expansion and contraction of arable land on floodplains was influenced by fluctuations in the floodplain watertable and flooding before humans constructed drainage systems and flood defences.

Sites similar in location but with less environmental data have been excavated in Britain. In the Middle Thames, a Neolithic causewayed enclosure was exca-vated at Staines in 1961–3 (Robertson-Mackay, 1987). It is located in the valley, about 1 km north of the Thames, on a tongue of floodplain terrace gravel, bounded to the south by the meandering course of a small stream and a marsh. This camp, sitting on an island of gravel, was of some importance as indicated by evidence of settlements and a multiplicity of on-site activities associated with it. The site at Staines it not atypical; indeed there is another similar site further upstream in the Thames valley at Abingdon (Leeds, 1928).

During the Mid-Holocene the floodplains of Europe were probably at their most diverse with regional variations in climate, soils and groundwater condi-tions largely unmitigated by human impact. Neolithic cultures must have been profoundly affected by natural environmental change, both gradual (e.g. changing forest composition) and abrupt (storms and floods). From the Neolithic onwards adaptation to this change is increasingly replaced by a mini-misation of the impact of natural environmental change through agriculture and the management of floodplain environments.

Many valleys with catchments containing carbonate rocks in North-West Europe contain extensive deposits of tufa; examples already mentioned include Shippea Hill and other Fenland sites and Thatcham. Tufa is a deposit of calcium carbonate precipitated from waters rich in calcium bicarbonate. Its precipitation is favoured by increased temperatures, abundant organic matter such as aquatic plant stems onto which it forms and clear water with low levels of suspended sediment. Further details of the classification of tufa and its environment of deposition can be found in Pedley (1990).

Work in the Dour valley on the south coast of England has revealed both *in situ* and reworked tufa within the valley fill (Bates and Barham, 1993). A well-preserved Middle Bronze Age boat excavated at Dover (Fenwick *et al.*, in press) was found to rest on *in situ* tufa and contain reworked tufa in the form of rounded tufa clasts (oncoliths). Dating evidence suggests that the tufa in the Dour valley and elsewhere in the British Isles and Ireland was being deposited during the Mid-Holocene between *c.* 7500 bp and *c.* 4000 bp (Evans, 1975). It is actively forming in significant quantities today only in the extreme west of Ireland and in southern Europe. The precise reasons for this phase of deposition are unknown but the most likely cause is river and floodplain stability with carbonate rich waters flowing in relatively wide and shallow anastomosing channels containing abundant growth of aquatic plants. A slightly higher mean annual temperature may have also encouraged extensive tufa deposition; indeed it has traditionally been associated with the Mid-Holocene climatic optimum (Evans, 1975). This environment with low levels of suspended sediment, high groundwater tables and a quiescent hydrological regime is supported by the molluscan evidence and the common interstratification of tufa with peats, and it is compatible with largely forested catchments and floodplains. The common reworking of the tufa in the Middle to Late Bronze Age and the Iron Age is another indication of a change in fluvial regime causing the ripping up of tufa beds and the abrasion of tufa into balls transported as part of the bedload. This process has been observed in present-day streams in Cambridgeshire (Fritsch and Pantin, 1946). In the Dour valley the tufa was quarried as a building material during the Roman period, when it was used in the construction of a naval fort, and in the medieval period.

6.4 Floodplain deforestation

By *c.* 6000 bp pollen evidence would suggest that most lowland floodplains in Britain and northern France were covered by alder-dominated woodland (the only native British species being *Alnus glutinosa*) or alder–hazel (*Corylus*) woodland, although there would undoubtedly have been regional variations in species composition with more oceanic elements in the west and continental elements in the east. There are two problems here, related to the limitations of pollen analysis. One is that the proportion of pollen from trees such as hazel, oak (*Quercus*) and ash (*Fraxinus*) derived from the floodplain is unknown and the second is that the importance of some tree species has undoubtedly been underestimated owing to low pollen productivity and/or poor pollen transport and preservation. An example of a tree under-represented in pollen diagrams is poplar (*Populus*), but its ecology and ecological affinities in mainland Europe would suggest it was a component of the floodplain forest. However, in floodplain pollen diagrams, alder and hazel are generally the dominant Mid-Holocene taxon, frequently reaching 90% of the TLP (total land pollen). As Janssen (1959) pointed out, this can present counting problems, if it is the non-local vegetation that is of interest to the palynologist or archaeologist. In

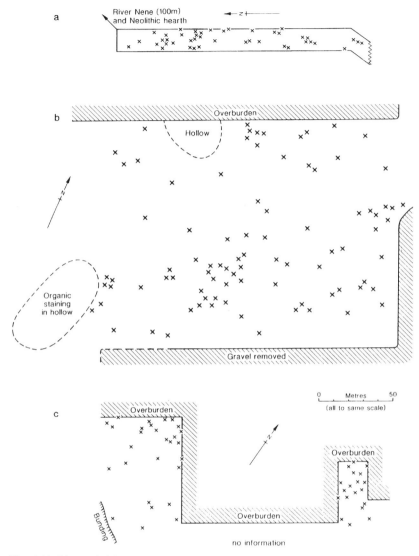

Fig. 6.12 Plans of alder woods derived from *in situ* tree roots. The sites are: (a) upstream site at Raunds, (b) Little Houghton and (c) Wollaston. Reproduced from Brown and Keough in *Lowland Floodplain Rivers: A Geomorphological Perspective*, Carling and Petts (1992), by permission of John Wiley and Sons Ltd.

addition to pollen, there is wood evidence from many floodplains and even *in situ* remains of alder carrs (on peat) and alder wet woodland (on mineral soils), preserved by burial by sediment in many valleys, including the Thames at Runnymede (Needham, 1992).

Brown and Keough (1992c) have excavated three alder woodland sites from the Middle Nene valley in the East Midlands, as shown by their plans in Figure 6.12. The stability of the alder woodland suggests that the community became

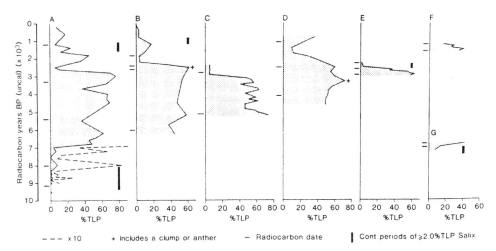

Fig. 6.13 The alder decline in the Severn valley, England. Comparison of alder percentage of TLP at Widen Marsh (A), Ashmoor Common (B), Longney (C), Callow End (D, Brown, 1982) and two sites in the Perry catchment; Ruyton-IX-Towns (F) and Tetchill Brook Junction (G). From *New Phytologist*, Brown (1988), by permission of the New Phytologist Trust.

non-invadable by other species probably as a result of waterlogging and substrate stability. There is very little evidence of the cyclic changes in vegetation that one would expect if there had been successional waves associated with channel migration. Alder also has the ability to survive flooding and a rise in the local watertable, through the production of adventitious roots (McVean, 1954). The decrease in the number of pollen types that are recorded accompanying high alder values is probably due not entirely to the 'drowning-out' effect, but also to the limited diversity of alder woodland. The alder decline seen in nearly all pollen diagrams is highly diachronous. If we look at sites just within a small part of the river Severn catchment in western Britain, we can see that it varies from as early as 3100 bp to 2500 bp (Figure 6.13), and in the Nene valley it occurs in one site as early as 5200 bp. Many of these sites show a two-stage decline, with an initial fall, a recovery or standstill and a second decline to very low values; at a few sites there are three stages (Brown, 1988). This feature is also found with some other declines in tree pollen types such as lime (Baker *et al.*, 1978). At all the non-coastal pollen sites in Britain known to the author, the declines are ascribed to human deforestation. The step-like declines have been ascribed to management and abandonment, but they may simply be caused by the spatial pattern of deforestation in relation to the core location, i.e. block deforestation at some distance from the core, which, for obvious reasons, is likely to be the last site deforested. The observation that this phenomenon is less common or pronounced with other tree types (Brown, 1988) would fit, as they would rarely form such pure stands. There is ample evidence

Plate 6.2 An *in situ* root cluster of alder (*Alnus glutinosa*) from the Raunds reach
of the Nene floodplain, Northamptonshire, England.

of the management of alder in later prehistory; in fact, coppicing of alder is
known from as early as the Neolithic from the Somerset Levels (Coles and
Coles, 1986), and Brown and Keough (1992c) have suggested that the seem-
ingly multiple-stemmed alder root clusters found in the Nene valley may have
been coppiced (Plate 6.2). Several sites, including four in the West Midlands,
show an increase in willow after the alder decline, which may be at least partly
natural, as alder had out-competed both birch and willow on floodplains
during the Early Holocene. In historical times willow species were planted for
wood and to line rivers and ditches, osiers (*Salix viminalis*, *Salix triandra* and
Salix purpurea) were extensively planted for the basket industry and most
recently *Salix alba coerulea* was planted for cricket bats.

Since the clearance of floodplain woodland is so diachronous and universally ascribed to human activity, it is therefore likely to be closely related to
the exploitation of valley reaches and to human factors such as population
density, settlement history and land use control. In this context, it is interesting
to note the good evidence of Neolithic clearance and cultivation of floodplains
in the Thames basin and in the valleys of the Wiltshire Downs (Limbrey, 1992).
In Britain and most of North-West Europe there was eventually almost total
deforestation of floodplains for pasture and arable cultivation, the few large
exceptions generally being forests preserved for hunting.

BURIED SITES

This chapter considers the alluviation and the burial of floodplain surfaces and sites that is such a common feature of the later Holocene in many different climatic environments. Just as the record is spatially variable so too are the causes and particularly the balance between the human and climatic signal contained within the alluvial record.

7.1 Late Bronze Age and Iron Age alluviation in the British Isles

From the Bronze Age onwards in the lowlands of North-West Europe, floodplain and fen-margin sites reveal evidence for increased flooding and alluviation. The picture is much less clear for upland sites (Richards, *et al.*, 1987). This is partly due to the lack of preserved archaeological sites on the valley floors and the more dynamic response of upland rivers to individual storms. Before describing some of the evidence for lowland alluviation, it is worth considering the types of data that may be available, other than a dated increase in overbank-silt deposition. First, pedological data: a lack of soil development and soil structure, caused by a lack of bioturbation and soil development. Soil micromorphology frequently reveals a decrease in pedological fabric and an increase in unbioturbated sedimentary micro-features (Limbrey, 1992). This could be caused by an increase in flood frequency and/or an increase in the sediment loading of overbank flows. The former is probably more important than the latter as fine sediment is supply- rather than transport-limited although both may be the result of climate and land use change. A second, more ambiguous, data type is the existence of an *in situ* peat horizon or tree stumps, which may result from a rise in the floodplain watertable, which may, or may not, be accompanied by increased alluviation (Robinson, 1992). A third data type is a coarsening up sequence, especially a band of fine gravel or coarse sand, traceable laterally across a site, and a fourth, the partial destruction of a site by channel change or catastrophic flooding. Just as the nature of the evidence varies, so does the nature of the hydrological change implied, from the lumped hydroclimatic response of watertable variations to the episodic response exemplified by flood sediments. In this context, we have to remember that one flood does not imply hydrological change, in contrast to evidence of a permanent rise in floodplain watertables which does. Variations in the frequency of flooding and rates of alluviation change the floodplain environment; for example, floodplain 'islands' or terrace remnants may

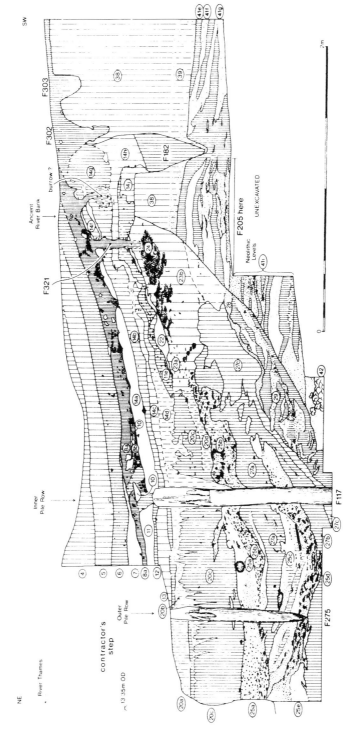

Fig. 7.1 Runnymede: the Late Bronze Age river edge with structures. From Needham and Longley (1980), reproduced by permission of the authors.

disappear – as alluviation raises the floodplain around them and may even bury them completely.

The Thames basin provides two sites which show good evidence of flood-plain change in later prehistory. These are the Neolithic–Late Bronze Age sites at Runnymede, near Egham (Needham and Longley, 1980; Longley,1980; Needham, 1985; 1992), and further upstream, the Iron Age site at Farmoor near Oxford (Lambrick and Robinson, 1979). The Runnymede site is particu-larly interesting, as the interstratified alluvial and settlement record is unusu-ally detailed and well recorded. The site consists of an occupation floor with post-holes, cultural material, and a midden, all under a metre of alluvium. Cultural remains include domestic refuse, pottery, bronzes and burnt flint. The Late Bronze Age settlement seems to have consisted of a single-phase wooden building which was burnt down. Occupation of the rest of the site continued and there was some rebuilding. Waterlogging of the entire site most probably caused abandonment after a relatively short period of time. In 1978, some 80 m of excavations revealed a silted-up river channel with a double row of pile-driven timbers and a prehistoric landsurface behind it (Figure 7.1). This was interpreted by the excavators as a wharfage, which fits well with the evidence of long-distance trade deduced from the bronzes discovered at the site (Needham, 1985). The position of the wharf and the evidence of channel erosion may be reconciled by the existence in this reach of an anastomosing channel or simply a main channel with some smaller secondary channels.

The Runnymede sites have produced abundant environmental evidence including mollusca and pollen. The mollusca point to damp conditions during the period of occupation and a cleared landscape but with some light wood-land in the vicinity. The economy of the site seems to have been reliant upon cattle, and to a lesser extent pigs and possibly sheep/goats for wool and milk. Wild boar (*Sus scrofa*) and red deer (*Cervus elaphus*) were hunted and the river provided wildfowl and perhaps fish. Horses seem to have been kept for riding. Human remains, mostly leg bones, were scattered across the site, some showing evidence of having been gnawed by dogs. The site shows ample evidence of the local economy, but very little evidence of any ceremonial or ritual activity. The bronzes, other exotic items and wharf all suggest that the site was an important inland port on the Thames trade route. If we regard the site as a port and farming village, we must remember that its low social prestige is largely because it was the creator of wealth for one or more prestigious sites near by. The Runnymede site displays evidence of increased flooding at the beginning and towards the end of the Bronze Age. There is evidence from an overbank gravel spread of a large flood at *c.* 4000 bp.

Similar flood layers have been dated to *c.* 3000 bp from the river Stour in the West Midlands (Brown, 1988). The identification of discrete events is relatively rare in predominantly silt and clay alluvial systems, probably because these result from a combination of an unusually large flood event (mega-flood) and continued floodplain aggradation, preventing the pedological reworking of the flood layer. The Bronze Age channel at Runnymede into which piles had been driven silted up, and more significantly, a blanket of archaeologically sterile brown alluvium about a metre thick began to be deposited over the entire site. However, whether the site abandonment was due to socioeconomic factors or repeated flooding is still not clear.

The Iron Age and Roman sites at Farmoor lie on the first gravel terrace of the Upper Thames and also on the Holocene floodplain close to an infilled cutoff (Lambrick and Robinson, 1979). On the dry land of the terrace, storage pits were found along with daub, suggesting the existence of an Iron Age building of some kind. After a gap in occupation, settlement was resumed on the floodplain, as evidenced by a Middle Iron Age farmstead. The excavators of this site employed a wide range of environmental techniques, including analysis of pollen, seeds, wood, plant macrofossils, mollusca and insects. Pollen, from all the contexts sampled, showed a cleared floodplain with very low tree percentages, but high percentages of grasses and herbs. The herbs were indicative of both grazing or pasture and arable land. The arable indicators included cereal pollen, some of which may have been transported to the site on cereal grains themselves. The non-cereal seeds indicated a variety of habitats, including marshland, grassland, woodland, disturbed ground and scrub. Not surprisingly in the light of the pollen analytical results, the wood discovered on the site was mostly from dryland trees, especially the cherry family (*Prunus*). The Early Iron Age deposits at Farmoor contained relatively few mollusca, mostly those with terrestrial affinities; however, the Middle Iron Age deposits produced a large number of aquatic mollusca, including the common bithynia (*Bithynia tentaculata*) and the flat valve snail (*Valvata cristata*), both indicative of flooding. The molluscan evidence for the Roman flooding is less strong. Taken along with the archaeological remains, the environmental evidence indicates that the farmstead was located in open wet grassland which was used for pasture and was liable to flooding. The rich floodplain grassland was probably being seasonally utilised, perhaps in spring. From both environmental and stratigraphic evidence, there seems to have been a marked increase in flooding after the Middle Iron Age, with seeds of aquatic plants and aquatic mollusca brought onto the site, along with increased sedimentation. At this time, flooding did not reach the lower terrace; however, by the Roman period it had. This increased flooding may well have been instrumental in the abandonment of the site. The gravel terrace at Farmoor is bisected by a palaeochannel only some 250 m from the main archaeological site. Although it is difficult to date, the infilling of Lateglacial peat stratified with sands suggests a Devensian date for channel excavation and, on archaeological evidence, it must have been abandoned by the river by the Iron Age. However, as Lambrick and Robinson (1979) point out, it probably functioned as a flood-channel for a considerable period of time after the

Iron Age and it remained a marshy depression providing valuable summer grazing.

In the valley of the Kennet, a tributary of the Thames, environmental work has revealed two episodes of accelerated alluviation: one Late Neolithic/Early Iron Age, the other post-medieval. Snail analysis indicates that the valley bottom was cleared in the Neolithic to provide dry grassland and at various times the valley was dry enough for occupation (Evans *et al.*, 1988).

Robinson and Lambrick (1984) have integrated the evidence of alluviation in the Upper Thames from several sites; their conclusion is that extensive alluviation is largely restricted to the last 3000 years and that it was particularly severe during the Late Iron Age/Roman period and during the Late Saxon/medieval period. Other evidence of Roman and medieval alluviation will be discussed in more detail later in the next section. Largely on the basis of waterlogged ditch deposits, Robinson and Lambrick (1984) also argue that there was a rise in the floodplain watertable which preceded alluviation as early as *c.* 2500 bp. There is also evidence of a lagged alluvial response from the river Nene, but during the Late Neolithic/Early Bronze Age (Brown and Keough, 1992a). Although it is clearly diachronous, even within a reach, owing to the uneven nature of the floodplain topography, all sites investigated by Brown *et al.* (1994) were subject to alluviation by 2500 bp. Another cause of diachrony can be the timing of land use change in different sub-catchments and in order to resolve this there have been several studies of the alluvial history of small catchments in the British Isles (Brown and Barber, 1985; Macklin, 1985) and mainland Europe (Bork, 1989).

Using pollen, diatoms and stratigraphic evidence from the floodplain of a small catchment in the West Midlands, called Ripple Brook, Brown and Barber (1985) attempted to relate a dramatic increase in alluviation around 2900 to 2300 bp to changes in the catchment environment. This was feasible because of the small size of the pollen sources areas (because of small site size), which meant that pollen input must have been largely restricted to the slopes of the catchment. The evidence shows a lag between slope deforestation and increased alluviation of about 300–400 years, which may be the result of sedimentary storage processes; or, more likely, it was the conversion of pasture to arable cultivation, rather than deforestation, that was responsible for the increased availability of fine sediment. The authors also, with the aid of some simplifying assumptions, estimated the catchment sediment yield. As can be seen in Figure 7.2, during the Early to Mid-Holocene, the average rate was around 20 tons $km^{-2}yr^{-1}$, but after 2300 bp it rose to 140 tons $km^{-2}yr^{-1}$. The Holocene mean rate is 50 tons $km^{-2}yr^{-1}$, which is not out of line with estimates from other sources including lakes (Brown, 1987b). This Late Bronze Age/Early Iron Age increase in alluviation seems to be widespread throughout the Severn basin: Shotton (1978) has dated the base of the rather uniform superficial unit common in the basin, called the Buff-Red Silty-Clay, at several sites and all fall

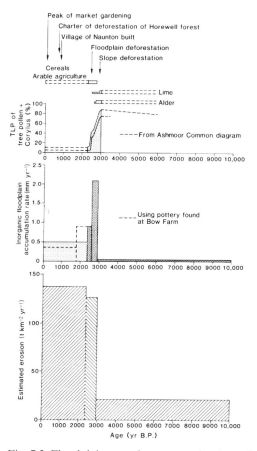

Fig. 7.2 Floodplain accretion rates and estimated erosion rates for the Ripple Brook catchment, Worcestershire, England, with additional information on vegetation change from within the catchment. Ashmoor Common is a similar floodplain pollen site, 8 km north of Ripple Brook. Reproduced from *Quaternary Research*, Brown and Barber (1985), by permission of the University of Washington.

into the time range 3100 bp to 2600 bp (Plate 7.1). During this period, accelerated fine alluviation took place in several other river valleys in Britain, including the rivers Ouse and Cuckmere (Burrin and Scaife, 1984; Scaife and Burrin, 1985) and another tributary of the river Thames, the Windrush (Hazelden and Jarvis, 1979). There seems to have been more limited sedimentation during this period in northern valleys, examples being the river Coe in Northumberland and valleys in Cumbria, whereas more countrywide alluviation episodes occurred at 2000–1600 bp and 1200–800 bp (Macklin and Lewin, 1993).

The phases recorded predominantly in southern England at 3800–3300 bp and 2800–2400 bp almost certainly reflect changing land use controls in increasingly agricultural catchments, coupled with erosive storms. The spatial

Plate 7.1 The Buff-Red Silty-Clay of the Severn Valley, exposed at Powick near Worcester, England.

distribution of alluviation in response to climatic deterioration is at the regional scale, catchment dependent, and so reflects the spatial distribution of erodible soils and erosive land uses. Land use change such as deforestation, the conversion of pasture to arable and drainage alters storm response not only by increasing sediment supply but often by increasing the volume and peak height of the flood hydrograph, especially in headwater catchments (Hollis, 1979).

7.2 Roman and medieval alluviation and channel change in the British Isles

There is evidence from several valleys in Britain of an increase in, or sustained, flooding and alluviation during the Roman occupation of Britain. As has already been mentioned, the evidence in the Upper Thames, of a rise in the watertable accompanied by increased flooding, began in the Middle to Late Iron Age; however, the increase in alluviation started a little later. Robinson and Lambrick (1984) ascribe the increased alluviation to the development of large villas with extensive arable field-systems (especially on the Cotswold hills), and continued farming on the clay slopes. They in fact ascribe all the hydrological changes seen in the Upper Thames after the Neolithic to human activity, but as is discussed later in this chapter, the probability of a climatic component cannot be dismissed. They also suggest that the reduction in alluviation after the Roman occupation was due to the collapse of the villa system, and that its increase again in the Late Saxon period was due to an agricultural revival on the Cotswolds and the reduction in the size of the Forest of Wychwood. Another important aspect of the work in the Upper Thames is that it has shown virtually no evidence for substantial lateral channel movement since at least the Neolithic.

Moving to the Midland valley of the Nene, at the margin of the Fens, the multi-period site at Fengate near Peterborough has also yielded evidence of Roman alluviation. The lower part of the site was covered by Roman freshwater clays which helped preserve the site. From the sedimentary evidence, Pryor (1984) concludes that there was freshwater flooding in the later part of the second century and third century AD. Other local sites also suggest flooding between about 230 and 270 AD. Although it is not impossible, it is rather unlikely that this was caused, as has been suggested, by backwater flooding associated with the so-called Romano-British marine transgression; it is more likely that it is a catchment-produced response. Fengate also provides some evidence of a hydrological change prior to the alluviation in the form of brushwood drains constructed during the Iron Age. Upstream in the Nene valley, at Redlands Farm, near Stanwick, the Roman period saw a rising watertable and overbank alluviation, preserving the villa buildings from robbing and ploughing in the Saxon and medieval periods (Keevil, 1992). There is also evidence of late Roman flooding at Aldwincle on the Nene (Jackson and Ambrose, 1976). Elsewhere, to the south of the Midlands, Roman alluviation has been identified at Braughing in Hertfordshire (Potter, 1976a).

Moving further north, evidence of increased alluviation has also come from the excavation of a Romano-British settlement at Sandtoft, South Humberside, beside the former course of the river Idle. From ditch infills and the spread of alluvium from the river, Samuels and Buckland (1978) and Buckland and Dinnin (1992) have argued for an increase in alluviation and a rise in the watertable of the Humberhead levels during the Late Roman period; they suggest that this was caused by agricultural change, although this interpretation is complicated by the possible effects of the construction of the artificial Turnbrigg Dyke waterway. It is, after all, from the Roman period onwards that the management of rivers begins. There is also evidence of Late and post-Roman flooding in York (Ramm, 1971), Brough-on-Humber (Wacher, 1969) and Watercrook in Cumbria (Potter, 1976a). Several studies of floodplain evolution, including work on the Sussex Ouse (Burrin and Scaife, 1984) and the Trent (Salisbury *et al.*, 1984), have also highlighted Roman alluviation.

Apart from a lack of positive evidence of Saxon alluviation in Britain, and Northern Europe generally, some sites such as Farmoor strongly suggest a decrease in the rate of alluviation, to the point where it may even have ceased (Robinson, 1992). In contrast, mid to late medieval alluviation is widespread in all lowland and piedmont river valleys in Britain and much of Northern Europe. Prior to this, there is evidence from several sites of renewed arable cultivation on floodplains, creating alluvial brown earths and decalcifying Iron Age and Roman alluvium (Limbrey, 1992). While this does not preclude flooding, it does represent a decreased rate of alluviation, coupled no doubt with population pressure. It was this increase in population which, in the fourteenth century, saw more land under the plough than ever before: this was primarily responsible for the widespread valley alluviation and colluviation. There is also later evidence of a climatic signal (Little Ice Age *c.* AD 1550–1800), especially evident in British uplands and where mining provided an over-supply of sediment to steep river valleys (Macklin and Lewin, 1993). Accelerated alluviation is also seen in mainland Europe at this time, as documented by detailed studies in northern Germany discussed in the next section.

The majority of *lowland* floodplains in Britain show remarkably little *channel* change during the Roman and medieval periods. The location of structures such as settlements, quays, bridges and weirs and the distribution of rigg and furrow provide ample evidence of stability from floodplains of large rivers such as the Thames and Severn. This is not to imply that there has been *no* channel change, especially since there are obvious problems with using the survival of constraining structures as evidence of little channel change. However, change seems to have been restricted to alterations in the number and dominance of channels where there were originally a multichannel system, siltation, occasional cutoffs, and locally active reaches. The Severn shows all of these features. At Gloucester, a map dated AD 1455 shows a third, easterly, channel which seems to have progressively silted-up, and then been built over in the eighteenth century as shown in Figure 7.3. A medieval bridge over this channel was excavated, and indicated a channel width of about 40 m (Hurst, 1974). In general, the history of channel change at Gloucester has been one of the maintenance of anastomosing channel pattern, although reduced to two channels, with siltation of the smaller branches. A similar pattern of development seems to have occurred at Runnymede on the Thames (Needham, 1992). The changes that have occurred are often relatively minor, and involve little or no reworking of the floodplain. For example, at Powick on the Lower Teme, a meander loop was abandoned by a chute cutoff across its neck some time after the establishment of the medieval parish boundary, but before AD 1740 (Brown, 1983a).

The entire Lower Severn has been plotted (Brown, 1983a), using 1st edition Ordnance Survey maps of the 1830s and 1840s, and compared to modern maps, using fixed ground control points. The conclusion reached was that very little lateral channel change has occurred over the majority of the reaches during the last 150 years. At some sites, there has been limited lateral channel shifting; for example, the Roman quay at Wroxeter stands 16.5 m from the present channel bank, and at Aylburton, near Gloucester, the Roman quay is approximately 40 m to the east of the present channel; but even these sites suggest very low rates of change. Even just upstream of Ironbridge Gorge, between Leighton and Buildwas, where the river displays a classic highly meandering planform, there

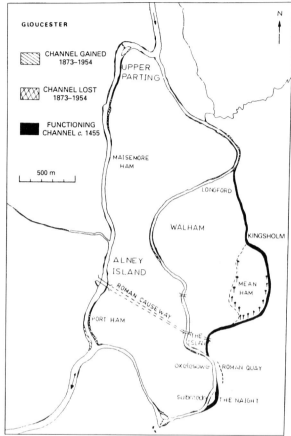

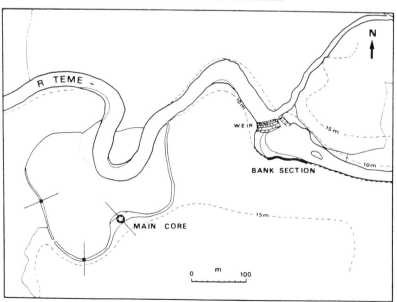

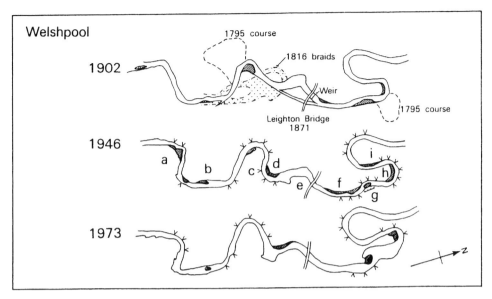

Fig. 7.4 Historical channel changes from the Middle Severn at Welshpool, Wales. Reproduced from *Palaeohydrology in Practice,* Lewin in Gregory, Thornes and Lewin (1987), by permission of John Wiley and Sons Ltd.

has been remarkably little channel change over the last 150 years. However, as soon as we move into the piedmont zone, close to the Welsh mountains, the Severn shows evidence of being far less laterally stable.

Lewin (1987) has shown significant channel change, some constrained, at sites such as Welshpool, Penstrowed, Llandinam, Lanidloes and Maesmawr since 1897 (Figure 7.4). A tributary of the Severn, the Vyrnwy, also displays evidence of post-Roman incision, and active migration over the last 200 years, although, as Lewin (1992) shows, there is also a reach of lower gradient which has been laterally stable in the historical period, with overbank sedimentation dominant. Although, as the Vyrnwy shows, the gross pattern, at the catchment scale, is fundamentally related to stream power (Ferguson, 1981; Lewin, 1987; Brown, 1987a) it does not explain the amount of change at the local level without the addition of a resistance factor. As Lewin (1987) points out, the pattern is complex since different reaches, bends and cutoffs have responded differently to the same event. Comparable studies of smaller piedmont or lowland rivers initiated on recently glaciated terrain (e.g. last Glacial outwash), such as the Dane (Hooke *et al.*, 1990) or the Bollin both in Cheshire (Mosley,

Opposite
Fig. 7.3 Historical river channel changes in the Lower Severn basin, England. (a) channel changes of the river Severn at Gloucester, (b) an historical cutoff on the lower river Teme at Powick near Worcester. After Brown (1983a).

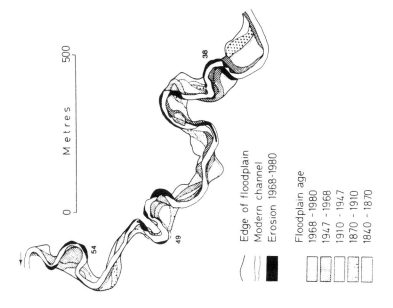

Metres

0   500

Edge of floodplain
Modern channel
Erosion 1968-1980

Floodplain age
1968 - 1980
1947 - 1968
1910 - 1947
1870 - 1910
1840 - 1870

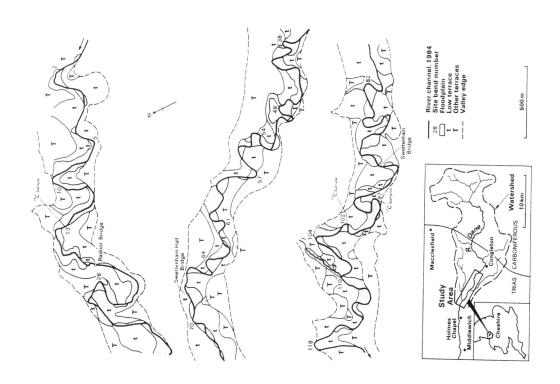

River channel, 1984
Site bend number
Floodplain
Low terrace
Other terraces
Valley edge

28
t
T

500 m

Radnor Bridge
Swettenham Hall Bridge
Swettenham Bridge
¹⁴C Sample

Study Area
Macclesfield
Holmes Chapel
Middlewich
Cheshire
Congleton
R. Dane
Watershed
10 km
TRIAS
CARBONIFEROUS

1975), have revealed considerable channel change over the last 150 years. Hooke *et al.* (1990) have been able to date much of the floodplain and the terraces of the river Dane at Swettenham; from their map (Figure 7.5), it can be seen that a considerable proportion of the floodplain area has been reworked since 1840. They have also shown that there was a major phase of aggradation caused by soil erosion in the medieval period, followed by dissection in the last 300 years which created a low terrace approximately 2 m above the modern floodplain.

Even within the active zone (as mapped by Ferguson, 1981), there is a considerable problem associated with the assessment of regional channel change. It lies in site selection, as there is bound to be a bias in favour of the most active sites, because of the existence of visible evidence of channel change. These studies have given us a useful insight into the classic processes associated with active reaches, which often exist within a general pattern of predominantly less activity. The pattern of fluvial activity in the uplands of Britain has clearly been different from that in lowland valleys during the last 1000 years or so. Since upland valley history has been characterised by more activity, especially erosion, these valleys are less likely to provide single stacked sequences, but more likely to produce terraces (Harvey and Renwick, 1987). Terraces can provide evidence of Holocene channel activity, as shown by the study of the Rheidol valley in Wales (Macklin and Lewin 1986). Out of five terraced fills, at least three are Holocene in age; they consist of high-sinuosity stream sediments with episodes of what the authors regard as human-induced accelerated deposition of fine-grained alluvium. Because of this, and the intrinsic causes of this activity, it seems likely that the pattern of activity in the uplands over the last 1000 years may not be dissimilar to that during most of the Holocene. The evidence of recent alluviation can vary from one valley to the next: in the case of the North York Moors, it varies from small-scale terracing to burial of the floodplain by silty overbank sediments. So Richards *et al.* (1987) caution against over-sophisticated mechanistic explanations, owing to the sensitivity of small upland catchments and the general lack of a proven causal chain based on physical processes observed in the catchment.

Returning to lowland valleys in the British Isles, the general pattern, even if we exclude the rivers Thames and Severn, is still of limited channel change and lateral stability. This is true of the Midland valleys, such as the Great Ouse, Soar and Nene (Rose *et al.*, 1980; Brown and Keough, 1992c). One obvious cause of this, which is of increasing importance during the historical period, is the 'taming' or management of rivers. However, the reasons for the channelisation

Opposite
Fig. 7.5 Channel changes on the river Dane at Swettenham, Cheshire, England. Reprinted from *Earth Surface Processes and Landforms*, Hooke, *et al.* (1990), by permission of John Wiley and Sons Ltd.

Plate 7.2 An aligned oak (*Quercus*) trunk from Colwick in England (photo:
C. Salisbury).

and control of British rivers were rarely associated with excessive lateral mobility, but instead with navigation needs, fishing and flood control (Petts, 1989).
The taming of British rivers was not difficult, in comparison with many continental and North American rivers. As this implies, stability is not as common
in continental Europe; there is also at least one major exception in lowland
Britain: the river Trent around Nottingham.

Salisbury *et al.* (1984) have provided unusually detailed evidence of rapid and
substantial channel change during the last 2000 years at Colwick (Plate 7.2,
Figure 7.6). Here gravel extraction revealed buried tree trunks and fish weirs in
abandoned channels. This allowed Salisbury *et al.* to date the channels rather
precisely using dendrochronology and radiocarbon dating, and to reconstruct
the old channel pattern. They also produced estimates of meander migration
rates for the medieval period, which are all of the order of 0.2–0.5 m per year.
These rates are high and comparable with those reported from historical
studies of rivers in the piedmont zone. At Hemington, 18 km upstream of
Colwick, opposite the Derwent junction, excavations have revealed three
bridges of different designs which were constructed across the Trent in the
eleventh and twelfth centuries (Plate 7.3). All three failed – the earliest possibly
lasting under sixty years – and were buried by gravel (Salisbury, pers. comm.).
The Trent in this reach has a mobile gravel bed and has reworked and redeposited Devensian gravel as it migrated, burying bridges, fish weirs and a
Norman mill (Salisbury, 1992; Clay, 1992). The reasons for the anomalous

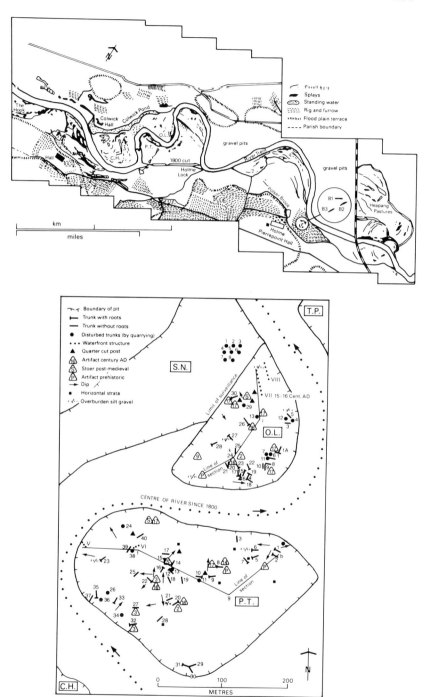

Fig. 7.6 Medieval channel changes on the river Trent at Colwick, near Nottingham, England: (a) the whole reach and (b) detail of two bends and the distribution of tree trunks recovered from gravel pits. From Salisbury *et al.* (1984), by permission of the authors.

Plate 7.3 The excavated remains of an eleventh-century bridge across the river Trent, England.

behaviour of this reach of the Trent are not known, but are probably related to a rather high local stream power, due to the entry of three sizeable tributaries within 22 km – two of which (the rivers Dove and Derwent) drain upland catchments – a feature not found in the lower reaches of any other major British river. This style of river activity has associated with it a specialised archaeology, characterised by the remains of mills utilising the high stream power (Clay, 1992), fish weirs utilising its lack of depth, anchor weights and bridge piers. Owing to the rapid overwhelming of sites in this environment, it can have a surprisingly high preservation potential, analogous to some of the continental Mesolithic sites, such as Noyen-sur-Seine discussed in chapter 6.

Until recently less was known about the alluvial history of Irish valleys than about valleys elsewhere in North-West Europe. With often extremely low slopes, to the point where some river reaches are interconnected ribbons of lakes (e.g. the Shannon), it might be suspected that overbank, lacustrine and peaty deposits would predominate over lateral deposits, except in the mountains. There is, however, evidence of accelerated soil erosion in the Middle Neolithic from Fornaught Strand in south-eastern Ireland (Macklin and Needham, 1992) and from dated silts in south Wexford (Culleton and Mitchell, 1976). The Wexford erosion is attributed to forest clearance and the establishment of raths (small farmsteads) at the beginning of the Christian period around AD 500. The raths had a mixed economy and heavy ploughs were used to till the soil.

Work on the Little Brosna valley, which is part of the Shannon system, has shown that a fluvial system only replaced a lacustrine system *c.* 4300–4150 bp and was accompanied by the development of raised bogs (Aalbersberg, 1994). It is not until AD 1200–1750 that the anastomosing river system deposits extensive overbank clays and the characteristic callows of the Shannon are formed. The callows are river meadows of considerable ecological value (Heery, 1993) and it would seem that they and species-rich hay meadows once characteristic of English floodplains are largely an artifact of river alluviation associated with land use change (Lambrick and Robinson, 1988). The difference in timing between the Irish and English sites probably reflects a different land use history, with widespread arable cultivation of the Irish Midlands only occurring in the post-medieval period.

The distribution of fluvial activity in historical times illustrates how unrealistic it is to separate climate and land use factors at the extra-regional scale. The expansion of intensive arable farming known to be associated with accelerated erosion has predominantly occurred in the drier east of the British Isles. These areas are also characterised by greater inter-annual variability of precipitation in contrast to the wetter maritime western regions, and especially Ireland, which have largely remained under pasture.

7.3 Historical channel change and alluviation in mainland Europe

In mainland North-West Europe, there are several large rivers which have displayed considerable channel instability during the historical period. Two examples are the Danube and Main rivers in southern Germany. Using dendrochronological dating of fluvially deposited tree trunks (or rannen), Becker and Schirmer (1977) have shown that the Middle Ages were characterised by increased fluvial activity, which, in this case, took the form of erosion into older Iron Age and Roman gravels and the deposition of cross-bedded channel gravels and flood sands. Indeed, the work on these rivers shows that they have been far more active than large British rivers throughout the Holocene, with many phases of lateral erosion and deposition, as is shown by the representative cross-section of the Upper Main in Germany in Figure 7.7. Many large rivers in Central Europe have also displayed high rates of lateral migration, including the Slupia in Poland (Floreck and Floreck, 1986), the Vistula (Starkel, 1991b), the Wisloka (Starkel, 1981) and the Warta (Kozarski, 1991).The most likely cause of this difference between these and other westerly non-continental rivers, including British rivers, is generally the contribution they received during the Holocene from valley glaciers and snowmelt, giving them a much greater sensitivity to climate change during the historical period, including the 'Little Ice Age', than the lowland rivers of the maritime western seaboard.

Late Holocene silts, called *Auelehm*, are common in much of Germany. These silts are generally of the Late Bronze/Early Iron Age and/or the Middle

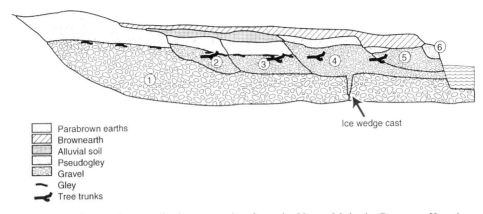

Parabrown earths
Brownearth
Alluvial soil
Pseudogley
Gravel
Gley
Tree trunks

Ice wedge cast

Fig. 7.7 A generalised cross-section from the Upper Main, in Germany. Key: 1 Wurm (Devensian/Wisconsinian) age gravel (low terrace), 2 Middle Atlantic gravels, 3 Sub-Boreal gravels, 4 Iron-Age Roman gravels, 5 Middle age to modern gravels with pile constructions, 6 last-century gravels. Adapted from Becker and Schirmer (1977). For a histogram of the rannen (fossil tree trunks) from the valley see Figure 2.6.

Ages, although it varies from valley to valley, both with the period of agricultural expansion and with agricultural intensity.

Geomorphological investigations of valleys in Lower Saxony, north Germany (Rother, 1989; Bork, 1989), have produced a rather precise and integrated picture of accelerated alluviation and colluviation during the late prehistoric to medieval period. The stratigraphy of valleys such as the Weser, Leine, Ilme and Werra generally contains Lateglacial sediments which include a volcanic tuff, a lower or earlier valley loam and at least a couple of later 'meadow loams' (Plate 7.4). These meadow loams which post-date c. 3000 bp contain a detailed history of alluviation. Younger meadow loams are distinguished from older meadow loams by their slightly coarser grain size (silty clay with some fine sand) and their higher calcium carbonate content. Interdigitating with these alluvial units are colluvial units, including alluvial fans (Figure 7.8). Brown (1992) has shown that some of these colluvial units are magnetically enhanced, and that the peak enhancement occurs at the base of the unit, which suggests the surface stripping or inter-rill erosion of enhanced topsoil. A chronology of these units shows that they are clearly related to variations in the intensity of farming during the last 2000 years. In the valleys of the Ilme, Weser and Werra, the older meadow loams date from the eighth to fourteenth centuries, while the younger meadow loam is post-fifteenth-century. Typical colluvial rates for the eighth to fourteenth centuries are around 1.7 mm yr^{-1} and the rates after the fifteenth century are lower, at around 0.3 mm yr^{-1} (Bork, 1989). Particularly high rates during the early fourteenth century were most probably associated with climatic instability, includ-

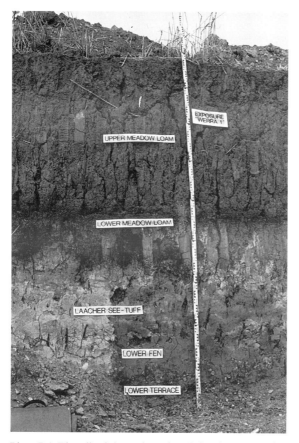

Plate 7.4 The alluvial stratigraphy of the river Werra in north Germany. See text for explanation of the labels.

ing the most devastating flood Europe has suffered in the last 1500 years, which occurred in 1342 (Bork, 1989). The overall higher rate during this period was, however, also related to the intensive use of strip-terraces.

7.4 The Mediterranean record

Environments with a Mediterranean-type climate are highly susceptible to erosion, owing to the combination of infrequent but intense rainstorms, and vegetation cover limited by drought, grazing and fire (Brown, 1990). The Mediterranean basin itself displays some spectacular eroded landscapes, including badlands, alluvial fans and limestone hills denuded of soil. There is also abundant evidence of the deposition of the eroded soil at slope-bases and in river valleys (Macklin and Lewin 1993; Woodward, 1995).

In his classic study of Mediterranean alluviation, Vita-Finzi (1963; 1969) recognised two common alluvial units, one of which is of historical age and has a widespread occurrence throughout the Mediterranean basin: the so called

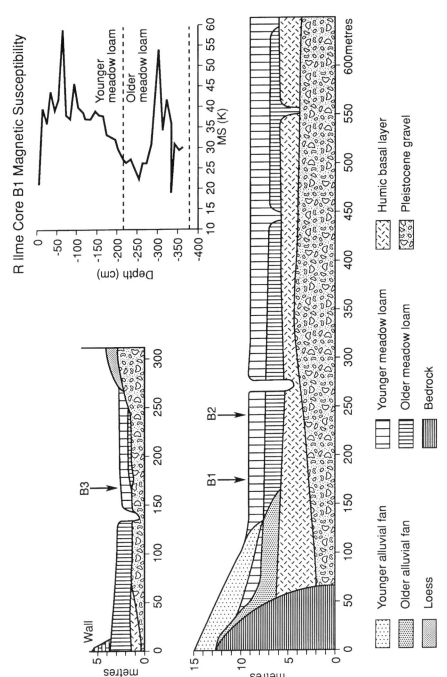

Fig. 7.8 Cross-sections of the Leine, Ilme and Weser valleys, northern Germany, and magnetic susceptibility profiles. From data by Rother (1989) and taken from Brown (1992).

'Younger Fill'. This unit is often cut into, and partly derived from, an 'Older Fill' which is generally regarded as being of Pleistocene age. The Younger Fill is generally buff/grey/brown in colour and composed of silty fine sand with some rounded/subrounded gravel lenses. It forms the floodplain of most valleys and is effectively a low terrace, resulting from post-medieval stream incision. In many cases, it was probably deposited relatively quickly by just a few flash-floods, causing some erosion of existing valley sediments, of both channel and overbank origin. The major period of deposition was from the Late Roman to early medieval period, *c.* AD 300–1500, but with a distinct north–south gradient. Vita-Finzi (1976) regards the cause of deposition as primarily climatic – the result of a temporary southward shift in the depression belts of Europe – citing as key evidence a decrease in the antiquity of the fill from north (45° N) to south (30° N) (Vita-Finzi, 1976). This interpretation of the data originally led to some debate with those who favoured a primarily anthropogenic origin (Eisma, 1964; Davidson, 1980; van Andel *et al.*, 1986 and Wagstaff, 1981), partly on the basis of observations of peak deposition just after the break-up of the Roman Empire, when it is known that agricultural decline took place and terraces commonly fell into disrepair. It was also pointed out that the diachrony of the Younger Fill is probably the result of the complex response of alluviation to climatic change and land use history. The Younger Fill is, in reality, a complex unit or units and need not have the same primary cause in every location. Work in the Voidomatis basin, Epirus, in northern Greece has shown how much more complex the fill sequence is than a simple bipartite division. This basin, in which is located the Klithi rock shelter, contains four terraces (Figure 7.9), distinguishable using lithological and mineralogical techniques. One of these terraces can be directly related to glacial deposits in the headwaters (Bailey *et al.*, 1990). Major episodes of aggradation occurred before 150,000 bp, *c.* 26,000–20,000 bp and *c.* 20,000–15,000 bp; and the lowest seems to have been related to overgrazing some time around the eleventh century (Lewin *et al.*, 1991). On the basis of this and other work in Greece (Pope and van Andel, 1984), Lewin *et al.* (1991) question the validity and utility of the 'Older and Younger Fill' model.

There is little doubt that the original Older Fill/Younger Fill model is in need of refinement. This is now possible because of advances in dating techniques, particularly luminescence and palaeomagnetic methods and provenancing techniques. More systematic surveys are required at the regional scale, where the degree of diachrony/synchrony can be assessed basin to basin and within basins, related to both detailed archaeological surveys and independent indicators of climate change.

One suitable region is that of central Italy, the location of some of the initial observations of Holocene alluviation (Judson, 1963; Vita-Finzi and Judson, 1964; see Figure 7.10). The volcanics of central Italy provide an excellent marker horizon, capping the gravels and lacustrine deposits of the palaeo-Tiber

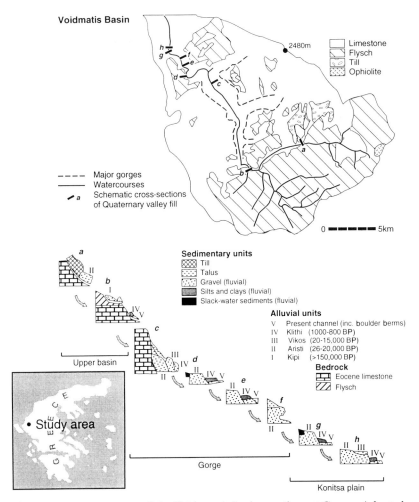

Fig. 7.9 Terrace sequence of the Voidomatis basin, north-west Greece. Adapted from Lewin *et al.*, 1991.

and blanketing the Tertiary–Pleistocene landscape through which the drainage net was established in the Late Pleistocene and Holocene. The tuffs are of variable age, but in places are as late as *c.* 30,000 bp (Locardi *et al.*, 1976). From sites at La Crescenzo and the Valchetta valley near Veio, Judson (1963) reports a single phase of alluviation between the Late Roman and medieval periods, whereas more complex sequences in Sicily suggest alluviation between the eighth and third centuries BC and, after a period of erosion, renewed alluviation in the medieval period. A detailed picture of alluviation at one site has been provided by geoarchaeological work at the Faliscan site of Narce (Potter, 1976b). Trenches in the lower terrace/floodplain of the river Treia revealed a complex stratigraphy of interbedded gravel lag, riffle, pool, bank and overbank

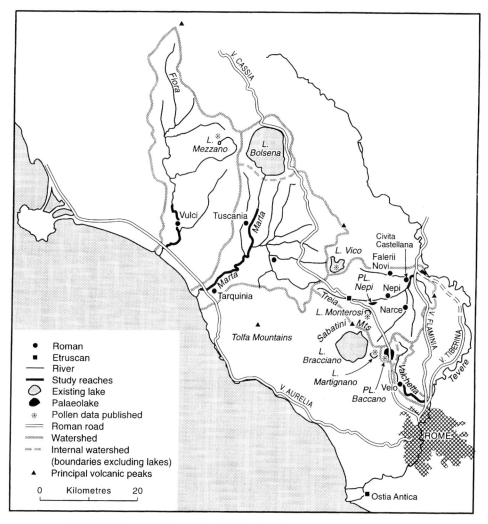

Fig. 7.10 A map of central Italy showing rivers and sites mentioned in the text.

sediments. Because the trenches traversed the majority of the floodplain width and contained abundant archaeological material, it was possible for Cherkauer (in Potter, 1976a) to trace the migrating thalweg, both horizontally and vertically (Figure 7.11). The sequence indicates deposition (undated) prior to 200 BC, a phase of erosion 200 BC to AD 200, deposition AD 200 to 800, minor erosion AD 800 to 1000 and then deposition until AD 1800 when incision began. This sequence has been regarded as consistent with other evidence in Italy and global climate change (Potter, 1976b). Mediterranean rivers in their upper-middle reaches of young valleys naturally transport considerable quantities of bedload and are quite prone to changes in bed elevation, relative to the height of the surface of the alluvial floodplain or terrace. Periods of rapid

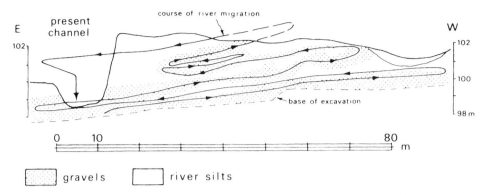

Fig. 7.11 The alluvial cross-section at Narce, Etruria, Italy, and its interpretation. From Cherkauer in Potter (1976a), by permission of *World Archaeology*.

migration and erosion of older terrace material will produce an episodic record, relating to local factors such as gradient, valley width, sediment supply and flood history. Owing to a combination of steep gradients and constrained width (both partly the result of the geological youth of the drainage network) and the Mediterranean climate, valley history is characterised by aggradation and erosion cycles, producing cut and fill stratigraphy (Brunsden and Thornes, 1979; Delano-Smith, 1981).

It is the last of these cycles that forms the Younger Fill, with evidence of earlier cycles either having been removed by erosion or being invisible beneath the floodplain watertable. Studies of the stratigraphy of the lower reaches of valleys are more likely to preserve evidence of changes in the sediment budget of catchments in earlier periods, as indicated by the rapid regression of river mouths that so adversely affected so many Roman ports, including Ostia Antica (Rome's ancient port) and Luni in Liguria (Ward-Perkins *et al.,* 1986). Studies in Foggia, southern Italy, also show downstream evidence of Iron Age downcutting and Roman aggradation, whilst upper reaches do not (Delano-Smith; 1981, Figure 7.12).

Work in the lower reaches of the Marta, Treia and other smaller valleys in Etruria all show considerable channel migration in the Roman period and vertical alluviation in the medieval and post-medieval periods (especially the Renaissance), but considerable variations in the rates of this alluviation (Figure 7.13, Plates 7.5 and 7.6). Whilst the fills of the lower reaches of the valleys in the north of the region are dominated by coarse channel sediments, similar sediments have been buried by several metres of vertically accreted silts in the southern valleys, most of it post-medieval in age. This may be related to intensification of agriculture around Rome in the Renaissance, combined with a period of frequent storms, as registered in the flood records of both the Tiber and the Arno (D'Onofrio, 1980). The alluvial record from middle and lower valley reaches, whether climatically or anthropogenically driven, can be related

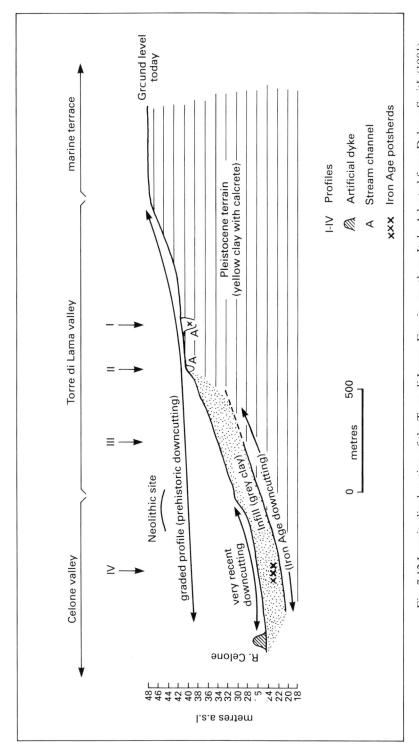

Fig. 7.12 Longitudinal section of the Torre di Lama, Foggia, southern Italy. Adapted from Delano-Smith (1981).

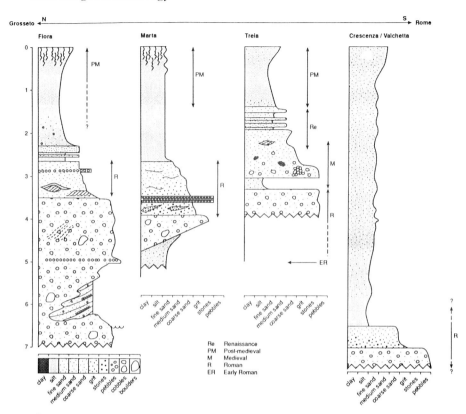

Fig. 7.13 Generalised average floodplain logs from the lower reaches of five valleys in southern Etruria, Italy. For location of the valley reaches, see Figure 7.10.

to changes in catchment vegetation. Central Italy is unusually suitable in this respect, because of a number of existing and drained crater lakes, from which pollen sequences have been derived. Lakes Martignano, Vico, Monterosi and Baccano all show an accelerated rate of vegetation change in the last 2500 years (Kelly and Huntley, 1991; Frank, 1968; Hutchinson, 1970; Bonatti, 1963). The sequences do, however, vary considerably in both the dominant species recorded and their history, at least in part because of local factors, such as altitude and soils.

Lake Monterosi has a small catchment but exhibits an increase in sedimentation and water depth and a change in water chemistry during the Roman period. This event correlates well with the construction of the Via Cassia in 171 BC and villa construction around the lake. There is also an increase in weeds of disturbed ground (e.g. *Urticaceae* and *Chenopodiaceae*) in the Late Roman period, suggesting less intensive cultivation or even abandonment of agricultural land. The Lake Martignano pollen profile shows important fluctuations of both mesophyllous and sclerophyllous trees, owing to climate change prior to human impact. In the last 2500 years, there is an accelerated

Plate 7.5 A typical `Younger Fill' type alluvial unit from the Marta valley, near Tarquinia in southern Etruria, Italy. The section grades up from a gravel basal unit to a banded sandy silt. The top metre covers post-medieval ridge and furrow and the whole section is post-Roman.

Plate 7.6 A 4 m accumulation of banded sand and silt adjacent to and partly burying a Roman structure. The structure is believed to be the viaduct built to carry the Via Tiburina over the river Treia, southern Etruria.

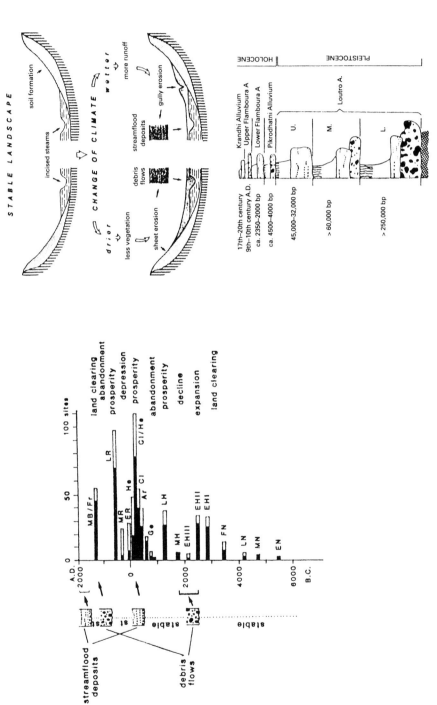

Fig. 7.14 The history of alluviation, vegetation and culture in the southern Argolid, Greece, over the last 5000 years. Inset, a composite alluvial sequence. Reproduced from Pope and van Andel (1984) and van Andel et al. (1986).

fall in the mesophyllous trees with the sclerophyllous component remaining approximately constant. A notable feature of several of these lake diagrams is a period of woodland regeneration some time, probably late, in the second millennium BC. Documentary evidence attests to the fact that much of southern Etruria was still wooded in the second millennium BC (Ward-Perkins, 1962).

Geomorphological work on the rivers draining the eastern slopes of the central Apennines, Marche region, has set Holocene fluvial activity into a Pleistocene framework. In the Upper Esino basin, there have been thirteen fluvial phases from the last Interglacial to the present (Calderoni *et al.*, 1991). Again, we see in the Holocene a difference in coastal and upper-middle valley reaches, related not to sea level or tectonic factors but to basin sediment output and the pattern of alluvial activity. The Musone river deposited a beach-barrier in the Bronze and Iron Ages, behind which sedimentation continued up until medieval times (Coltorti *et al.*, 1991). Coastal recession due to fluvial deposition is also seen in the Misa and Cesano rivers (Coltorti, 1991). Sections of these rivers were meandering in the Early Holocene to Roman periods, but then became braided, owing to an increase in sediment load (Coltorti, 1991). This transition is, however, diachronous by as much as 1000 years between one basin and another in the region. These and other intra-regional variations are most easily explained by catchment factors overriding or greatly modifying any climatic signal – in these cases an increase in sediment supply from spatially non-uniform deforestation in the Bronze and Iron Ages, and again in the Renaissance. Work in the Bifferno valley, in the region of Molise, has combined archaeological survey with studies of the alluvial sediments. Barker and Hunt (1994) identify eight valley floors (floodplain surfaces), all of which correspond to periods of significant intensification in settlement forms and land use from the late prehistoric to post-medieval.

A regional scale approach to alluviation and land use history in the southern Argolid, Greece, has provided a complex but unusually complete picture for the Late Pleistocene and Holocene. Pope and van Andel (1984) have identified eight alluvial units separated by periods of stability and soil formation. Three of these pre-date 6000 BC and, although they are of climatic origin, do not correspond to north European terrace chronology, as none date to the last glacial maxima or the Lateglacial. Neither do any date to the Early Holocene – a period of postulated monsoonal intrusions into the Aegean (Kutzbach, 1981). The units are most probably associated with warmer wetter periods, with little geomorphological activity during the colder steppe-climate periods corresponding to the northern hemisphere glaciations. Post 2000 BC, van Andel *et al.* (1986a; 1990) equate alluvial episodes with cultural change, in particular periods of economic decline and a lack of terrace maintenance and soil conservation measures (particularly in the Early Bronze Age and Late Classical to Hellenistic times, Figure 7.14). In the Southern Argolid and most of the Mediterranean, a distinction can be drawn between poorly sorted, matrix-supported, unstructured debris flow deposits and better supported lenticular alluvial units. The debris flows are ascribed by van Andel *et al.* (1986a) to periods of drier climate and less vegetation or extensive hillslope clearance, whilst they ascribe the alluvial units to wetter conditions or the neglect of terraces, producing gully erosion and concentrated runoff. The Argolid study illustrates how the complexity of both cultural and natural factors, and the interactions between them, may produce an environmental history lacking a one-to-one match with either set of controls.

Because the Mediterranean is a zone susceptible to erosion, because of high erosivities, erodibilities and tectonic activity, it needs only a small push for positive feedback mechanisms to lead to severe soil erosion. This has happened further back in the past before the major anthropogenic impact, as revealed by the realisation that the badlands of the Tabernas area in southern Spain pre-date the Bronze Age archaeological landscape (Thornes and Gilman, 1983). There is, however, little doubt that the documented human manipulation and management of the Mediterranean flora and the development of agriculture (Pons and Quezel, 1985) have had major effects on soil erosion, by increasing soil erodibility, making even small variations in climate important in transporting this soil in pulses down-valley, and in the subsequent trenching of these deposits. The cultural factor is equally variable, not only because of population and technological changes, but also because of economic factors influencing the construction, maintenance or abandonment of terraces and the clearance of scrub and woodland. More detailed sedimentological work and intra-unit dating is required, but it does seem that the variability of the Younger Fill(s) probably reflects the coincidence between high sediment availability, caused by post-Roman changes in land use, with a climate of variable erosivity. The problems of differentiating the human signal from the climatic signal are discussed further in section 7.6.

7.5 The North American experience

The European colonisation of North America led to profound changes in the physical environment, largely as a result of a sudden wave-like replacement of existing woodlands by arable and pastoral agriculture. Studies of the effects of this land use change have been greatly assisted by the existence of surveys of vegetation and rivers at the time of European settlement. These land use changes led to major changes in rivers and floodplains, which can be used, with caution, as a proxy-analogue of events and processes that operated much earlier in the prehistory of the Old World. However, before looking at the North American experience, it must be remembered that there are significant differences between it and possible Old World scenarios. These are listed below:

1   The land use change in North America was many times more rapid than it was in the Old World.
2   Although we really know very little about the spatial pattern of land use change in European prehistory, it was probably far more patchy

and fragmentary than the changes in North America, and it definitely included major episodes of woodland regeneration.

3 The methods of deforestation used were different, and this factor is known to affect sediment yield.

4 The subsequent agricultural systems were technologically very different.

5 The climatic environment cannot be assumed to have been the same; indeed, we know it was not.

However, with these provisos in mind, the North American experience does throw considerable light on the processes and mechanisms of fluvial response to land use change. Knox (1977) has shown that rapid land use change between 1833 and 1940, in the Platte River watershed in Wisconsin, caused a 300–500% increase in the magnitude of floods, with a recurrence interval of once in five or more years. It also caused major channel metamorphosis throughout the system, which, in this case, took the form of widening and shallowing in upland bedload streams and the opposite in downstream mixed and suspended load channels. Survey data, collected by Happ in the early days of the United States Soil Conservation Service (Happ *et al.*, 1940), was used by Trimble (1981) to examine changes in the sediment budget of Coon Creek, also in Wisconsin, over the period 1853 to 1975. The budgets for the periods 1853–1938 and 1938–75, as shown in Figure 7.15, indicate that the vast majority of eroded sediment went into floodplain and colluvial storage, some of which is now being remobilised, thereby increasing the unit sediment yield well after the peak of soil erosion in the catchment. Trimble and Lund (1982) used the Universal Soil Loss Equation (USLE) to estimate catchment erosion and, along with sediment yield estimates derived from floodplain storage, were able to plot a hysteresis loop, illustrating the storage lag for the catchment (see Figure 7.15). Knox (1991) has shown how these culturally accelerated accumulation rates are affected by the differing hydroclimatic controls on catchments of different sizes, including the relative contribution of anomalously large floods. As stated earlier, these studies cannot be used uncritically as scenarios for the European experience in prehistory for several reasons, but they do highlight several important processes which may have been equally important in both contexts including:

1 varied channel response depending upon the nature of the channel, including morphology, stream power and sediment load;

2 the importance of both hydrological and sedimentary changes;

3 the movement of sediment short distances, to slope bases, upstream sediment stores and alluvial fans;

4 significant lags between land-use change and maximum sediment yield;

5 implied temporal and spatial changes in the sediment delivery ratio caused by storage of sediment within the floodplain system.

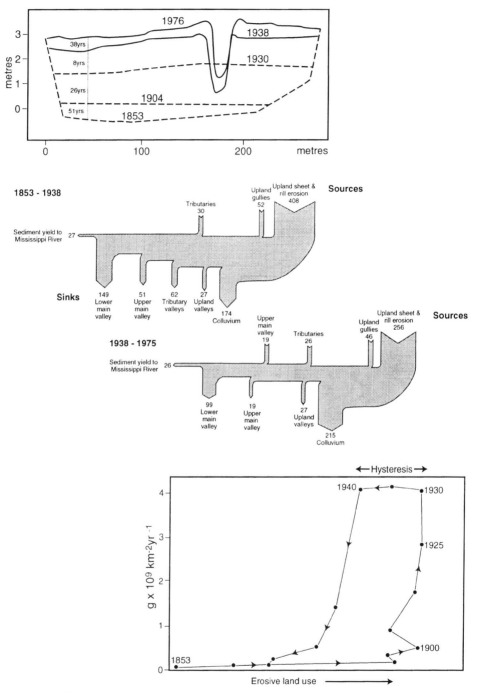

Fig. 7.15 Sediment budget studies in Coon Creek, Wisconsin: (top) a representative cross-sectional profile, (centre) the sediment budgets for the periods 1853–1938 and 1938–75 and (bottom) a hysteresis loop of estimated erosion against floodplain sedimentation. All adapted from Trimble (1983), by permission of *American Journal of Science*.

Some of these effects have been demonstrated for European rivers, in particular the lagged response (Brown and Barber, 1985) and the occurrence of both hydrological and sedimentary changes (Robinson and Lambrick, 1984). However, although the effect of most consequence to geoarchaeological studies of floodplains is the first (varied response), it remains difficult to investigate, because of the limitations of the stratigraphic record and our inability to reconstruct channel dimensions accurately from contexts other than perfectly preserved palaeochannels.

7.6 The role of climatic change

In reality, the recurrent question as to whether the changes outlined in this and the previous chapter were caused by human activity *or* climatic change is misleading, since all human activities take place within a climatic context and it is climatic events which transport sediment. The question should be rephrased as: what is the relative importance of climatic change or land use change during any particular period and can it be detected from the alluvial record? In order to investigate the role of climatic change, we need independent evidence of it. Fortunately, there are several sources of palaeoclimatic data available in later prehistory and the historical period, including dendroclimatology, written records, and the fluctuations of glaciers. Another data source is changes in peat humification recorded in raised peat bogs. Since raised peat bogs are only fed by rainfall and are sensitive to changes in climate, they can provide a truly independent record.

Barber (1981; 1982) has constructed a bog wetness curve for the last 2000 years, based on humification studies of Bolton Fell Moss in north-west Britain and this has been transformed using general linear modelling into a proxy climate record which for the recent period is highly correlated with known climatic change (Barber *et al.*, 1994). Shifts of the bog surface to pools, reflecting wet periods, occurred in AD 900–1100, 1300–1500 and 1740–1800. An alternative method of independent climatic reconstruction at the appropriate scale is dendroclimatology (see section 4.8 and chapter 10).

As yet, there have been few attempts to correlate these independent measures with pseudo-continuous alluvial variables, such as overbank accretion rates. Some authors have tried to link the regional pattern of alluviation to global climatic discontinuities (Potter, 1976b; Macklin and Lewin, 1993). There are several problems which need to be overcome here. The first is that, without some form of statistical evaluation of the data, false patterns may easily be identified and false correlations postulated. Secondly, temporal coincidence does not necessarily imply a common causality. Both these points are especially important, given the relatively poor dating accuracy and precision of alluvial units. Lastly, the climatic data used may not be entirely independent. The climatic discontinuities identified by Wendland and Bryson (1974), in all eleven (or more depending upon the data and criteria used), came from geological–botanical radiocarbon dates (including alluvial units) and 'cultural' radiocarbon dates, neither of which are truly independent or direct evidence of climatic change. Indeed, it is not entirely clear what the discontinuities really represent, although they do show some relationship to the traditional sequence of Holocene climatic change which formed the basis of the Blytt-Sernander climatic division of the Holocene.

For these reasons and the complexity of the Old World alluvial record, the search for correlations with so-called climatic discontinuities must be viewed with caution. This is not to say that we cannot expect to see climatic signals in the European alluvial data, but that we should expect them to be far less clear than those identified from the North American alluvial record by Knox (1983). However, in general, the considerable evidence of channel stability, and a relative lack of alluviation in the period 8000–5000 bp, does seem to be common both in Europe and in North America. Also, there is considerable independent evidence of significant hydrological changes across Europe around 2600–2300 bp (the Bronze Age/Iron Age transition in Britain). However, this is not mirrored in North America, where 2000–1800 bp is the nearest climatically induced fluvial phase identified by Knox (1983). The closest climatic discontinuity identified by Wendland and Bryson (1974) is at 2760 bp. This again highlights the problem with the methodology. Considering the number and duration of the climatic and alluvial discontinuities, it may be statistically improbable for them not to overlap, even if they were truly independent. However, the question as to the relative role of climatic changes remains important and the most fruitful avenues for future research lie in the identification of hydrological changes not inferred from alluviation (such as raised watertables and independent flood series changes derived from biological systems). These data can be compared with the results of catchment models, where both vegetation and climatic inputs can be varied, in an attempt to predict the mix of changes in catchment characteristics that was most probably the cause of the observed outcome.

With the historical period, there are more independent climatic data. There is, for example, ample evidence of the fifteenth- to nineteenth-century climatic deterioration in Europe called the Little Ice Age (Lamb, 1982; Grove, 1988). Indeed, it is known to have had direct effects on rivers, largely through freezing, as shown by records of Ice Fairs on the Thames (Lamb, 1982) and from flow records from the Severn (Brown, 1983a). It did not, however, produce significant channel changes in either case, nor is there any evidence that it affected alluviation. There are, however, some data to suggest that it may have been related to alluviation in upland Britain (Lewin *et al.*, 1991) and this is probably because it was primarily a thermal climatic event and would, therefore, have had maximum effect upon those catchments with the greatest relative contribution from snowmelt. This reminds us that the form of climatic change is important, that small changes in magnitude and frequency may be just as important as longer-term aggregate changes and that the effect of these changes will vary spatially because of differing climatic sensitivity of catchments.

That there is a climatic component in the alluvial record cannot be doubted, but further advances will only come from differentiating those changes that are primarily a response to increased sediment availability from those that are related to changes in the magnitude and frequency of transporting events. In this context, geoarchaeological work on soil erosion, colluvium and alluvial sediment stores is of great significance and potential (Bell and Boardman, 1992). However, archaeologists must remember that climatic events are responsible for the transport and redistribution of sediment which may or may not be produced by human land use changes; thus, in reality, the anthropogenic and climatic records can never be regarded as being truly independent of one another.

8

MANAGED FLOODPLAINS

The almost imperceptible shift from the opportunistic utilisation of resources to the management and control of those resources is composed of many human innovations. Alluvial environments can be seen as one of the key environments for innovations including: irrigation, river, road and bridge engineering, and drainage. Of these, irrigation is generally regarded as being both the earliest and the most important in socioeconomic and political terms. While this is not the place to cover the history of irrigation, drainage or river training (see Biswas, 1970; Purseglove, 1989; Sheail, 1988), the relationship between flood-plain exploitation and management is highly relevant to alluvial sites, and so will be considered here.

8.1 Flood farming and irrigation

The origins of irrigation are generally associated with the civilisations of the great alluvial valleys of Mesopotamia (Tigris and Euphrates), Egypt (Nile), India (Indus) and China (Hwang-Ho). These societies, which are associated with distinctively hierarchical modes of production, transformed their physical environments by the control of water. In the Euphrates valley, the control of water levels – high enough for seed germination but low enough to avoid damage – has its origins in floodwater farming during the Neolithic. A site at the edge of the floodplain at Chogi Mami, dated to 7500 bp, provides probably the earliest evidence of irrigation canals (Roberts, 1989). Later occupation of the floodplain (6500 bp) took place on levées and allowed the abstraction of water through the levées down onto the flood basins, the edges of which could be used for crops. From this manipulation of a natural process over time, channels were straightened or created from scratch. One of the problems associated with this form of irrigation was salinisation, a problem which became increasingly serious, and forced crop changes later in the Dynastic period (Jacobsen, 1982). The fact that this irrigation system was based upon a centrally organised and codified system of regulation is clear; however, the Wittfogel model (Wittfogel, 1957), which proposes that it was the need to control the distribution of water that produced this form of social organisation, can be criticised on the grounds that it puts the cart before the horse. Similar environmental conditions existed elsewhere in the semi-arid zone, even in the fertile crescent, but so-called hydraulic civilisations did not appear. Therefore it seems likely that it was a sociocultural climate favourable for a centralised and highly

254

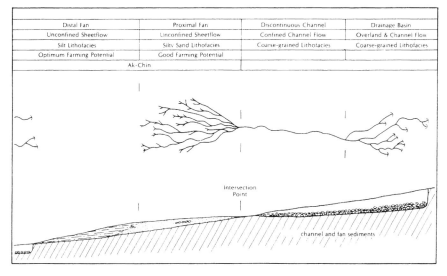

Distal Fan	Proximal Fan	Discontinuous Channel	Drainage Basin
Unconfined Sheetflow	Unconfined Sheetflow	Confined Channel Flow	Overland & Channel Flow
Silt Lithofacies	Silty Sand Lithofacies	Coarse-grained Lithofacies	Coarse-grained Lithofacies
Optimum Farming Potential	Good Farming Potential		

Fig. 8.1 The alluvial fan, discontinuous channel system and optimum location for Ak-Chin farming. From Waters and Field (1986), reproduced by permission of *Geoarchaeology*.

organised social system that may have allowed the potential of the environment to be exploited initially, whence, no doubt, technological, social and political changes occurred together.

In most valleys, centralised irrigation systems did not evolve, and flood farming remained the norm. The nilotic agriculture of Egypt was a natural flood-basin system (Butzer, 1976) with local water administration. Flood farming was also practised in the North American Southwest. An example is the use of ephemeral drainage systems by aboriginal peoples on the flanks of the Tortolita mountains, Arizona (Waters and Field, 1986). Crops were planted by the Pima, Papago and Hopi Indians on alluvial fans, at the point where the flow becomes unconfined and spreads out across the fan surface. This is called 'Ak-Chin' farming, from a Papago word for the mouth of an arroyo. It is a precarious form of farming as it depends upon adequate rainfall to produce floods and a location where seed and plants will not be washed out or buried by sediment. In this respect, the distal fan is best (see Figure 8.1), because of the higher moisture-holding capacity of the fine sand and silt sediment (Foged, 1975). Ak-Chin fields were regularly abandoned as a result of fan-head entrenchment. Waters and Field (1986) suggest there is a correlation between the Late Period Hohokam settlements and optimal floodwater farming areas especially on the smaller alluvial fans. A detailed description of the Ak-Chin system, its geomorphic setting and related ethnographic studies has been presented by Nabhan (1986a,1986b).

Flood farming technologies were also common in North Africa from the

Neolithic onwards. In Tripolitania, north Libya, structures for water control (e.g. low walls) were built and used from the first to fourth centuries AD (Barker and Jones, 1982). There have even been attempts to revive the practice (Gale and Hunt, 1986). Gale and Hunt have estimated total runoff and maximum discharge from floodwater systems using the Darcy-Weisbach equation (see chapter 3 and appendices) and an equation for estimating roughness for turbulent flow in rough channels. One problem with these calculations is that relatively small changes in storm frequency would have produced large variations in the usable potential yield, making it difficult to have much confidence in estimated input parameters.

An even more opportunistic irrigation system is that employed by the Owen's valley Paiute who diverted streams to water patches of self-propagating wild plants (Steward, 1929). Sherratt (1980) has suggested that similar practices may have been employed in the early phases of occupation of sites like Jericho, and Vita-Finzi (1969) has pointed out that suitable conditions existed for flood farming in parts of Jordan in the Early Holocene. The successful management of floodwater farming systems implies sophisticated and long-term knowledge of rare events in the arid environment. As Gilbertson (1986) notes, more field surveys, field trials and experimental farms are needed to publicize floodwater farming; the same is true for our understanding of how the systems functioned in the past and how they related to the organisation of society.

8.2 Temperate flood-meadows

In the temperate maritime zone, irrigation is only really needed on droughty (generally sandy) soils and where drainage has over-lowered the watertable. A modern exception to this is horticulture which often does require irrigation, especially in rain-shadow areas such as eastern Britain. However, another form of irrigation, the control of flooding in order to add nutrient-rich sediment to floodplains, has been practised extensively in the temperate region, and has produced flood- or water-meadows, still quite common in Europe until recently. In such areas where flooding has been managed for irrigation or nutrients, warp soils are created. These soils can be found in many British floodplains, including the Lower Trent where they probably date from the eighteenth century (Bridges, 1973). Evidence of the maintenance of alluvial meadows, known from the archaeological and historical records, suggests the practice considerably pre-dates the eighteenth century and may extend back into the medieval period or even earlier. Flood-meadows generally consist of a network of shallow channels which distribute sediment-laden floodwater across the floodplain, starting before the river would have naturally gone overbank (by means of channels cut through the levées). This increases the rate of alluviation partly because the highest concentration of suspended sediment normally occurs on the rising limb of the hydrograph (Gregory and Walling, 1973). The accumulation rate of warp soils can be measured using radioisotopes and has been used to test models of soil nitrogen cycling (Sasscer *et al.*, 1971). Flood-meadows also develop rich and diagnostic floras because of the particular combination of abundant nutrients and water with cutting or grazing (Girel, 1994).

Managed water-meadows such as those on the river Frome in Dorset, were undoubtedly more widespread in England until as late as the Second World War (Dudley Stamp, 1948). The creation of mill leats may have had a very similar effect to flood channels, and the beneficial effects of flooding would have been realised well before flooding was controlled.

A variant of the managed flood-meadows – the floated water meadows – was a significant feature of the agricultural revolution in the Wessex chalk valleys in the seventeenth century (Cowan, 1982). Weirs were constructed to divert water into artificial channels to flood the meadows along the Wyle valley in 1635. They are really a form of irrigation network which formed part of the sheep and corn system. One meadow is still functioning today at Lower Woodford near Salisbury. The water enters the meadows along a raised major 'carriage' and is taken off into smaller carriages, then let down through gates and sluices onto the meadow. It flows across the meadow surface and converges into a system of drains and then into the main river again (Figure 8.2). This is, therefore, the combination of an irrigation and a drainage system designed to flush nutrients and silt onto the meadow, increasing its grazing quality. Archival work has shown that these or similar warping systems were widespread in Europe in the sixteenth to eighteenth centuries (Girel, 1994) and particularly well-preserved examples exist on the Seine, Moselle and Isère in France, the Po in Italy and the Upper Rhine in Switzerland. These systems demonstrate the vital link and similarity in form between irrigation and drainage networks, a link essential in the semi-arid zone if salinisation is to be prevented.

8.3 River management: from early obstructions to well-behaved rivers.

Early obstructions
It is probably impossible for us to know where and when the first permanent or fixed structures were placed in rivers, either with the aim of controlling water depth or for fishing. In the temperate environment, they could have easily been adapted opportunistically from fallen trees, log jams or beaver dams. Indeed early fishing techniques may have included ambushing fish at natural debris dams, especially during the migration of salmonids.

The manufacture of traps at Noyen-sur-Seine and the construction of wooden waterfronts from the Neolithic onwards illustrate that the technology was available for sophisticated structures, and if we presume fish formed a significant food source (probably underrepresented in archaeological data), it seems highly probable that weir-type structures were extensively used in later prehistory. However, the oldest definite weirs recorded from excavations in the

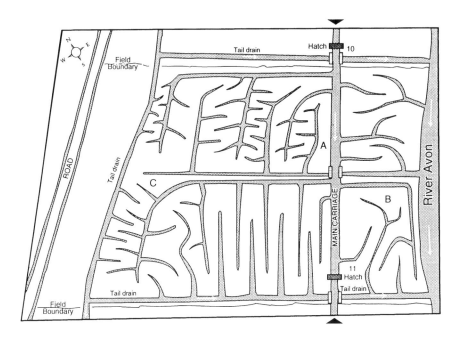

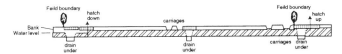

Fig. 8.2 Part of the floated meadow system at Lower Woodford in the Avon valley near Salisbury, England. Redrawn from Cowan (1982), by permission of the author.

British Isles are Anglo-Saxon, dating from the sixth and seventh centuries, although structures believed to be weirs are known that are of Neolithic age (Salisbury, pers. comm.). Excavations in the Middle Trent floodplain have revealed several of these weirs, which consist of a row of posts extending in a V-shape from the shallows, with wattle hurdles between the posts (Salisbury, 1981; Figure 8.3; Plate 8.1). These hurdle 'hedges' are a common fish-catching device known from many parts of the world (Van Brant, 1984). The Middle Trent has been unusually active for a lowland British river during the Holocene, depositing sand and gravel in shallow, actively migrating channels. Indeed, the Trent remained unnavigable in the dry season because of numerous shoals, until the turn of the eighteenth and nineteenth centuries and was one of the last rivers in England to be controlled (Petts, 1989). The mobile channel laid down sheets of gravel and this has facilitated the excavation of the weirs during gravel quarrying, but it is also likely that this river morphology made the reach a particularly favourable location for weir construction with shallow wadeable chan-

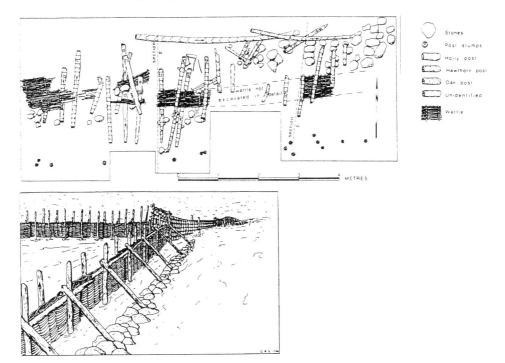

Fig 8.3 An excavated Saxon fish weir from Colwick in the Trent valley near
Nottingham, England (top) and a tentative reconstruction of it (below). Both
from Losco-Bradley and Salisbury (1988), by permission of the authors.

nels making it easy to drive the posts into the bed. These weirs have been tree-
ring dated, showing the expansion of the meander at Colwick, the channel
moving 200 m in a period of about sixty years (Losco-Bradley and Salisbury,
1988). Over sixty other weirs have been found in Britain and Ireland, with the
best-documented being on the river Severn in western Britain and on the river
Suir in Ireland. The Middle Severn was, and is, a relatively narrow and deep
channel, so weirs had to be more substantial, with timber braces and piles sup-
porting the wattle fence (Pannett, 1981; Figure 8.3).

Inevitably, these weirs caused a conflict of interest by hindering river navigation: Magna Carta in AD 1215 called for all inland weirs on the Thames and
Medway to be removed. Somewhat ironically the agreement was signed on a
small island in the Thames at Runnymede typical of those used for the construction of fish weirs (as the channels are narrow and shallow). Many such islands
were created for that purpose by digging a second channel at the point of a slight
inflection in the main channel. In 1392 the Lords of Colwick (Middle Trent) were
even prosecuted for obstructing the river with fish weirs (Losco-Bradley and
Salisbury, 1988). Alternatives were either to leave a gap, which was probably
more difficult in deeper channels, or to dig a bypass channel or 'barge-gutter'
around the weir. This was common on the Severn and resulted in many small

Plate 8.1 The remains of a medieval (Norman) fish weir excavated from the Trent valley at Colwick (photo: C. Salisbury).

and thin islands called bylets or eyots. These are not easy to distinguish from natural islands and islets but are generally rather more angular and less irregular. Pannett (1971) has identified the sites of sixteen of these medieval weirs upstream of the Ironbridge Gorge (Figure 8.4) and five more are known to have existed from documentary evidence. Many have remained visible (although the barge gutters may have silted up), because of the channel stability of the Severn during the Late Holocene; this is largely the result of its tall cohesive banks (Dury *et al.*, 1972; Brown, 1987a; Carling, 1991). In Ireland, some of these hedge and basket type weirs were still being used until very recently.

Water mills and channels

The other major river engineering works undertaken in the late prehistoric, Roman and medieval periods was the construction of mills and their associated mill ponds and leats. Mills were generally located either on gravel islands, at the edges of the floodplain or where tributaries joined the main river. A channel was dug from the main channel (if it was a large river), and taken down the floodplain at a very low fall (gradient), in order to generate a sufficient hydraulic head to power the mill wheel. The actual plan of the mill, weirs, leat and mill pond(s) was extremely variable, according to the size of the stream, capital investment and many other factors. Some mills were constructed on islands, others were on the main channel with underground bypass channels

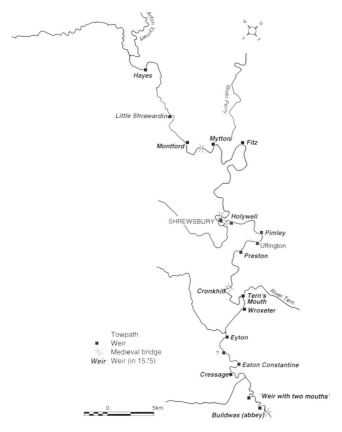

Fig. 8.4 A map of medieval fish weirs on the Middle Severn, England. Adapted from Pannett (1981).

and others were of the open bypass type (Figure 8.5). There is obviously an advantage to be derived from using a natural multi-channel reach or a natural island and this makes it very difficult to disentangle the effects of mills from the past occurrence of naturally anastomosing reaches. The capital available was important as is revealed by some of the monastic mills which had leats up to 3 km long. Because of the high capital cost of watermills, they were generally long-lived (Holt, 1988), so many Victorian mills sit on the site of Domesday mills. The leats and ponds had to be cleared out regularly, as they were very prone to siltation.

At Wharram Percy in Yorkshire, England, in the late Saxon and early medieval periods fish ponds were impounded by the construction of a series of clay dams and in one case the pond of a watermill disused in the thirteenth century was also converted into a fish pond (Beresford and Hurst, 1990). The dams were strengthened using wattle hurdling and a wide range of delicate arti- facts found preserved in the pond, including wooden shovel blades, leather

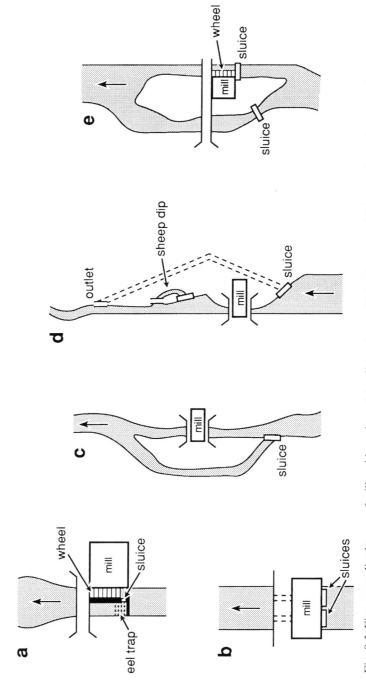

Fig. 8.5 Five generalised types of mill and leat plans: (a) collateral type, (b) bridge type with internal wheel, (c) island type, (d) subterranean type and (e) bypass type. Based partly on Vince (1987).

shoes, basketry and textiles. Pollen analysis of the sediments indicated that the surrounding area was completely cleared and under mixed arable agriculture. The dams were constantly repaired and rebuilt, together with the pond and channels which needed frequent clearing (Hurst, 1984), as was the case at Bordesley Abbey in Warwickshire, central England (Astill, 1993). This problem was undoubtedly exacerbated by the high suspended sediment loads during the thirteenth and fourteenth centuries, when more land in England was under the plough than today. The leats and ponds were often multi-purpose, an exceptional example being at Carmarthen in Wales, where a landowner was allowed to build a watermill only on condition that the leat be run around the town perimeter to act as a defensive barrier (James, 1980). More commonly, traps for eels and other fish were placed in leats and mill ponds. Although mills probably had most effect on smaller streams and rivers their effects on channel form and sedimentation rates have yet to be fully investigated. As the distribution map of the 6082 Domesday mills shows, there was hardly a reach of any lowland river in England that was not occupied by a mill (see Hodgen, 1939).

A surviving medieval floodplain
Since the intensification of agriculture began after the Second World War the vast majority of floodplains in Britain and North-West Europe have been drained or ploughed up and rivers have been channelised and embanked. The result is that survival of the form of a medieval floodplain is now extremely rare. However, in Central Europe such floodplains stiĺl exist. In southern Moravia, in the Czech Republic, there is a national wildlife reserve called the Litovelské Pomoraví. It covers about 90 km^2 of the floodplain of the Moravia river and is an ecologically rich mosaic of woodland, pasture and arable land bisected by cross-cutting channels (Figure 8.6). Some of the alder and oak woodland is known to be over 600 years old and alluvial woodland management has been practised continuously from the medieval period up until today (Klostan, 1992). The area is surrounded by medieval flood banks, as is the village of Strěn which was an island of pasture in the alluvial forest, isolated for at least a week each year by floods. Many of the channels were created as leats for mills and these have been left high and dry, while the main channel has incised, migrated and created cutoffs. Similarly, because of the rise of the floodplain, surface tributary channels have been culverted under leat channels, rather than follow the edge of the floodplain downstream, as would naturally happen. The result is a patchwork of areas with channels at different heights and of different types and an extremely rich aquatic-terrestrial system. The town of Litovel was the main centre for mills – channels remain running through the town square and seven of the mills have been converted into small hydroelectric power stations. The action of the small weirs in many ways mimics natural beaver dams, and Litovelské Pomoraví has been one of the sites for the reintroduction of beaver into Central Europe (Klostan, pers. comm.).

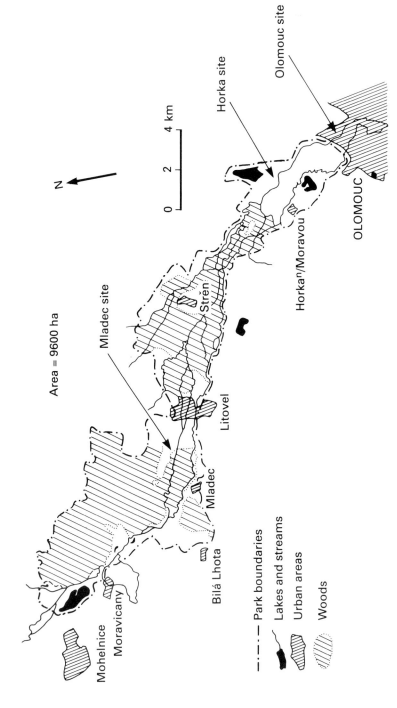

Fig. 8.6 A map of the floodplain reserve of Litovelské Pomoraví, Czech Republic. Adapted from Klostan (pers. comm.).

This medieval floodplain system perpetuated the biological diversity that had been created by beavers in the preceding natural system, largely through the creation of multiple channels with varying physical and chemical in-channel environments. In many other parts of Europe, the channel pattern remains but the essential component – the woodland – has gone. The re-afforestation of these floodplains has tremendous potential for the creation of rich ecosystems which may also act as natural purifiers in the drainage basin.

River channelisation and flood protection
By the seventeenth century, the need for water transport throughout Europe had led to major navigation works on most large rivers, including the construction of weirs, towpaths and jetties, with dredging, straightening and bank protection works. The North American experience is obviously rather different, with no management of large rivers prior to European colonisation. Thus, in the case of the Middle Mississippi, we see the conversion of a natural channel and floodplain system to a managed system completed in a period of just over 100 years (Stevens *et al.*, 1975). In the early nineteenth century, navigation on the river was extremely difficult and valley settlements were frequently flooded. The Federal Government was petitioned to provide adequate low flow depths, through the construction of a narrower navigation channel and of embankments to reduce flooding. First, snags such as debris (including many wrecks) and trees were removed and then between 1824 and 1881 private landowners constructed low embankments. Comprehensive improvement with Government funds took place between 1880 and 1907, and in 1927 the Corps of Engineers were authorised by Congress to create a navigation channel by the construction of dyke fields to reduce channel width. It is not surprising that this has only been partially successful, considering the great lateral mobility of the natural channel and its propensity to cut off meander loops. The floodplain has, as a result, been opened up for agriculture and urbanisation; as Figure 8.7 shows, a discharge of 36,816 m^{3}s^{-1} (1,300,000 cfs) can be accommodated in the channel, which previously would have inundated the floodplain.

The major navigational problem with British rivers was, in fact, not lateral stability but the shoaling and siltation of the bed (Bradley, 1948). Although the history of every river is different for both physical and economic reasons, the case of the Severn is not atypical of such works in the British Isles. In 1575, Acts of Parliament facilitated the 'cleansing' of parts of the Severn by the Commissioners of Sewers. This would have aided navigation to some extent, although lack of depth over shoals was the main problem. Around 1727, Thomas Harrison recorded all the shoals between Stourport and Gloucester (Figure 8.8; Williams, 1846, 1860). All except four were reidentified by Richardson (1964). The locations of these shoals correlate well with the locations of fords and ferries, suggesting the latter originated from the former. This

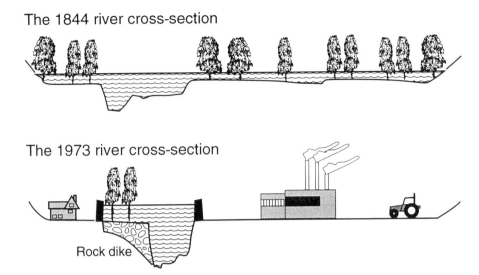

Fig. 8.7 A generalised 1944 and 1973 cross-section across the Middle Mississippi floodplain with the maximum containable flood in 1973. Adapted from Stevens *et al.* (1975).

situation led to demands for channel 'improvements'. In the seventeenth century Andrew Yarrenton contemplated the partial canalisation of the Severn, and partially canalised a small tributary (Dick Brook), installing a lock at its junction with the Severn (Smith, 1974). In 1784, William Jessop surveyed the river from Coalbrookdale to Gloucester. He proposed dredging to maintain a depth of 4 ft (1.2 m) below Worcester. Although the scheme was never implemented, some early river training was tried; timber-framed jetties filled with stones were placed above some shoals, which, by contracting the width and increasing velocities, 'enabled it [the Severn] to wash away the gravel which occasioned the shallows' (Williams, 1860). Unfortunately, the structures caused inconvenience to navigation and so their removal was ordered. In the late eighteenth century, towpaths were improved, some of which had been constructed prior to the sixteenth century. Calls for canalisation of the river in the late eighteenth century were a result both of the industrial revolution – a major centre of which was on the banks of the river around Ironbridge – and the associated period of 'canal mania' (Hadfield, 1979). Telford surveyed parts of the river in 1800 and ordered the monitoring of river levels at Coalport. He was concerned at the piecemeal nature of the embankments and the lack of provision of flood storage (Plymley, 1803). Telford's embankment, called the 'argy', was deliberately set back from the river to provide this storage. He also proposed locks and weirs to aid navigation, supply water power and aid abstraction. During the nineteenth century, this canalisation was completed, made possible by a series of Acts of Parliament (1842, 1853, 1870, 1890) and despite

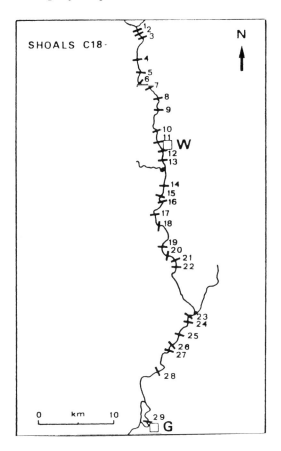

Fig. 8.8 A map of the eighteenth-century shoals in the river Severn between
Gloucester and Stourport, England. G is Gloucester and W Worcester.
Constructed from data collected by Harrison reported in Richardson (1964).

local opposition. It involved not only the construction of oblique weirs
(designed by Leeder Williams supposedly to attenuate the flood hydrograph),
but also revetting and mattressing, bed armouring (by dropping stones and
even stone-laden barges), cutting off some tight meanders, dredging and even
the blasting of some solid riffles. Since the nineteenth century, there has been
a concern for the maintenance of adequate depths in the face of siltation problems and the construction of several flood relief schemes which have involved
increasing the height of embankments and the provision of some areas for spill
storage.

Sheail (1988) points out that the regulation of British rivers has always been
a matter of public concern and the management of very few other natural
resources has been subjected to as much public scrutiny. Attempts to reach con-
sensus and accept the multipurpose nature of the resource have generally

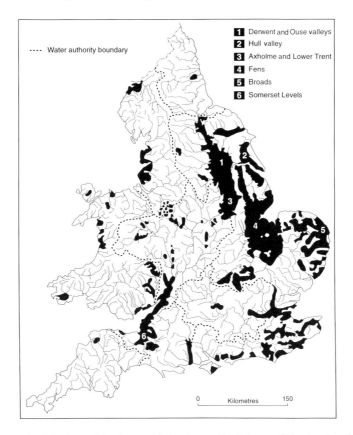

Fig. 8.9 A combined map of the channelised rivers of England and areas of predominantly wetland prior to this century. Various sources, including Brookes *et al.* (1988).

triumphed over conflicting interests. However, the vast majority of British rivers have now been canalised or channelised, with profound effects upon their dynamic behaviour and ecology and therefore also their floodplains (Figure 8.9; Brookes, 1988).

8.4 Land drainage

On the wet low-lying North-West European seaboard, the drainage of excess waters has been attempted over 2000 years. There is, of course, a classical record of drainage and reclamation which extends back to at least the late second millennium BC, when Lake Copais in Boeotia, Greece, was drained with canals and dykes by the Myceneans (Potter, 1981). The lake was formed in a polje (which is a structural basin in limestone) and embanked dykes discharged into natural swallow-holes; but these became blocked and a tunnel had to be constructed. The southern Po valley was an area of extensive and successful Roman reclamation, and other areas included parts of Rome itself, the

Pontine Marshes, Lake Baccano, the valle di Castiglioni and Tavoliere near Lucera. Settlements on the reclaimed areas were linked by drainage canals and the land was subject to systematic division by centuration. Essential to these works was engineering expertise in the construction of dams and sluices, although the use of the lock was unknown.

We cannot satisfactorily separate river engineering and drainage, as they are often closely connected, both functionally and legally. For example, it was a common accusation that fish weirs and other river obstructions were the cause of a perceived increase in flooding. Even the Roman Senate was very reluctant to build flood abatement works in the cities of Florence, Terni and Rieti (Potter, 1981) through fear of aggravating the situation. Where multiple bifurcating and cross-connected channel systems existed, they were converted into one- or two-channel systems in order to facilitate the evacuation of floodwaters and make the construction of river crossings cheaper. This also happened inadvertently because of the siltation of side-arms, often assisted by the habit of using them as dumps, especially in towns. On the river Trent, groynes were constructed to concentrate the flow (i.e. the thalweg and higher-velocity water) into only one channel, leaving the other to 'warp', i.e. fill with silt and clay (Salisbury, 1992). The earliest evidence of land drainage in the British Isles is, as has already been mentioned, from the Iron Age at Fengate, where drains consisting of brush-wood bundles were discovered by Pryor (1984). It seems that only the occupation site was drained and the drainage could not prevent the site from increased flooding towards the end of its occupation history. The evidence at Fengate does suggest that the drainage of the floodplain site was a response to a flood problem, a technical innovation that would probably have proved more successful at sites other than Fengate.

The first evidence of extensive drainage in Britain is from the Roman period. The Roman expertise in water control for irrigation derived from techniques practised by the Greeks and Etruscans. The best-known example of Roman drainage in Britain is the Car Dyke, draining part of the Fens, which was built by Hadrian in the second century AD. It was a catch-water designed to collect runoff from upland slopes at the edge of the Fens. Although the other Roman canals are not dated, there does seem to have been an expansion of settlement between 125 and 150 AD (Phillips, 1970), although this may also have been related to natural drying out. There was then freshwater flooding in the third century AD and drastic marine flooding in the fifth century (the so-called Romano-British transgression) which temporarily terminated occupation in the Fens.

A similar history, including the fifth century flooding, characterises the Somerset Levels in south-west England (Williams, 1971). With the decline of the Roman Empire, land drainage and reclamation became more piecemeal and it is not until the thirteenth and fourteenth centuries that major works are undertaken, funded and executed by the Church. The marshes around many great abbeys, including Glastonbury in the Somerset Levels and Ely in the Fens, were drained by the monks to provide high-quality grazing land for sheep. The drainage of these valleys and fenlands helped sustain the power and wealth of the Church up until the Reformation. Also, during the Middle Ages, land drainage, water abstraction and fishing were increasingly regulated and codified by water bailiffs and Commissioners of Sewers who reported to the government; later Courts of Sewers administered an increasing volume of legislation concerning land drainage. After the dissolution of the monasteries, the Church's role in land drainage and reclamation was replaced by propagandists who saw the profits to be made from grazing and arable farming on the flat and fertile reclaimed soils. The process of large-scale reclamation began again under Elizabeth I and continued under the Stuarts, with foreign expertise, especially from the Netherlands. The most famous of these was Cornelius Vermuyden, responsible for the main arterial drainage system of the Fens in East Anglia. The result was, within a couple of hundred years, the drainage of all of the large fens and river valleys in England. From the seventeenth century onwards, drainage was a business; a combination of engineering expertise with capital, as it has remained to this day, even if the capital is in the form of subsidies. The drainage of wetlands has left a rural industrial landscape with the remains of wind-pumps, pump-houses, drains, sluices and embankments. It has also caused the lowering of peaty fenlands through peat wastage. The best example is in the East Anglian Fens at Holme Fen where the ground surface has been lowered by 3.87 m since 1848 (see Plate 8.2; Hutchinson, 1980). It is now the lowest point in Britain, at –2.75 m OD, and the potential threat of sea flooding has increased, leading to the treadmill of drainage, increased sea protection, increased shrinkage, increased sea protection – an environmental situation worsened by the possibility of sea level rise, associated with the effects of global warming on the Earth's climate.

8.5 The reconstruction of historical flood magnitude and frequency

Probably the most obvious method of reconstructing past hydrological and climatic conditions is from written records, or flood marks, of floods and drought, as used in the introduction to this book. These records are relatively common because of the economic and social impact of floods and droughts, and probably the easiest extreme event to quantify is the height of a flood. The recording of flood heights is common to many early civilisations, including the officials of the Chinese Shang Dynasty, centred on Am Yang in the valley of the Yellow river, who kept records of weather conditions and floods on sacred carved bones. More commonly flood heights were recorded on stone pillars, walls or buildings (Plates 8.3 and 8.4). All historical flood records, including physical flood marks, should be regarded critically, as not infrequently the day, month or even year may be wrong and flood marks have frequently been moved from one building to another with little guarantee that it remains, or originally

Plate 8.2 Holme Fen post, Fenland England, showing the shrinkage of the peat since 1848. The top of pillar marks the original land surface.

was, at the correct height (Archer, 1995). The safest procedure is to compare flood heights and reject any which are only recorded at a single location. Flood markers do, however, remain extremely useful, allowing the reconstruction of the floodwater surface (Archer, 1993). Even if not of agricultural or religious importance, flood records were frequently kept because of the threat to life and property, as part of the management of the river and floodplain. Because flooding of the Arno in Florence has been a persistent problem, it has been recorded in some detail, if not necessarily with great accuracy, for the last 800 years (Losaco, 1967). As the city was a great centre for art and learning there were many representations of the floods, such as drawings and maps, including enough information for the production of accurate flood maps for 1333, 1740, 1844 and 1966 (Figure 8.10). During the sixteenth century even Leonardo da Vinci was employed to produce drawings and maps of the Arno. Table 8.1 gives the major floods recorded for each century; the largest of these, in order, were

Plate 8.3 The Ripetta pillar marking flood heights of the river Tiber in Rome.

probably 1557, 1740, 1547, 1758, 1844 and 1966, although this is not certain as the earlier flood heights are not as accurately known as the later ones. Although the floods caused a great deal of damage and many deaths, they certainly did not prevent the city becoming one of the richest in Europe. In cool temperate environments such as North-West Europe such excellent early records are generally lacking for many reasons, but, in order to show what can be done, the historical hydrological records from the Severn basin in western Britain will be briefly described.

The majority of the floods recorded are for the Middle and Lower Severn, the earliest quantified being the 'High Flood' of 1672. There are, however,

Plate 8.4 Flood heights on the Water Gate of Worcester Cathedral on the banks of the river Severn, England.

unquantified flood records prior to this (Table 8.2). Worcester, like many other towns including Gloucester on the Lower Severn, had a 'water gate' by the Cathedral where, from the seventeenth century onwards, flood heights were notched into the stone (Plate 8.4). At Tewkesbury the exceptional flood of 1795 is marked by a plaque, as it reached halfway up the nave of the Abbey, which is located at the highest point of the terrace island on which the town sits. As it is not recorded as an exceptionally high flood at Worcester, it is likely that it was predominantly an Avon event.

From 1850 onwards, the lock records give an almost complete flood series, which has been analysed by Brown (1983a) using Benson's (1950) flood frequency method for historical series (see appendix 2). The river Severn also has among the earliest semi-continuous river records in Europe: from Coalport, covering the years 1789–1800. They appear in the Shropshire County Agricultural Report and were to be included in an article by Telford for Plymley's *General View of the Agriculture of Salop*, 1803. The records are daily staff gauge records with an unknown datum level which is reached only once in the array. The quay on which the staff gauge was probably located was built in 1775 but no traces of this have been found. The data vary in quality during the eleven years; for the first seven years Sundays are not recorded and Figure 8.12 shows that the levels cluster around certain heights, although the overall frequency distribution is as would be expected. The modal distance between

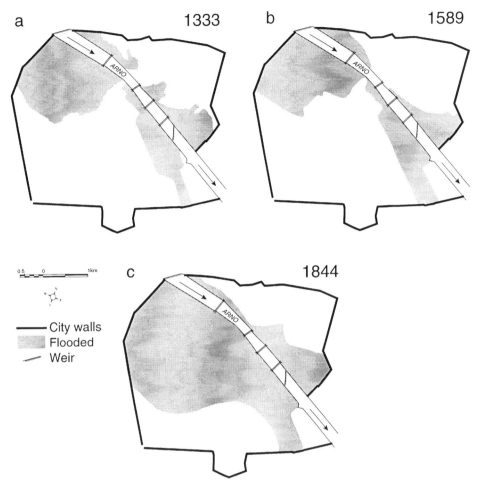

Fig. 8.10 Flood maps from Florence, Italy, for: (a) AD 1333, (b) AD 1589, and (c) AD 1844. Adapted from plates in Losaco (1967).

each 'spike' is 6 in., suggesting a rounding, or that the markings on the gauge were 6 in. apart. Another problem with the data is that large overbank events are not recorded but simply given as 'out of bounds' or 'overflowed' and a constant height recorded. Unfortunately, this 'bankfull' height seems to have varied, probably because of different readers (Figure 8.11).

An attempt was made to recreate ten of the highest single-peak in-bank storm hydrographs, using a spline fitting technique (Figure 8.12 a and b). Only hydrographs with more than two points on the rising limb were used. The same operation was performed for ten hydrographs from the nearby gauging station at Ironbridge, 1951–62. A curvature of peak index was than calculated for six- and twelve-hour intervals from the non-dimensionalised hydrographs. The means for both the six- and twelve-hour measures were found to be higher for

Table 8.1. *Recorded floods from Florence, 1100 to 1899 (data from Losaco 1967).*

Dates AD	Flood years
1100–99:	1168, 1177,
1200–99:	1269, 1282, 1284, 1288
1300–99:	1333, 1334, 1335(2), 1380
1400–99:	1456, 1457, 1466,
1500–99:	1511, 1516, 1532, 1543, 1544, 1547, 1579, 1589(2), 1590
1600–99:	1646, 1676, 1677, 1679, 1687, 1688(3)
1700–99:	1714, 1719, 1740, 1745, 1758, 1761
1800–99:	1809, 1844, 1864

Table 8.2. *Unquantified Severn floods (source: Waters, 1949 and Worcester Cathedral records).*

Date	Estimated rank	Flood name and comments
1483	1	Buckingham's flood, water on the floodplain for ten days
1606	3	January flood
1620	2	29 November onwards
1672	?	High Flood, the first quantified

the Coalport data, i.e. the hydrographs were more peaked. This trend is indicative of the hydrological trend associated with urbanisation and increased land drainage but could also be caused by a change in storm intensities. The data were also used to generate a non-dimensional flow duration curve. A bankfull height was used as a cutoff for the Ironbridge data. As can be seen from the curves (Figure 8.13), the Coalport flow data seem to have been more variable than the recent Ironbridge data. This may also be related to land use change and the construction of the Vyrnwy reservoir, although this only affects a relatively small percentage of the flow volume at Ironbridge. Another explanation is the 'Little Ice Age' (*c.* 1430–1850) (Grove, 1988), as there is other evidence of this climatic event in the data. Between 1780 and 1820, annual temperatures across the North Atlantic everywhere above 50° North were 1–3°C lower than today (Lamb and Johnson, 1966; Grove, 1988). Out of approximately 4000 readings, 86 (2%) are listed when the river was frozen over; this is extremely rare today. It is likely that many of the larger overbank events were related to even greater snowmelt effects than are experienced today. While the aim of this discussion has been to show how such data can be analysed, it is worth mentioning that the conclusions reached relate to both climate change and land use change,

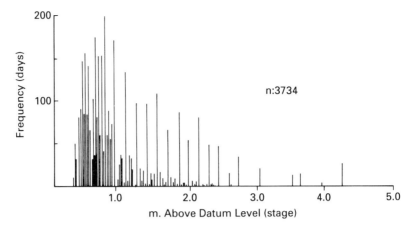

Fig. 8.11 The frequency of levels taken at Coalport, Shropshire, England, 1789–1800. From Brown (1983).

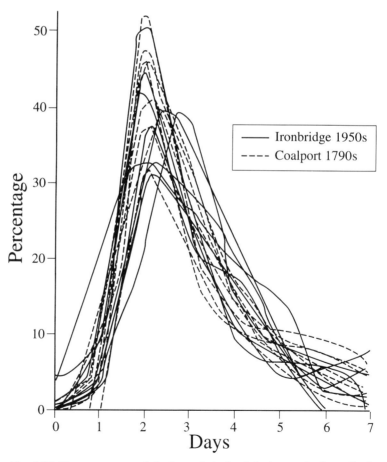

Fig. 8.12 The reconstructed single-peak, in-bank hydrographs from Coalport, 1789–1800 and Ironbridge 1951–62. From Brown (1983a).

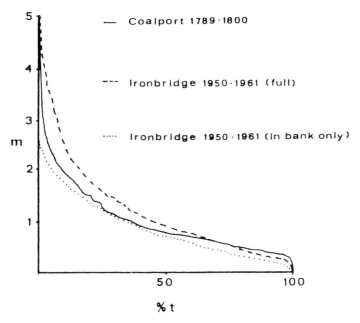

Fig. 8.13 Non-dimensional curtailed flow duration curves for the Coalport data (1789–1800) and the Ironbridge data (1951–62). From Brown (1983).

as both have occurred simultaneously. Other analyses of flow records from the Severn have come to broadly the same conclusion (Howe *et al.*, 1967; Higgs, 1987).

The fish weir, the mill, the floodplain drainage system and the flood record should not be seen independently, but should be seen as integrated parts of the floodplain landscape. The management of rivers and floodplains had major consequences for settlement. As the problems associated with floodplain occupation were reduced, so the economic advantages of the location could be grasped. Rivers and floodplains became sources of wealth for each generation: fisheries and mills in the medieval period, then centres of trade, and sources of mechanical power for early industry. This has led to a vast expansion of settlement on floodplains and further pressure to reduce the risks and inconvenience of flooding and channel change. Only recently, because of a combination of national recession, more concern for the environment and the knowledge that flood relief schemes are rarely justified in cost-benefit terms, has the pace of channelisation slowed.

The history of river management has probably had important effects upon floodplain sedimentation rates, although long runs of data confirming this are not available. The frequency of inundation of most floodplains has been engineered to be less frequent than once in five years, and many areas of floodplains are now out of the reach of all probable floods. This has led to a reduction in the natural addition of nutrients to floodplain soils from floods, a shortfall which has probably been more than made up for by the use of artificial fertilisers. However, the addition of fertilisers to floodplain soils is particularly problematic, because of their proximity to watercourses and the high watertable. As we have seen in previous periods, changes to one part of the floodplain system have repercussions on other parts of the system, and our management of floodplains has rarely been integrated or coercive enough to incorporate all effects. Even the hydraulic civilisations, which most nearly achieved this, were not immune to high social and environmental costs in the longer run.

9

THE CULTURAL ARCHAEOLOGY OF FLOODPLAINS

The last chapter outlined the impact of humans on the floodplain system through the management and control of floodplain resources. This begs several questions; were floodplains preferentially settled and if so why, and how have people coped with the negative as well as positive aspects of floodplain locations? This chapter explores these questions and the data that archaeology can generate that can be used to test such hypotheses and other hypotheses concerning relationships between culture and environment. Floodplains not only have particular sets of positive and negative resources (in the widest sense) but also may have ritual or mythic significance – all of which is part of the cultural archaeology of floodplains.

9.1 Locational data and alluvial environments

Any explanatory theory of the location for any activity, excluding enforcement but including inertia, must relate to the perceived advantages and disadvantages of that location as opposed to other locations. When we are dealing with a single or primary site function (such as mining), this seems obvious, but in reality this is rarely, if ever, the case. Even when there was no relocation decision, as is implied by the occurrence of continuously occupied multi-period sites, the perception of positive and negative factors is important in preventing abandonment. This is especially true in the case of dynamic, or hazardous, environments, such as steep slopes, volcanoes and floodplains. In these cases, we can rephrase the locational problem as: why do people persist in living and working in areas subject to hazardous events? The hazardousness of a place is not a simple matter, either from the physical perspective or from the social. For example, the hazard (or negative resource) must be perceived as hazardous if it is to affect behaviour. In considering this question, the distinction between the operational environment (Eo) and the cognised environment (Ec) made by Rappaport is useful, and even those who accept the general principle of maximisation, as a rule guiding the necessary choices in palaeoeconomic behaviour, must recognise the variability and variety of possible satisfactions to be maximised (Jochim, 1976). It is, however, extremely difficult not to let our prejudices concerning negative and positive factors dictate our interpretations; indeed, a consideration of the positive and negative significance of past environmental factors is part of a questioning archaeology which also has contemporary significance. This chapter discusses the assumed attractions of floodplain

279

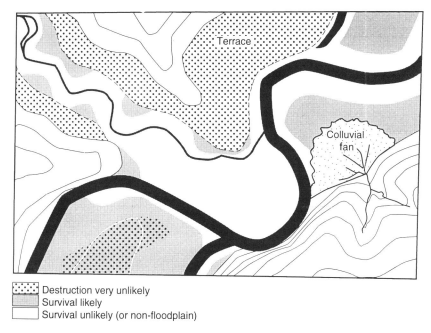

Destruction very unlikely
Survival likely
Survival unlikely (or non-floodplain)

Fig. 9.1 The preservation potential of a hypothetical floodplain.

locations, the negative factors, and evidence of the importance of these factors in the past by way of a synthesis. First of all, some consideration must be given to the integrity of locational data in alluvial environments.

By their very nature alluvial environments are liable to impart bias on the preservation of settlement patterns. The factors responsible for this bias include:

1 Erosion and destruction of sites by channel activity. This is likely to be greater closer to the channel or, in the long term, greater towards the middle of the floodplain and on the outer edges of valley meanders, because of the preferred position of channels in alluvial valleys (Palmquist, 1975). Fluvial systems are, however, only ever semi-predictable, so caution should be used in the assumption of general trends.

2 Deposition preserving sites but rendering them invisible. This is likely to be greater on the lower parts of the floodplain and on sites which have not been artificially built up or which were not occupied for very long. In mid-latitudes this is the greatest problem and effectively renders distribution maps with significant proportions of alluvial cover difficult to use. On the basis of excavated areas it may be possible to apply weighting factors (Bradley, 1978).

The location of both erosion and deposition may alter over time (Figure 9.1). The result is that, in general, sites located at the edges of floodplains and on terraces, terrace remnants or abandoned levées will tend to be preferentially recorded by ground survey and aerial photography. Indeed, while crop-marks are often particularly clear on gravel terraces, such as in the Thames valley, they are rather rare on the silty and clay soils of the active floodplain. Some improvement in the detection of buried alluvial sites may be possible in some cases and under certain conditions, using airborne thermal infra-red remote sensing (Allsop and Greenbaum, 1991). Geophysical methods, such as ground resistivity, are also less successful on deep clay-rich soils and, in any case, they cannot provide survey data over large areas. The existence of previously unknown sub-alluvial sites is attested to by the large number which have been discovered during gravel extraction and development. The bias is more worrying than that imposed upon dry land sites by the autocorrelation of discovery, because the bias acts in the same direction as we might intuitively expect, i.e. higher, drier ground close to water being preferred for settlement. The result of this is that maps of site locations covering alluvial environments are difficult to use in any form of quantitative locational analysis, and a safer alternative is through the identification and analysis of site activities and functions in different floodplain environments.

9.2 Positive factors

Positive factors will vary with site type, i.e. between temporary sites or areas visited for food procurement and settlement sites which may be seasonal but are to some degree permanent. In environments where nearly all land is habitable, even at a cost, it is assumed that a locational decision is the outcome of the balancing of perceived positive against perceived negative factors. There are several related points that have to be remembered about this type of reasoning. First, perceived hazards and resources are not real hazards and resources: the decision may turn out to have been wrong, and there are convincing examples of this. Real hazards and resources change and some sites lose while others gain. Secondly, it assumes there is unoccupied space, space not under the polity of already existing settlements, and lastly it assumes that all relevant information is available, which, of course, can never be the case. The hazard versus advantage argument is often criticised as being (a) unrealistically formal, which is true but unavoidable, and (b) fundamentally economic and non-cultural. This is not true, since any factors can be included: economic, political or ritual.

Positive factors can be invoked, either explicitly or more commonly implicitly, to explain continued occupation and site function. There is a danger of circular reasoning here and these arguments are only useful when either the site function is not known or there is some change in the environment of the site. Although geological opportunism (*sensu* Higgs and Vita-Finzi, 1972) does not necessarily explain the location of a site, it may help identify site function or render improbable other functions. Other than in the case of the prediction of unknown settlement locations, the one fact we know is that a settlement existed; the more useful question is therefore not why it existed at that spot but what was it 'doing' there.

Resources and palaeoeconomy

The permanent or ephemeral water supply to floodplains means that they are biologically highly productive, relatively diverse, and less liable to drought than surrounding lands. Their diversity is caused by the variety of micro-environments, including hydroseres in various seral stages providing patches of different plant communities. Food procurement activities have included fishing, fowling, gathering and hunting and, in agricultural communities, watering and grazing stock, and cultivation. In addition floodplains provide other resources, including drift-wood, material for shelters, matting and baskets, osiers and coppice poles and, probably most important of all, water for cooking, drinking and washing (Coles and Coles, 1989). Unfortunately, many of these resources, especially gathered plants, are archaeologically rather invisible. Fish bones are less well preserved in the archaeological record than mammal bones. It may also not be possible to differentiate between materials brought on to the site from other areas and those from the alluvial parts of the site catchment – two examples being wood and terrestrial mollusca. In addition to being archaeologically invisible, these resources tend to be regarded, even in recent studies, as secondary, even when in reality they may be a vital part of a village economy (Madge, 1993).

Evidence from intensively excavated alluvial sites, such as Newferry in Ireland (Brinkhuizan in Woodman, 1977), gives us some idea of the wide range of both fish and birds eaten in prehistory. However, Simmons *et al.* (1981) have pointed out the surprising lack of fish bones and fishing equipment from Mesolithic sites in Britain. There is a serious problem of differential preservation here, as the bones of salmonids and eels are less well preserved than those of primary freshwater fish such as pike and perch (Simmons *et al.*, 1981). This means that on present evidence we cannot accurately determine the importance of fish in prehistoric diets and therefore the full palaeoeconomic importance of the riverine habitat. In addition, it is believed that all indigenous freshwater fish entered Britain via the land bridge which was severed at the end of the Boreal period (*c.* 8200 bp), populating only the river catchments bordering the eastern English Channel and the southern North Sea (Wheeler, 1972). This means that in catchments outside this area, including those further north than the Yorkshire Ouse, freshwater primary fish were probably introduced. This does not, of course, apply to eels and salmonids, because of the oceanic segments of their life cycle. In the absence of bone evidence, there may be a role here for biomolecular work on skeletons exploiting the relationship between the ^{13}C:^{14}C ratio of our food and our bodies.

Both the biophysical and social roles of different subsistence bases have yet to be explored. Interestingly it has been known for some time that New World societies based on anadromous fish consumption tend to have high populations and large residential groups and are more sedentary than other hunter-gatherers (Suttles, 1968). As well as fish, rivers provide shellfish, amphibians and reptiles which may act as supplementary food resources; frogs, toads and lizards are commonly found on Bronze Age sites (Tinsley, 1981). Rivers would also have attracted game, including ungulates, especially during dry summers, and they facilitated ambush just as dry land clearings would have done. Bones of riverine mammals, such as beaver (*Castor fiber*) and otter (*Lutra lutra*), may indicate hunting or trapping.

In the natural environment, the location of edible plants is not random and there are a large number of both edible and medicinal plants that are restricted to floodplain environments (Table 9.1). Nearly 25% of the poisonous plants found in Britain are restricted to wet and riverine habitats. Natural or primeval floodplains were therefore km^2 for km^2 probably more attractive in terms of food resources than most of the intervening land and must always have attracted preferential human exploitation. Studies of the Mississippian culture of North America have emphasised adaptation to the floodplain niche which is reflected in settlement patterns (Smith, 1978). This adaptation involved selective utilisation of a small number of plants and animals that were dependable, seasonally abundant energy sources that could be exploited at a 'relatively low level of energy expenditure' (Smith, 1978). The five main species groups are:

1 backwater fish species
2 migratory waterfowl
3 the terrestrial trinity of white-tail deer, racoon and turkey
4 nuts, fruit and berries, primarily hickory nuts, walnuts, acorns, persimmons, cherries, plums and hackberries
5 seed-bearing pioneer plants, e.g. *Polygonum* spp. and *Chenopodium* spp.

Additionally natural vegetation was removed from areas of better (drier) soil to grow maize, beans, squash, sunflower, marsh elder and gourd.

For agriculturalists, the floodplain provides the best seasonal grazing and water for cattle, even prior to deforestation, as oxbow lakes and backswamp marshes provide excellent grazing, even in times of drought. Floodplain soils are also very fertile if dry enough or if drained, as illustrated by the particularly high utilisation of floodplains for strip farming in medieval Europe.

An increase in our knowledge of the ways in which riverine resources were used will only come from detailed environmental studies, but they must be coupled with the analysis of social factors. This information, along with more reliable evidence of past settlement patterns and densities, can be used in the production of new narratives of cultural difference and cultural change.

Non-subsistence attractions
Floodplain settlements have often been 'explained' by reference to several non-subsistence locational advantages, including transport, floatability,

Table 9.1. *A list of some of the plants known to be used as food or poison from British floodplains. The list is undoubtedly not complete and does not include fungi but does illustrate the potentially wide range of species that could have been used. Some of the species are not restricted to floodplains but are most commonly found in that environment. Compiled from several sources including Mabey (1972).*

EDIBLE roots

White water lily	*Nymphaea alba*
Silverweed	*Potentilla anserina*
Flowering rush	*Butomus umbellatus*
Early purple orchid	*Orchis mascula*

EDIBLE leaves or foliage

Watercress	*Rorippa nasturtium-aquaticum*
Lady's smock	*Cardamine pratensis*
Common wintercress	*Barbarea vulgaris*
Brooklime	*Veronica beccabunga*
Hawthorne	*Crataegus monogyna*
Fat hen	*Chenopodium album*
Wild hop	*Humulus lupulus*
Bistort	*Polygonum bistorta*
Common sorrel	*Rumex acetosa*
Stinging nettle	*Urtica dioica*
Common comfrey	*Symphytum officinale*

EDIBLE stems

Marsh thistle	*Cirsium palustre*

HERBS

Meadowsweet	*Filipendula ulmaria*
Wild angelica	*Angelica sylvestris*
Sweet gale	*Myrica gale*
Water mint	*Mentha aquatica*
Ground ivy	*Glechoma hederacea*

EDIBLE fruits and flowers

Elder	*Sambucus nigra*
Crab apple	*Malus* spp.
Water chestnut	*Trapa natans*

POISONS

Buttercup	*Ranunculus* spp.
Ivy	*Hedera helix*
Hemlock	*Conium maculatum*
Water dropwort	*Oenanthe* spp.
Dog's mercury	*Mercurialis perennis*
Woody nightshade	*Solanum dulcamara*
Fritillary	*Fritillaria meleagris*
Meadow saffron	*Colchicum autumnale*

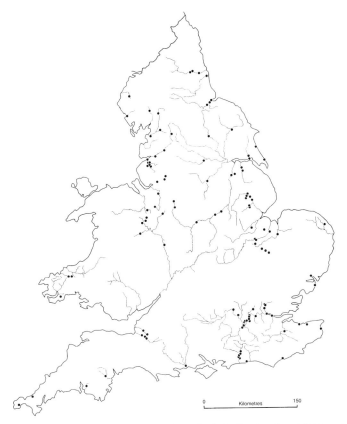

Fig. 9.2 The distribution of log-boat finds in England and Wales. Adapted from McGrail (1978).

fording, exchange, burial, cult, ritual and combat (Needham, 1989). In fully forested environments such as the Amazon basin, there is a strong tendency for settlements to be located along rivers which are the main means of intervillage transport. Boats have been found in many archaeological excavations in the Old World, from the Swiss lake villages to the early historic crannogs of Scotland and Ireland. The earliest craft seems to have been the familiar log-boat made from a single tree trunk. Unsurprisingly, many have been found in old river beds such as that of the rivers Trent, the Ancholme in Nottinghamshire and the Witham in Lincolnshire (Cummins and Rundle, 1969; White, 1979). In his comprehensive survey of English and Welsh log-boats, McGrail (1978) lists over 179 finds with groupings in most large river basins and wetlands, but a concentration in the south and east, particularly the Middle Thames, the Arun in Sussex, the Witham and Fenland rivers (Figure 9.2). There is probably considerable bias to this distribution operating through the ground conditions required for preservation, and the distribution of building activity on floodplains. Some were surprisingly large; those found at

Brigg and Hasholme in eastern England were capable of carrying over twenty humans or 10,000 kg (10 tonnes) of cargo (Millett and McGrail, 1987). Log-boats of varying designs seem to have been in use from *c.* 3500 bp until as late as the medieval period *c.* 1000 bp (McGrail, 1978). Coracle-type craft are less well preserved but have been inferred from decayed remains and carvings from the European Bronze Age (Coles and Coles, 1989). Some of the earliest planked craft come from the Bronze Age shipyard at North Ferry on the banks of the river Humber, also in eastern England (Wright, 1976). These unique craft made of oak planks with yew bindings were undoubtedly for river rather than sea travel. Further evidence of early waterborne transport is provided by the discovery of paddles (assuming they are paddles). Two examples are the birch-wood paddles from the Mesolithic site of Star Carr, Yorkshire, and the decorated Bronze Age paddles from Lake Keitele in Central Finland (Vilkuna, 1987). As the discovery of the remarkably well-preserved Viking longboats in Denmark and the Bronze Age boat in Dover, southern England (Fenwick *et al.*, in press) illustrates, boats have relatively high preservation potential, either because of high ritual value or the ease with which they may be sunk and preserved by anaerobic sediments. The true economic role of inland ports therefore may best be illustrated by excavations of ships and boats.

One of the simplest use of rivers is for the uncontrolled floating of objects – floatability (Beckinsale, 1969a). The easiest way to transport large floatable objects such as timber is to float them down river. In the northern forests of Canada, Scandinavia and Russia which have suitable river regimes with spring and early summer floods, this has remained a common method of transporting lumber. It can also be used in the tropics, although many tropical hardwoods will not float while they are still green. There is therefore a considerable advantage to locating a building which requires large timbers close to the banks of a relatively large river.

However, when thinking about either inland navigation or floatability, it should be remembered that all rivers have changed during the Holocene and in many places the relatively deep, shoal- and weed-free channels common in low-lands today are the result of management (Petts, 1989). In the more forested environments of the Mesolithic and Neolithic in Europe small and medium-sized rivers may have been frequently obstructed and far less navigable than today. Even large rivers in dry areas can be obstructed by tree debris; the Murray in Australia used to be cleared at an expense of $60,000 annually at the turn of the century, in order to facilitate paddlesteamer traffic into the interior. This has stopped in the last sixty years and the river is impassable because of jams of red gum. Changes in the morphology and activity of rivers, especially tendencies to braiding, have profound effects on navigability as do changes from flood- to drought-dominated flow regimes. In turn, changes in navigability can isolate one location and revitalise another or cause the diversion of community wealth and resources to river management.

The early function of many river sites was clearly as crossing points, where travellers had to stop, either to pay to cross or just to rest. Indeed, with fords and ferries, there were frequently times when the river was in flood and could not be crossed, leaving travellers requiring food and accommodation for hours, days or even weeks (a captive market). River crossings, therefore, often developed as small service-sector towns, a function which often continued after a bridge was constructed. This function has frequently been used to explain the site of a riverine settlement, i.e. by a shoal (riffle) forming the lowest bridging/fording point, but, in reality, the existence and growth of any such settlement is dependent entirely upon socioeconomic factors, primarily trade. It is a necessary but not sufficient criterion for any particular crossing site, given the pattern of prevailing trading routes and technology.

The defence argument is more problematic. Rivers may have always been invested with some political significance as one of the most obvious boundaries in the landscape; however, this could militate as much against as for settlement. While rivers are often used as minor administrative boundaries within Old World states, they do not *generally* form major internal administrative or international boundaries (Beckinsale, 1969b). There are of course exceptions such as part of the Rhine, and the river Thames which acted as a defensive barrier between the kingdoms of Wessex and Midland Mercia and which has remained as a county boundary for most of its length. River boundaries are far more common in areas carved up by European colonisers, such as in Australia and North America, where the need to establish identifiable boundaries quickly, over-rode the problems associated with using rivers, problems which seem to have been recognised by indigenous inhabitants (Strehlow, 1947). The first of these problems is that rivers can and do change their courses; the second is that population is attracted to them and therefore away from the interior, where a capital or main settlement would ideally be located, for both safety and political control; i.e. as far away from the external borders as possible but preferably either at the coast or on a large river. These locational conditions are clearly in conflict. The last problem is that cooperation would be required, to utilise the river for safe transport or to control it for navigation, fishing, abstraction or power (Beckinsale, 1969b). Overall, the positive factors favour the establishment of major centres on rivers, thus making them inappropriate for boundaries in settled societies; this does not apply in the same way to mobile societies where rivers probably form important territorial boundaries. If rivers have a defensive role it is normally restricted to a first or last line of defence or as a refuge once hostilities have broken out. Historical examples of this abound, from the problems the invading Romans faced from marsh-dwelling Britons to Alfred the Great's retreat to the Isle of Athelney in the Somerset Levels (south-west England) in the face of invading Danes. It can be argued that, except for extremely large rivers, the defence factor is not a reason for floodplain settlement, as floodplains are difficult to defend. This is also implied by the lack of Iron Age floodplain sites with defences, in comparison with the defensive hilltop forts so common in the period. However, if location on the floodplain occurs, for whatever reasons, the most easily defendable site often seems to have been chosen – the two most common being the core of an overgrown meander incised into a terrace or bedrock, or a terrace island. However, both locations also offer other major advantages, as they may be relatively free-draining, free from flooding but close to the river for transport and water. As discussed in previous chapters, earlier in the Holocene North-West European floodplains were very different from those that exist today, being dry enough for settlement in some periods, and in other periods wetter, with large areas covered by marshes and shallow lakes (Brown, 1987b). Similar problems exist with attempts to assign ritual or cult importance to riverine locations, although there is evidence from old river-names (see appendix 3.1). The occurrence of barrows and cemeteries on terraces or terrace islands may suggest that isolation was important, perhaps to prevent desecration, but it should not be forgotten that this may also just be a reflection of the fact that it is impossible to build a barrow or dig a grave in an area with a watertable at or near the surface. More work is required to substantiate these claims, but there does seem to be evidence that dry 'islands' may have had ritual significance in a number of cultures; indeed, the concept of a sacred island has continued into the religious baggage of the twentieth century. River islands are also preferentially associated with riverine settlement sites for the obvious reason that this is where the river is at its narrowest and easiest to bridge.

Several authors have suggested that finds from river beds may be related to water cults of various kinds, and there are numerous contemporary examples where springs and rivers have acquired religious significance. For example, in India, the source of the Bhagirati and the junction of this headstream with the other headstream of the Ganges at Devaprayag are famous pilgrimage sites, as also is Allahabad where the Jumna enters the Ganges. Over a million people have regularly assembled at Allahabad this century, almost certainly the largest gathering of humans in the history of humankind. The best archaeological example of the ritualistic importance of a river is the role of the Nile in the Egyptian world view (Sack, 1980). The Nile not only formed the economic basis of the Upper Kingdom but influenced its religion as well. It is notable that flood epics are common to many cultures. There are clear parallels between the Hebrew story of Noah and the Ark and the earlier Babylonian flood saga of King Atra-hasiś, his boat, its passengers and the seven-day flood (Lambert and Millard, 1969). There would seem to be little doubt that any religion based on Gods of the elements would be bound to regard water and water sources as in some sense sacred. One of the most obvious signs of God's power is the flood. Although their meanings are complex and little understood, flood myths are one of the most widely diffused narratives known (except in Africa) and probably the most studied of all narratives (Dundes, 1988). Interpretations of flood myths have varied from straightforward narratives of environmental history and danger, punishment for sin and retribution, to a 'male' myth of the creation (Dundes, 1988). Whatever their contextual meaning, they play a significant part in many systems of belief, inculcating reverence for divine authority. The attraction of river locations for all the reasons mentioned above is illustrated by some of the earliest structures that have been archaeologically recorded.

The existence of wooden structures to facilitate habitation of extremely wet alluvial and lacustrine environments such as the Mesolithic platform at Star Carr (Clark, 1972), the lake villages in the Somerset Levels and in Switzerland or crannogs in Scottish lochs indicates that such locations had a pull which is cross-cultural and most likely to be based upon the exploitation of natural resources. There is, however, a danger that in emphasising the palaeoeconomic role of these sites we divorce them from their neighbouring dryland resources which were an integrated part of their existence (J. Evans, 1990; Louwe Kooijmans, 1993).

Depending upon the landscape, high/dry land may be terraces or sand dunes only a few metres above the floodplain or it may be the valley slopes and inter-fluves. In both cases the soils, drainage and ecology will be different, presenting complementary resources. As in the case of the Dutch Delta where all year round occupation is often possible, settlement location and size and economic interdependency/self-dependency will change over time as a result of popula-tion pressure, technology, social factors and environmental change. Louwe Kooijmans (1993) has evaluated these factors in the light of the settlement and environmental history of the Dutch Delta period by period:

> *Mesolithic 10,000–6400 cal. BC:* broad-spectrum gathering/for-aging, fowling, fishing and hunting.
>
> *Late Mesolithic/Early Neolithic 5300–4200 cal. BC:* 'the availability phase'; cattle herding associated with Linear Bandekeramik (LBK) settlements.
>
> *Late Neolithic 3300–2600 cal. BC:* end of the natural bioresource exploitation and final substitution (initial consolidation), settle-ment sites in all ecological zones varying from 10–90% agrarian (long-fallow), restricted residential mobility systems.
>
> *Late Beaker/Early Bronze Age 2600–1700 cal. BC:* short-fallow agrarian, initial mixed farming, wild animal bones absent from sites, draught animals common, increase in ploughing.
>
> *Middle/Late Bronze Age 1700–700 cal. BC:* a rigid self-sufficient mixed-farming economy, winter stalling, manuring, fields fenced and ditched, little or no hunting or fowling, some fishing. Settlement located to facilitate access to sandy soils for arable and wet pastures for herding e.g. dune margins, creek ridges, levée splays and roddons.
>
> *Iron Age 700–0 cal. BC:* diversified mixed farming and high interde-pendency, cattle less prominent, horse-breeding common, new arable crops: gold of pleasure (*Camelina sativa*), Celtic bean (*Vicia fabia*), carrot (*Daucus carota*) and rapeseed turnip (*Brassica campestris*). Domestic/internal differentiation of space, revived interest in wet environments.

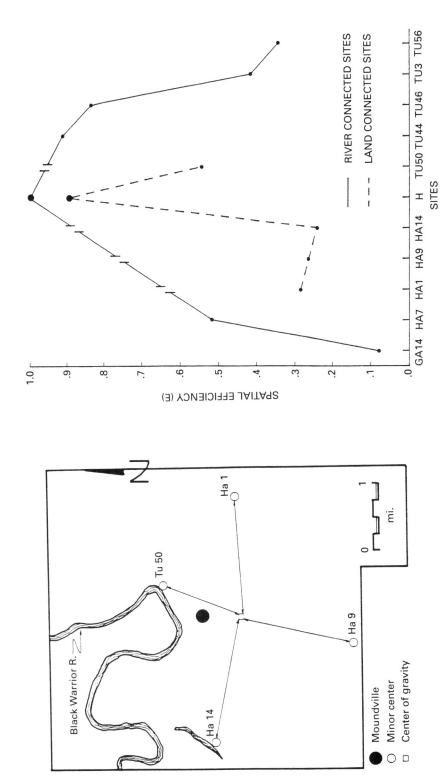

Fig. 9.3 Spatial efficiency of the Mississippi Moundsville sites, West Virginia. Adapted from Steponaitis (1978), by permission of Academic Press Inc.

A combination of subsistence and non-subsistence factors (from both flood-plain and dryland sites) can be subsumed when looking at the spatial efficiency of a location. The concept of spatial efficiency is derived from central place theory (Berry, 1967). It can be measured using straight-line distances to other centres by calculating the coordinates of the demographic centre of gravity. However, in order to do this, the population of the centres must be known (or a surrogate used). When it is not, and all the centres are assumed to have the same population, the approach is reduced to a purely spatial measure of central place. This technique has been used in the study of the Mississippian complex chiefdom sites around Moundville by Steponaitis (1978). He has also calcu-lated the spatial efficiency of river-connected sites and found that Moundville had the highest spatial efficiency for both land and river (Figure 9.3). The analysis suggested that Moundville was the central place with four subsidiary centres around it. Since these four sites and Moundville are located on poorer soil than the surrounding sites in the hierarchy, Steponaitis (1978) suggests that sociopolitical factors related to the minimisation of movement were influ-encing the spatial distribution of the sites, or the development of those sites which were the centres of chiefly power. Steponaitis's key variables include the flow of tribute and administrative information, but many more could be impor-tant, including warfare, political alliance and locational inertia. The method-ology does, however, allow some evaluation of the relative importance of subsistence and non-subsistence factors in alluvial and other environments.

9.3 Negative factors

Despite the obvious point that a floodplain location is more hazardous than most dryland locations, it is a relative risk; that is, relative to other risks and relative to the pull of the location. Secondly, the risk depends upon the river size and regime and so the risk of catastrophic flooding is greatest in semi-arid and subtropical monsoonal environments, since in non-coastal tropical zones a regular annual flood cycle exists which is easily adapted to. In temperate environments, catastrophic flooding is rare except in mountainous environ-ments. Figure 9.4 gives a selection of generalised flood frequency curves for different environments. In all non-coastal environments, even today with dense floodplain occupation, floods kill relatively few people in relation to earth-quakes, disease, famine and war – some of which would have been even worse in prehistory. Indeed, the flood risk is not independent of technology, urban fabric and socioeconomic status; death from catastrophic river flooding could possibly have been less common in prehistory than in historical times or today. The exception to this is coastal wetlands and the lower valleys of rivers within the reach of surge tide effects, tsunamis and hurricanes, where flooding is and probably always has been a major hazard and cause of loss of life.

The effects of nuisance as opposed to catastrophic flooding are more difficult to evaluate. If it occurs extremely regularly it would presumably be common

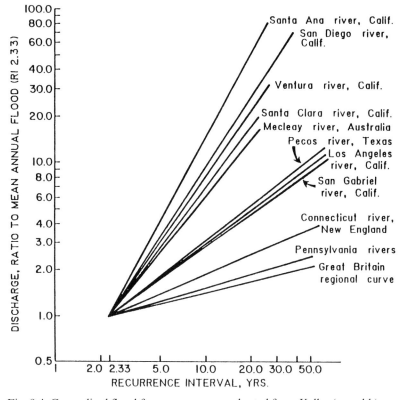

Fig. 9.4 Generalised flood frequency curves, adapted from Keller (unpubl.).

knowledge and lead to avoidance of the site. There is also evidence that occupation has continued at many prehistoric sites despite flooding. All locational decisions in the face of hazard are taken with incomplete knowledge and against a background hazard frequency distribution. A structure may be located in what turns out to be a poor location and even a safe location may be an illusion caused by a run of non-average years. We can therefore only specify an approximate space on a risk graph, outside which occupation would seem to be unlikely (Figure 9.5). In contemporary studies of flood hazard, the problem has been rephrased: 'why do people persist in living and working in areas subject to repeated floods?' (Kates, 1962). Studies by Kates (1962) and Burton and Kates (1964) which investigated this question produced five reasons:

1 Occupants did not know about the flood hazard.
2 They knew about the flood hazard but personally did not expect a future flood, and were therefore not unduly concerned.
3 They expected a flood but did not expect to bear a loss.
4 They expected to bear a loss but not a serious one.
5 They expected to bear a serious loss; were concerned and had therefore undertaken, or were planning to undertake, some action to reduce the losses.

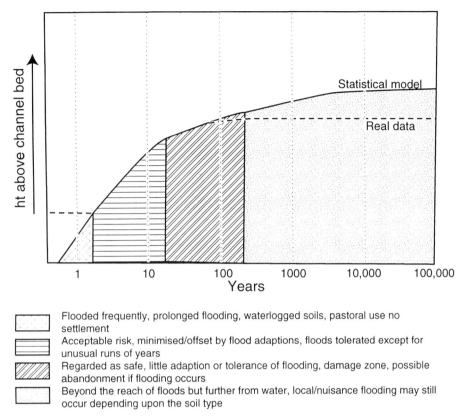

Fig. 9.5 A generalised graph of floodplain risk in relation to flood frequency and magnitude.

To this culturally specific list must be added a fatalist acceptance or even a celebration of flooding as the will of God or Gods. This work illustrates that, within one culture at one time and in the face of community knowledge, 'there is a variety of personal perceptions of hazard and potential loss' (Kates, 1962). These studies also reveal that perception depends to some extent upon the householder's location on the certainty–uncertainty scale (i.e. statistical flood threat), but in a non-linear manner. Harding and Parker (1972) interviewed a sample of occupants who lived on those areas of the river Severn floodplain near Shrewsbury which were inundated by the extreme flood of 1947 and found that only 45% of them felt there was a flood problem in the area and only 27% thought there would be another flood in the future.

That contemporary Westerners' perception of the hazard is still influenced by their ideology is demonstrated by studies of perceived causes of flooding also on the Lower Severn (Waller and Shaw, 1970; Penning-Rowsell, 1976). Six percent of the interviewees regarded nuisance flooding as an act of God, and as one interviewer puts it, 'if one should have so incurred His displeasure that one is swept away, then that is a flood'. These studies and others from different environments show the perception of the risk is in many ways more important than the risk itself. Since perception is culturally, socially and politically deter-mined, it must have changed throughout prehistory. Indeed the 'problem' of adjustment does not seem to have existed at all for aboriginal floodwater-farming groups in southern Arizona and northern Mexico (Cooke and Dornkamp, 1974). That the attractions of the floodplain or even channel bed can outweigh the perceived risk is clearly demonstrated by the practice of using ephemeral river beds as markets in towns in southern Spain. Occasionally, 'dis-aster' strikes, as at Orviedo in Murcia Province in the 1960s, where 147 people were killed by a flash flood, while setting up market stalls (J. Thornes, pers. comm.) The knowledge of flash flooding existed throughout the community but economic factors compelled risk-taking behaviour in the face of a low fre-quency and very unpredictable risk.

There has been archaeological interest in individuals', as opposed to society's, risk-taking strategies (Van der Leeuw, 1989). However, there is little reason to think that it is biologically rather than culturally controlled, making contemporary psychological studies of limited value in the direct interpreta-tion of the past. Although the concept of risk, in the sense of the *a priori* calculation of the chances of success or failure, may be a useful way to analyse behaviour from our perspective, it is probably an inappropriate concept for most past communities. Unlike today, the risk takers may never have seen themselves as taking risks; they may not have had any concept of risk at all, although they may have had a normal expectation of event magnitude (see chapter 10). The application of risk theory and probability theory, outside the sphere of gambling, is a modern Western invention and related to a decline in views of certainty. Although modern Western society has not reached it yet, it is on the way to becoming what Beck (1992) calls the 'risk society', where social control is routed through the management of largely human created risks asso-ciated with development. Most prehistoric societies probably had ideologies that 'explained' all natural phenomena; they were deterministic and so the concept of risk would have been redundant. This does not make risk analysis worthless, but means that we must take all social factors into account and not just those that we think would have been relevant to the subjects.

The prevailing ideology of the rule makers of the society may have incorpo-rated rules, commands, stories, etc. which effectively reduced risk, and this struc-tural risk avoidance may also have operated at the individual level through negative perceptions of the environment, which remain common even to the present day (see notes in appendix 3.2 and Purseglove, 1989). One obvious reason for these fears is disease, especially malaria, but also bubonic plague and cholera. Before river channelisation and floodplain drainage and from at least the thirteenth century onwards, malaria was endemic in many north European wetlands. Although not as deadly as tropical malaria (*Plasmodium falciparum*), the north European strain (*Plasmodium vivax*) is spread by the mosquito *Anopheles atroparvus*, which breeds in saline water as far north as Finland. The disease has been shown to have been endemic in coastal wetlands and the Lower Thames valley until the nineteenth century (Dobson, 1980) and was one of the causes of a perception of fens and marshes as unhealthy places, especially for children and outsiders, i.e. the non-immune section of the population. Fen and marsh dwellers were probably immune and both opium poppy (*Papava somniferum*) and cannabis (*Cannabis sativa*) were used to counteract the effects of the disease (Purseglove, 1989). Bubonic plague was associated with wetlands, because the black rat (*Rattus rattus*) which carried the flea vector (*Xonopsylla cheopis*) was accidentally introduced, possibly by returning Crusaders, and spread from wharfs and ports to neighbouring marshes, and cholera was spread by the pollution of wetlands and rivers by untreated human sewage. The result was that, even as late as 1827, the Fens of East Anglia, were avoided by travellers fearful of the 'marsh miasma' (Watson, 1827). Although largely unfounded the fear of wetlands which is common in eighteenth- and nineteenth-century writings can be seen as both a lack of understanding and a disregard for land regarded as unproductive or unimproved in a post-agricultural-revolution world (see appendix 3.2). However, the settlement and exploitation of floodplains has produced many adaptations, both technological and behavioural.

Flood adaptations
There are several means by which nuisance flooding or its risk to life and damage can be minimised. These range from low-cost/labour modifications to buildings, such as the fitting of flood boards (Plate 9.1), to flood embankments. On the floodplains of the Lower Rhine and its distributaries in the Netherlands, villagers built refuge mounds, or terps, after disastrous floods in the sixteenth century. A list of some traditional measures is given below:

> Emergency, labour-intensive flood fighting
> Flood boards for doors (Plate 9.1)
> Raised walkways (Plate 9.2)
> Buildings on stilts
> Buildings on mounds
> Refuge mounds
> Flood embankments

Because of the pull of rivers for trading, industrial processes, sport and recreation, many of these measures are common today; examples include buildings on stilts and raised walkways (Plate 9.2). If the premium of the riverside location is great enough, as it can be with riverside inns, then even frequent flooding and its costs will be tolerated (Plate 9.3). This should make us wary about assigning flooding as an overridingly negative factor in relation to floodplain occupation.

It is far from straightforward to infer hazard from archaeology (Bell, 1992); coping strategies will be related to the magnitude of the hazard within limits

Plate 9.1 A flood door on a seventeenth-century cottage on the floodplain of the river Axe in Devon, England.

set by the collective memory of the community. We must therefore look at adaptations to the stress and information flow, including the transfer of environmental information from generation to generation.

Catastrophe and abandonment

It has frequently been suggested that floodplain sites have been abandoned because of flooding. Classic examples include Mohenjo-daro on the Indus (Piggott, 1950), Sybaris in southern Italy (Raikes, 1967) and Petra in modern Jordan. However, upon further excavation and geoarchaeological work catastrophic flooding has, in most cases, either been rejected as the cause of abandonment or substantially amended in favour of adaptation, with

Plate 9.2 A flood walkway, near the village of Sutton Bonnington, Leicestershire, England.

abandonment occurring as a result of several factors one of which may have been increasing flooding (Raikes, 1964; 1965; 1967; Lambrick, 1967). The identification of an environmental cause for abandonment is an extremely important archaeological statement, in that it is taken to override political and economic factors. The thesis always requires sceptical scrutiny on several grounds. First, the evidence of water-deposited silts sealing an occupation surface is not enough: it needs to be shown that the silts originated from the flooding of the river (and not just nuisance flooding of the site itself) and preferably that the silts immediately post-date or are contemporary with some use of the site.

The abandonment of settlements because of flooding in the historical period is extremely rare, even in the case of catastrophic losses of human life. One rather revealing exception is in the case of colonisation, when the settlers have little or no experience of the environment in which they are living. A rather vivid example of the mislocation of settlements by pioneers during colonisation is the town of Gundagai, New South Wales. The town stands at the point where the floodplain of the Murrumbidgee widens to approximately 1 km and leaves the mountains. The floodplain was settled at this location, because it was the crossing point for explorers and travellers travelling west into the Riverine Plain, and, owing to the fact that the river was frequently too high to be crossed, traders set up on the banks providing services to the travellers' camps. Buildings were constructed on the floodplain, and the town was gazetted and surveyed in 1838. There are historical records (Crooks, 1989) of frequent warnings given to the Europeans by the local Aborigines that the location was not

Plate 9.3 The Ferry Boat Inn at Stoke Bardolph, Nottinghamshire, England. The sign by the door reads. 'This pub regularly floods on average once every three years damaging beyond repair the seating and other fixtures. No insurance company will cover the damage but we keep the pub open and in pristine condition – because we love it and you love it.'

safe. The town was flooded to a depth of 1 m in 1844 and again in 1851, the response being to construct upper storeys presumed above any flood height. Then, on 25 June 1852, the town was destroyed by a flood 4–5 m deep which killed eighty-nine people (over 30% of the population) and destroyed seventy-one buildings. The buildings were smashed by the flow and particularly by floating tree trunks. This remains Australia's worst flood disaster and it would have been even worse but for an Aboriginal named Yarri who saved many lives

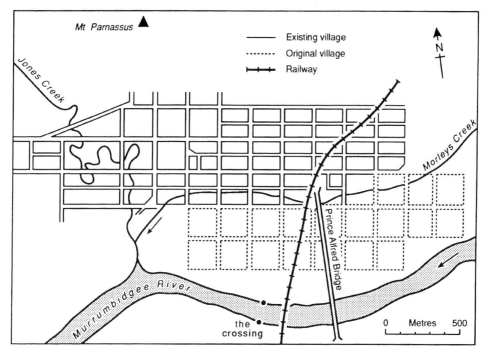

Fig. 9.6 Map of the old and new north town of Gundagai, New South Wales. Adapted from Crookes (1986).

during the flood using a bark canoe. After an even greater flood in 1853, the present town was built on the valley slopes to the south and north of the flood-plain. The lowest street of the new north town was the highest street of the old town (Figure 9.6). Plate 9.4 shows the floodplain where the original town was located, a unique metal bridge completed in 1867 and railway viaduct built in 1901.

The floodplain form does give some indication of the power of overbank flow in this environment, as it is uneven, with several flood channels, scour depressions and flood levées. The name Murrumbidgee is also derived from the Aboriginal word Morambeedja which means 'one big water' or 'mother of waters'.

This sort of flood disaster is unusual and related fundamentally to cultural factors, such as colonialism and unregulated development. Whether by song, story or myth, hazards were probably avoided until population pressure and free-market gains forced risk-taking activities. The record of flooding that is preserved in flood sediments along with settlement sites is rarely catastrophic in nature (otherwise the site would not survive), often reinforcing arguments in favour of gradual abandonment as does the common lack of finds on such sites, as valuable items go with people. Several sites such as the medieval village of West Cotton in Northamptonshire show valiant efforts to combat a flood

Plate 9.4 The floodplain at Gundagai, New South Wales, showing the new north and south towns each side of the floodplain and the railway viaduct (right) and Prince Alfred Bridge (left) which cross the floodplain over where the original town was sited.

hazard; here a flood embankment was constructed in order to protect the site. A larger-scale example is the repeated raising of floor levels in Rome's imperial port at Ostia. If abandonment does occur, it is probably due to a combination of factors, the most important being economic, so that it no longer becomes worth coping with persistent flooding. The most obvious cases would be a loss of river traffic or the loss of arable land on the floodplain causing a shift to higher ground.

9.4 Locational synthesis

As the lake and bog dwellers of northern Europe show, either the pull of the environment or the push from dry land was so great as to recompense for the considerable 'costs' of construction. While some sites may have been short-lived (e.g. Flag Fen in the Cambridgeshire Fens), others have long occupation histories. One of the most persistent and stable cultures remained, until recent times, the Marsh Arabs who live in the marshland at the junction of the Tigris and Euphrates in southern Iraq (Thesiger, 1967). While the emphasis on the negative factors associated with floodplain occupation has waned, the full importance of the floodplain corridor for dry-landscape archaeology is just beginning to be perceived. The balance between negative and positive factors will have changed over time, as a result not only of environmental change, but

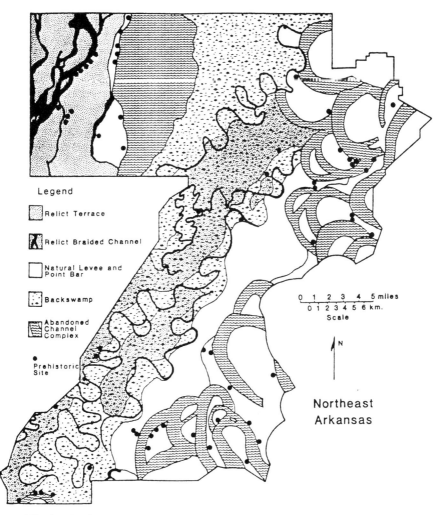

Fig. 9.7 Settlement patterns in the Lower Mississippi valley. From Guccione *et al.* (1988), reproduced by permission of *Geoarchaeology*.

also of socioeconomic factors. Labour, for example, might be drawn from wetland activities, in order to intensify dryland farming. The capacity of humans to tolerate change should not be underestimated. In their study of the environmental constraints on human settlement on the Lower Mississippi, Guccione *et al.* (1988) showed that, despite quite profound changes in the floodplain environment, it was continuously settled and exploited for 3000 years. A statistical analysis of site catchments in the valley also showed that the sites most likely to be occupied were well-drained surfaces in proximity to a stream course. This can be seen from Figure 9.7, where the prehistoric sites clearly cluster close to the present and former channels. However, the full extent of preservation bias in this, as in other studies, is not known, although in this

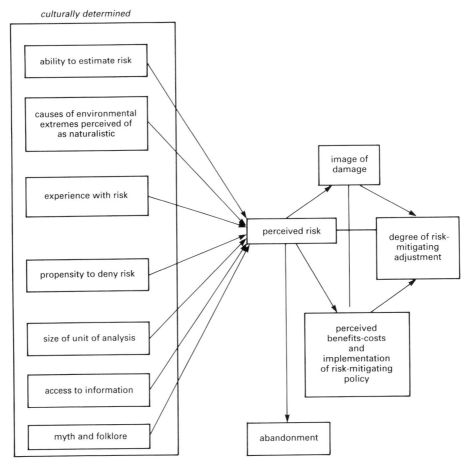

Fig. 9.8 The chain of factors between hazard/resource and behaviour, modified from Mitchell (1984).

case it would require over thirty sites (or 50% more) to be located in the empty space in order to redress the balance.

The relationships between environmental factors implicitly used in any site catchment analysis and the reason why a site is where it is, even in a functional sense, remain far from resolved in most cases. The economic models of Von Thunen, Weber or Christaller are inappropriate for prehistoric communities. Although it has proven useful, it is not essential to take an entirely resource maximising/economically rational view of the relationships between resources and behaviour. The binary opposition of negative and positive factors, push and pull, can only be a first step in the search for more comprehensive explanations which reflect the complexity of human society. One person's hazard may be another person's opportunity, depending upon the structure of society. We need to know more about the management of risk and how it was distributed amongst social and economic groups. We should seek archaeological evidence for the links in the chain (Figure 9.8) which might partially explain how resources were perceived and prioritised and by whom. Important factors must include information collection and flow, and an unbiased picture of the subsistence base.

The unavoidable conflict of negative and positive aspects of riverine habitation are well illustrated by flood myths. Flood myths can be thought of as confronting the primeval conflict of good and evil through the creation (guilt)–flood-solution (absolution) problem (Frymer-Kensky, 1988). Floods tend to be more beneficial in those myths where drought means famine (Follansbee, 1988) and this illustrates the contextual nature of the river as resource and hazard. An interesting illustration of this can be seen in the experience of a flood by archaeologists and local inhabitants. In 1931, the excavators of Nuzi, an alluvial site in northern Iraq, were working when a flood occurred. Despite the damage to the site, which disrupted excavation, and devastation of the nearby village, the local inhabitants, although disturbed at losing their possessions, 'cheerfully set about rebuilding, joyful in the knowledge that the rain from heaven assured a particularly abundant harvest' (Follansbee, 1988). In Semitic mythology, fertility is associated with the Tammuz ritual. Tammuz is called the 'bringer of beneficent floods'. The almost certain polygenesis of the flood myth suggests that irrespective of its cultural, societal or psychoanalytical meanings it is one of the most pervasive and accessible metaphors humans can use.

10

PEOPLE, FLOODPLAINS AND ENVIRONMENTAL CHANGE

This final chapter further develops the theme of human–environment interactions in alluvial contexts. It aims to show how environmental change at a variety of temporal scales and human response can be viewed not as being deterministic, but, owing to sociocultural factors, as semi-predictable if enough is known about human perceptions of environmental change and the socioeconomic structure of society. A simplistic neo-classical model is used as the springboard for exploring the many social, cultural and political factors which cause this to be so. It is argued that at the root of past simplistic views of human–environment interactions has been a deep-seated conceptualised dichotomy between humans and environment most poignantly illustrated in the false dichotomy of the 'human versus climate' debate over the causes of alluviation.

10.1 Palaeohydrology, climate and resources

In 1967, Sir Mortimer Wheeler commented caustically on the 'established belief in recurrent changes of climate, the imprecise usage of the term such as "wetter", "drier", "warmer", "more genial": "wetter" etc. than what?' (Wheeler in Raikes, 1967). In chapters 3, 4 and 8 various methods of reconstructing past river flow and climate were introduced. The reasoning employed in palaeohydrology is typical of that used in the interpretation of environment–climate interactions (Figure 10.1). Deductive reasoning is used to determine level 2 information. Implications for levels 3, 4 and 5 are considerably more speculative. One way of reducing this speculative element is by using some model of the hydrological system. The palaeohydrological estimates can be used as inputs to, or tests of, hydrological models. These may be simple balance-type models, as shown below;

$$Q = P - E_t \pm G_s \pm S_s \pm I_t$$

where Q is discharge, P is precipitation, E_t is evapotranspiration, G_s is groundwater storage, S_s is soil moisture storage and I_t is any inter-basin transfer. The use of water-balance models with estimates of global warming due to the burning of fossil fuels has suggested that climatic sensitivity will be greatest in drier zones (Shaake, 1990). Sophisticated hydrological models such as the Stanford Watershed model may be used in conjunction with General Circulation Models (GCMs); however, because these models include as many

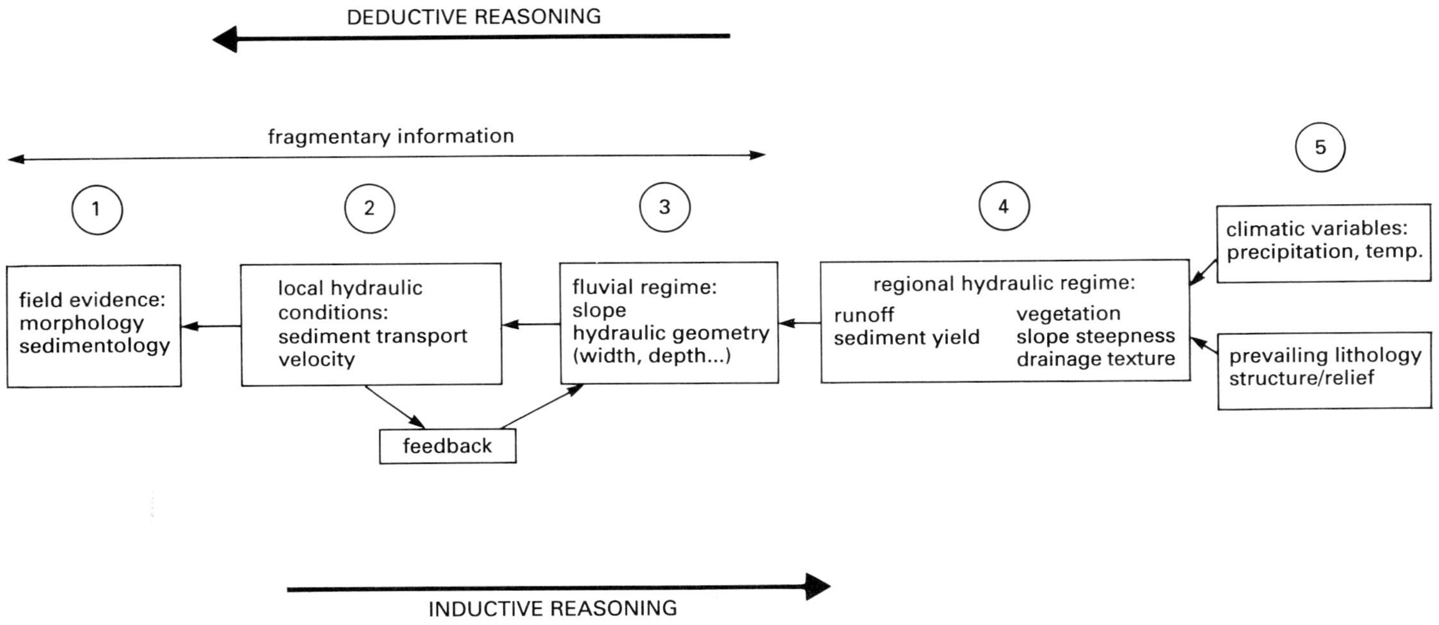

DEDUCTIVE REASONING

fragmentary information

① field evidence:
    morphology
    sedimentology

② local hydraulic
    conditions:
    sediment transport
    velocity

    feedback

③ fluvial regime:
    slope
    hydraulic geometry
    (width, depth....)

④ regional hydraulic regime:
    runoff   vegetation
    sediment yield slope steepness
                    drainage texture

⑤ climatic variables:
    precipitation, temp.

    prevailing lithology
    structure/relief

INDUCTIVE REASONING

Fig. 10.1 The reasoning chain in palaeohydrology. Adapted from Baker (1974a).

of the processes in the hydrological system as possible they require heavy parameterisation. The water-balance approach has been used by Lockwood (1979; 1983) to estimate the hydrological regime of a lowland catchment in central England during the Atlantic/Neolithic (*c.* 6000 bp). He has shown that, despite higher annual precipitation, streamflow may have been marginally less than it is today; it was probably also, and more importantly, less variable. This is due to the forest cover that is assumed to have existed; this would have increased interception and decreased storm runoff. Soils would also probably have had a higher infiltration capacity and a higher moisture storage capacity, also tending to reduce storm runoff.

The input to these models can also come from palaeoecological data including tree rings and Coleoptera (Barber and Coope, 1987). Data from the productivity, growth and decay rates of biological systems such as peat bogs may also produce proxy palaeoclimatic estimates (Barber, 1981; Barber *et al.*, 1994). We now have a reasonably good outline of temperature and rainfall (less good) variations throughout the Holocene for many parts of the globe, but far less is known about variation in the magnitude and frequency of climatic events (Flohn and Fantechi, 1984; Gregory, 1988). We need to know this, because it is events that have the most immediate effect on human populations, whether they are droughts, floods or fires. Although we may be facing a slow rise in global sea level at the moment, it is the increasing incidence of coastal flooding that will have a direct effect on society. As has already been discussed in chapter 9, it is through phenomena that most people in most societies perceive their environment. These can be reconstructed using palaeohydrological methods which can potentially provide quantitative estimates with a reasonable range of likely error for hydrological parameters against which settlement history can be evaluated. They can, for example, provide a measure of hazard or negative resources in terms of both flood and drought. Positive resources or resource potential can be estimated using productivity models for the past, just as they have been used for the future (Parry, 1975; 1978; 1990), but they can only be used with a sound understanding of other inputs, including technology and labour. In order to estimate resource implications we have to convert our model of climate change into a form appropriate for management and the assessment of human response.

Flood frequency and magnitude: the nested frequency concept
Even in countries which have been collecting both meteorological and hydrological records for a century or more, such as Britain or the United States of America, it remains difficult to obtain an accurate assessment of the flood risk under the current climatic regime (Bevan, 1993). This is particularly true where extreme floods result from a combination of processes such as snowmelt, rain and high tides, as is the case with most large centres of population located on large floodplains. There is an assumption that the occurrence of events con-

forms to an underlying probability distribution of some sort (e.g Generalised Extreme Value distribution), the parameters of which have to be calculated from river records or estimated from catchment characteristics. The problem is that this assumes that the processes that produce floods do not change and so the parameters used to estimate the flood distribution will remain constant. This is not the case, as palaeohydrological studies show. The period 1920s–60s, from which our modern averages are calculated, is now known to have been atypical with low inter-annual variability and the warmest mean temperatures of the last half millennium. In Southern Europe the 30-year mean rainfall has varied by 40% and in Northern Europe by 15% (Flohn and Fantechi, 1984).

Floods are affected not only by changes in climate but also in land use; so, an assumption of stationarity of the magnitude/frequency distribution of flood events is unhelpful in the analysis of both past and future changes in floodplain environments in response to climate change. An alternative conceptual framework is a nested frequency distribution, giving a mixed signal in the long-term record (Figure 10.2; Brown, 1991). Two approaches can be taken to modelling the impact of future climate change on flooding, the waterbalance approach and stochastic simulation, but given the inadequate representation of basin response in these models (Bevan, 1993) predictions must be regarded as subject to considerable uncertainty. Given the present climatic change scenario, of about 2°C rise in temperature and an increase on average of both winter and summer rainfall, we would expect the frequency of floods to increase although extreme flood peaks may not. Although not catastrophic there may be significant implications for society, including a need for mitigating measures such as land use and drainage management in order to reduce peak runoff, and investment in flood defences, although, given the tendency of flood defenses to relocate and worsen the problem floodplain zonation would be more advisable. What measures will be taken over the next thirty years can be only semi-predicted, on the basis of the perceived threat and present economic trends.

Integrating environmental change and risk
The impact of any environmental change, such as an increase in the frequency or magnitude of flooding or drought, depends upon a complex interaction between many variables. These include: access to information, understanding of likely or possible consequences, political will and economic resources. Since these factors will vary from society to society, it follows that response will vary irrespective of the size of the threat. The importance of the affluence of the society in hazard impact is illustrated by the abundant data on differential death tolls in developed and non-developed countries resulting from similar catastrophes. Owing to overcrowding, poor medical facilities, vulnerable housing and occupation of the most vulnerable land, hazards such as floods, hurricanes and earthquakes kill many times more people in developing than developed countries, irrespective of the geological hydrological magnitude. An

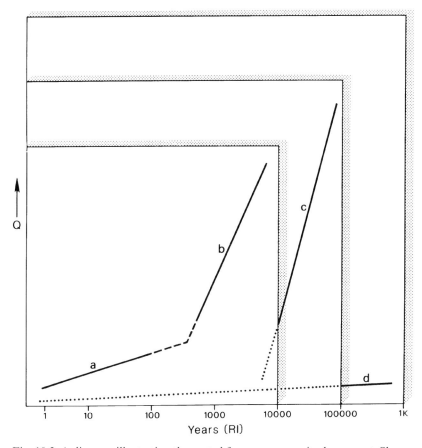

Fig. 10.2 A diagram illustrating the nested frequency-magnitude concept. Slope a is the flood series produced by 'normal' interglacial maritime processes, e.g. westerly air masses crossing the British Isles, and floods are rainfall generated. Slope b is the flood series produced by coincidence of rainfall and/or snowmelt (maximum controlled by maximum rainfall intensity + maximum melt rate). Some historical floods fall into this series, including the 1947 flood and probably floods that occurred in the 'Little Ice Age'. Slope c represents large floods caused by a sudden change in the thermal regime resulting in rapid melting of ice-fronts, glacial-lake bursts, etc. Slope d represents rather low variance regimes produced by cold continental conditions, low rainfall and limited summer melting. Cold ice conditions unfavourable for surges or jokulahaups. Reproduced from Brown in *Temperate Palaeohydrology*, Starkel, Gregory and Thornes (1991), by permission of John Wiley and Sons Ltd.

example is the effects of Cyclone Tracey which struck Darwin, Australia, in 1974 and killed sixty-four people and Hurricane Fifi which struck Honduras in the same year killing 8000 people. Both areas are prone to tropical cyclones, both storms were of the same intensity and both destroyed over 80 % of the buildings in the main impact zones (Bryant, 1991).

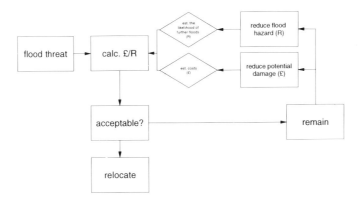

Fig. 10.3 A simple rational model of floodplain dwellers' response to flood hazard. See the text for a discussion of the naïvety of such a model and other important factors and constraints.

It can be argued that archaeology illustrates the evolution of this situation through the emergence and development of inequality and its material consequences in housing quality, residential location and population density. While this is often regarded as a Marxist analysis (Bryant, 1991) it is shared by a wide spectrum of authorities with differing ideological positions, and only becomes strictly Marxist when the assumption is made that, if workers were able to control their own labour, they would be better adapted to contend with the vagaries of the natural environment.

As a starting point, a simple rational model would suggest that flooding will be accepted and adapted to (or coped with) *in situ* as long as the combination of the costs of moving elsewhere and the opportunity costs of the riverside location exceed the costs of damage, rebuilding and flood defences (Figure 10.3). Work on individual choice and decision making has further refined this model into three variants: expected utility, subjective expected utility and bounded rational choice (Burton *et al.,* 1978). Expected rationality is where a choice is made on the basis of an assessment of all the expected outcomes. Subjective expected utility choice is where a choice is made on the basis of a person's subjective view of the probability of expected outcomes. Bounded rational choice is where a judgement is arrived at by a subjective assessment of utility with something less than the goal of choosing the maximum returns. If we take the case of riverside dwellers who have been warned of a flood but do not know if the flood will breach the levée: if the property is worth two units and the cost of evacuation is one unit, then there are four possible outcomes. If they do not evacuate and the river does not breach the levée, then nothing is lost; whereas if it does breach the levee, they lose all. If they evacuate they lose the cost of evacuation, regardless of the height of the flood. If we assume that the probability of the flood breaching the levée is known accurately and is 4 out of 10, then the expected utility of the choice can be calculated

Table 10.1. *Payoff matrices for flood: expected utility and known*
probability (adapted from Burton et al., 1978 and Slovic et al., 1974).

	Flood breaches the levee	Flood fails to breach the levee	Expected utility
Evacuate	pay for evacuation $0.4\times1=0.4$	pay for evacuation $0.6\times1=0.6$	1.0
Remain	lose all $0.4\times0=0$	no loss $0.6\times2=1.2$	1.2

(see Table 10.1): in this case the greater expected utility is derived by remaining put! If, however, the probability of the levee being overtopped has increased unbeknownst to the dwellers, and it is now 6 out of 10, then the decision would result in a loss. This analysis also assumes that the values and probabilities accurately represent those of the floodplain dweller. With subjective expected utility, the dwellers may attach quite different values to their property or to the evacuation than might an outsider and the chances of the levée being breached may be estimated in another way. These judgements would then determine the payoff using the same method as for expected utility. An alternative is that the dwellers are offered inducements to stay or leave, which might or might not be determined from expected or subjective utility, and a further alternative is that the dwellers are not interested in maximising the payoff, but want to follow a course of action by which they are assured that the costs do not exceed one unit. In this case of bounded rationality, the difference between 1.2 and 1 is immaterial and they would evacuate. These different strategies may in a broad sense relate to opportunistic and conservative behaviours at the individual scale (Van der Leeuw, 1989).

As the above example shows, in theory the outcome depends on access to information, the ability to process it and the values of the individual or society and social structure. Studies of human response to flooding show, however, that this is not entirely the case even in developed countries today. The reasons for the failure of these economic models to predict hazard response are illuminating for both explaining the past and predicting the future:

1 Information on the probability distribution of flooding is never complete or entirely accurate.
2 The opportunity costs of floodplain abandonment are not easily estimated and will change if some abandonment occurs.
3 Optimism, or extreme risk-taking behaviour.
4 Transfer of the costs of the location to another body, e.g. landlord or state.
5 Inability to move owing to political control.
6 Fatalistic beliefs.

Information on the likelihood of an event of a certain magnitude is extremely useful and there are a variety of ways in which such information may be stored. In some ancient societies, such as ancient Egypt, and in modern times, written environmental records can form the basis of risk estimation, which since the seventeenth century has been based in the formal application of probability theory. The very action of recording the magnitude of events allows comparisons to be made year to year and so implies that there will be developed a *normal expectation of the magnitude of the event* (as the ancient Egyptians clearly had), which is the basis of unformalised probability. In other societies, environmental history may only be communicated orally through stories and song and so will depend upon individual and community memory and cultural continuity. The role of the elderly as the keepers of community memory may have been important in some societies; however, unfortunately this is rather invisible archaeologically.

Chapter 9 described some of the opportunity costs of floodplain abandonment and how they vary naturally and with technology. If, in the face of a hazard, some abandonment occurs, the returns on the floodplain resources could easily increase for those who are left, so raising the threshold at which they would leave and reducing the overall response. This is one of the reasons why partial abandonment is common, with a small settlement persisting often for hundreds of years. This is closely related to risk-taking behaviour, which although it can be seen as being a fundamental part of human biology can also be seen, as above, as just one economic strategy, even though it is often misguided. Likewise the costs of coping can be reduced, if part or all is shouldered by someone else. This may be through beneficence or charitable action or an accepted responsibility by landlord or government. It is a combination of this strategy with formal estimation of the risk that has been developed as flood insurance and has allowed the settlement of many flood-prone areas in developed countries, and fuelled the engine of flood protection.

There are many reasons why relocation may not be possible under almost any circumstances (such the strategic importance of a bridge), but whatever the reason this will operate through power structures within society. Indeed, the idea of not coping, but moving, is inappropriate in highly authoritarian systems, just as it is if fatalistic beliefs are predominant in society.

The benefits of coping through the reduction of loss is undoubtedly one of the forces promoting technological change, as discussed in chapter 9: the invention of the stilt house, flood barrage or early warning system as an important response. One problem which the past highlights is that these responses have tended to be either individual and/or piecemeal and, owing to society's lack of understanding of the mechanics of the process, have actually increased the risk in the longer term and/or for others. The embanking of towns and rivers has dramatically reduced the area available for flood storage on most large floodplains. The result is that peak flood heights increase and so flooding may be worse, especially for those areas not embanked (Richards, 1982). The technological treadmill of increased embanking, flood insurance, increased flood heights, increased embanking etc. has been questioned on both environmental and economic grounds in recent years. The adoption of alternatives such as floodplain zonation and management depends upon political control, which varies with perception, ideology and resources.

Beck (1992) argues that risk, its sources, perception and management, are increasingly taking a central role in capitalist post-industrial cultural change. Beck emphasises that physical risks are created and affected in social systems, but that, prior to industrialisation, risks were generally local in nature and external (natural); technology has, through the conquest of these risks of survival, created the new risks of technology which are generally invisible and often regional or even global (e.g. radioactivity, acid rain, global warming). Pre-industrial risks were visible in the widest sense whereas modern and future risks can escape perception. It follows that the individual or group cannot, under these circumstances, make the sort of choices outlined earlier; so, an elite emerges through which both the risks and society are managed. Depending upon the prevailing ideology of a state, this may vary from the corporate view of the state's responsibility and little direct involvement of the population to capitalist privatisation of the problem through individualisation of the risks and solutions.

The changing nature of environmental risk and the variety of societal factors that may be responsible for human responses are illustrated in both the archaeological and historical records and clearly show us that there has never been and will not be in the future a single determinable response to a set of environmental parameters. This realisation allows us to face possible future changes in climate and other human-induced environmental change with a possibilistic theory of likely response based upon economic, cultural and political analysis.

Apportioning blame: alluviation and the false human–environment dichotomy
Contemporary studies of recent environmental change, such as global warming, show just how difficult, and some would argue unrealistic, it is to separate natural from human impacts (Goudie, 1981). It is also becoming evident with post-industrial climate change that it may not matter, in that since the climate of the future is determined by *both* human and natural factors which are probably beyond practical control (given the distribution of wealth and the marginal effect of controlling emissions), then it is the impacts and repercussions on agricultural and economic systems which must be the focus of our attention. The apportioning of blame to nature and human actions may have psychological-cultural origins and management implications but can obscure the reality of the *combined* nature of causality in all but the most excep-

tional contexts. This is illustrated by the climate versus human debate over the causes of periods of increased alluviation in the archaeological record (see chapter 7, section 7.4). In reality, ever since there has been *any* human impact on vegetation there has been *some* human impact on catchment hydrology and sediment yield. The magnitude of the effect can be assumed to increase with the proportion of the catchment so affected. In conceptual terms the alluvial response can be thought of as:

$$A/dt = Q_{cf}/dt . S_{av}/dt$$

where A is the rate of alluvial deposition, Q_{cf} is discharges competent to transport sediments above bankfull, and S_{av} is sediment available for transport. Given that in the case of suspended sediment flood flows can normally transport all sediment available to them, transport and deposition is a function of channel erosion and erosive land uses since both increase sediment availability. So a change in flood frequency and magnitude can affect both the availability of sediment, through erosion, and its transport and deposition. Human alteration of land use affects both terms in this equation and so in conceptual terms we should think of the alluvial record as being the *product* of climate as modified by human alterations of catchment characteristics *and* human land use. The balance between these two terms has clearly altered during the Holocene; so whereas in the Mesolithic it might be accurate to regard the alluvial record as essentially a climatic signal blurred by human impact, by historical times it can be argued, as it is in this book, that we have a land use signal blurred by climatic variation. Discovering the changing balance of these factors over time, and from region to region, should be one of the prime aims of future geoarchaeological research into alluvial environments. The question of a climatic or human causality of a particular alluvial episode is therefore a falsely dichotomous view of the problem.

10.2 Floodplain settlement and environmental change: past and future
Present concerns over human impact on the Earth's climate – global warming and its effects on sea level – have forced both environmental and social scientists to re-examine the relationships between society and environmental change. While this was once a major theme in the social sciences, it has largely been replaced by sociopolitical studies, in which the natural environment is not a major concern in comparison with the built environment. Archaeology has, however, neglected the natural environment far less than the other social sciences, partly because of the development of scientific and environmental archaeology.

One of the major research themes of environmental archaeology has been the effects of environmental change on past societies and this is directly relevant to contemporary questions concerning the social impact of predicted

THE CO$_2$ PYRAMID

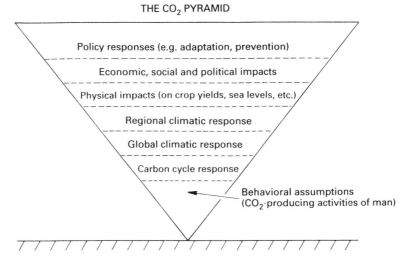

Fig. 10.4 A schematic representation of the cascading pyramid of uncertainties associated with the global warming problem.

climate change. The view that the past is the key to a better understanding of the future lies at the heart of several major research programmes on global environmental change including: CLIMAP (past climate mapping program – funded by the International Quaternary Association – INQUA), PAGES (Past Global Changes Project of the International Geosphere-Biosphere Programme – IGBP) and GLOCOPH (Commission on Global Continental Palaeo-hydrology) and other programmes funded by research councils and national and international scientific bodies. A major goal of the World Climate Programme started in 1979, later incorporated into the United Nations Environmental Programme (UNEP), was to develop a better understanding of the interaction of climate and society, so that policy makers can predict effects and formulate responses to climate change. Although we believe we under-stand, at least in outline, the processes responsible for greenhouse-gas-induced global warming, this will not inevitably lead to a solution (Houghton *et al.,* 1990). This is because, at the base of the cascading pyramid of uncertainty (Figure 10.4), is the amount of carbon dioxide injected into the atmosphere over the next few decades. This depends upon society and is not easy to predict. One can suggest, based upon past responses to generalised threats, that responses will be of two kinds: geotherapeutic measures to reduce carbon dioxide and other greenhouse gas emissions (probably a marginal effect given the inequality of global development) and impact alleviation to minimise dis-benefits (Perry, 1992).

An alternative view, based upon the analysis by Beck (1992), would be that, since the magnitude of the problem is difficult to know precisely, it is not possible for society to calculate the associated risks; in this situation, it becomes the construction and management of human perception of the risk that will determine response. The fact that we have limited room to change, in terms of carbon dioxide emissions, means that this environmental crisis is not fundamentally different from those past crises which may have impacted upon societies who did not understand their causes, irrespective of whether they thought they did or not. Adjustments will be political, such as the call for increased nuclear power production in order to reduce carbon dioxide emissions, the promotion of energy conservation, or government attempts to influence personal lifestyles. Depending upon the nature of the society, they may also be social and economic, individual or collective, democratic or dictatorial. Adjustments will vary according to the complexity of the society and can lead to changes in the organisation of that society. Integrated studies of environmental change and societal response illustrate this. Reference to two examples will suffice.

The response to regional desiccation in central North America around AD 1100 by the Mill Creek Indians was a change in subsistence to hunting. Maize cultivation was completely abandoned and there was a retreat from the cultivation of marginal areas. Here, we see a shift in the subsistence base – an adjustment at the household level which was aggregated up to the level of the culture (Barreis and Bryson, 1968). In contrast, if we look at the societal response to the 1627 flood in Mexico City, we see an institutional response. The response was that of an imposed colonial bureaucracy which converted the drama for all into a crisis for the indigenous peoples, with far more dying of disease than were killed by the flood itself (Hoberman, 1978). The seventeenth-century history of flood protection and response in Mexico City is a political–environmental story.

The response of any society to environmental change is fundamentally a product of its social, cultural and political identity. Most archaeological interpretations of human response to environmental change have been criticised as being deterministic and simplistic. This is not inherent in the topic but the result of using over-simplistic models of climate–society relationships, more like type (a) in Figure 10.5, rather than types (b) to (d). Since floodplains are one of the environments where the links between occupancy and resources, both negative and positive, are closest and floodplains can yield a high-quality geoarchaeological record, they have great potential for the examination of past societies' responses to environmental change, at a variety of scales from the Bronze Age household on the Thames floodplain at Runnymede to the decline of civilisations. As illustrated by the recent increase in geoarchaeological floodplain projects throughout Europe, and hopefully by this book, floodplains provide unparalleled opportunities for truly integrated multidisciplinary studies of environmental change and human causes and impacts which may point to future threats and management solutions.

(a) Input-output model

(b) Interactive model

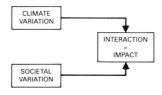

(c) Interactive model with feedback

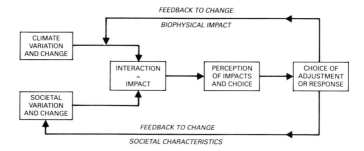

(d) Interactive model with feedback and underlying process

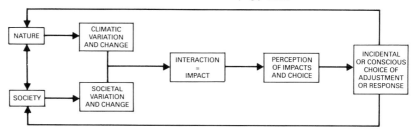

Fig. 10.5 A hierarchy of models of climate–society relationships. Adapted from Kates (1978).

APPENDICES

The aim of these appendices is to provide some theoretical background to parts of the thematic chapters and to provide supplementary information and comment on aspects related to the perception of alluvial environments. Appendix 1 provides the theory behind chapter 3 and palaeohydrology, whilst appendix 2 provides the theoretical background to flood frequency analysis, an important method used frequently throughout the book. Appendix 3 includes material which whilst, not central to the book, does illustrate and elaborate the discussions of the human use and perceptions of alluvial environments in chapters 8 and 9.

NOTATION

V   velocity
R   hydraulic radius (close to the mean depth for most natural channels)
v   kinematic viscosity
RI   return interval of an event (e.g. flood)
n   number of events
Re   Reynold's number
τ shear stress
Dv   velocity difference
ε eddy viscosity
g   acceleration due to gravity (approx. 9.81 m s^{-2})
F   Froude number
k   constant
S   slope
n   Manning's roughness coefficient
P_e potential energy
m   water mass
h   height above a datum
Q   discharge
W   width
D   depth
p_w specific weight of water
p_s specific weight of sediment particles
Ω power
ω specific power or power per unit of bed
τ_0 downslope shear stress component
τ_{th} shear stress at the threshold of entrainment
J   transport weight per unit width
f function
V_{th} flow velocity at the threshold of sediment entrainment
Q_s sediment discharge
J_b bedload transport rate per unit width
J_s suspended sediment transport rate

m_s suspended mass per unit area

V_s mean suspended load velocity

e_b bedload efficiency (dimensionless)

e_s suspended sediment efficiency (dimensionless)

$\varnothing$ dynamic friction coefficient (approximately the static angle of internal friction for a cohesionless mass of sand grains)

r   radius

V_f fall velocity

μ dynamic viscocity

d   grain size

Appendix 1

RIVER FLOW AND SEDIMENT TRANSPORT

1.1 Flow

The water which falls on a drainage basin but does not enter into groundwater storage is, at some point, conveyed by channels which may sit either in bedrock or on relatively unconsolidated alluvial deposits. For any channel we can measure the steady-flow or discharge by multiplying the cross-sectional area below the water level by the velocity of flow (Figure A.1). Water is a Newtonian fluid, unlike a flow of rock debris or tomato ketchup, and as such it cannot resist stress applied to it but shears in *direct proportion to that stress*. The behaviour of water in rivers and streams is controlled by viscosity and inertia because these forces govern the resistance of the fluid to acceleration caused by slope. The inertial resistance of water is controlled by mass density, and the ratio of inertial to viscous forces is described by the dimensionless Reynold's number (Re):

$$Re = VR/v$$

where V is velocity (ms^{-1}), R is hydraulic radius of flow (m) and v is kinematic viscosity (m^{2}s^{-1}). For low values of Re viscous forces prevail and flow is laminar, which can be conceptualised as parallel layers of water shearing over one another (Figure A1). But as velocity increases inertial forces increase, and above a critical Re number fluid motion becomes turbulent with random secondary motions or eddies superimposed upon the main downstream direction of flow. With laminar flow the shearing stress (τ) of fluid motion is proportional to the kinematic viscosity (v) and the velocity difference between two layers (i.e. a segment of the velocity profile):

$$\tau = v(Dv)$$

where D is the depth of flow. In turbulent flow additional viscous resistance is generated by the random movements of molecules (which results in a diffusion effect). This additional resistance is called eddy viscosity (ε) and shear stress in this case is calculated as:

$$\tau = (v + \varepsilon)Dv$$

The addition of ε which is generally much larger than v is the reason that for the same slope turbulent flow exerts a greater shear stress on bed and banks. In fact the laminar flow type is rare in rivers and most flow is of the turbulent type. Two types of turbulent flow may be differentiated on the basis of whether a

320

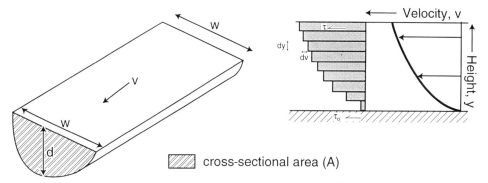

Fig. A1 A diagram of channel geometry and hydraulic parameters.

gravity wave can travel both upstream and downstream from a point. If it can, the flow is tranquil or subcritical turbulent flow, if it can only travel downstream it is called shooting or supercritical turbulent flow. The distinction is given by the Froude number (F) which is calculated from the equation below:

$$F=\frac{V}{\sqrt{(gD)}}$$

where g is the acceleration due to gravity. Subcritical flow occurs when the Froude number is under 1, and supercritical flow occurs when it is over 1. When the river is in flood, often with a choppy surface and breaking surface waves, the flow is turbulent and probably shooting. Although river velocity obviously varies (in general between about zero and 3m s^{-1}) it is kept from increasing further by the roughness of the river boundary, i.e. the rougher the surface the more the water will be slowed down. Indeed by measuring or estimating the roughness we can calculate the likely river velocity for a given slope and therefore the discharge using the Manning equation below (Figure A.1 and Table 3.2).

$$V=k_1R^{\frac{2}{3}}S^{\frac{1}{2}}n^{-1}$$

where V is velocity, k_1 is a constant, R is the hydraulic radius (equivalent to the mean depth for most channels), S is slope and n is Manning's roughness coefficient which varies from 0.014 for a concrete channel to 0.70 for a wide natural channel with sluggish weedy pools. There are several other flow formulae but all are based upon the depth–slope product with some constant or constants for friction losses of energy caused by the channel shape or perimeter characteristics. Earlier we referred to measuring steady flow; this is when discharge is constant over a period of time. There is another type of flow, which is unsteady, associated with varying discharge as for example when a flood wave passes down a channel. In practice most situations lie in-between (depending upon climate and river size) with gradually varying unsteady flow.

1.2 Sediment transport

Of particular importance to us is when, and how, the river does work, i.e. erodes and moves materials. Rivers obviously can have the power to do a lot of work, despite most of their energy being lost to heat, and the calculation of this power is the basis of sediment transport equations. Streams convert potential energy to kinetic energy. From basic physics we can calculate the power of the stream (called stream power) and the stream power per unit area of stream bed, as below: the potential energy of water (P_e) is given by:

$$P_e = mgh$$

where m is water mass, g is gravitational acceleration and h is height above the datum. If we want to measure the mass of water in a river passing a point for a given time period (discharge or Q), conventionally per second (s^{-1}) we can do this from the flow equation below:

$$Q = W\overline{D}V$$

where W is the river width, $\overline{D}$ is the mean depth and V is the velocity of water. This water flowing downslope will lose this potential energy at the rate:

$$\Omega = pgQS$$

where Ω is power in Watts per metre (Wm^{-1}), p is the specific weight of water (e.g. 1000 kg m^{-3}), g is gravitational acceleration (9.8 m s^{-1}), Q is discharge (where $Q = W\overline{D}V$ in $m^{-3}s^{-1}$) and s is slope. This is normally converted into a specific power or power per unit of bed (ω) by:

$$\omega = \Omega/W$$

This power is available to transport particles of various sizes and it is related to the shear stress (Ω) that we have previously defined, thus:

$$\omega = \tau_0 \overline{V}$$

where τ_0 is the downslope shear stress component calculated from the equation below:

$$\tau_0 = pgh \sin S$$

Most sediment transport equations have one of two forms (Allen, 1977):

$$J = f_1(\overline{V} - V_{th})$$

or

$$J = f_2(\omega)$$

where J is dry-mass transport rate per unit width, $\overline{V}$ is the mean flow velocity, V_{th} is the flow velocity at the threshold of sediment entrainment, ω is specific stream power and *f* is a function. $\overline{V}$ and V_{th} can be replaced by τ_0 and τ_{th} representing the respective boundary downslope shear stress and the boundary shear stress at the threshold of entrainment. Greater values of J will be required to move more sediment, which is the *capacity* of the flow, and larger particles, which is the *competence* of the flow. The boundary shear stress describes the forces applied to the channel which must be balanced by the channel resistance if erosion is not to occur. In order to apply flow equations appropriately we must recognise that there are different types of river sediment load. There is the load in solution called the *dissolved load*; that which is, or may be suspended, called the *suspended load*; and lastly the *bedload* which is bed material which moves by rolling, sliding and jumping, or to put it another way particles which are not supported by the flow except momentarily. The solution load moves at the velocity of water or diffuses to an equilibrium concentration in response to a concentration gradient. Despite the fact that the dissolved load is probably responsible for at least as much of the sediment leaving the continents as the suspended load (Walling and Webb, 1986) it is not of relevance here because it is the product of biochemical weathering of rocks and soils which, although important on the geological time-scale, and the day-to-day scale in soils, has only indirect relevance to geoarchaeological problems. It is, however, closely related to the prime causes of the destruction of archaeological evidence such as bone dissolution through leaching!

The suspended load is of importance because it represents much of the removal of eroded soil into and out of floodplain systems. The suspended load is subdivided into the wash load which is in almost permanent suspension and the coarser saltation or suspended bedload which is only suspended above certain flow velocities or shear stresses. The wash load therefore is largely supply-controlled, i.e. by the severity of catchment erosion now and in the past, and primarily not by flow conditions. Through flooding it is the suspended load that is often responsible for the burial and preservation of archaeological sites and the characteristics of floodplain soils. We therefore need to understand the controls on suspended sediment transport. As has already been implied, it is possible to define a critical velocity representing the ability of a flow to carry material of a given size, or competence of a flow, as the lowest velocity at which a particle of a given size, density and shape will move. In general it requires higher shear stresses and velocities to move larger and heavier particles, but as the modified Hjulstrom curve shows (Figure A.2), below a particle diameter of about 0.5 mm increased velocities are required; this is because cohesion increases with decreasing particle grain size, and so those particles which are silts and clays (under 0.063 mm) clump together forming larger aggregates. Indeed sometimes these aggregates can be so large that they cannot be suspended at all and form part of the bed material (e.g. mudballs which are occasionally revealed in excavations). The curve also shows a fall velocity line demarcating sedimentation from transportation. This indicates that the initial

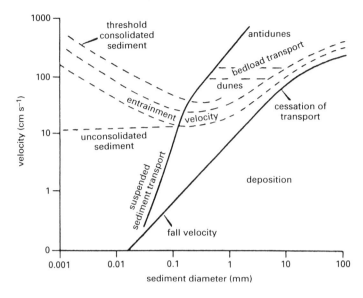

Fig. A2 A modified Hjulstrom curve.

critical velocity required for movement or entrainment is greater than that
required to sustain transport. The bedload and suspended load will now be
dealt with in a little more detail.

The critical tractive force, or force required to move a particle on the channel
bed, can be calculated using the Du Boys equation as given below:

$$Q_s = k\tau_0(\tau_0 - \tau_{th})$$

where Q_s is the sediment discharge and k is a constant. This equation is the
basis of tractive force equations, the most widely used of which are the Shield's
formula:

$$Q_s = \frac{10QS\,(\tau_0 - \tau_{th})\,d_{50}}{(p_s/p - 1)^2}$$

and the Meyer-Peter and Muller (1948) equation:

$$Q_s^{2/3} = 250Q^{2/3}S - 42.5d_{50}$$

Assuming a water density of 988kKg m^{-3} an equivalent simplified formula
(Richards, 1982) is:

$$Q_s = 0.253\,(\tau_0 - \tau_{th})^{2/3}$$

Like all tractive force equations it is limited in its applicability, in this case to
relatively low bedload transport conditions with medium sand–gravel beds and
not much saltating or suspended load. A slightly different approach is based
on stream power expenditure which follows the second of the generalised trans-

port equations given earlier in this appendix (Yang, 1972). This has particular applicability to the coarse suspended load sediment as is described in the next section. An alternative and very different approach was formulated by Einstein (1950). Einstein's stochastic model of bedload transport is based upon the probability distribution of lift forces in turbulent flow and a transport intensity function based upon the probability of particle exchange at the bed. So far it has been the first of these approaches, which is known as tractive force theory, which has been used to try and predict past flows from sediments (palaeohydraulics) and to model the transport of artifacts and bones, as is discussed later in this appendix and in chapter 3.

Some particles or aggregates will be transported in suspension at moderate flows well below the velocities required to initiate bedload transport. As long as the vertical component of lift by turbulent eddies is great enough particles will remain in suspension. As flow increases so a particle will first vibrate, start rolling, then start saltating in an interrupted jump, be involved in collisions (imparting energy to other saltating grains) and eventually go into uninterrupted suspension (Leeder, 1982). As previously mentioned, excess stream power can be used to estimate the transport of coarser suspended load. The immersed weight transport rate can be given by:

$$J_s = [(p_s - p)p]m_s g \overline{V}_s$$

where p_s is the sediment specific weight, p the specific weight of water, m_s the suspended mass per unit area. The friction coefficient is not bed related as in the case of bedload but given by the ratio of the fall velocity V_f to the suspended sediment velocity V_s, i.e. the particle will be kept in suspension if the turbulence provides a vertical velocity component equal to the particle fall velocity. The work rate will be maintained by the power remaining after power use in bedload transport and so this suspended load fraction is in essence suspended bedload. The suspended load equation based on the above theory is:

$$J_s V_f / V_s = \omega e_s (1 - e_b)$$

where e_b is the bedload efficiency which is zero below the transport threshold but increases rapidly as transport begins as it is affected by bedform development because form roughness reduces the power available for transport, and e_s is the suspended sediment efficiency. Bagnold (1966) gives the efficiency of $e_s(1 - e_b)$ as around 0.01.

Other equations for predicting suspended load transport are based on the diffusion (the result of turbulent eddies) and the velocity profile. Since fine suspended load can be transported even by moderate flows, most river regimes allow transport of fine sediment and so more attention is often given to the volume of material that can be transported and the conditions under which sedimentation occurs. As we have seen, the bedload capacity of a stream depends upon stream gradient and discharge. This is not the case with wash and fine suspended load as transport rates are generally set by the supply of fine sediment to the stream. This is indicated by the extremely high concentrations of suspended sediment reached by rivers such as the Yellow river in China. One of its tributaries, the Dali river, has a mean annual sediment yield of 25,600 t $km^{-2}yr^{-1}$ which is the highest known annual value on Earth (Walling and Webb, 1983). If suspended sediment is over about 10% by volume the nature of fluid flow is changed and non-Newtonian hydraulics apply.

As water velocity decreases so material may start to fall out of suspension as suggested by the sedimentation line on the Hjulstrom curve. For spherical grains under 2 mm in size the well known Stoke's Law applies. The drag resistance of a spherical particle fall through a fluid depends upon the area of the grain ($6\pi r$), the viscosity of the fluid which is temperature dependent and the velocity of fall. This is added to the buoyancy force tending to hold the particle up. For suspension this must equal the downward force which is related to the volume of the sphere and its density (or submerged weight). This is simplified to the equation given below:

$$V_f = \frac{[(p_s - p_w)g]d^2}{18\mu}$$

where d is the grain diameter, p_s is the particle density, p_w is the water density and μ is the dynamic viscocity. The equation only strictly applies to particles below 0.1 mm in diameter as above this some account should be taken of inertial forces and above 2 mm inertial forces are dominant. Also, even in low concentrations, wash load can retard settling. Since gravity, density of water and viscosity remain constant (or nearly so) we can see that the settling velocity of a spherical grain depends upon its size and density. In general this means that for small grains (under 2 mm) velocity increases with the square of grain diameter. In clear water at a temperature of 20°C and assuming the sediment has a density of 2.65 g cm^{-3} (i.e. that of quartz) this simplifies to:

$$V_f = 9000d^2$$

Stoke's or similar equations can be used to calculate the upward velocity required to keep grains in suspension or the size of grains that will settle out under still-water conditions in a given period of time. For example during flood inundation, water 1 m deep and at 20°C would have to remain still for over 2½ hours to allow all the sand and coarse silt grains (over 0.06 mm) to settle out, and over 17 hours to allow all the fine silt grains (between 0.006 mm and 0.002 mm) to settle out. Since water is agitated by winds and thermal turbulence this means that particles of this size may remain suspended or take many hours or days to settle out. Particles smaller than 0.001 mm (1 micron) are so affected by Brownian motion that they will not settle out at all even with zero velocity unless flocculation occurs or the water column disappears through infiltration into the floodplain soil, or evaporation. Flocculation and the formation of aggregates is the dominant process of sedimentation in this case. This has important implications for floodplain sediments, including the potential role of aggregating agents and plants in affecting the rate of deposition of fine suspended sediment, both in and out of channels. It may also be the scientific basis for the processes of warping discussed in chapter 8. It is these principles and Stoke's equation which is utilised in grain size analysis of fine sediments by either the pipette or hydrometer methods and also by methods based on the transmission of light, laser energy or X-rays across a settling tube (see later in appendix 1 for more on methods).

Bagnold (1966) produced an equation for total load (suspended and bedload) derived from first principles. It is based upon the transport rate calculated as the product of available stream power and stream efficiency using the equations we have already introduced. Assuming $V_s = V$ the total load is given by bedload plus suspended load thus:

$$J = J_b + J_s$$

which equals:

$$\omega \left(\frac{e_b}{\tan\varnothing} + \frac{e_s V_s}{v_f} . (1 - e_b) \right)$$

which simplifies to:

$$\omega \left(\frac{e_b}{\tan\varnothing} + 0.01 . \frac{V}{v_f} \right)$$

where $\varnothing$ is the dynamic friction coefficient. However, this does not apply to the fine wash load of a stream, only to the bedload and suspended bedload in the plane-bed regime. It should be clear from the preceding discussion that bedload and the coarse suspended load cannot be treated as being independent.

1.3 Grain size analysis and palaeohydraulics

As mentioned earlier, for the bedload the entrainment of particles is a function of the energy available for transport. It is the estimation of this energy and its conversion into velocity and depth of flow that is the basis of the palaeohydraulic estimation of past flows. Other factors being equal (such as bed conditions), and in the absense of cohesion, the velocity required to move a particle is directly proportional to the diameter of the particle. In extremely well-sorted sediments there may be one grain size, but in most fluvial sediments there is a range of grain sizes which is measured by grain or particle size analysis. Grain size analysis is a quantitative description of non-consolidated sediments which is used to aid facies identification and can be used to reconstruct past hydraulic parameters. The methods all involve the separation of a bulk sample into size fraction and then the measurement of the mass in each fraction. The mass is then plotted against the size classes to give a grain size curve for the sediment.

The curve is generally cumulative and log-transformed to produce a near-straight or typically S-shaped curve. Statistical parameters can then be read off the graph (or calculated directly be computer) such as the median grain size (d_{50}), the 84th percentile (d_{84} where 84% is finer) or other statistical measures such as the sorting, skewness or kurtosis (Folk and Ward, 1957; Briggs, 1977). The method used will vary with the sediment size and range (Table A1). The largest pebbles and cobbles can be individually measured (long and short axes) using callipers or a tape-measure but dry sieving using a sieve shaker is the most suitable method for gravels and coarse sand. Wet sieving is particularly suitable for fine sands and silts and sedimentation techniques are suitable for silts and clays. Sedimentation techniques, either pipette analysis or hydrometer analysis has in most laboratories been replaced by the use of either an X-ray method (e.g. sedigraph), light transmission (photometry) or a coulter counter. It should be remembered that below-sand-size particles form aggregates and so it may be the aggregate size which is the effective (i.e. transported) grain size rather than the actual particle size. The random nature and size of samples is important if the curve is to be truly representative of the unit sampled. For coarse gravels large samples are essential (e.g. 10–20 kg) whereas for silts and sands samples can be 1–2 kg and for silt and clay 0.1 kg is enough.

In practice only the bedload fraction can be used to estimate past flow velocities using tractive force theory as outlined in appendix 2.1. This can be done using the largest grain transported, but since this is one clast which may not be representative of the conditions (i.e. it could have toppled into the river) it is more sensible to take a statistically 'largest' size (e.g. d_{95}). It is also possible in some cases to use boulders which did not move in the flow to produce an upper envelope curve. These are frequently artifacts such as anchor stones, and the remains of bridges or revetments (all designed not to move!). Standard hydraulic relationships can then be used to predict the velocity required to entrain the clast size and critical depth. A typical method is the use of Shield's function for particle entrainment and the Du Boys equation for the calculation of flow depth. The flow depth can then be used as input to the Manning–Limerinos equation (see appendix 1.2 and chapter 3, Table 3.2) or the Colebrook–White equation. Several studies have used this tractive-force approach, with the field data being gravel unit grain size (e.g. d_{97}) and grain size range, reconstructed bed slopes and an estimate of the former bed widths based upon the geometry of channel units (Cheetham, 1976; 1980; Church, 1978; Maizels, 1983; Dawson, 1989). In his classic palaeohydrological study Baker (1974b) used hydraulic theory to estimate past flow intensity from alluvial deposits. The simplified expression used (for clear water) was:

$$DS/1.65d = 0.06$$

where D is depth of flow, S is energy slope (approximately equal to water surface slope) and d is the intermediate particle diameter.

Table A1. *Grain size scale and ranges of different techniques*

Methods applicable	microns	phi (φ)	Classification (Wentworth)
CC, SG, CF	0.24	12	
CC, SG, CF	0.49	11	
CC, SG, CF	1.00	10	
CC, SG	1.26	9.6	clay
CC, SG	1.58	9.3	
CC, SG	2.00	9.0	
CC, SG	2.52	8.6	
CC, SG	3.17	8.3	fine silt
CC, SG	4.00	8.0	
CC, SG	5.04	7.6	
CC, SG	6.35	7.3	
CC, SG	8.00	7.0	
CC, SG	10.08	6.7	
CC, SG	12.70	6.3	medium silt
CC, SG	16.00	6.0	
CC, SG	20.16	5.6	
CC, SG	25.4	5.3	
CC, SG	32.0	5.0	coarse silt
CC, SG	40.4	4.6	
CC, SG, WS	50.8	4.2	
CC, SG, WS	64.0	4.0	
CC, SG, WS, DS	80.6	3.5	very fine sand
CC, SG, WS, DS	125	3.0	
WS, DS	180	2.5	fine sand
WS, DS	250	2.0	
WS, DS	355	1.5	medium sand
WS, DS	500	1.0	
WS, DS	710	0.5	coarse sand
WS, DS	1000	0.0	
DS	1400	−0.5	granules
DS	2000	−1.0	(grit or pea
DS	2800	−1.5	granules)
DS	4000	−2.0	
DS	5600	−2.5	fine pebbles
DS	8000	−3.0	
DS	11,200	−3.5	medium pebbles
DS	16,000	−4.0	
DS	22,400	−4.5	
DS	32,000	−5.0	coarse pebbles
DS	48,000	−5.5	
DS	64,000	−6.0	
DS, CA	128,000	−7.0	cobbles
CA	256,000	−8.0	
T	512,000	−9.0	

Table A1 (*cont.*)

Methods applicable	microns	phi (ϕ)	Classification (Wentworth)
T	1,024,000	-10.0	boulders
T	2,048,000	-11.0	

Notes:
CC Coulter Counter   WS wet sieving   CA calipers
SC Sedigraph (x-ray)   DS dry sieving   T tape measure
CF centrifugation

All tractive force methods require several assumptions including the assumption of steady uniform flow, the availability of all grain sizes, loose bed conditions (i.e. no armouring and imbrication), and the statistical variability within some of the empirical relationships as well as the validity of the shear stress models themselves. For this reason the error of any one method may exceed an order of magnitude and several methods are usually used and a range of probable discharges computed, and outliers rejected (Rotnicki, 1991).

Appendix 2

FLOOD FREQUENCY ANALYSIS

2.1 Standard flood frequency analysis

The most used method of flood prediction is based on the assumption of the random occurrence of floods of a given magnitude. This means that the longer the time period the larger would be the expected flood, i.e. if camping by a river for a month you would be unlikely and unlucky to experience a massive flood; however, living by the river for tens of years you should expect to experience large floods. The average time which elapses between two events of equal magnitude, or exceeding a common level, is the *return period* or *recurrence interval* (RI). So the flood with a 100-year return interval would be much larger than that with a 2-year return interval. This does not, however, mean that the 100-year flood cannot occur tomorrow or twice in a year, what it means is that *on average* it can be expected to occur only once in a 100-year period. It follows from this that the probability analysis of floods is rather more useful for describing past hydrological trends and the design criteria of structures, embankments and bridges (i.e. built to withstand the once in 500 years flood) than it is for flood warning. The calculation is fundamentally simple; the floods over a particular threshold are ranked from largest to smallest and assigned return periods with the largest flood having the return period of the time over which the floods were recorded (i.e. for a 100 years of flood the largest flood has a return period of 100 years). This is called a partial (flood) duration series; if only the largest flood each year is used it is called the annual duration series. The flood magnitude is then plotted against the return period in order to obtain a curve which is relatively straight if logarithmic or extreme value transformations are used (e.g. semi-log graph paper, or Gumbel's extreme value paper or equivalent computer transformations). These curves have been frequently used to extrapolate outside the period of record. However, this is not accurate, especially for long return periods, and in practice the palaeoflood methodology of Costa (1978) and Baker (1987) is probably more reliable (see chapter 3). This is in part because the method has theoretical weaknesses as floods do not necessarily conform to one population distribution (Brown, 1991; 1996). There is also evidence that there is an absolute upper limit to flood magnitudes from a given area (Georgiadi, 1979; Enzel *et al.*, 1993) and it is clear that the relationship between flood magnitude and return interval changes as climate changes (see papers in Gregory, Branson and Brown, 1996). However, the method remains an important way of comparing and describing floods and it has

331

remained in engineering use in Europe and Asia although less so in North America. The probability approach can also be used to analyse historical data in order to describe the flood environment and provide evidence of climate change. More details of the methods and pitfalls of the probability analysis of floods and the choice of frequency distributions can be found in Ward (1978).

2.2 Historical flood frequency analysis

Benson (1950) has devised a method for incorporating historical (or archaeological) floods into flood series. The formula used for the partial duration as described above is:

$$RI = n + 1/m$$

where RI is the recurrence interval in years, n is the number of years of record and m is the rank of the item in the array. Benson's revised formula uses an amended rank (m_1), which is calculated as below:

$$m_1 = A + (H - A/T - A)(m - A)$$

where m_1 is the raised rank, A is the number of annual floods equalling or exceeding the smallest historical flood, H is the length of total flood record in years and T is the length of the record or monitored period for which all events are known. However, one of the problems with this approach is that the date of commencement of the series must still be known, and this is rarely the case. It is also not applicable if only one historical event is known and there is a large gap in magnitude between it and the highest in the recorded series. So in most cases the record is too incomplete and not amenable to quantitative analysis. Flood heights can still, however, provide a benchmark against which more recent floods can be judged, although care must be taken to exclude local influences which may have altered the local flood rating curve (the relationship between discharge and stage or water surface height). Potter (1978) has provided a guide to the types of historical data that can be used for Britain and methodological problems. More discussion of the use of historical records can also be found in chapter 9.

Appendix 3

DOCUMENTARY EVIDENCE AND
WETLAND PERCEPTIONS

3.1 Place- and river-name evidence

The study of place- and river-names, which has seen a revival in recent years, has two principal aims. One aim is fundamentally a part of historical linguistics, the study of the history of early languages, elements of which may only survive as place-names from pre-literate languages. The other is archaeological, providing supplementary data on the character and history of landscapes or the perceptions of landscape by prehistoric peoples (Gelling, 1988). River-names are a particularly important sub-set of place-names as it would appear that they may preserve some of the earliest evidence of prehistoric languages and have often remained relatively unchanged or mediated by subsequent languages. In Britain most recent work still uses as its starting-point the classic work by Ekwall (1928), supplemented by Jackson (1953) and Rivet and Smith (1979).

Place- and river-names have a remarkable longevity, often being used long after the local language has been forgotten or suppressed, and so they can provide indications of the form of early languages (Renfrew, 1987). In his classic work on river-names (hydronomy) Hans Krahe (1957) pointed out the similarity of river-names in Central Europe (e.g. Ara in Germany, Holland, England, Scotland and Spain, or Soar, England and Saar, Germany) and he suggested that this indicated a common root in Old European or pre-Indo-European languages. It is also possible that the similarity stems from an early stage in the differentiation of an undifferentiated early Indo-European language spoken in Europe north and west of the Alps that eventually produced the Celtic languages (Renfrew, 1987). This accords with Georgiev's (1973) view that some place-names reveal an intermediate stage between pre-Indo-European and Indo-European languages. The use of place-names has also been associated with a belief that natural barriers such as mountains and seas can act as linguistic barriers. Accordingly isolated areas such as Iberia or Italy might be expected to have had a more stable linguistic history than an area such as Central Europe and this would be reflected in the homogeneity and antiquity of river-names. However, at least in the case of large rivers, this would seem not to be the case. Place-names are also one of the few cases where words are borrowed from a 'lower' language spoken by a subjugated people by a 'dominant' language spoken by conquering peoples (Bloomfield, 1935; Renfrew, 1987), although notions of a contact zone (Pratt, 1992) and two-way exchange are now seen as being more appropriate for colonial situations (King, 1976). It is interesting to note that, in comparison with other natural features such as mountains or seas, the existing river-name is often adopted, even if amended (e.g. Murrumbidgee and Mississippi). Tempting though the use of place- and river-names in historical linguistics is, caution is essential, as pointed out by Chadwick (1973); 'the study of place-names and loan words is rather more complicated than many have thought, and the certain facts are few'.

In Britain the pattern of river-names relates to the history of conquest and settlement of the British Isles. The names of the large rivers such as Severn and Trent have similarities with European names and are probably pre-Celtic or proto-Celtic (Brythonic or Old European) and may go as far back as the Bronze Age. Jackson (1953) suggested that the pattern of Celtic river- and place-names in Britain reflected the history of Anglo-Saxon invasion. He divided Britain into four broad regions from the south-east to the north and south-western peripheries. In the south-east (area I), which was invaded earliest (AD 550) Celtic river-names are rare, whilst in the Midlands (area III, invaded during the seventh and eighth centuries) more Celtic names appear and in the south-west and north-west peripheral regions (area IV) Celtic place- and river-name evidence is overwhelming.

Place- and river-names have been used by archaeologists to indicate either the character of a past landscape or the perception of a past landscape (i.e. part of cognitive archaeology). There are, however, many pitfalls, as Cameron (1961) warns: 'unless early spellings of a place-name are known we can never be absolutely certain of its original meaning'. In many cases the meaning can be very general, such as the river-names Avon and Exe which both mean 'river' in Celtic (Cameron, 1961), or it is unknown, as in the case of the river Severn, which is definitely of Celtic or pre-Celtic origin as it is derived from the name Sabrina recorded by Tacitus in the second century AD (Cameron, 1961; Gelling, 1988) and has similarities with many mainland European river-names. However, in many cases the names reflect either some characteristic of the river or its environs or some perception of the river. For example there are several river-names in Britain which seem to refer to the pattern of the river, including Ivel/Yeo (Somerset) which in Celtic means 'forked river', Cam (Gloucestershire), Weaver (Cheshire), Anker (Warwickshire) and Wharfe (Yorkshire) which all mean crooked, and Ince (Lancashire) which means 'river island' as does the Old English word part '–eg'. Other river and floodplain features may be recorded such as gravel banks in the old name 'eyrr' or oxbow lakes in the later name 'Mortlake'. Physical characteristics may by recorded, such as the colour of the water as may be the case for the Thames, Tame and Tamar which have been taken to mean 'dark waters' and the Dove which means 'black river' (Cameron, 1961). Other characteristics may be recorded, such as the speed of flow (Calder – 'rapid stream'), presence of bedrock reaches

(Catterick from the Latin *cataracta* meaning waterfall or rapids) or regime such as in the use of the word-part 'hamps' (as in Hampshire) to refer to rivers which dry up in summer. Rivers may also be named after characteristics of the area around them such as trees (e.g. Andover – ash tree stream), or characteristics of the valley as with names which mean 'abounding in' – as with the river Cole (abounding in hazels) or the river Leam (abounding in elms). A faunal example is the common derivation of names such as Beferic meaning 'place of beavers' or 'abounding in beavers', an intriguing example being one of the islands on the river Severn which is called Bevere island. However, great caution is required here as the reference may be to a distinguishing feature which might be just one ash tree in an area of oak woodland (Gelling, 1988; Rackham, 1986). However, the careful and systematic use of river-names may well reveal spatial patterns of environmental variables which may accord with data derived from environmental archaeology in the same way it has been used to document the land use and boundaries of multiple estates (Jones, 1976) and forest history through the use of distribution maps (Rackham, 1986). It is possible that the many names referring to river pattern, islands and trees may be an indication of the tortuous, tree-lined and divided (i.e. multiple-channel) nature of most European rivers in late prehistory.

Names may also provide a glimpse of the perception of rivers and their use as in the case of superlative descriptions (e.g. Perry meaning 'bright, beautiful') and indications of ritual significance as in the case of the river Dee which means literally 'the goddess' or 'holy river' (Cameron, 1961). This aspect has been taken further by Coies (1994) who has proposed a landscape approach to the interpretation of river-names. By exploring similarities or consistencies in the character or uses of rivers with similar names Coles suggests that a 'meaning' may be proposed. Meaning can be taken here simply to refer to the association of a name with a particular feature or attribute as it may have an unrecoverable meaning such as an action associated with the place or attribute. The example Coles uses is a British (Celtic or pre-Celtic) name Trisantona, root of the river-names Trent (four in England), Tarrant (two in England), Trannon (Wales) and Trisanna (Austrian Tyrol). She concludes from archaeological and geographical evidence that Trisantona may indicate an important route or thoroughfare. The application of this approach to the common-root European rivers identified by Krahe (1957) could give us new insights into late prehistoric European culture and language.

3.2 Literary evidence of the human perception of wetlands

It is worth examining very briefly the varied and variable historical perception of wetlands and wetland dwellers since this has coloured our view of the attractiveness of floodplains most of which were wetlands before drainage. The most obvious way of doing this is through the analysis of literary and other texts. However, it must be remembered that texts, including those aspiring to be objective or scientific, reflect prevailing sociocultural factors such as power relations, cultural differences, imperialism and vested interests (Barnes and Duncan, 1992). It is, of course only the view of the educated elite that can be seen through literature; however, these people (or others of the same class – engineers, estate managers, politicians) have disproportionate power over the environment. Wetlands as seen through the writing of eighteenth and nine-teenth scholars, novelists and the clergy were generally still places of flood and disease (Purseglove, 1989). In Anglo-Saxon traditions wetlands or 'mores' were associated with swamp monsters, disease and death. They were regarded as hostile, god-forsaken, empty (which they were not), unproductive (again which they were not) and, all in all, to be avoided. Many words derived from wetland environments have become pejorative, e.g. morass, bogy-man, bog-standard, dank and quagmire. Wetlands also produced strange and incomprehensible phenomena, from the common and very local dense fog (Shakespeare's 'fen-sucked fog', *King Lear*) to marsh-fires caused by methane and known locally as 'corpse-candles', 'jack-o'-lanterns' and 'will-o'-the-wisp'. One obvious reason for these fears is disease, especially malaria, but also bubonic plague and cholera (see chapter 9), but differences between writers of different outlooks and periods suggest other factors are also responsible. Probably one of the best illustrations of the differing views of outsiders and locals of the riverine environment can be seen in the writings of two eminent nineteenth-century novelists on the Mississippi river. Dickens wrote in 1878:

> At the junction of the two rivers, on ground so flat and low and marshy, that at certain seasons of the year it is inundated to the house tops, lies a breeding place of fever, ague, and death; vaunted in England as a mine of Golden Hope, and specu-lated in, on the faith of monstrous representations, to many people's ruin. A dismal swamp, on which the half-built houses rot away: cleared here and there for the space of a few yards; and teeming, then, with rank, unwholesome vegetation, in whose baleful shade the wretched wanderers who are tempted hither droop, and die, and lay their bones; the hateful Mississippi circling and eddying before it, and turning off upon its southern course, a slimy monster hideous to behold; a hotbed of disease, an ugly sepulchre, a grave uncheered by any gleam of promise: a place without one single quality, in earth or air or water, to commend it: such is this dismal Cairo.

Whereas in 1883 Twain wrote the following about the same reach of the river:

> The scenery, from St Louis to Cairo – two hundred miles – is varied and beautiful. The hills were clothed in the fresh foliage of spring now and were a gracious and worthy setting for the broad river flowing between.

While acknowledging the poverty and devastation caused by flooding, his atti-tude to the river and its 'life' differs markedly from Dickens's.

By the end of the nineteenth century the general perception had changed slightly to viewing alluvial wetlands as primarily a barrier to progress (Petts, 1989). It is, however, essential to remember that all of these accounts were written by writers, academics and clergy, all generally urban dwellers and ignorant of the economic and social importance of wetlands. Indeed these views found their way into archaeology under the guise of the avoidance of heavy (i.e. alluvial) soils and dense, impenetrable vegetation, a perception only recently redressed by the rise of wetland and alluvial archaeology. It has been argued that this negative view is part of the habit of using the past 'as a stick to beat the present' (Williams, 1973).

REFERENCES

Aaby, B. and Berglund, B. E. 1986. Characterisation of peat and lake deposits. In B. E. Berglund (ed.), *Handbook of Holocene Palaeoecology and Palaeohydrology.* Wiley, Chichester, 231–46.

Aalbersberg, G. 1994. The Little Brosna River valley: Quaternary geology and palaeo-ecology. Unpublished report and thesis for the Faculty of Earth Sciences, Free University of Amsterdam, Amsterdam.

Abdul, A. S. and Gilham, R. W. 1984. Laboratory studies on the effect of the capillary fringe on streamflow generation. *Water Resources Research* 20, 691–8.

Adams, R. M. 1965. *Land Behind Baghdad: A History of Settlement on the Diyala Plains.* University of Chicago Press, Chicago.

1981. *Heartland of Cities: Surveys of Ancient Settlement and Land Use on the Floodplain of the Euphrates.* University of Chicago Press, Chicago.

Adamson, D. A., Gasse, F., Street, F. A. and Williams, M. A. J. 1980. Late Quaternary history of the Nile, *Nature* 287, 50–5.

Aitken, M. J. 1990. *Science Based Dating in Archaeology.* Longman, London.

Alexander, C. S. and Prior, J. C. 1971. Holocene sedimentation rates in overbank deposits in the Black Bottom of the Lower Ohio river, Southern Illinois. *American Journal of Science* 270, 361–72.

Alexander, E. B. 1974. Extractable iron in relation to soil age on terraces along the Truckee River, Nevada. *Soil Science Society of America Proceedings* 38, 121–4.

Allen, J. R. L. 1965. A review of the origin and characteristics of recent alluvial sediments. *Sedimentology* 5, 89–191.

1977. Changeable rivers: some aspects of their mechanics and sedimentation. In K. J. Gregory (ed.), *River Channel Changes.* Wiley, Chichester, 15–46.

Allsop, J. M. 1992. The British Geological Survey: geoprospection techniques applied to the archaeological landscape. In P. Sperry (ed.), *Geoprospection in the Archaeological Landscape.* Oxbow Monograph 18, Oxbow Books, Oxford, 121–40.

Allsop, J. M. and Greenbaum, D. 1991. Airborne remote sensing of alluvial deposits and the detection of potential archaeological sites (abstract). *Geophysical Journal International* 104, 689.

Amoros, C., Roux, A. L., Reygrobellet, J. L., Bravard, J. P. and Pautou, G. 1987. A method for applied ecological studies of fluvial hydrosystems. *Regulated Rivers* 1, 17–36.

Amoros, C. and Van Urk, G. 1989. Palaeoecological analysis of large rivers: some principles and methods. In G. E. Petts, H. Moller and A. L. Roux (eds.), *Historical Change of Large Alluvial Rivers.* Wiley, Chichester, 143–65.

Anderson, M. G. and Calver, A. 1977. On the persistence of landscape features formed by a large flood. *Transactions of the Institute of British Geographers*, New Series 2, 243–54.

Andrews, E. D. 1983. Entrainment of gravel from naturally sorted river-bed material. *Bulletin of the Geological Society of America* 94, 1225–31.

Archer, D. R. 1995. Tablets of stone. *Circulation: The Newsletter of the British Hydrological Society* 45, 3.

Archer, N. 1993. Discharge estimates for Britain's greatest flood: river Tyne, 17th November

1771. *Procs. British Hydrological Society 4th National Hydrology Symposium*, Cardiff, 4.1–4.6.

Astill, G. G. 1993. *A Medieval Industrial Complex and Its Landscape: The Metalworking Watermills and Workshops of Bordesley Abbey*. Council for British Archaeology Research Report 92.

Atkinson, T. C., Briffa, K. R., Coope, G. R., Joachim, M. J. and Perzy, D. W. 1986. Climatic calibration of coleopteran data. In B. E. Berglund (ed.), *Handbook of Palaeoecology and Palaeohydrology*. Wiley, Chichester, 851–8.

Avery, B. 1980. *System of Soil Classification for England and Wales (Higher Categories)*. Technical Monograph 14, Soil Survey of Great Britain, Harpenden.

Bagnold, R. A. 1966. An approach to transport problems from general physics. Professional Paper of the United States Geological Society 422 I.

Bailey, G. N., Lewin, J., Macklin, M. G. and Woodward, J. C. 1990. The 'Older Fill' of the Voidomatis Valley, northwest Greece and its relationship to the Palaeolithic archaeology and glacial history of the region. *Journal of Archaeological Science* 17, 145–50.

Bailiff, I. 1992. Luminescence dating of alluvial deposits. In S. Needham and M. M. Macklin, (eds.), *Archaeology Under Alluvium*. Oxbow Books, Oxford, 27–36.

Baker, C. A. and Jones, D. K. C. 1980. Glaciation of the London Basin and its influence on the drainage pattern: a review and appraisal. In D. K. C. Jones (ed.), *The Shaping of Southern England*. Institute of British Geographers Special Publication no. 11, London, Academic Press, 131–76.

Baker, C. A., Moxey, P. M. and Oxford, P. M. 1978. Woodland continuity and change in Epping Forest. *Field Studies* 4, 645–69.

Baker, V. R. 1974a. Techniques and problems in estimating Holocene flood-discharges. American Quaternary Association, *Abstracts of the Third Biannual Meeting*. University of Wisconsin, Madison, 63.

1974b. Palaeohydraulic interpretation of Quaternary alluvium near Golden, Colorado. *Quaternary Research* 4, 95–112.

1983. Large-scale fluvial paleohydrology. In K. J. Gregory (ed.), *Background to Palaeohydrology*, Wiley, Chichester, 453–78.

1987. Paleoflood hydrology and extraordinary events. *Journal of Hydrology* 96, 79–99.

1989. Magnitude and frequency of palaeofloods. In K. Bevan and P. Carling (eds.), *Floods: Hydrological, Sedimentological and Geomorphological Implications*. Wiley and Sons, Chichester, 171–84.

Baker, V. R., Kochel, R. C., Patton, P. C. and Pickup, G. 1983. Palaeohydrologic analysis of Holocene flood slack-water sediments. In J. D. Collinson and J. Lewin (eds.), *Modern and Ancient Fluvial Systems*. International Association of Sedimentologists. Special Publication 6, 229–39, Blackwell, London.

Baker, V. R., Pickup, G. and Polach, H. A. 1985. Radiocarbon dating of flood events, Katherine Gorge, Northern Territory, Australia. *Geology* 13, 344–7.

Bannister, P. 1976. *Introduction to Physiological Plant Ecology*. Blackwell, Oxford.

Barber, K. E. 1976. History of vegetation. In P. D. Moore and S. B. Chapman (eds.), *Methods in Plant Ecology*. Blackwell, Oxford.

1981. *Peat Stratigraphy and Climatic Change*. Balkema, Rotterdam.

1982. Peat-bog stratigraphy as a proxy climate record. In A. F. Harding (ed.), *Climatic Change in Later Prehistory*. Edinburgh University Press, Edinburgh, 103–13.

Barber, K. E. and Brown, A. G. 1987. Late Pleistocene organic deposits beneath the floodplain of the river Avon at Ibsley, Hampshire. In K. E. Barber (ed.), *Fieldguide to Wessex and the Isle of Wight*. Quaternary Research Organisation, Cambridge, 65–74.

Barber, K. E., Chambers, F. M., Maddy, D., Stoneman, R. and Brew, J. S. 1994. A sensitive high-resolution record of late Holocene climatic change from a raised bog in northern England. *The Holocene* 4, 198–205.

Barber, K. E. and Coope, G. R. 1987. Climate history of the Severn valley during the last 18,000 years. In K. J. Gregory, J. E. Lewin and J. Thornes (eds.), *Palaeohydrology in Practice.* Wiley, Chichester, 201–16.

Barker, G. and Hunt, C. O. 1994. The dynamics of human activity and valley fill processes in the Biferno valley, Molise, Italy. In J. Lewin and J. Woodward (eds.), *Mediterranean Quaternary Environments.* Balkema, Rotterdam, 145–59.

Barker, G. and Jones, B. 1982. The UNESCO Libyan Valleys Survey 1979–1981: palaeoeconomy and environmental archaeology in the pre-desert. *Libyan Studies* 18, 1–34.

Barnes, T. J. and Duncan, J. S. (eds.), 1992. *Writing World: Discourse, Text and Metaphor in the Representation of Landscape.* Routledge, London.

Barreis, D. A. and Bryson, R. A. 1968. Climate change in the Mill Creek Culture. *Journal of the Iowa Archaeological Society* 15, 1–25.

Barton, D. R. and Smith, S. M. 1984. Insects of extremely small and extremely large aquatic habitats. In V. H. Resh and D. M. Rosenberg (eds.), *The Ecology of Aquatic Insects.* Praeger, New York, 456–83.

Bates, M. R. and Barham, A. J. 1993. Recent observations of tufa in the Dour valley, Kent. *Quaternary Newsletter* 71, 11–25.

Batt, C. M. and Noel, N. 1991. Magnetic studies of archaeological sediments. In P. Budd, B. Chapman, C. Jackson, R. C. Janaway and B. S. Ottoway (eds.), *Archaeological Sciences 1989: Proceedings of a Conference on the Application of Scientific Techniques to Archaeology.* Oxbow Books, Oxford, 234–41.

Batterbee, R. W. 1986. Diatom analysis. In B. E. Berglund (ed.), *Handbook of Holocene Palaeoecology and Palaeohydrology.* Wiley, Chichester, 527–70.

  1988. The use of diatoms in archaeology: a review. *Journal of Archaeological Science* 15, 621–44.

Batterbee, R. W. and Charles, D. F. 1986. Diatom-based pH reconstruction studies of acid lakes in Europe and North America: a synthesis. *Water, Air and Soil Pollution* 30, 347–54.

Beck, U. 1992. *Risk Society: Towards a New Modernity.* Sage Publications, London.

Becker, B. 1975. Dendrochronological observations on the postglacial river aggradation in the southern part of Central Europe. *Biuletyn Geologiczny* 19, 127–36.

Becker, B. and Schirmer, W. 1977. Palaeoecological study on the Holocene valley development of the river Main, Southern Germany. *Boreas* 6, 303–21.

Beckinsale, R. P. 1969a. The human use of open channels. In R. J. Chorley (ed.), *Introduction to Geographical Hydrology.* Methuen, London, 83–95.

  1969b. Rivers as political boundaries. In R. J. Chorley (ed.), *Introduction to Geographical Hydrology.* Methuen, London, 96–107.

Behrensmeyer, A. K. and Hill, A. P. (eds.) (1980). *Fossils in the Making.* University of Chicago Press, Chicago, 527–70.

Bell, B. 1970. The oldest records of the Nile floods. *Geographical Journal,* 569–73.

  1971. Climate and the history of Egypt. *American Journal of Archaeology* 79, 223–69.

  1975. The dark ages in ancient history. I The first dark age in Egypt. *American Journal of Archaeology* 75, 1–26.

Bell, F. G., Coope, G. R., Rice, R. J. and Riley, T. H. 1972. Mid-Weichselian fossil-bearing deposits at Syston, Leicestershire. *Proceedings of the Geological Society* 83, 197–221.

Bell, M. 1983. Valley sediments as evidence of prehistoric land-use on the South Downs. *Proceedings of the Prehistoric Society* 49, 119–50.

  1992. Archaeology under alluvium: human agency and environmental process. Some concluding thoughts. In S. Needham and M. G. Macklin (eds.), *Archaeology Under Alluvium.* Oxbow Books, Oxford, 271–6.

Bell, M. and Boardman, J. 1992. *Past and Present Soil Erosion.* Oxbow Monograph 22, Oxbow Books, Oxford.

Bennett, K. D. 1983. Postglacial population expansion of forest trees in Norfolk, U.K. *Nature* (London) 303, 164–7.

1989. A provisional map of forest types for the British Isles 5000 years ago. *Journal of Quaternary Science* 4, 141–4.

Benson, M. A. 1950. Use of historical data in flood frequency analysis. *Transactions of the American Geophysical Union* 31, 419–24.

Beresford, M. and Hurst, J. 1990. *Wharram Percy Deserted Medieval Village.* English Heritage, London.

Berger, G. W. 1984. Thermoluminescence dating studies of glacial silts from Ontario. *Canadian Journal of Earth Science* 21, 1393–9.

Berry, B. J. L. 1967. *Geography of Market Centres and Retail Distribution.* Prentice Hall, Englewood Cliffs, NJ.

Bevan, K. 1993. Riverine flooding in a warmer Britain. *The Geographical Journal* 159, 157–61.

Bhowmik, N. G. 1984. Hydraulic geometry of floodplains. *Journal of Hydrology* 68, 369–401.

Binford, L. 1977. General introduction. In L. Binford (ed.), *For Theory Building in Archaeology.* Academic Press, London.

Bintliff, J. L. 1977. *Natural Environment and Human Settlement in Greece.* British Archaeological Reports, International Series 528, Oxford.

Birks, H. J. B., Line, J. M., Juggins, S., Stevenson, A. C. and ter Braak, C. F. J. 1990. *Diatoms and pH Reconstruction. Philosophical Transactions of the Royal Society, London, B* 327, 263–78.

Biswas, A. K. 1970. *A History of Hydrology.* North-Holland, Amsterdam.

Blake, D. H. and Ollier, C. D. T. 1971. Alluvial plains of the Fly river, Papua. *Zeitschrift für Geomorphologie* Suppl. 12, 1–17.

Bliss, E. W. 1995. The Nile floods and world weather. *Memoirs of the Royal Meteorological Society* 1, 79–84.

Bloomfield, L. 1935. *Language.* Allen and Unwin, London.

Bohncke, S. J. P. and Vandenberghe, J. 1991. Palaeohydrological development in the Southern Netherlands during the last 15,000 years. In L. Starkel, K. J. Gregory and J. B. Thornes (eds.), *Temperate Palaeohydrology.* Wiley, Chichester, 253–82.

Bonatti, E. 1963. Stratigraphia pollinica dei sedimenti postglaciali di Baccano, lago craterico del Lazio. *Atti della Scieta Toscana di Scienze Naturali Residente in Pisa. Memoriel Serie A, Processi Verbali* 70, 40–8.

Bork, H.-F. 1989. Soil erosion during the past millennium in Central Europe and its significance within the geomorphodynamics of the Holocene. In F. Ahnert (ed.), *Landforms and Landform Evolution in West Germany.* Catena Supplement 15, 121–32.

Bowen, D. Q. 1978. *Quaternary Geology.* Pergamon, Oxford.

Bowen, D. Q., Hughes, S. A., Sykes, G. A. *et al.* 1989. Land–sea correlations in the Pleistocene based on isoleucine epimerization in non-marine molluscs. *Nature* 340, 49–51.

Bowler, J. M. 1978. Quaternary climate and tectonics in the evolution of the Riverine Plain, Southeastern Australia. In J. L. Davies and M. A. J. Williams (eds.), *Landform Evolution in Australia.* Australian National University Press, Canberra, 70–112.

Brackenridge, G. R. 1984. Alluvial stratigraphy and radiocarbon dating along the Duck river, Tennessee. Implications regarding flood-plain origin. *Bulletin of the American Geological Society* 95, 9–25.

Bradley, C. and Brown, A. G. 1992. Floodplain and palaeochannel wetlands: geomorphology, hydrology and conservation. In C. Stevens (eds.), *Conserving Our Landscape: Evolving Landforms and Ice-Age Heritage.* English Nature, Peterborough, 101–12.

Bradley, E. J. 1917. The Severn: as it was, as it is, and as it should be. *Transactions of the Worcestershire Naturalists Club* 6, 237–45.

1948. Making the Severn navigable. Unpublished Report for the Severn River Commission.

Bradley, R. 1978. *Prehistoric Settlement in Britain.* Routledge and Kegan Paul, London.

1990. *The Passage to Arms: An Archaeological Analysis of Prehistoric Hoards and Votive Deposits*, Cambridge University Press, Cambridge.

Bradley, R. S. 1985. *Quaternary Paleohydrology: Methods of Paleoclimatic Reconstruction*. Allen and Unwin, Boston.

Braga, G. and Gervasoni, S. 1989. Evolution of the Po river: an example of the application of historic maps. In G. E. Petts (ed.), *Historical Change of Large Alluvial Rivers: Western Europe*. Wiley, Chichester, 113–26.

Brammer, H. 1971. Coatings in seasonally flooded soils. *Geoderma* 6, 5–16.

Branson, J., Gregory, K. J. and Brown, A. G. 1996. *Global Continental Changes: The Context of Palaeohydrology*. Geological Society Monograph, Geological Society, London.

Brasier, M. D. 1980. *Microfossils*. Allen and Unwin, London and Boston.

Brewer, R. 1976. *Fabric and Mineral Analysis of Soils*. Robert E. Krieger, Huntington, NY.

Bridge, J. S. and Leeder, M. R. 1979. A simulation model of alluvial stratigraphy. *Sedimentology* 26, 617–44.

Bridges, E. M. 1973. Some characteristics of alluvial soils in the Trent valley, England. *5th and 6th Commission International Soil Science Society Transactions*, 247–53.

Bridgland, D. R. 1985. Uniclinal shifting: a speculative reappraisal based on terrace distribution in the London basin. *Quaternary Newsletter* 47, 26–33.

1988. The Pleistocene fluvial stratigraphy and palaeogeography of Essex. *Proceedings of the Geologists' Association* 99, 291–314.

1994. *Quaternary of the Thames*. Chapman and Hall, London.

Briffa, K. R., Jones., P. D., Wigley, T. M. L., Pilcher, J. R. and Baillie, M. G. L. 1983. Climate reconstruction from tree rings: part I, basic methodology and preliminary results for England. *Journal of Climatology* 3, 233–42.

Briggs, D. 1977. *Sediments*. Butterworths, London.

Briggs, D. J., Coope, G. R. and Gilbertson, D. D. 1985. *The Chronology and Environmental Framework of Early Man in the Upper Thames Valley: A New Model*. British Archaeological Reports, British Series 137, Oxford.

Brinkhuizan, D. C. 1977. The fish remains. In P. C. Woodiman, Recent excavations at Newferry, Co. Antrim. *Proceedings of the Prehistoric Society* 43, 197–8.

Brinson, M. M.1990. Riverine forests. In A. E. Lugo, M. M. Brinson and S. Brown (eds.), *Forested Wetlands*. Ecosystems of the World 15, Elsevier, Amsterdam, 35–61.

Brookes, A. 1988. *Channelized Rivers: Perspectives for Environmental Management*. Wiley, Chichester.

Brown, A. G. 1982. Human impact on the former floodplain woodlands of the Severn. In M. Bell and S. Limbrey (eds.), *Archaeological Aspects of Woodland Ecology*. British Archaeological Reports, International Series 146, Oxford, 93–105.

1983a. Late Quaternary palaeohydrology, palaeoecology and floodplain development of the lower River Severn. Unpublished PhD thesis, University of Southampton.

1983b. An analysis of overbank deposits of a flood at Blandford Forum, Dorset, England. *Revue de Géomorphologie Dynamique* 32, 95–9.

1985a. Traditional and multivariate techniques in the interpretation of floodplain sediment grain size variations. *Earth Surface Processes and Landforms* 10, 281–91.

1985b. The potential of pollen in the identification of suspended sediment sources. *Earth Surface Processes and Landforms* 10, 27–32.

1987a. Holocene floodplain sedimentation and channel response of the lower River Severn, United Kingdom. *Zeitschrift für Geomorphologie* N.F. 31, 293–310.

1987b. Long-term sediment storage in the Severn and Wye catchments. In K. J. Gregory, J. Lewin and J. B. Thornes (eds.), *Palaeohydrology in Practice*. Wiley, Chichester, 307–32.

1988. The palaeoecology of *Alnus* (alder) and the Postglacial history of floodplain vegetation.

Pollen percentage and influx data from the West Midlands, United Kingdom. *New Phytologist* 110, 425–36.

1989. Holocene floodplain diachronism and inherited downstream variations in fluvial processes: a study of the river Perry, Shropshire, England. *Journal of Quaternary Science* 5, 39–51.

1990. Soil erosion and fire in areas of Mediterranean type vegetation: results from chaparral in southern California, USA and matorral in Andalucia, southern Spain. In J. B. Thornes (ed.), *Vegetation and Erosion*. J. Wiley, Chichester, 269–87.

1991. Hydrogeomorphological changes in the Severn basin during the last 15,000 years: orders of change in a maritime climate. In L. Starkel, K. J. Gregory and J. B. Thornes (eds.), *Temperate Palaeohydrology*, Wiley, Chichester, 147–69.

1992. Slope erosion and colluviation at the floodplain edge. In M. Bell and J. Boardman (eds.), *Past and Present Soil Erosion*. Oxbow, Oxford, 77–87.

1996. Human dimensions of palaeohydrological change. In J. Branson, A. Brown and K. J. Gregory (eds.), *Global Continental Changes: The Context of Palaeohydrology*. Geological Society Special Publication No. 115, Geological Society, London, 57–72.

Brown, A. G. and Barber, K. E. 1985. Late Holocene palaeoecology and sedimentary history of a small lowland catchment in Central England. *Quaternary Research* 24, 87–102.

Brown, A. G. and Bradley, C. 1996. *Past and Present Alluvial Wetlands and the Archaeological Resource: Implications from Research in East Midland Valleys, U.K.* Proceedings of Wetland Conference, Bristol, English Heritage, HMSO, 189–203.

Brown, A. G. and Brookes, A. in prep. The nettles effect: vegetation-induced differential deposition of suspended sediment on floodplains.

Brown, A. G. and Ellis, C. 1995. People, climate and alluviation: theory, research design and new sedimentological and stratigraphic data from Etruria, Italy. *Papers of the British School in Rome* 63, 45–73.

Brown, A. G., Gregory, K. J. and Milton, E. J. 1987. The use of Landsat multispectral scanner data for the analysis and management of flooding on the river Severn, England. *Environmental Management* 11, 695–701.

Brown, A. G. and Keough, M. 1992a. Holocene floodplain metamorphosis in the East Midlands, United Kingdom. *Geomorphology* 4, 433–45.

1992b. Palaeo-channels, palaeo-landsurfaces and the 3–D reconstruction of floodplain environmental change. In P. A. Carling and G. E. Petts (eds.), *Lowland Floodplain Rivers: A Geomorphological Perspective*. Wiley, Chichester, 185–202.

1992c. Palaeochannels and palaeolandsurfaces: the geoarchaeological potential of some Midland (U.K.) floodplains. In S. Needham and M. G. Macklin (eds.), *Archaeology under Alluvium*. Oxbow Books, Oxford, 185–96.

Brown, A. G., Keough, M. K. and Rice, R. J. 1994. Floodplain evolution in the East Midlands, United Kingdom: The Lateglacial and Flandrian alluvial record from the Soar and Nene valleys. *Philosophical Transactions of the Royal Society Series A*, London, 261–93, 348.

Brown, A. G., Stone, P. and Harwood, K. 1995. *The Biogeomorphology of a Wooded Anastomosing River: The Gearagh on the River Lee in County Cork, Ireland*. Occasional Papers in Geography 32, University of Leicester.

Brunsden, D. and Thornes, J. B. 1979. Landscape sensitivity and change. *Transactions of the Institute of British Geographers* 4, 463–84.

Brush, G. S. and Brush, L. M. 1972. Transport of pollen in a sediment laden channel: a laboratory study. *American Journal of Science* 272, 359–81.

Brush, L. M. and Wolman, M. G. 1960. Knickpoint behaviour in non-cohesive material: a laboratory study. *Bulletin of the Geological Society of America* 71, 59–74.

Bryan, K. 1954. The geology of Chaco Canyon, New Mexico. *Smithsonian Miscellaneous Collection* 122, 1–65.

Bryant, E. A. 1991. *Natural Hazards.* Cambridge University Press, Cambridge.

Buckland, P. and Dinnin, M. H. 1992. Peatlands and floodplains: the loss of a major palaeontological resource. In *Conserving Our Landsape: Evolving Landforms and Ice-Age Heritage.* Papers from a Conference in Crewe, Cheshire, May 1992, English Nature, Peterborough, 145–50.

Bull, W. L. and Knuepfer, P. L. K. 1987. Adjustment by the Charwell river, New Zealand, to uplift and climatic change. *Geomorphology* 1, 15–32.

Bullock, P., Federoff, N., Jongerius, A., Stoops, G., Tursina, T. and Babel, U. 1985. *Handbook for Soil Thin Section Description.* Waine Research Publications, Wolverhampton.

Burgess, C. 1980. *The Age of Stonehenge.* Dent, London.

Burnett, A. W. and Schumm, S. A. 1983. Neotectonics and alluvial river response. *Science* 222, 49–50.

Burrin, P. J. and Scaife, R. G. 1984. Aspects of Holocene valley sedimentation and floodplain development in southern England. *Proceedings of the Geologists' Association* 95, 81–96.

Burton, I. and Kates, R. W. 1964. The perception of natural hazards in resource management. *Natural Resources Journal* 3, 412–41.

Burton, I., Kates, R. W. and White, G. F. 1978. *The Environment As Hazard.* Oxford University Press, New York.

Butzer, K. W. 1959. Environment and human ecology in Egypt during predynastic and early dynastic times. Bulletin, Société de Géographie d'Egypte 32, 43–87.

  1976. *Early Hydraulic Civilisation in Egypt: A Study in Cultural Ecology.* University of Chicago Press, Chicago.

  1982. *Archaeology as Human Ecology.* Cambridge University Press, Cambridge.

Butzer, K. W. and Hanson, C. L. 1968. *Desert and River in Nubia: Geomorphology and Prehistoric Environments at the Aswan Reservoir.* University of Wisconsin Press, Madison.

Calderoni, G., Coltorti, M., Dramis, F., Magnetti, M. and Cilla, G. 1991. Sedimentazione fluviale e variazioni climatche nell'alto bacino del fiume Esino drante il Pleistocene Superiore. In Proceedings of a Conference: *Fenomeni di Erosione e Alluvionamenti Degli Alvei Fluviali,* Università degli studi di Ancona, Ancona, 14–15 Ottobre 1991, 171–90.

Cameron, K. 1961. *English Place-Names.* Batsford, London.

Campbell, C. J. and Dick-Peddie, W. A. 1964. Comparison of phreatophyte communities on the Rio Grande in New Mexico. *Ecology* 45, 492–502.

Carling, P. A. 1991. An appraisal of the velocity reversal hypothesis for stable pool-riffle sequences in the river Severn, England. *Earth Surface Processes and Landforms* 16, 19–31.

Carling, P. A. and Petts, G. E. 1992, *Lowland Floodplain Rivers: Geomorphological Perspectives.* Wiley, Chichester.

Carlston, C. W. 1965. The relation of free meander geometry to stream discharge and its geomorphic implications, *American Journal of Science* 263, 864–85.

Carson, M. A. and Lapoint, M. F. 1983. The inherent asymmetry of river meander planforms. *Journal of Geology* 91, 41–55.

Casteel, R. W. 1976. *Fish Remains in Archaeology and Palaeoenvironmental Studies.* Academic Press, London, New York and San Francisco.

Castleden, R. 1976. The floodplain gravels of the river Nene. *Mercian Geologist* 6, 33–47.

Caton-Thompson, G. and Gardner, E. W. 1932. The prehistoric geography of the Kharg oasis. *Geographical Journal* 80, 369–409.

Chadwick, J. 1973. Discussion of V. I. Georgiev, 'The arrival of the Greeks, linguistic evidence'. In R. A. Crossland and A. Birchall (eds.), *Bronze Age Migrations in the Aegean.* Duckworth, London, 254–5.

Chambers, F. M. and Elliott, L. 1989. Spread and expansion of Alnus Mill. in the British Isles: timing, agencies and possible vectors. *Journal of Biogeography* 16, 541–50.

Chartres, C. J. 1980. A Quaternary soil sequence in the Kennet Valley, central southern England. *Geoderma* 23, 125–46.

Chatters, J. C. and Hoover, K. A. 1986. Changing Late Holocene flooding frequencies on the Columbia River, Washington. *Quaternary Research* 26, 309–20.

Cheetham, G. H. 1976. Palaeohydrological investigation of river terrace gravels. In D. A. Davidson and M. R. Shackley (eds.), *Geoarchaeology*, Duckworth, London, 76–89.

1980. Late Quaternary palaeohydrology: the Kennet valley case study. In D. K. C. Jones (ed.), *The Shaping of Southern England.* Institute of British Geographers, Special Publication 11, 203–23.

Chorley, R. J. and Kennedy, B. A. 1971. *Physical Geography: A Systems Approach.* Prentice Hall, London.

Church, M. 1978. Palaeohydrological reconstructions from a Holocene valley fill. In A. D. Miall (ed.), *Fluvial Sedimentology.* Canadian Society of Petroleum Geology Memoir 5, 743–72.

1992. Channel morphology and typology. In P. Calow and G. E. Petts (ed.), *The Rivers Handbook.* Blackwell Scientific Publications, Oxford 126–43.

Church, M. and Jones, D. 1982. Channel bars in gravel-bedded rivers. In R. D. Hey, J. C. Bathurst and C. R. Thorne (eds.), *Gravel-bed Rivers.* Wiley, Chichester, 291–323.

Churchill, D. M. 1962. The stratigraphy of the Mesolithic sites III and V at Thatcham, Berkshire, England. *Proceedings of the Prehistoric Society* 14, 362–70.

Clark, A. 1989. *Seeing Beneath the Soil.* Batsford, London.

1992. Palaeomagnetic dating of sediments and its calibration. In S. Needham and M G. Macklin (eds.), *Archaeology Under Alluvium.* Oxbow Books, Oxford, 43–9.

Clark, J. G. D. 1972. *Star Carr: A Case Study in Bioarchaeology.* Publications in Anthropology No. 10, Reading, MA.

Clark, J. G. D. and Godwin, H. 1962. The Neolithic in the Cambridgeshire Fens. *Antiquity* 36, 10–32.

Clark, R. M. 1975. A calibration curve for radiocarbon dates. *Antiquity* 49, 251–66.

Clarke, D. L. 1972. Models and paradigms in contemporary archaeology. In D. L. Clarke (ed.), *Models in Archaeology.* Methuen, London, 1–60.

1973. Archaeology: the loss of innocence, *Antiquity* 47, 6–18.

Clay, P. 1992. A Norman mill at Hemington fields, Castle Donington, Leicestershire. In S. Needham and M. G. Macklin (eds.), *Archaeology Under Alluvium.* Oxbow Books, Oxford, 163–8.

Cloutman, E. W. 1988. Palaeoenvironments in the Vale of Pickering. Part I: stratigraphy and palaeogeography of Seamer Carr, Star Carr and Flixton Carr. *Proceedings of the Prehistoric Society* 54, 1–19.

Cloutman, E. W. and Smith, A. G. 1988. Palaeoenvironments in the Vale of Pickering. Part III: Environmental history at Star Carr. *Proceedings of the Prehistoric Society* 54, 37–58.

Coleman, J. M. 1969. Brahmaputra river: channel processes and sedimentation. *Sedimentary Geology.* 3, 129–239.

Coles, B. J. 1992a. The possible impact of beaver on valleys big and small in a temperate landscape. In S. Needham and M. G. Macklin (eds.), *Archaeology Under Alluvium.* Oxbow Books, Oxford, 93–9.

1994. *Trisantona* rivers: a landscape approach to the interpretation of river names. *Oxford Journal of Archaeology* 13, 295–312.

1995. Archaeology and the restoration of wetlands. In B. D. Wheeler, S. C. Shaw, W. J. Fojt and R. A. Robertson (eds.), *Restoration of Wetlands.* Wiley, Chichester, 19–32.

Coles, B. J. (ed.) 1992b. *The Wetland Revolution in Prehistory.* The Prehistoric Society and WARP, Exeter.

Coles, B. and Coles, J. 1986. *Sweet Track to Glastonbury.* Thames and Hudson, London.

1989. *People of the Wetlands: Bogs, Bodies and Lake Dwellers.* Thames and Hudson, London.

Coles, J. M. 1990. *Waterlogged Wood: Guidelines on the Recording, Sampling, Conservation and Curation of Structural Wood.* English Heritage, London.

Colinvaux, P. 1987. Amazon diversity in light of the palaeoecological record. *Quaternary Science Reviews* 6, 93–114.

Collins, D. 1978. *Early Man in West Middlesex: The Yiewsley Palaeolithic Sites.* HMSO, London.

Coltorti, M. 1991. Modificazioni morfologiche Oloceniche nelle piane alluvionali Marchigiani: alcuni esempi nei fiumi Misa, Cesano e Musone. *Geografica Fisica e Dinamica Quaternaria* 14, 73–86.

Coltorti, M., Consoli, M., Dramis, F., Gentili, B. and Pambianchi, G. 1991. Evoluzione geomorfologica delle piane alluvionale deele Marche Centro-Meridionale. *Geografica Fisica e Dinamica Quaternaria* 14, 87–100.

Conway, B. W. 1968. Preliminary geological investigations of Boyn Hill terrace deposits at Barnfield Pit, Swanscombe, Kent during 1968. *Proceedings of the Roya! Anthropological Society of Great Britain and Ireland for 1968,* 58–61.

Cooke, R. U. and Dornkamp, J. C. 1974. *Geomorphology in Environmental Management.* Clarendon Press, Oxford.

Coope, G. R. 1986. Coleopteran analysis. In B. E. Berglund (ed.), *Handbook of Holocene Palaeoecology and Palaeohydrology.* Wiley, Chichester, 703–14.

Coope, G. R. and Lister, A. M. 1987. Late-glacial mammoth skeletons from Condover, Shropshire, England. *Nature* 330, 472–7.

Corfield, in press. Monitoring the condition of waterlogged archaeological sites. In *Proceedings of the Waterlogged Organic Archaeological Materials Working Group of the Conservation Committee of the International Council of Museums,* Portland, Maine, August 1993.

Costa, J. E. 1978. Holocene stratigraphy in flood frequency analysis. *Water Resources Research* 14, 626–32.

   1983. Palaeohydraulic reconstruction of flash flood peaks from boulder deposits in the Colorado front range. *Bulletin of the Geological Society of America* 94, 986–1004.

Coster, H. P. and Gerrard, J. A. F. 1947. A seismic investigation of the history of the river Rheidol in Cardiganshire. *Geological Magazine* 84, 360–8.

Courty, M. A., Goldberg, P. and Macphail, R. 1989. *Soils and Micromorphology in Archaeology.* Cambridge University Press, Cambridge.

Cowan, M. 1982. *Floated Watermeadows in the Salisbury Area.* South Wiltshire Industrial Archaeology Society, Historical Monograph 9, Salisbury.

Croke, J. and Nanson, G. C. 1991. Floodplains; their character and classification on the basis of stream power, sediment type, boundary resistance and antecedency. *Geomorphology* 3, 13–26.

Crookes, A. 1989. *Yarri Hero of Gundagai.* Second edition, Allen Crooks, Gundagai, New South Wales.

Crowder, A. A. and Cuddy, D. G. 1973. Pollen in a small basin: Wilton Creek, Ontario. In H. J. B. Birks and R. G. West (eds.), *Quaternary Plant Ecology,* Cambridge University Press, Cambridge, 61–76.

Culleton, E. G. and Mitchell, G. F. 1976. Soil erosion following deforestation in the early Christian period in southern Wexford. *Journal of the Society of Antiqueries of Ireland* 106, 120–3.

Cummins, W. A. and Rundle, A. J. 1969. The geological environment of the dug-out canoes from Holme Pierrepoint, Nottinghamshire. *Mercian Geologist* 3, 177–88.

Cushing, E. J. 1967. Evidence for differential pollen preservation in Late Quaternary sediments in Minnesota. *American Journal of Science* 262, 1075–88.

Cutler, D. F., Rudall, D. J., Gasson, P. E. and Gale, R. M. O. 1987. *Root Identification Manual of Trees and Shrubs.* Chapman and Hall, London.

Dansgaard, W., White, J. W. C. and Johnson, S. J. 1989. The abrupt termination of the Younger Dryas climate event. *Nature* 339, 532–3.

Davidson, D. A. 1980. Erosion in Greece during the first and second millennia BC. In R. A. Cullingford, D. A. Davidson and J. Lewin (eds.), *Timescales in Geomorphology*. Wiley, Chichester, 143–58.

Davidson, D. A. and Shackley, M. R. (eds.) 1976. *Geoarchaeology*. Duckworth, London.

Davis, W. M. 1902. Base-level, grade and peneplains. *Journal of Geology* 10, 77–111.

Dawson, M. 1989. Flood deposits present within the Severn main terrace. In K. Bevan and P. Carling (eds.), *Floods: Hydrological, Sedimentological and Geomorphological Implications*. Wiley, Chichester, 253–64.

Delano-Smith, C. 1981. Valley changes: some observations from recent field and archive work in Italy. In G. Barker and R. Hodges (eds.), *Archaeology and Italian Society: Prehistoric, Roman and Medieval Studies*. British Archaeological Reports, International Series 102, Oxford, 239–47.

Delcourt, P.A. and Delcourt, H. R. 1981. Vegetation maps for eastern North America: 40,000 B.P. to the present. In R. C. Romans (ed.), *Geobotany II. Plenum* New York, 123–65.

Demumbrum, L. E. and Bruce, R. R. 1960. Mineralogy of three soils of the Mississippi river alluvial plain. *Soil Science* 89, 333–7.

Desheng, J. and Schumm, S. A. 1986. A new technique for modelling river morphology. In V. Gardiner (ed.), *International Geomorphology 1986* Part I. Wiley, Chichester, 681–90.

Dethier, D. P. 1988. The soil chronosequence along the Cowlitz river, Washington. *United States Geological Survey Bulletin* 1590–F, 1–25.

Dickens, C. 1842. *American Notes*. 1910 edn. Chapman and Hall, London.

Dister, E. 1985. *Taschenpolder als Hochwasserschutzmabnahme am Oberrhein*. GR 37, Aven, 241–7.

Dobbie, C. H. and Wolfe, P. O. 1953. The Lynmouth flood of August 1952. Part II. *Proceedings of the Institution of Civil Engineers* 2, 522–88.

Dobson, M. 1980. 'Marsh fever' – the geography of malaria in England. *Journal of Historical Geography* 6, 357–89.

Doelle, W. H., Dart, A. and Wallace, H. D. 1985. The southern Tucson basin survey: intensive survey along the Santa Cruz river, Tucson, Arizona. *Institute for American Research Technical Report* 85, Tucson, 1–97.

D'Onofrio, C. 1980. *Il Tevere: L'Isola tiberina, le inondazioni, i molini, i porti, le rive, i muraglioni, i ponti di Roma*. Romana Società Editrice, Rome.

Dudley Stamp, L. 1948. *The Land of Britain: Its Use and Misuse*. Longman, London.

Dugmore, A. J. 1991. International tephrochronological studies in the NE Atlantic region. Paper given to QRA annual discussion meeting, 3–4 January 1991, International Research Initiatives and Data-banks, 16–21.

Dundes, A. (ed.) 1988. *The Flood Myth*. University of California Press, Berkeley and Los Angeles.

Dury, G. H. 1965. Theoretical implications of underfit streams. *United States Geological Survey Professional Paper* 452B.

Dury, G. H., Sinker, C. A. and Pannett, D. J. 1972. Climate change and arrested meander development on the river Severn. *Area* 4, 81–5.

Dyakowska, J. 1937. Researches on the rapidity of the falling down of pollen of some trees. *Bulletin of the International Academy of Polish Science and Letters. Clinical Sciences, Mathematics and Nature*. Series B1. Bot. 1936, 155.

Edelman, C. H. and Van der Voorde, P. K. J. 1963. Important characteristics of alluvial soils in the tropics. *Soil Science* 95, 258–63.

Ehrenberg, M. R. 1977. *Bronze Age Spearheads from Berkshire, Buckinghamshire and Oxfordshire*. British Archaeological Reports, British Series 34, Oxford.

Einstein, H. A. 1950. The bedload function for sediment transport in open channel flows. *Technical Bulletin United States Department of Agriculture* 1026.

Eisma, D. 1964. Stream deposition in the Mediterranean area in historical times. *Nature* 202, 1061.

Ekwall, E. 1928. *English River-Names.* Clarendon Press, Oxford.

Enzel, Y., Ely, L. L., House, P. K., Baker, V. R. and Webb, R. H. 1993. Paleoflood evidence for a natural upper bound to flood magnitudes in the Colorado river basin. *Water Resources Research* 29, 2287–97.

Erdtman, G. 1969. *Handbook of Palynology.* Munksgaard, Copenhagen.

Erdtman, G., Berglund, B. E. and Praglowski, J. 1961. *An Introduction to a Scandinavian Pollen Flora.* Volume I. Almquist and Wicksell, Stockholm.

Erskine, W., Melville, M., Page, K. J. and Mowbray, P. D. 1982. Cutoff and oxbow lake. *Australian Geographer* 15, 174–80.

Erskine, W. D. and Warner, R. F. 1988. Geomorphic effects of alternating flood and drought dominated regimes on NSW coastal rivers. In R. F. Warner (ed.), *Fluvial Geomorphology of Australia.* Academic Press, Australia, 223–39.

Evans, J. G. 1975. *The Environment of Early Man in the British Isles.* Elek, London.

1990. Review of B. A. Purdy (ed.) 1988, 'Wet Site Archaeology'. Caldwell, New Jersey: The Telford Press. *Proceedings of the Prehistoric Society* 56, 339–40.

1992. River valley bottoms and archaeology in the Holocene. In B. Coles (ed.), *The Wetland Revolution in Prehistory.* The Prehistoric Society and WARP, Exeter, 47–53.

Evans, J. G., Davies, P., Mount, R. and Williams, D. 1992. Molluscan taxocenes from Holocene overbank alluvium in southern central England. In S. Needham and M. G. Macklin (eds.), *Archaeology Under Alluvium.* Oxbow Books, Oxford, 65–74.

Evans, J. G., Limbrey, S., Mate, I. and Mount, R. J. 1988. Environmental change and land-use history in a Wiltshire river valley in the last 14000 years. In J. C. Barrett and I. A. Kinnes (eds.), *The Archaeology of Context in the Neolithic and Bronze Age: Recent Trends.* Sheffield, Department of Archaeology and Prehistory, 97–104.

Evans, T. 1990. History of Nile flows. In P. P. Howell and J. A. Allen (eds.), *The Nile, Resource Evaluation, Management, Hydropolitics and Legal Issues*, SOAS/Royal Geographical Society, Telford, 20–38.

Everitt, B. L. 1968. The use of cottonwood in an investigation of the recent history of a flood-plain. *American Journal of Science* 266, 417–39.

Faegri, K. and Iversen, J. 1990. *Textbook of Pollen Analysis.* Third edition, Munksgaard, Copenhagen.

Fenneman, N. M. 1906. Floodplains produced without floods. *Bulletin of the American Geographical Society* 38, 89–91.

Fenwick, V., Parfitt, K., Bates, M. R. and Barham, A. J. (in press). A Bronze Age stitched-plank boat discovered in Dover, Kent: a preliminary report. *International Journal of Nautical Studies.*

Ferguson, R. I. 1981. Channel form and channel changes. In J. Lewin (ed.), *British Rivers.* Allen and Unwin, London, 90–125.

Ferring. C. R. 1986. Rates of fluvial sedimentation: implications for archaeological variability. *Geoarchaeology* 1, 259–74.

Ferring, C. R. and Peter, D. E. 1987. Geoarchaeology of the Dyer site, a prehistoric occupation in the Western Ouachitas, Oklahoma. *Plains Anthropology* 32, 351–66.

Fiedel, S. J. 1987. *Prehistory of the Americas.* Cambridge University Press, Cambridge.

Fisk, H. N. 1944. *Geological Investigations of the Alluvial Valley of the Lower Mississippi Valley.* Mississippi River Commission Publication 52, Vicksburg, Mississippi.

Fitzpatrick, E. A. 1984. *Micromorphology of Soils.* Chapman and Hall, London.

Flohn, H. and Fantechi, R. 1984. *The Climate of Europe: Past, Present and Future.* D. Rheidel Publishing Co., Dordrecht.

Floreck, E. and Floreck, W. 1986. Age and development of the Slupia river floodplain terrace, Pomerania, Poland. *Quaternary Studies in Poland* 7, 5–24.

Foged, M. M. 1975. Runoff agriculture: efficient use of rainfall. In J. L. Thames and J. N. Fischer (eds.), *Watershed Management in Arid Zones*. AID/University of Arizona, Tucson, 130–46.

Foged, N. 1947–48. Diatoms in watercourses in Funen. I–VI. *Dansk Botanica Arkiv* 12(5), 12(6), 12(9), 12(12).

1978. *Diatom Analysis: The Archaeology of Svendborg, Denmark* 1. Odense University Press, Odense.

Folk, R. and Ward, W. 1957. Brazos river bar: a study of the significance of grain size parameters. *Journal of Sedimentary Petrology* 27, 3–26.

Follensbee, E. 1988. The story of the flood in the light of comparative semitic mythology. In A. Dundes (ed.), *The Flood Myth*. University of California Press, Berkeley and Los Angeles, 75–88.

Foss, J. E. and Segovia, A. V. 1983. Rates of soil formation. In T. G. LaFleur (ed.), *Groundwater as a Geomorphic Agent*. London, Allen and Unwin, 1–17.

Frank, A. H. E. 1968. Pollen stratigraphy of the Lake of Vico (Central Italy). *Palaeogeography, Palaeoclimatology, Palaeoecology* 6, 67–85.

Franks, J. W. 1960. Interglacial deposits at Trafalgar Square, London. *New Phytologist* 59, 145–52.

French, C. I. A. 1988. Aspects of buried prehistoric soils in the fen margin northeast of Peterborough, Cambridgeshire. In P. Murphy and C. I. A. French (eds.), *The Exploitation of Wetlands*. British Archaeological Reports, British Series 186, Oxford, 193–211.

1990. Neolithic soils, middens and alluvium in the lower Welland valley. *Oxford Journal of Archaeology* 9, 305–11.

Frey, D. G. 1964. Remains of animals in Quaternary lake and bog sediments and their interpretation. *Arch. Hydrobiol. Beih.* 2, 1–114.

1986. Cladoceran analysis. In B. E. Berglund (ed.), *Handbook of Holocene Palaeoecology and Palaeohydrology*. Wiley, Chichester, 667–92.

Frison, G. C. 1976. Cultural activity associated with prehistoric mammoth butchering and processing. *Science* 194, 728–30.

Fritsch, F. E. and Pantin, C. F. A. 1946. Calcareous concretions in a Cambridgeshire stream. *Nature* 30, 397–9.

Fritts, H. C. 1976. *Tree Rings and Climate*. Academic Press, London and New York.

Frostick, L. and Reid, I. 1983. Taphonomic significance of sub-aerial transport of vertebrate fossils on steep semi-arid slopes. *Lethaia* 16, 157–64.

Frymer-Kensky, T. 1988. The Atrahasis epic and its significance for our understanding of Genesis 1–9. In A. Dundes (ed.), *The Flood Myth*. University of California Press, Berkeley and Los Angeles, 61–74.

Gale, S. J. and Hunt, C. O. 1986. The hydrological characteristics of a floodwater farming system. *Applied Geography* 6, 33–42.

Gamble, C. 1986. *The Palaeolithic Settlement of Europe*. Cambridge University Press, Cambridge.

Gardiner, V. and Dackombe, R. V. 1983. *Geomorphological Field Manual*. Allen and Unwin, London.

Garrison, E. G., Rowlett, R. M., Cowan, D. L. and Holroyd, L. V. 1981. ESR dating of ancient flints. *Nature* 290, 44–5.

Gatewood, J. S., Robinson, T. W., Colby, B. R., Horn, J. D. and Halpenny, L. C. 1950. Use of water by bottomland vegetation in Lower Stafford Valley, Arizona. *United States Geological Survey Water Supply Paper* 1103.

Gelling, M. 1984. *Placenames in the Landscape*. J. M. Dent, London.

1988. *Signposts to the Past: Place-Names and the History of England*. Second Edition, Phillimore, Chichester.

Georgiadi, A. G. 1979. Upper limits of the elements of the hydrologic regime. *Soviet Hydrology* 18, 225–30.

Georgiev, V. I. 1973. The arrival of the Greeks: the linguistic evidence. In R. A. Crossland and A. Birchall (eds.), *Bronze Age Migrations in the Aegean*. Duckworth, London, 243–54.

Gerrard, J. (ed.) 1987. *Alluvial Soils.* Van Nostrand Reinhold, New York.

Gibbard, P. L. 1985. *Pleistocene History of the Middle Thames Valley*. Cambridge University Press, Cambridge.

1994. *The Pleistocene History of the Lower Thames Valley.* Cambridge University Press, Cambridge.

Gibbard, P. L., Bryant, I. D. and Hall, A. R. 1986. A Hoxnian interglacial doline infilling at Slade Oak Lane, Denham, Buckinghamshire, England. *Geological Magazine* 123, 27–43.

Gibbard, P. L. and Cheshire, D. A. 1983. Hatfield Polytechnic (Roe Hyde Pit). In J. Rose (ed.), *Field Guide. Diversion of the Thames.* Quaternary Research Association, Hoddesdon, 110–19.

Gibbard, P. L., Switsur, V. R. and Wintle, A. G. 1986. A reappraisal of the age of silts in the Wrecclesham gravel at Alton Road, Farnham, Surrey. *Quaternary Newsletter* 50, 6–13.

Gibbard, P. L., Wintle, A. G., and Catt, J. A. 1987. Age and origin of clayey silt `Brickearth' in West London, England. *Journal of Quaternary Science* 2, 3–9.

Gilbert, G. K. 1877. *Report on the Geology of the Henry Mountains*. United States Geological and Geographical Survey, Rocky Mountains Region, General Printing Office, Washington DC.

Gilbertson, D. D. 1986. Runoff (floodwater) farming and rural water supply in arid lands. *Applied Geography* 6, 5–12.

Gilham, R. W. 1984. The effect of the capillary fringe on water-table response. *Journal of Hydrology* 67, 307–24.

Gillespie, R. 1986. *Radiocarbon User's Handbook*. Oxford University Committee for Archaeology, Monograph 3.

Girel, J. 1994. Old distribution procedures of both water and matter fluxes in floodplains of Western Europe: impact on present vegetation. *Environmental Management* 18, 203–21.

Girling, M. A. 1988. The bark beetle *Scolytus scolytus* (Fabricius) and the possible role of elm disease in the early Neolithic. In M. Jones (ed.), *Archaeology and the Flora of the British Isles*. Oxford Committee for Archaeology, Monograph 14, 34–8.

Girling, M. A. and Greig, J. R. A. 1985. A first fossil record for *Scolytus scolytus* (F.) (Elm Bark Beetle): its occurrence in elm decline deposits from London and the implications for Neolithic elm disease. *Journal of Archaeological Science* 12, 347–52.

Gladfelter, B. G. 1975. Middle Pleistocene sedimentary sequences in East Anglia (United Kingdom). In K. W. Butzer and G. L. Isaac (eds.), *After the Australopithecines: Stratigraphy, Ecology and Culture Change in the Middle Pleistocene.* Mouton, The Hague, 225–58.

Godłowska, M., Kozłowski, J., Starkel, L. and Wasylikowa, K. 1987. Neolithic settlement at Pleszow and changes in the natural environment in the Vistula valley. *Przeglad Archeologiczny* 34, 133–59.

Godwin, H. 1940. Studies in the post-glacial history of British vegetation. III. Fenland pollen diagrams. *Philosophical Transactions of the Royal Society Series B* 230, 239–61.

1978. *Fenland: Its Ancient Past and Uncertain Future.* Cambridge University Press, Cambridge.

Gosselink, J. G. and Turner, R. E. 1978. The role of hydrology in freshwater wetland ecosystems. In R. E. Good, D. F. Whigham and R. L. Simpson (eds.), *Freshwater Wetlands: Ecological Processes and Management Potential.* Academic Press, London and New York, 63–78.

Goudie, A. 1981. *The Human Impact.* Basil Blackwell, Oxford.

1987. Geography and archaeology: the growth of a relationship. In J. M. Wagstaff (ed.), *Landscape and Culture*. Basil Blackwell, London, 11–25.

1992. *Environmental Change*. Third edition, Clarendon Press, Oxford.

Graf, W. L. 1977. The rate law in fluvial geomorphology. *American Journal of Science* 277, 178–91.

1979. Catastrophe theory as a model for change in fluvial systems. In D. D. Rhodes and G. P. Williams (eds.), *Adjustments of the Fluvial System*. Kendall/Hunt Publishers, Dubuque, Iowa, 13–32.

Gray, H. H. 1984. Archaeological sedimentology of overbank silt deposits on the floodplain of the Ohio river near Louisville, Kentucky. *Journal of Archaeological Science* 11, 421–32.

Green, C. P. and McGregor, D. F. M. 1980. Quaternary evolution of the upper Thames. In D. K. C. Jones (ed.), *The Shaping of Southern England*. Institute of British Geographers Special Publication 11, 177–202, Academic Press, London.

Gregory, K. J. 1983. *Background to Palaeohydrology*. Wiley, Chichester.

Gregory, K. J., Branson, J. and Brown, A. G. 1996. *Global Changes: The Context of Palaeohydrology*. Geological Society Special Publication, London.

Gregory, K. J., Lewin, J. and Thornes, J. B. 1987. *Palaeohydrology in Practice*. Wiley, Chichester.

Gregory, K. J. and Walling. D. E. 1973. *Drainage Basin Process and Form*. Edward Arnold, London.

Gregory, S. 1988. *Recent Climatic Change*. Belhaven Press, London.

Griffin, J. B. 1978. Foreword. In B. D. Smith (eds.), *Mississippian Settlement Patterns*. Academic Press, New York, 15–22.

Grime, J. P., Hodgson, J. G. and Hunt, R. 1979. *The Abridged Comparative Plant Ecology*. Unwin Hyman, London.

Grosse-Bruckman, G. 1986. Analysis of vegetative plant macrofossils. In B. E. Berglund (ed.), *Handbook of Holocene Palaeoecology and Palaeohydrology*. Wiley, Chichester, 591–618.

Grove, J. 1988. *The Little Ice Age*. Methuen, London.

Guccioni, M. J., Laffert, R. H. and Scott Cummings, L. 1988. Environmental constraints of human settlement in an evolving Holocene alluvial system, the Lower Mississippi valley. *Geoarchaeology* 3, 65–84.

Gurnell, A. M. and Gregory, K. J. 1984. The influence of vegetation on stream channel processes. In T. P. Burt and D. E. Walling (eds.), *Catchment Experiments in Geomorphology*. Geo Books, Norwich, 515–35.

Hack, J. T. 1942. The changing physical environment of the Hopi Indians of Arizona. *Harvard University Peabody Museum Papers* 35, 1–85.

1965. Postglacial drainage evolution and stream geometry in the Ontonagon area, Michigan. *United States Geological Survey Professional Paper* 504B, 1–40.

Hadfield, C. 1979. *British Canals*. Sixth edition, David and Charles, Newton Abbott.

Hagberg, J. K. 1988. The bronze shield from Fröslunda near lake Vänern, West Sweden. In B. Hårdh, L. Larsson, D. Olavsson and R. Petré (eds.), *Trade and Exchange in Prehistory: Studies in Honour of Berta Stjernquist*. Histoiske Museum, Lund, 119–26.

Hanson, C. B. 1980. Fluvial taphonomic processes: models and experiments. In A. K. Behrensmeyer and A. P. Hill (eds.), *Fossils in the Making*. University of Chicago Press, Chicago, 156–81.

Happ, S. C., Rittenhouse, G. and Dobson, G. C. 1940. Some principles of accelerated stream and valley sedimentation. *United States Department of Agriculture Technical Bulletin* 695.

Harden, J. W. 1982. A quantitative index of soil development from field descriptions: examples from a chronosequence in Central California. *Geoderma* 28, 1–28.

Harding, D. M. and Parker, D. J. 1972. A study of the flood hazard at Shrewsbury, U.K. *Twenty-Second Geographical Congress Proceedings*, Calgary.

Harding, P., Gibbard, P. L., Lewin, J., Macklin, M. G. and Moss, E. H. 1987. The transport and abrasion of flint handaxes in a gravel-bed river. In G. de G. Sieveking and M. H. Newcomer (eds.), *The Human Uses of Flint and Chert*. Papers from the fourth International Flint Conference, Cambridge.

Hare, F. K. 1947. The geomorphology of a part of the Middle Thames. *Proceedings of the Geologists' Association* 16, 271–81.

Harvey, A. M., Oldfield, F., Baron, A. F. and Pearson, G. W. 1981. Dating of post-glacial landforms in the central Howgills. *Earth Surface Processes and Landforms* 6, 401–12.

Harvey, A. M. and Renwick, W. H. 1987. Holocene alluvial fill and terrace formation in the Bowland Fells, northeastern England. *Earth Surface Processes and Landforms* 12, 249–57.

Harwood, K. and Brown, A. G. 1993. Changing in-channel and overbank flood velocity distributions and the morphology of forested multiple channel (anastomosing) systems. *Earth Surface Processes and Landforms* 18, 741–8.

Hassan, E. A. 1979. Geoarchaeology: the geologist and archaeology. *American Antiquity* 44, 267–70.

Havlicek, P. 1991. The Moravian river basin during the last 15,000 years. In L. Starkel, K. J. Gregory and J. B. Thornes (eds.), *Temperate Palaeohydrology.* Wiley, Chichester, 319–42.

Haynes, C. V. 1971. Geochronology of man–mammoth sites in the Great Plains and their bearing upon the origin of the Llano complex. In W. Dart and J. K. Jones (eds.), *Pleistocene and Recent Environments of the Great Plains.* Lawrence University of Kansas, special publication 3, 77–92.

1981. Geochronology and palaeoenvironments of the Murray Springs Clovis sites, Arizona. *National Geographic Society Research Reports* 13, 243–51.

1982. Archaeological investigation of the Lehner site, Arizona. *National Geographic Society Research Reports* 14, 325–34.

1990. The Antevs–Bryan years and the legacy for paleoindian studies. In L. F. Laport (ed.), *Establishment of a Geologic Framework for Paleoanthropology.* Geological Society of America Special Publication 242 Boulder, Colorado, 55–68.

Haynes, C. V. and Huckell, B. B. 1986. *Sedimentary Successions of the Prehistoric Santa Cruz River, Tucson, Arizona.* Arizona Bureau of Mines and Geology, Open File Report.

Hayward, M. and Fenwick, I. 1983. Soils and hydrological change. In K. J. Gregory (ed.), *Background to Palaeohydrology*, Wiley, Chichester, 167–88.

Hazelden, J. and Jarvis, M. G. 1979. Age and significance of alluvium in the Windrush valley, Oxfordshire. *Nature* 282, 291–2.

Hedges, R. E. M. 1991. AMS dating: present status and potential applications. *Quaternary Proceedings* 1, 5–11.

Heery, S. 1993. *The Shannon Floodlands: A Natural History.* TírEolas, Kinvara.

Heinzelin, Jean de. 1964. Le sous-sol du temple d'Aksha. *Kush* 12, 102–10.

Helck, W. 1966. Nilhöhe und Jubiläumsfest. *Zeitscrift Agypt. Sprache* 93, 74–9.

Henderson, F. M. 1966. *Open Channel Flow.* Macmillan, London.

Herath, J. W. and Grimshaw, R. W. 1971. A general evaluation of the frequency distribution of clay and associated minerals in the alluvial soils of Ceylon. *Geoderma* 5, 119–30.

Hester, J. 1972. *Blackwater Locality No. 1: A Stratified Early Man Site in Eastern New Mexico: Dallas, Texas.* South Methodist University Fort Burgwin Research Centre, Dallas.

Hey, R. D. and Thorne, C. R. 1975. Secondary flow in river channels. *Area* 7, 191–5.

Higgs, E. S. and Vita-Finzi, C. V. 1972. Prehistoric economies: a territorial approach. In E. S. Higgs (ed.), *Papers in Economic Prehistory*, Cambridge University Press, Cambridge, 27–36.

Higgs, G. 1987. Environmental change and hydrological response: flooding in the Upper Severn catchment. In K. J. Gregory, J. Lewin and J. B. Thornes (eds.), *Palaeohydrology in Practice.* Wiley, Chichester, 131–59.

Hoberman, L. 1978. Bureaucracy and disaster: Mexico City and the flood of 1629. *Journal of Latin American Studies* 6, 211–30.

Hodgen, M. 1939. Domesday watermills. *Antiquity* 13, 261–79.

Hoffman, W. 1986. Chironomid analysis. In B. E. Berglund (ed.) *Handbook of Holocene Palaeoecology and Palaeohydrology.* Wiley, Chichester, 715–28.

Holliday, V. T. 1985. New data on the stratigraphy and pedology of the Clovis and Plainview sites, Southern High Plains. *Quaternary Research* 23, 388–402.

1987. Geoarchaeology and late Quaternary geomorphology of the Middle South Platte river, Northeastern Colorado. *Geoarchaeology* 2, 317–29.

Hollis, G. E. (ed.) 1979. *Man's Impact on the Hydrological Cycle in the United Kingdom.* Geo Books, Norwich.

Holloway, R. G. 1981. Preservation and experimental diagenesis of pollen exine. Unpublished PhD thesis, Texas A. and M. University.

Holmes, D. A. and Western, S. 1969. Soil-texture patterns in the alluvium of the lower Indus plain. *Journal of Soil Science* 20, 23–37.

Holt, R. 1988. *The Mills of Medieval England.* Basil Blackwell, Oxford.

Hooke, J. M. 1977. The distribution and nature of changes in river channel pattern. In K. J. Gregory (ed.) *River Channel Changes.* Wiley, Chichester 265–80.

Hooke, J. M., Harvey, A. M. Miller, S. Y. and Redmond, C. E. 1990. The chronology and stratigraphy of the alluvial terraces of the river Dane valley, Cheshire. *Earth Surface Processes and Landforms* 15, 717–37.

Houghton, J. T., Genkins, G. J. and Ephraums, E. (eds.) 1990. *Climate Change: The IPCC Scientific Assessment.* Cambridge University Press, Cambridge.

Howe, G. M., Slaymeker, H. O. and Harding, D. M. 1967. Some aspects of the flood hydrology of the upper catchments of the Severn and Wye. *Transactions of the Institute of British Geographers* 41, 33–58.

Howell, P. P. and Allen, J. A. 1994. *The Nile: Sharing a Scarce Resource.* Cambridge University Press, Cambridge.

Huckleberry, G. A. 1985. 'Palaeoenvironmental interpretation from soils in the Sunlight Basin Area, Park County, Wyoming'. MA Thesis, University of Wyoming, Laramie.

Hughes, D. A. 1980. Floodplain inundation: processes and relationships with channel discharge. *Earth Surface Processes* 5, 297–304.

Huntley, B. and Birks, H. J. B. 1983. *An Atlas of Past and Present Pollen Maps for Europe: 0–13000 Years Ago.* Cambridge University Press, Cambridge.

Huntley, D. J., Godfrey-Smith, D. I. and Thewalt, M. L. W. 1985. Optical dating of sediments. *Nature* 313, 105–7.

Hurst, H. 1974. Excavations at Gloucester, 1971–1973. Second interim report. *The Antiquarians' Journal* 54, 8–51.

Hurst, J. G. 1984. The Wharram Percy research project: results to 1983. *Medieval Archaeology* 28, 101–2.

Hustedt, F. 1937–9. *Die Susswasser-Flora Mitteleuropas. Heft 10: Bacillarriophyta (Diatomaceae).* Jena, Verlag Von Gustav Fischer.

Hutchinson, E. (ed.) 1970. *Ianula: An Account of the History and Development of the Lago di Monterosa, Latium, Italy.* Transactions of the American Philosophical Society 40.

Hutchinson, J. N. 1980. The record of peat wastage in the East Anglian Fenland at Holme Fen Post, 1848–1978 AD. *Journal of Ecology* 68, 229–49.

Iversen, J. 1944a. *Viscum, Hedera* and *Ilex* as climatic indicators. *Geolohie Fören. Stockholm förh* 66, 463–83.

1944b. Landnam i Denmarks Stenlader. *Denmaks Geologiska Undersolgelse,* series 11, 1–68.

1958. The bearing of glacial and interglacial epochs on the formation and extinction of plant taxa. *Uppsala Universitets Arssfrift* 6, 210–15.

Jackson, D. A. and Ambrose, T. M. 1976. A Roman timber bridge at Aldwincle, Northamptonshire. *Britannia* 7, 39–72.

Jackson, K. 1953. *Language and History in Early Britain.* Nelson, Edinburgh.

Jacobi, R. M., Tallis, J. H. and Mellars, P. A. 1976. The southern Pennine Mesolithic and the ecological record. *Journal of Archaeological Science* 3, 307–20.

Jacobsen, G. L. and Bradshaw, R. H. W. 1980. The selection of sites for palaeovegetational study. *Quaternary Research* 16, 80–96.

Jacobsen, T. 1982. *Salinity and Irrigation Agriculture in Antiquity.* Bibliotheca Mesopotamica 14, Chicago.

Jacobsen, T. and Adams, R. H. 1958. Salt and silt in ancient Mesopotamian agriculture. *Science* 128, 1251–8.

James, C. S. 1985. Sediment transfer to overbank sections. *Journal of Hydraulic Research* 23, 435–52.

James, T. 1980. *Camarthen: An Archaeological and Topographical Survey.* Dyfed Archaeological Trust. Monograph Series 2.

Jane, F. W. 1956. *The Structure of Wood.* Adam and Charles Black, London.

Janssen, C. R. 1959. *Alnus* as a disturbing factor in pollen diagrams. *Acta Botanica Neerlandica* 8, 55–8.

1972. The palaeoecology of plant communities in the Dommel valley, North Brabant, Netherlands. *Journal of Ecology* 60, 411–37.

1986. The use of pollen indicators and of the contrast between regional and local pollen values in the assessment of the human impact on vegetation. In K.-E. Behre (ed.), *Anthropogenic Indicators in Pollen Diagrams* Balkema, Rotterdam, 203–8.

Jennings, S. 1992. A ceramic fish trap. In D. Gaimster and M. Redknap (eds.), *Everyday and Exotic Pottery from Europe c. 650–1900.* Oxbow Books, Oxford, 66–9.

Jenny, H. 1962. Model of a rising nitrogen profile in Nile valley alluvium, and its agronomic and pedogenic implications. *Proceedings of the American Society of Soil Science* 26, 588–91.

Jochim, M. A. 1976. *Hunter-Gatherer Subsistence and Settlement: A Predictive Model.* Academic Press, New York.

Johnson, D. L., Keller, E. A. and Rockwell, T. K. 1990. Dynamic pedogenesis: new views on some key soil concepts and a model for interpreting Quaternary soils. *Quaternary Research* 33, 306–19.

Johnson, G. A. 1972. A test of the utility of central place theory in archaeology. In P. J. Ucko, R. Tringham and G. W. Dimbleby (eds.), *Man, Settlement and Urbanism.* Duckworth, London, 769–85.

Jones, G. 1976. Multiple estates and early settlement. In P. H. Sawyer (ed.), *Medieval Settlement: Continuity and Change.* Edward Arnold, London, 15–40.

Jones, P. D., Ogilvie, A. E. J. and Wigley, T. M. L. 1984. *Riverflow Data for the United Kingdom: Reconstructed Data Back to 1844 and Historical Data Back to 1556.* Climatic Research Unit, University of East Anglia Research Paper 8, Norwich.

Jones, R. (ed.) 1985. *Archaeological Research in Kakadu National Park.* Australian National Parks and Wildlife Service, Special Publication 13, Australian National University, Canberra.

Jones, R. L. and Keen, D. H. 1993. *Pleistocene Environments of the British Isles.* Chapman and Hall, London.

Judson, S. 1963. Erosion and deposition of Italian stream valleys during historic time. *Science* 140, 898–9.

Kates, R. W. 1962. *Hazard and Choice Perception in Flood Plain Management.* Department of Geography Research Paper 78, University of Chicago, Chicago.

1978. *Risk Assessment of Environmental Hazard.* Wiley, Chichester.

Keevil, G. D. 1992. Life on the edge: archaeology and alluvium at Redland's Farm, Stanwick, Northants. In S. Needham and M. G. Macklin (eds.), *Archaeology Under Alluvium.* Oxbow Books, Oxford, 177–184.

Keller, E. A. 1971. Areal sorting of bed load material: the hypothesis of velocity reversal. *Bulletin of the Geological Society of America* 82, 753–6.

1972. Development of alluvial stream channels: a five stage model. *Bulletin of the Geological Society of America* 83, 1531–6.

Keller, E. A. and Florsheim, J. 1993. Velocity-reversal hypothesis: a model approach. *Earth Surface Processes and Landforms* 18, 733–40.

Kellerhals, R. and Church, M. 1989. The morphology of large rivers: characterisation and management. In D. P. Dodge (ed.), *Proceedings of the International Large Rivers Symposium*. Canadian Special Publication of Fisheries and Aquatic Sciences 106, 31–48.

Kelly, M. G. and Huntley, B. 1991. An 11000-year record of vegetation and environment from Lago di Martignano, Latium, Italy. *Journal of Quaternary Science* 6, 209–24.

Kemp, R. A. 1985a. The decalcified Lower Loam at Swanscombe Kent: a buried Quaternary soil. *Proceedings of the Geologists' Association* 96, 343–55.

1985b. *Soil Micromorphology and the Quaternary.* Quaternary Research Association Technical Guide 2, Cambridge.

Kennedy, B. A. 1972. 'Bankfull' discharge and meander forms. *Area* 4, 209–12.

Kerney, M. P. 1971. Interglacial deposits in Barnfield Pit, Swanscombe, and their molluscan fauna. *Journal of the Geological Society of London* 127, 69–93.

Kidson, C. 1962. The denudation chronology of the river Exe. *Transactions of the Institute of British Geographers* 31, 43–99.

King, A. 1976. *Colonial Urban Development: Culture, Social Power and Environment.* Routledge and Kegan Paul, London.

King, W. B. R. and Oakley, K. P. 1936. The Pleistocene succession in the lower part of the Thames valley. *Proceedings of the Prehistoric Society* 1, 52–76.

Kirby, A. and Kirkby, M. J. 1976. Geomorphic processes and the surface survey of archaeological sites in semi-arid areas. In D. A. Davidson and M. L. Shackley (eds.), *Geoarchaeology: Earth Science and the Past.* Duckworth, London, 229–54.

Klein, J., Lerman, J. C., Damon, P. E. and Linick, T. W. 1980. Radiocarbon concentrations in the atmosphere, 8000 year record of variations in tree-rings. *Radiocarbon* 22, 950–61.

Klein, P. *et al.* 1995 *Reserve Naturelle Offendorf.* Conservatoire des Sites Alsaciens, France.

Klink, A. 1989. The Lower Rhine: palaeoecological analysis. In G. E. Petts, H. Moller and A. L. Roux (eds.), *Historical Change of Large Alluvial Rivers.* Wiley, Chichester and New York, 183–202.

Klostan, V. 1992. Research and management of the headwater area Litovelské Pomoraví. In J. Krecek and M. J. Haigh (eds.), *Proceedings of the Symposium on Environmental Regeneration in Headwaters.* Prague/Sec, Czech Republic, 336–41.

Knighton, D. 1984. *Fluvial Forms and Processes.* Edward Arnold, London.

Knox, J. C. 1977. Human impact on Wisconsin stream channels. *Annals of the Association of American Geographers* 67, 323–42.

1983. Responses of river systems to Holocene climates. In H. E. Wright Jr (ed.), *Late-Quaternary Environments of the United States, The Holocene.* Volume II, University of Minnesota Press, Minneapolis, 26–41.

1991. Rates of floodplain overbank vertical accretion. *Geomorphology* 3, 20–38.

Kochel, R. C. and Baker, V. R. 1982. Paleoflood hydrology. *Science* 215, 353–61.

Koutaniemi, L. 1979. Late-glacial and post-glacial development of the Oulanka river basin, north-eastern Finland. *Fennia* 157, 13–73.

1991. Glacio-isostatically adjusted palaeohydrology, the rivers Ivalojoki and Oulankajoki, Northern Finland. In L. Starkel, K. J. Gregory and J. B. Thornes (eds.), *Temperate Palaeohydrology.* Wiley, Chichester, 65–78.

Kozarski, S. 1991. Warta – a case study of a lowland river. In L. Starkel, K. J. Gregory and J. B. Thornes (eds.), *Temperate Palaeohydrology.* Wiley, Chichester, 189–215.

Krahe, H. 1957. Indogermanisch und Alteuropäisch. *Saeculum* 8, 1–16. Reprinted in A. Scherer (ed.), *Die Urheimat der Indogermanen.* 1968, Darmstadt, Wissenschaftliche Buchgesellschaft, 426–54.

Ku, T.-L. 1976. The uranium-series method of age determination. *Annual Review of Earth and Planetary Science* 4, 347–79.

Kutzbach, J. E. 1981. Monsoon climate of the early Holocene: climate experiment with the Earth's orbital parameters for 9,000 years ago. *Science* 214, 59–61.

Kutzbach, J. and Street-Perrott, F. A. 1985. Milankovitch forcing of fluctuations in the level of tropical lakes from 18 to 0 K yr BP. *Nature* 317, 130–4.

Lamb, H. H. 1982. *Climate, History and the Modern World.* Methuen, London.

Lamb, H. H. and Johnson, A. E. 1966. *Secular Variation of the Atmospheric Circuation Since 1750.* HMSO, London.

Lambert, W. G. and Millard, A. R. 1969. *Atra-hasiś – The Babylonian Story of the Flood.* Oxford University Press, Oxford.

Lambrick, G. H. and Robinson, M. A. 1979. *Iron Age and Roman Riverside Settlement at Farmoor, Oxfordshire.* Council for British Archaeology Report 32.

    1988. The development of floodplain grassland in the Upper Thames valley. In M. Jones (ed.), *Archaeology and the Flora of the British Isles.* Oxford Committee for Archaeology Monograph 14/Botanical Society of the British Isles Report 19, Oxford, 55–75.

Lambrick, H. T. 1967. The Indus flood-plain and the 'Indus' civilisation. *Geographical Journal* 133, 483–95.

Langbein, W. B. and Leopold, L. B. 1966. River meanders - theory of minimum variance. *United States Geological Survey Professional Paper* 422H.

Langford, M., Taylor, G. and Flenley, J. R. 1986. *The Application of Texture Analysis for Automated Pollen Identification.* Proceedings of Conference on Identification and Pattern Recognition, Toulouse, France, Université de Paul Sabatier, Volume II, 729–39.

Lattman, L. H. 1960. Cross section of a floodplain in a moist region of moderate relief. *Journal of Sedimentary Petrology* 30, 275–82.

Leeder, M. R. 1982. *Sedimentology: Process and Product.* George Allen and Unwin, London.

Leeds, E. T. 1928. A Neolithic site at Abingdon, Berkshire, second report. *Antiquitarian Journal* 8, 461–77.

Leopold, L. B. and Bull, W. B. 1979. Base level, aggradation and grade. *Proceedings of the American Philosophical Society* 123, 168–202.

Leopold, L. B. and Miller, J. P. 1954. A Postglacial chronology for some alluvial valleys in Wyoming. *United States Geological Survey Water Supply Paper* 1261, 1–90.

Leopold, L. B. and Wolman, M. G. 1957. River channel patterns: braided, meandering and straight. *United States Geological Survey Professional Paper* 282C, 1–85.

Lewin, J. 1978. Floodplain geomorphology. *Progress in Physical Geography* 2, 408–37.

    1987. Historical river channel changes. In K. J. Gregory, J. Lewin and J. B. Thornes (eds.), *Palaeohydrology in Practice: A River Basin Analysis.* Wiley, Chichester, 161–70.

    1992. Alluvial sedimentation style and archaeological sites: the Lower Vyrnwy, Wales. In S. Needham and M. G. Macklin (eds.), *Archaeology Under Alluvium.* Oxbow Books, Oxford, 103–10.

Lewin, J. and Brindle, B. J. 1977. Confined meanders. In K. J. Gregory (ed.), *River Channel Changes.* Wiley, Chichester, 221–33.

Lewin, J. and Hughes, D. A. 1980. Welsh floodplain studies II: application of a qualitative inundation model. *Journal of Hydrology* 46, 35–49.

Lewin, J, Macklin, M. G. and Woodward, J. C. 1991. Quaternary fluvial sedimentation in the Voidomatis basin, Epirus, northwest Greece. *Quaternary Research* 35, 103–15.

Lewis, G. W. and Lewin, J. 1983. Alluvial cutoffs in Wales and the Borderland. In J. D. Collinson and J. Lewin (eds.), *Modern and Ancient Fluvial Systems.* International Association of Sedimentologists, Special Publication 6. Blackwell, London, 145–54.

Lewis, J. S. C. and Wiltshire, P. E. J. 1992. Late glacial and early Flandrian archaeology in the Colne valley (Middlesex); possible environmental implications. In S. Needham and M. G. Macklin (eds.), *Archaeology Under Alluvium.* Oxbow Books, Oxford, 235–48.

Lewis, R. B. 1974. *Mississippian Exploitative Strategies: A Southeast Missouri Example.* Missouri Archaeological Society Research Series 11.

Libby, W. F. 1955. *Radiocarbon Dating.* University of Chicago Press, Chicago.

Limbrey, S. 1992. Micromorphological studies of buried soils and alluvial deposits in a Wiltshire river valley. In S. Needham and M. G. Macklin (eds.), *Archaeology Under Alluvium.* Oxbow Books, Oxford, 53–64.

Limbrey, S. and Robinson, S. 1988. Dry land to wet land: soil resources in the Upper Thames valley. In P. Murphy and C. I. A. French (eds.), *The Exploitation of Wetlands.* British Archaeological Reports, British Series 186, Oxford, 129–44.

Lisle, T. 1979. A sorting mechanism for a riffle pool sequence. *Bulletin of the Geological Society of America* 90, 1142–57.

Lister, A. M. 1986. New results on deer from Swanscombe, and the stratigraphic significance of deer in the Middle and Upper Pleistocene of Europe. *Journal of Archaeological Science* 13, 319–38.

Locardi, E., Lombardi. G., Funiciello, R. and Parotto, R. 1976. The main volcanic groups of Latium (Italy): relations between structure, evolution and petrogenesis. *Geologica Romana* 15, 179–300.

Lockwood, J. G. 1979. Water balance of Britain 50,000 BP to the present. *Quaternary Research* 12, 297–310.

1983. Modelling climate change. In K. J. Gregory (ed.), *Background to Palaeohydrology.* Wiley, Chichester, 25–50.

Long, D. and Morton, A. C. 1987. An ash fall within the Loch Lomond Stadial. *Journal of Quaternary Science* 2, 97–102.

Longley, D. 1980. Runnymede Bridge 1976: excavations on the site of a late Bronze Age settlement. *Surrey Archaeological Society Research Volume* 6.

Losaco, U. 1967. Notizie e considerazioni sulle inondazioni d'Arno in Firenze. *L'Universo* 47, 720–820.

Losco-Bradley, P. M. and Salisbury, C. R. 1988. A Saxon and a Norman weir at Colwick, Nottinghamshire. In M. Aston (ed.), *Medieval Fish, Fisheries and Fishponds in England.* British Archaeological Reports, British Series 182, Oxford, 329–51.

Louwe Kooijmans, L. P. 1993. Wetland exploitation and upland relations of prehistoric communities in the Netherlands. In J. Gardiner (ed.), *Flatlands and Wetlands: Current Themes in East Anglian Archaeology.* East Anglian Archaeology, Report 50, 71–116.

Lowe, J. J. and Walker, M. J. C. 1984. *Reconstructing Quaternary Environments.* Longman, London and New York.

Lugo, A. E., Brinson, M. M. and Brown, S. 1990. *Forested Wetlands.* Ecosystems of the World 15, Elsevier, Amsterdam.

Lynch, T. F. 1990. Glacial-age man in South America? A critical review. *American Antiquity* 55, 12–36.

Mabey, R. 1972. *Food for Free.* Fontana/Collins, Glasgow.

McDonald, A., Keller, E. A. and Tally, T. 1982. The role of large organic debris on stream channels draining Redwood forests in north-west California. In J. W. Harden, D. C. Marron and A. McDonald (eds.), *Friends of the Pleistocene 1982 Pacific Cell Fieldtrip Guidebook. Late Cenozoic History and Forest Geomorphology of Humbolt County, California*, 226–45.

McGrail, S. 1978. *Logboats of England and Wales. Parts I and II.* British Archaeological Reports, British Series 51, Oxford.

McGregor, D. F. and Green, C. P. 1983. Post-depositional modifications of Pleistocene terraces of the river Thames. *Boreas* 12, 23–33.

Mackin, J. H. 1948. Concept of the graded river. *Bulletin of the Geological Society of America* 59, 463–512.

Macklin, M. G. 1985. Floodplain sedimentation in the upper Axe valley, Mendip, England. *Transactions of the Institute of British Geographers* new series 10, 235–44.

Macklin, M. G. and Lewin, J. 1986. Terraced fills of Pleistocene and Holocene age in the Rheidol valley, Wales. *Journal of Quaternary Science* 1, 21–34.

1989. Sediment transfer and transformation of an alluvial valley floor: the river Tyne, Northumbria, U.K. *Earth Surface Processes and Landforms* 14, 233–46.

1993. Holocene river alluviation in Britain. *Zeitschrift für Geomorphologie* 88, 109–22.

McVean, D. N. 1954. Ecology of *Alnus glutinosa* (L.) Gaertn. Postglacial history. *Journal of Ecology* 44, 331–3.

Maddy, D., Keen, D. H., Bridgland, D. R. and Green, C. P. 1991. A revised model for the Pleistocene development of the river Avon, Warwickshire. *Journal of the Geological Society of London* 148, 473–84.

Madge, C. 1993. *Medicine, Money and Masquerades: Gender, Collecting and 'Development' in the Gambia.* Department of Geography Discussion Paper, Leicester University.

Maher, L. J. 1972. Nomograms for computing 0.95 confidence limits of pollen data. *Review of Palaeobotany and Palynology* 13, 95–124.

Maizels, J. K. 1983. Palaeovelocities and palaeodischarge estimation for coarse gravel deposits. In K. J. Gregory (ed.), *Background to Palaeohydrology.* Wiley, Chichester, 101–39.

Maizels, J. K. and Aitken, J. 1991. Palaeohydrological changes during deglaciation in upland Britain: a case study from north-east Scotland. In L. Starkel, K. J. Gregory and J. B. Thornes (eds.), *Temperate Palaeohydrology.* Wiley, Chichester, 105–46.

Mamakowa, K. and Starkel, L. 1974. New data about the profile of Quaternary deposits at Brzeznica in Wisloka valley. *Studie Geomorph. Carpatho-Balcanica* 8, 47–59.

Mansikkaniemi, H. 1991. Regional case studies in southern Finland with reference to glacial rebound and Baltic regression. In L. Starkel, K. J. Gregory and J. B. Thornes (eds.), *Temperate Palaeohydrology.* Wiley, Chichester, 79–104.

Marriott, S. 1992. Textural analysis and modelling of flood deposits: river Severn, U.K. *Earth Surface Processes and Landforms* 17, 687–98.

Marston, A. T. 1937. The Swanscombe skull. *Journal of the Royal Anthropological Institute* 67, 339–406.

Martin, P. 1973. The discovery of America. *Science* 179, 969–74.

Matthews, J. A. 1985. Radiocarbon dating of surface and buried soils: principles, problems and prospects. In K. S. Richards R. R. Arnett and S. Ellis (eds.), *Geomorphology and Soils.* Allen and Unwin, London, 269–88.

Meltzer, D. J. 1989. Why don't we know when the first people came to North America? *American Antiquity* 54, 471–90.

Mensching, H. 1951. Die entstehung der Auelehmdecken in Nordwestdeutschland. *Proceedings of the Third International Congress of Sedimentologists*, Groningen-Wageningen, Netherlands, 193–210.

Meyer-Peter, E. and Muller, R. 1948. Formulas for bed-load transport. *Proceedings of the International Association for Hydraulic Research, Third Annual Conference*, Stockholm, 39–64.

Miall, A. D. 1973. Markov chain analysis applied to an ancient alluvial plain succession. *Sedimentology* 20, 347–64.

1977. A review of the braided-river depositional environment. *Earth Science Reviews* 13, 1–62.

1983. Basin analysis of fluvial sediments. In J. D. Collinson and J. Lewin (eds.), *Modern and Ancient Fluvial Systems.* Special Publication 6 of the International Association of Sedimentologists, Blackwell Scientific Publishing, London, 279–86.

Miller, G. H., Hollin, J. T. and Andrews, J. T. 1979. Aminostratigraphy of U.K. Pleistocene deposits. *Nature* 281, 539–43.

Millett, M. and McGrail, S. 1987. The archaeology of the Hasholme logboat. *Archaeological Journal* 144, 69–155.

Mitchell, J. 1984. Hazard perception studies: convergent concerns and divergent approaches during the past decade. In T. F. Saarinen, D. Seamon and J. L. Sell (eds.), *Environmental Perception and Behavior: An Inventory and Prospect.* University of Chicago, Department of Geography Research Paper 209, 33–59.

Mitsch, W. J. and Gosselink, J. G. 1993. *Wetlands*. Second edition, Van Nostrand Rheinhold, New York.

Moore, P. D., Webb, J. A. and Collinson, M. E. 1991. *An Illustrated Guide to Pollen Analysis.* Second edition, Blackwell Scientific, Oxford.

Mordant, D. and Mordant, C. 1992. Noyen-Sur-Seine: a Mesolithic waterside settlement. In B. Coles (ed.), *The Wetland Revolution in Prehistory.* Wetland Archaeological Research Project Occasional Paper 6, Exeter, 55–64.

Morzadec-Kerfourn, M. T. 1974. Variations de la ligne de rivage armoricain au Quaternaire. *Mémoirs Société Geologique et Minéral de Bretagne* 17, 26–40.

Mosley, M. P. 1975. Channel changes on the river Bollin, Cheshire, 1872–1973. *East Midlands Geographer* 6, 185–99.

Muller, J. 1978. The Kincaid system: Mississippian settlement in the environs of a large site. In B. D. Smith (ed.), *Mississippian Settlement Patterns.* Academic Press, New York, 233–68.

Nabhan, G. P. 1986a. Papago Indian desert agriculture and water control in the Sonoran desert, 1697–1934. *Applied Geography* 6, 43–59.

1986b. 'Ak-chin' 'arroyo mouth' and the environmental setting of Papago Indian fields in the Sonoran desert. *Applied Geography* 6, 61–75.

Naiman, R., Décamps, H. and Fournier, F. 1989. *Role of Land/Inland Water Ecotones in Landscape Management and Restoration.* MAB Digest 4, UNESCO, Paris.

Nanson, G. C. 1981. New evidence of scroll-bar formation on the Beatton river. *Sedimentology* 28, 889–91.

1986. Episodes of vertical accretion and catastrophic stripping: a model of disequilibrium flood-plain development. *Bulletin of the American Geological Society* 97, 1467–75.

Nanson, G. C., East, T. and Roberts, R. G. 1993. Quaternary stratigraphy, geochronology and evolution of the Magela Creek catchment in the monsoon tropics of northern Australia. *Sedimentary Geology* 83, 277–302.

Nanson, G. C. and Erskine, W. D. 1988. Episodic changes of channels and floodplains on coastal rivers in New South Wales. In R. F. Warner (ed.), *Fluvial Geomorphology of Australia.* Academic Press, Australia, 66–87.

Nanson, G. C. and Page, K. 1983. Lateral accretion of fine-grained concave benches on meandering rivers. In J. D. Collinson and J. Lewin (eds.), *Modern and Ancient Fluvial Systems.* Special Publication 6 of the International Association of Sedimentologists, Blackwell Scientific Publishing, London, 133–44.

Nanson, G. C., Price, D. M. and Short, S. A. 1992. Wetting and drying of Australia over the past 300 ka. *Geology* 20, 791–94.

Nanson, G. C., Price, D. M., Short, S. A., Young, R. W. and Jones, B. G. 1991. Comparative uranium-thorium and thermoluminescence dating of weathered Quaternary alluvium in the tropics of northern Australia. *Quaternary Research* 35, 347–66.

Nanson, G. C. and Young, R. W. 1987. Comparison of thermoluminescence and radiocarbon age determinations from late-Pleistocene alluvial deposits near Sydney, Australia. *Quaternary Research* 27, 263–9.

Needham, S. 1985. Neolithic and Bronze Age settlement on the buried floodplain of Runnymede. *Oxford Journal of Archaeology* 4, 125–37.

1989. River valleys as wetlands: the archaeological prospects. In J. M. Coles and B. J. Coles (eds.), *The Archaeology of Rural Wetlands.* WARP and English Heritage, 29–34.

1992. Holocene alluviation and interstratified settlement evidence in the Thames valley at Runnymede Bridge. In S. Needham and M. G. Macklin (eds.), *Archaeology Under Alluvium*. Oxbow Books, Oxford, 249–60.

Needham, S. and Longley, D. 1980. Runnymede Bridge, Egham: a late Bronze Age riverside settlement. In J. Barrett and R. Bradley (eds.), *Settlement and Society in the British Later Bronze Age*. British Archaeological Reports British Series 83, Oxford, 397–436.

Needham, S. and Macklin, M. G. (eds.) 1992. *Archaeology Under Alluvium*. Oxbow Books, Oxford.

Newcomer, M. H. and Sieveking, G. de G. 1980. Experimental flake scatter patterns: a new interpretive technique. *Journal of Field Archaeology* 7, 345–52.

Nortcliffe, S. and Thornes, J. B. 1988. The dynamics of a tropical floodplain environment with reference to forest ecology. *Journal of Biogeography* 15, 49–59.

Novak, I. D. 1973. Predicting coarse sediment transport: the Hjulstrom curve revisited. In M. Morisawa (ed.), *Fluvial Geomorphology*. Binghampton, NY, 13–25.

Oakley, K. P. and Leakey, M. 1937. Report on excavations at Jaywick Sands, Essex (1934) with some observations on the Clactonian industry and on the fauna and geological significance of the Clacton channel. *Proceedings of the Prehistoric Society* 3, 217–60.

Odum, E. P. 1975. *Ecology*. Holt, Rinehart and Winston, New York.

O'Reilly, H. 1955. Survey of the Gearagh, an area of wet woodland on the river Lee, near Macroom, Co. Cork. *Irish Naturalist Journal* 11, 9–15.

Orrell, J. and Gurr, A. 1989. What the Rose can tell us. *Antiquity* 63, 421–9.

Orton, C., Tyers, P. and Vince, A. 1993. *Pottery in Archaeology*. Cambridge University Press, Cambridge.

Osborne, P. J. 1974. An insect assemblage from Lea Marston, Warwickshire, and its bearing on the contemporary climate and ecology. *Quaternary Research* 4, 471–86.

1988. A Late Bronze Age fauna from the river Avon, Warwickshire, England: its implications for the terrestrial and fluvial environment and for climate. *Journal of Archaeological Science* 15, 715–27.

Page, K. J., Nanson, G. C. and Price, D. M. 1991. Thermoluminescence chronology of Late Quaternary deposition on the Riverine Plain of south-eastern Australia. *Australian Geographer* 14–23.

Palmquist, R. C. 1975. Preferred position model and subsurface valleys. *Bulletin of the Geological Society of America* 86, 1392–8.

Pannet, D. J. 1971. Fish weirs of the river Severn. *Shropshire Conservation Trust Newsletter* 41, 4–7.

1981. Fish weirs of the river Severn. In P. Murphy (ed.), *The Evolution of the Marshland Landscape*. Shropshire Naturalists Trust, 144–57.

Parry, M. L. 1975. Secular climatic change and marginal agriculture. *Transactions of the Institute of British Geographers* 64, 1–13.

1978. *Climatic Change, Agriculture and Settlement*. Dawson, Folkestone.

1990. *Climate Change and World Agriculture*. Earthscan, London.

Passega, R. 1957. Texture as a characteristic of clastic deposition. *Bulletin of the American Society of Petroleum Geologists* 41, 1952–84.

1964. Grain size representation by CM patterns as a geological tool. *Journal of Sedimentary Petrology* 34, 830–47.

Passmore, D. G., Macklin, M. G., Brewer, P. A., Lewin, J., Rumsby, B. T. and Newson, M. D. 1993. Variability of Late Holocene braiding in Britain. In J. Best and C. Bristow (eds.), *Braided Rivers*. Geological Society Publication, 205–30.

Patrick, R. 1948. Factors affecting the distribution of diatoms. *Botanical Review* 14, 473–524.

Patrick, R. and Reimer, C. W. 1966. *The Diatoms of the United States*. 3 Vols. Monograph of the Academy of Natural Sciences of Philadelphia 13.

Pearson, G. W., Pilcher, J. R., Baille, M. G. L., Corbett, D. M. and Qua, F. 1986. High-precision measurements of Irish oaks to show the natural variations from AD 1840 to 5210 BC. *Radiocarbon* 28, 911–34.

Pearson, G. W., Pilcher, J. R., Baillie, M. G. L. and Hillam, J. 1977. Absolute radiocarbon-dating using a low altitude European tree-ring calibration. *Nature* 270, 25–8.

Pearson, G. W. and Stuiver, M. 1986. High-precision calibration of the radiocarbon time scale, 500–2500 BC. *Radiocarbon* 29, 839–61.

Peck, R. M. 1973. Pollen budget studies in a small Yorkshire catchment. In H. J. B. Birks and R. G. West (eds.), *Quaternary Plant Ecology.* Blackwell, Oxford, 43–60.

Pedley, H. M. 1990. Classification and environmental models of cool freshwater tufas. *Sedimentary Geology* 68, 143–54.

Penka, M., Vyskot, M., Klimo, E. and Vasicek, F. 1985. *Floodplain Forest Ecosystem.* Developments in Agricultural and Managed-Forest Ecology Series 15A, Elsevier, Amsterdam, Oxford and New York.

Penning-Rowsell, E. C. 1976. The effects of flood damage on land use planning. *Geographia Polonica* 34, 139–58.

Perry, A. 1992. The economic impact, costs and opportunities of global warming. *Progress in Physical Geography* 16, 97–100.

Petts, G. E. 1987. Ecological management of regulated rivers: a European perspective. *Regulated Rivers* 1, 363–9.

   1989. Historical analysis of fluvial hydrosystems. In G. E. Petts, H. Moller and A. L. Roux (eds.), *Historical Change of Large Alluvial Rivers: Western Europe.* Wiley, Chichester, 1–18.

Phillips, C. W. (ed.) 1970. *The Fenland in Roman Times.* Royal Geographical Society Research Publication No. 5, Royal Geographical Society, London.

Piggott, S. 1950. *Prehistoric India.* Penguin Books, Harmondsworth.

Pizzuto, J. E. 1987. Sediment diffusion during overbank flows. *Sedimentology* 34, 304–17.

Plymley, J. 1803. *General View of the Agriculture of Shropshire.* London.

Pohl, F. 1937. Die pollenerzeugnung der windbluter. *Botanischer Centrablattung* 56A, 365–470.

Pons, A. and Quezel, P. 1985. The history of the flora and vegetation and past and present human disturbance in the Mediterranean region. In C. Gomez-Campo (ed.), *Plant Conservation in the Mediterranean Area.* W. Junk, Dordrecht 25–43.

Pope, K. O. and van Andel, T. H. 1984. Late Quaternary alluviation and soil formation in the Southern Argolid: its history, causes and archaeological implications. *Journal of Archaeological Science* 11, 281–306.

Popov, I. V. and Gavrin, Y. S. 1970. Use of aerial photography in evaluating the flooding and emptying of river floodplains and the development of floodplain currents. *Soviet Hydrology* 5, 413–25.

Porter, S. C. (ed.) 1983. *Late Quaternary Environments of the United States. Volume 1. The Late Pleistocene* (series editor H. E. Wright). University of Minnesota Press, Minneapolis.

Potter, H. R. 1978. *The Use of Historic Records for the Augmentation of Hydrological Data.* Institute of Hydrology, Report 46.

Potter, T. W. 1976a. Valley and settlement: some new evidence. *World Archaeology* 8, 207–19.

   1976b. *A Faliscan Town in South Etruria: Excavations at Narce 1966–1971.* British School at Rome, London.

   1981. The Roman occupation of central Fenland. *Britannia* 12, 79–133.

Pratt, M. L. 1992. *Imperial Eyes: Travel Writing and Transculturation.* Routledge, London.

Prentice, I. C. 1985. Pollen representation, source area and basin size: towards a unified theory of pollen analysis. *Quaternary Research* 23, 76–86.

Pryor, F. 1984. *Excavations at Fengate, Peterborough, England: The Fourth Report.* Northamptonshire Archaeological Society Monograph 2.

Punt, W. (ed.) 1976–. *The Northwest European Pollen Flora.* Elsevier, Amsterdam.

Purseglove, J. 1989. *Taming the Flood.* Oxford University Press, Oxford.

Rackham, O. 1986. *The History of the Countryside.* Weidenfeld and Nicolson, London.

Raikes, R. 1964. The end of the ancient cities of the Indus. *American Anthropologist* 66, 196–203.

1965. The Mohenjo-daro floods. *Antiquity* 39, 284–9.

1967. *Water, Weather and Prehistory.* John Baker, London.

Ramm, H. G. 1971. The end of Roman York. In R. M. Butler (ed.), *Soldier and Civilian in Roman Yorkshire.* Leicester University Press, Leicester, 179–99.

Rapp, G. and Gifford, J. A. (eds.) 1985. *Archaeological Geology.* Yale University Press, New Haven.

Razzaq, A. and Herbillon, A. J. 1979. Clay mineralogical trend in alluvium-derived soils of Pakistan. *Pédologie* 29, 5–23.

Reider, R. G. and Karlstrom, E. T. 1987. Soils and stratigraphy of the Laddie Creek site (48BH345), an altithermal-age occupation in the Big Horn mountains, Wyoming. *Geoarchaeology* 2, 29–47.

Reineck, H.-E. and Singh, I. B. 1973. *Depositional Sedimentary Environments.* Springer-Verlag, New York.

Renfrew, C. 1987. *Archaeology and Language.* Penguin, Harmondsworth.

Renfrew, C. and Bahn, P. 1991. *Archaeology: Theories, Methods, and Practice.* Thames and Hudson, London.

Rhodes, E. J. and Aitken, M. J. 1988. Optical dating of archaeological sediment. *La Chronologie* 1, 117–20.

Rhodes, E. J. and Pownall, L. 1994. Zeroing of the OSL signal in quartz from young glaciofluvial sediments. *Radiation Measurements* 23, 581–55.

Richards, K. 1982. *Rivers.* Methuen, London.

Richards, K. S., Peters, N. R., Robertson-Rintoul, M. S. E. and Switsur, V. R. 1987. Recent valley sediments in the North York Moors: evidence and interpretation. In V. Gardiner (ed.), *International Geomorphology 1986*, Part I. Wiley, Chichester, 869–83.

Richardson, L. 1964. *The River Severn Between Upper Arley (Worcs.) and Gloucester.* Published privately, Worcester.

Riehl, H., El-Bakry, M. and Meitin, J. 1979. Nile river discharges. *Monthly Weather Review* 107, 1546–53.

Ritter, D. F., Kinsey, W. F. and Kauffman, M. E. 1973. Overbank sedimentation in the Delaware river valley during the last 6000 years. *Science* 179, 374–5.

Rivet, A. L. F. and Smith, C. 1979. *The Place-Names of Roman Britain.* Oxford University Press, London.

Roberts, M. B. 1986. Excavation of the Lower Palaeolithic site at Amey's Eartham pit, Boxgrove, West Sussex: a preliminary report. *Proceedings of the Prehistoric Society* 52, 215–45.

Roberts, N. 1989. *The Holocene.* Basil Blackwell, Oxford.

Roberts, R. G., Jones, R. and Smith, M. A. 1990. Thermoluminescence dating of a 50,000 year old human occupation site in northern Australia. *Nature* 345, 153–6.

Robertson-Mackay, R. 1987. The Neolithic causewayed enclosure at Staines, Surrey: excavations 1961–1963. *Proceedings of the Prehistoric Society* 53, 23–128.

Robertson-Rintoul, M. S. E. 1986. A quantitative soil stratigraphic approach to the correlation and dating of post-glacial river terraces in Glen Feshie, Western Cairngorms. *Earth Surface Processes and Landforms* 11, 605–17.

Robinson, M. 1992. Environment, archaeology and alluvium on the river gravels of the South Midlands. In S. Needham and M. G. Macklin (eds.), *Archaeology Under Alluvium.* Oxbow Books, Oxford, 197–208.

Robinson, M. and Lambrick, G. H. 1984. Holocene alluviation and hydrology in the Upper Thames basin. *Nature* 308, 809–14.

Roe, D. A. 1976. Palaeolithic industries in the Oxford region: some notes. In D. A. Roe (ed.), *Field Guide to the Oxford Region*, Oxford, Quaternary Research Association, 36–43.

1981. *The Lower and Middle Palaeolithic Ages in Britain.* Routledge and Kegan Paul, London.

Rose, J., Turner, C., Coope, G. R. and Bryan, M. D. 1980. Channel changes in a lowland river catchment over the last 13,000 years. In R. A. Cullingford, D. A. Davidson and J. Lewin (eds.), *Timescales in Geomorphology.* Wiley, Chichester, 159–76.

Rother, N. 1989. Holozane erosion und akkumulation in Ilmetal, Sudeniedersachsen. *Bayreuth Geowissenschaftliche Annaler* 55, 85–92.

Rotnicki, K. 1983. Modelling past discharges of meandering rivers. In K. J. Gregory (ed.), *Background to Palaeohydrology.* Wiley, Chichester, 321–54.

1991. Retrodiction of palaeodischarges of meandering and sinuous alluvial rivers and its palaeohydroclimatic implications. In L. Starkel, K. J. Gregory and J. B. Thornes (eds.), *Temperate Palaeohydrology.* Wiley, Chichester, 431–72.

Roux, A. L., Bravard, J.-P., Amoros, C. and Pautou, G. 1989. Ecological changes of the French Upper Rhone river since 1750. In G. E. Petts, H. Moller and A. L. Roux (eds.), *Historical Change of Large Alluvial Rivers.* Wiley, Chichester and New York, 323–50.

Rowlands, M. 1984. Conceptualising the European Bronze and early Iron Ages. In J. Bintliff (ed.), *European Social Evolution*, Bradford University Press, Bradford, 23–40.

Rybnicek, K. and Rybnickova, E. 1987. Palaeogeobotanical evidence of middle Holocene stratigraphic hiatuses in Czechoslovakia and their explanation. *Folio Botanische. Phytotaxia, Praha* 22, 313–27.

Sack, R. D. 1980. *Conceptions of Space in Social Thought.* Macmillan, London.

Salisbury, C. R. 1981. An Anglo-Saxon weir at Colwick, Nottinghamshire. *Transactions of the Thoroton Society* 84, 26–36.

1992. The archaeological evidence for palaeochannels in the Trent valley. In S. Needham and M. G. Macklin (eds.), *Archaeology Under Alluvium.* Oxbow, Oxford, 155–62.

Salisbury, C. R., Whitley, P. J., Litton, C. D. and Fox, J. L. 1984. Flandrian courses of the river Trent at Colwick, Nottingham. *Mercian Geologist* 9, 189–207.

Salmi, M. 1962. Investigations on the distribution of pollens in an extensive raised bog. *Bulletin of the Commission for Geology of Finland* 204, 152–93.

Salo, J., Kalliola, R., Hakkinen, I., Makinen, Y., Niemela, P., Puhakka, M. and Coley, P. D. 1986. River dynamics and the diversity of Amazon lowland rain forest. *Nature* 322, 254–8.

Samuels, J. and Buckland, P. C. 1978. A Romano-British settlement at Sandtoft, South Humberside. *Yorkshire Archaeological Journal* 50, 65–75.

Sandford, K. S. 1924. The river gravels of the Oxford district. *Quarterly Journal of the Geological Society of London* 80, 113–79.

Sandford, K. S. and Arkell, W. J. 1939. Paleolithic man and the Nile valley in Lower Egypt. *Publications of the University of Chicago Oriental Institute* 46, 1–105.

Sangster, A. G. and Dale, H. M. 1961. A preliminary study of differential pollen grain preservation. *Canadian Journal of Botany* 39, 35–51.

Sasscer, D. S., Jordan, C. F. and Kline, J. R. 1971. Mathematical model of tritiated and stable water movement in an old-field system. In *Radionuclides in Ecosystems.* Proceedings of the Third National Symposium on Radioecology, US Atomic Energy Commission, Washington, 915–23.

Saucier, R. T. 1974. *Quaternary Geology of the Lower Mississippi Valley.* Arkansas Archaeological Survey, Research Series 6.

1981. Current thinking on riverine processes and geologic history as related to human settlement in the Southeast. *Geoscience and Man* 22, 7–18.

Scaife, R. G. and Burrin, P. J. 1985. The environmental impact of prehistoric man as recorded in the upper Cuckmere valley at Stream Farm. *Sussex Archaeological Collections* 123, 27–34.

1992. Archaeological inferences from alluvial sediments: some findings from southern England. In S. Needham and M. G. Macklin (eds.), *Archaeology Under Alluvium*. Oxbow Books, Oxford, 75–92.

Schmudde, T. H. 1963. Some aspects of land forms of the lower Missouri river floodplain. *Annals of the Association of American Geographers* 53, 60–6.

Schumm, S. A. 1968. *River Adjustment to Altered Hydrologic Regimen – Murrumbidgee River and Palaeochannels, Australia.* United States Geological Survey Professional Paper 598.

1973. Geomorphic thresholds and complex response of drainage systems. In M. Morisawa (ed.), *Fluvial Geomorphology.* Binghamton Publications in Geomorphology, Suny, Binghamton, NY, 69–85.

1977. *The Fluvial System.* Wiley, New York.

Schumm, S. A. and Khan, H. R. 1972. Experimental study of channel patterns. *Bulletin of the Geological Society of America* 83, 1755–70.

Schumm, S. A. and Lichty, R. W. 1965. Time, space and causality in geomorphology. *American Journal of Science* 263, 110–19.

Schumm, S. A. and Parker, R. S. 1973. Implications of complex response of drainage systems for Quaternary alluvial stratigraphy. *Nature* 243, 99–100.

Schweingruber, F. H. 1978. *Microscopic Wood Anatomy.* Swiss Federal Institute for Forestry Research, Birmensdorf, Zurcher A.G.

Scott, G. R. 1963. *Quaternary Geology and Geomorphic History of the Kassler Quadrangle, Colorado.* United States Geological Survey Professional Paper 421A.

Scully, R.W. and Arnold, R.W. 1981. Holocene alluvial stratigraphy in the upper Susquehanna river basin, New York. *Quaternary Research* 15, 327–44.

Sealy, K. R. and Sealy, C. E. 1964. The terraces of the Middle Thames. *Proceedings of the Geologists' Association* 67, 369–92.

Sealy, R. S. 1979. Ancient courses of the Great and Little Ouse in Fenland. *Proceedings of the Cambridge Antiquarian Society* 69, 1–19.

Shaake, J. D. 1990. From climate to flow. In P. E. Waggoner (ed.), *Climate Change and US Water Resources.* Wiley, New York, 23–40.

Shackley, M. R. 1974. Stream abrasion of flint implements. *Nature* 248, 501–2.

Shanks, M. and Tilley, C. 1987. *Social Theory and Archaeology.* Polity Press, Oxford.

Sheail, J. 1988. River regulation in the United Kingdom: an historical perspective. *Regulated Rivers: Research and Management* 2, 221–32.

Sherratt, A. 1980. Water, soil and seasonality in early cereal cultivation. *World Archaeology* 11, 313–30.

Shipman, P. 1981. *Life History of a Fossil: An Introduction to Taphonomy and Palaeoecology.* Harvard University Press, Cambridge, Mass.

Shotton, F. W. 1978. Archaeological inferences from the study of alluvium in the lower Severn–Avon valleys. In S. Limbrey and I. G. Evans (eds.), *Man's Effect on the Landscape: The Lowland Zone.* Council for British Archaeology Research Report 21, 27–32.

Shotton, F. W. and Coope, G. R. 1983. Exposures of the Power House terrace of the river Stour at Wilden, Worcestershire. *Proceedings of the Geological Association* 94, 33–44.

Shotton, F. W. and Osborne, P. 1986. Faunal content of debris left by an exceptional flood of the Cuttle Brook at Temple Balsall Nature Reserve. *Proceedings of the Coventry Natural History Society* 10, 359–63.

Siddiqui, Q. A. 1971. The palaeoecology of non-marine ostracoda from Fladbury, Worcestershire and Isleworth, Middlesex. In H. J. Oertli (ed.), *Paléoécologie Ostracodes.* Bulletin de Centre Recherches de Pau- SNPA, 5 supplement, 331–9.

Simmons, I., Dimbleby, G. W. and Grigson, C. 1981. The Mesolithic. In I. Simmons and M. Tooley (eds.), *The Environment in British Prehistory.* Duckworth, London, 82–124.

Simola, H. 1977. Diatom succession in the formation of annually laminated sediments in Lovojarvi, a small eutrophicated lake. *Annales Botanica Fennica* 14, 143–8.

Singer, R., Wymer, J. J., Gladfelter, B. G. and Wolff, R. 1973. Excavation of the Clactonian industry at the golf course, Clacton-on-Sea, Essex. *Proceedings of the Prehistoric Society* 39, 6–74.

Sioli, H. 1975. Tropical river: the Amazon. In B. A. Whitton (ed.), *River Ecology*. Blackwell, Oxford, 461–91.

Sklash, M. G. and Farvolden, R. N. 1979. The role of groundwater in storm runoff. *Journal of Hydrology* 43, 45–65.

Slovic, P. *et al.* 1974. Decision processes, rationality and adjustment to natural hazards. In G. F. White (ed.), *Natural Hazards: Local, National, Global*. Oxford University Press, New York, 187–205.

Smith, A. G. 1981. The Neolithic. In I. G. Simmons and M. J. Tooley (eds.), *The Environment in British Prehistory*. Duckworth, London, 125–209.

1984. Newferry and the Boreal–Atlantic transition. *New Phytologist* 98, 35–55.

Smith, A. G. and Cloutman, E. W. 1988. Reconstruction of Holocene vegetation history in three dimensions at Waun-Fignen-Felen, an upland site in Wales. *Philosophical Transactions of the Royal Society of London*, Series B 322, 159–219.

Smith, A. G. and Pilcher, J. R. 1973. Radiocarbon dates and vegetation history of the British Isles. *New Phytologist* 72, 903–14.

Smith, A. G., Whittle, A., Cloutman, E. and Morgan, L. A. 1989. Mesolithic and Neolithic activity and environmental impact on the south-east Fen-edge in Cambridgeshire. *Proceedings of the Prehistoric Society* 55, 207–49.

Smith, B. D. 1978. *Mississippian Settlement Patterns*. Academic Press, New York.

Smith, D. G. and Smith, N. D. 1980. Sedimentation in anastomosing river systems: examples from alluvial valleys near Banff, Alberta. *Journal of Sedimentary Petrology* 50, 157–64.

Smith, L. P. and Stockton, C. W. 1981. Reconstructed stream flow for the Salt and Verde rivers from tree-ring data. *Water Resources Bulletin* 17, 939–47.

Smith, W. S. 1974. Industrial archaeology in the Dick Brook valley. In B. H. Adlam (ed.), *Worcester and Its Region*. Geographical Association, Worcester, 118–26.

Sparks, B. W. 1961. The ecological interpretation of Quaternary non-marine mollusca. *Proceedings of the Linnaean Society* 172, 71–80.

Stanley, D. J. and Maldonaldo, A. 1979. Nile cone: Late Quaternary stratigraphy and sediment dispersal. *Nature* 266, 129–35.

Starkel, L. 1991a. Characteristics of the temperate zone and fluvial palaeohydrology. In L. Starkel, K. J. Gregory and J. B. Thornes (eds.), *Temperate Palaeohydrology*. Wiley, Chichester, 3–12.

1991b. The Vistula valley: a case study for Central Europe. In L. Starkel, K. J. Gregory and J. B. Thornes (eds.), *Temperate Palaeohydrology*. Wiley, Chichester, 171–88.

Starkel, L. (ed.) 1981. The evolution of the Wisloka valley near Debica during the late Glacial and Holocene. *Folia Quaternaria* 53, 1–91.

Starkel, L., Gregory, K. J. and Thornes, J. B. 1991. *Temperate Palaeohydrology*. Wiley, Chichester.

Stein, J. K. 1983. Earthworm activity: a source of potential disturbance of archaeological sediments. *American Antiquity* 48, 277–89.

Stene, L. P. 1980. Observations on lateral and overbank deposition – evidence from Holocene terraces, southwestern Alberta. *Geology* 8, 314–17.

Steponaitis, V. P. 1978. Location theory and complex chiefdoms: a Mississippian example. In B. D. Smith (ed.), *Mississippian Settlement Patterns*. Academic Press, New York, 417–54.

Stevens, M. A., Simons, D. B. and Schumm, S. A. 1975. Man-induced changes of middle

Mississippi river. *Journal of the Waterways, Harbors and Coastal Engineering Division* May 1975, 119–33.

Steward, J. H. 1929. Irrigation without agriculture. *Papers of the Michigan Academy of Science, Arts and Letters* 12, 149–56.

Stolk, A., Hogervorst, J. J. and Berendsen, H. J. A. 1989. Correcting C-14 histograms for the non-linearity of the radiocarbon time scale. *Radiocarbon* 31, 169–78.

Stolk, A., Törnqvist, T. E., Hekhuis, K. P. V., Berendsen, H. J. A. and van der Plicht, J. 1994. *Radiocarbon* 36, 1–10.

Strautz, W. 1963. Auelehmbildung und -gliederung im Weser- und Leinetal mit vergleichenden Zeitbestimmungen aus dem Flussgebiet der Elbe. *Landespflege* 1, 273–314.

Street-Perrott, F. A., Marchand, D. S., Roberts, N. and Harrison, S. P. 1989. *Global Lake-level Variations from 18,000 to 0 Years Ago: A Palaeoclimatic Analysis.* US Department of Energy Report TR046, Springfield, Va.

Strehlow, T. 1947. *Aranda Traditions.* Melbourne University Press, Victoria.

Stuart, A. J. 1976. The history of the mammal fauna during the Ipswichian/last interglacial in England. *Philosophical Transactions of the Royal Society* B276, 221–50.

Stuiver, M. and Pearson, G. W. 1986. High-precision calibration of the radiocarbon time-scale, AD 1950–500 BC. *Radiocarbon* 28, 805–38.

Suess, H. E. 1970. Bristlecone-pine calibration of the radiocarbon time-scale 5,000 BC to the present. In I. U. Olsson (ed.), *Radiocarbon Variations and Absolute Chronology.* Wiley, New York and London, 303–11.

Suttles, W. 1962. Variation in habitat and culture on the Northwest Coast. *Proceedings of the 34th International Congress of Americanists*, Vienna, 1960, 522–37.

   1968. Coping with abundance: subsistence on the northwest coast. In R. B. Lee and I. Devore (eds.), *Man the Hunter.* Aldine Publication Co., New York, 56–68.

Swale, E. M. F. 1969. Phytoplankton in two English rivers. *Journal of Ecology* 57, 1–23.

Szabo, B. J. and Collins, D. 1975. Ages of fossil bones from British interglacial sites. *Nature* 254, 680–2.

Tauber, H. 1965. Differential pollen dispersal and the interpretation of pollen diagrams. *Danmarks Geologiska Undersogelse* 2, 89, 1–69.

Taylor, G. and Woodyer, K. D. 1978. Bank deposition in suspended-load streams. In A. D. Miall (ed.), *Fluvial Sedimentology.* Memoirs of the Canadian Society of Petroleum Geologists 5, 257–75.

Taylor, R. E. and Meighan, C. W. 1978. *Chronologies in New World Archaeology.* Academic Press, New York.

Thesiger, W. 1967. *The Marsh Arabs.* Penguin, Harmondsworth.

Thorne, C. R. and Zevenbergen, L. W. 1985. Estimating mean velocity in mountain rivers. *Journal of Hydraulic Engineering, American Society of Civil Engineers* 111, 612–24.

Thornes, J. B. and Gilman, A. 1983. Potential and actual erosion around archaeological sites in south-east Spain. *Catena Supplement* 4, 91–113.

Tinsley, H. M. 1981. The Bronze Age. In I. Simmons and M. Tooley (eds.), *The Environment in British Prehistory.* Duckworth, London, 210–49.

Tolonen, K. 1986. Rhizopod analysis. In B. E. Berglund (ed.), *Handbook of Holocene Palaeoecology and Palaeohydrology.* Wiley, Chichester, 645–66.

Törnqvist, T. 1993. *Fluvial Sedimentary Geology and Chronology of the Holocene Rhine–Meuse Delta, The Netherlands.* University of Utrecht, Utrecht.

Trigger, B. G. 1970. The cultural ecology of Christian Nubia. In A. Bengers (ed.), *Kunst und Geschichte Nubiens in Christlicher Zeit.* Recklinghausen, Germany, 346–79.

Trimble, S. W. 1981. Changes in sediment storage in the Coon Creek basin, Driftless Area, Wisconsin, 1853 to 1975. *Science* 214, 181–3.

1983. A sediment budget for Coon Creek basin in the driftless area, Wisconsin, 1853–1977. *American Journal of Science* 283, 454–74.

Trimble, S. W. and Lund, S. 1982. *Soil Conservation and the Reduction of Erosion and Sedimentation in the Coon Creek Basin.* United States Geological Survey Professional Paper 1234.

Troels-Smith, J. 1955. Characterisation of unconsolidated sediments. *Danmarks Geologiska Undersogelse* 4R, 3, 10.

1960. Ivy, misletoe and elm. Climatic indicators–fodder plants. *Danmarks Geologiska Undersogelse* 4, 1–3.

Tubbs, C. R. 1978. An ecological appraisal of the Itchen valley flood-plain. *Proceedings of the Hampshire Field Club and Archaeological Society* 34, 5–22.

Tucker, M. 1982. *The Field Description of Sedimentary Rocks.* Geological Society of London Handbook, London.

Turner, C. and West, R. G. 1968. The subdivision and zonation of interglacial periods. *Eiszeitalter und Gegenwart* 19, 93–101.

Turner, C. G. 1983. Dental evidence for the peopling of the Americas. In R. Shutler (ed.), *Early Man in the New World.* Sage Publications, Beverly Hills, 147–158.

Twain, M. 1883. *Life on the Mississippi* 1904 edn, Harper, New York.

Twigg, H. M. 1959. Freshwater studies in the Shropshire Union Canal. *Field Studies* 1, 1–27.

van Andel, T. H., Jacobsen, T. W., Jolly, J. B. and Lianos, N. 1986. Late Quaternary history of the coastal zone near Francthi cave, southern Argolid, Greece. *Journal of Field Archaeology*, 7, 389–402.

van Andel, T. H., Runnels, C. N. and Pope, K. O. 1986. Five thousand years of land use and abuse in the southern Argolid, Greece. *Hesperia* 55, 103–28.

van Andel, T. H., Zangger, E. and Demitrack, A. 1990. Land use and soil erosion in prehistoric and historical Greece. *Journal of Field Archaeology* 17, 379–96.

Van Brant, A. 1984. *Fish Catching Methods of the World.* London.

Van Cleve, K. and Viereck, L. A. 1981. Forest succession in relation to nutrient cycling in the Boreal forest of Alaska. In D. C. West, H. H. Shugart and D. B. Botkin (eds.), *Forests and Succession: Concepts and Application.* Springer-Verlag, New York, 188–201.

Vandenberghe, J. 1987. Changing fluvial processes in a small lowland valley at the end of the Weichselian pleniglacial and during the Late Glacial. In V. Gardiner (ed.), *International Geomorphology '86*, Part I, Proceedings of the International Geomorphology Congress, Manchester. Wiley, Chichester, 731–44

Vandenberghe, J. and Van Huissteden, J. 1989. The Weichselian stratigraphy of the Twente region, eastern Netherlands. In J. Rose and P. Schlücter (eds.), *Quaternary Type Sections: Imagination or Reality.* Quaternary Research Association, Cambridge, 93–9.

Vandenberghe, J. and de Smedt, P. 1979. Palaeomorphology in the eastern Scheldt basin (Central Belgium). *Catena* 6, 73–105.

Vandenberghe, J., Bohncke, S., Lammers, W. and Zilverberg, L. 1986. Geomorphology and palaeoecology of the Mark valley (southern Netherlands): geomorphological valley development during the Weichselian and Holocene. *Boreas* 16, 55–67.

Van der Leeuw, S. E. 1989. Risk, perception, innovation. In S. E. Van der Leeuw and R. Torrence (eds.), *What's New: A Closer Look at the Process of Innovation.* Unwin Hyman, London, 300–29.

Van der Valk, A. G. 1981. Succession in wetlands: a Gleasonian approach. *Ecology* 62, 688–96.

Van Geel, B. 1986. Applications of fungal and algal remains and other microfossils in palynological studies. In B. E. Berglund (ed.), *Handbook of Holocene Palaeoecology and Palaeohydrology.* Wiley, Chichester, 497–506.

Van Huissteden, J., Van Der Valk, L. and Vandenberghe, J. 1986. Geomorphological evolution of a lowland valley system during the Weichselian. *Earth Surface Processes and Landforms* 11, 207–16.

Van Leeuwaarden, W. and Janssen, C. R. 1987. Differences between valley and upland vegetation development in eastern Noord-Brabant, the Netherlands, during the late Glacial and early Holocene. *Review of Palaeobotany and Palynology* 52, 179–204.

Vannote, R. L., Minshall, G. W., Cummins, K. W., Sedell, J. R. and Cushing, C. E. 1980. The river continuum concept. *Canadian Journal of Fisheries and Aquatic Science* 37, 130–7.

Varallyay, G. 1968. Salt accumulation processes in the Hungarian Danube valley. *9th International Congress Soil Science Transactions* 1, 371–80.

Vepraskas, M. J. and Bouma, J. 1976. Model experiments on mottle formation simulating field conditions. *Geoderma* 15, 217–30.

Vilkuna, J. 1987. Prehistoric paddles from Finland. *News Warp* 3, 32–4.

Vince, J. 1987. *Discovering Watermills.* Fifth edition, Shire Publications, Aylesbury.

Vita-Finzi, C. 1963. Carbon-14 dating of medieval alluvium in Libya. *Nature* 198, 880.

   1969. *The Mediterranean Valleys: Geological Changes in Historical Times.* Cambridge University Press, Cambridge.

   1973. *Recent Earth History.* Macmillan, London.

   1976. Diachronism in Old World alluvial sequences. *Nature* 263, 218–19.

Vita-Finzi, C. and Judson, S. 1964. Recent deposition and erosion in valleys of the Mediterranean basin. *Geological Society of America Special Paper* 76, 172–3.

Wacher, J. S. 1969. Excavations at Brough-on-Humber 1958–1961. *Society of Antiquarians Research Report* 25, 76–81.

Wagstaff, J. M. 1981. Buried assumptions: some problems in the interpretation of the 'Younger Fill' raised by recent data from Greece. *Journal of Archaeological Science* 8, 247–64.

Walker, D. 1970. Direction and rate in some British post-glacial hydroseres. In D. Walker and R. G. West (eds.), *Studies in the Vegetational History of the British Isles.* Cambridge University Press, Cambridge, 117–39.

Walker, I. R. and Paterson, C. G. 1985. Efficient separation of subfossil Chironomidae from lake sediments. *Hydrobiologia* 122, 189–92.

Walker, L. R. and Chapin, F. S. 1986. Physiological controls over seedling growth in primary succession on an Alaskan floodplain. *Ecology* 67, 1508–23.

Walker, L. R., Zasada, J. C. and Chapin, F. S. 1986. The role of life history processes in primary succession on an Alaskan floodplain. *Ecology* 67, 1243–53.

Walker, P. H. and Coventry, R. J. 1976. Soil profile development in some alluvial deposits of eastern New South Wales. *Australian Journal of Soil Research* 14, 305–17.

Waller, M. 1994. Flandrian environmental change in Fenland. *East Anglian Archaeology* Report 70, Cambridgeshire Archaeology Committee/Cambridgeshire County Council.

Waller, R. S. and Shaw, T. L. 1970. Drainage and flooding in the Gloucester region. *Civil Engineering and Public Works Review* 65, 368–9.

Walling, D. E., Quine, T. A., and He, Q. 1992. Investigating contemporary rates of floodplain sedimentation. In G. E. Petts and P. Carling (eds.), *Lowland Floodplain Rivers: A Geomorphological Perspective.* Wiley, Chichester, 165–84.

Walling, D. E. and Webb, B. 1983. Patterns of sediment yield. In K. J. Gregory (ed.), *Background to Palaeohydrology.* Wiley, Chichester, 69–100.

   1986. Solutes in river systems. In S. T. Trudgill (ed.), *Solute Processes.* Wiley, Chichester, 261–93.

Wallis Budge, E. A. 1926 [republished 1977]. *The Dwellers of the Nile.* Dover Publications, New York.

Ward, R. 1978. *Floods: A Geographical Perspective.* Macmillan, London.

Ward-Perkins, B., Mills, N., Gadd, D. and Delano-Smith, C. 1986. Luni and the Ager Lunensis:

the rise and fall of a Roman town and its territory. *Papers of the British School at Rome* 54, 81–146.

Ward-Perkins, J. 1962. Etruscan towns, Roman roads and medieval villages. *The Geographical Journal* 128, 389–405.

Warner, R. F. (ed.) 1988. *Fluvial Geomorphology of Australia*, Academic Press, Australia.

Wasylikowa, K. 1986. Analysis of fossil fruits and seeds. In B. E. Berglund (ed.), *Handbook of Holocene Palaeoecology and Palaeohydrology*. Wiley, Chichester, 571–90.

Waters B. 1949. *Severn Stream*. Dent, Gloucester.

Waters, M. R. 1985. Late Quaternary alluvial stratigraphy of Whitewater Draw, Arizona: implications for regional correlation of fluvial deposits in the American Southwest. *Geology* 13, 705–8.

1986a. Sulphur Springs woman: an early human skeleton from southeastern Arizona. *American Antiquity* 51, 361–5.

1986b. The Sulphur Spring stage and its place in New World prehistory. *Quaternary Research* 25, 251–6.

1988. Holocene alluvial geology of the San Xavier reach of the Santa Cruz river, Arizona. *Geological Society of America Bulletin* 100, 479–91.

Waters, M. R. and Field, J. F. 1986. Geomorphic analysis of Hohokam settlement patterns on alluvial fans along the western flank of the Tortolita mountains, Arizona. *Geoarchaeology* 1, 329–45.

Waton, P. 1982. Pollen diagrams from Dorset. In M. Bell and S. Limbrey (eds.), *Archaeological Aspects of Woodland Ecology*. British Archaeological Reports International Series, Oxford, 146, 93–105.

Watson, W. 1827. *An Historical Account of the Ancient Town and Port of Wisbech*. Privately published.

Watts, W. A. 1978. Plant macrofossils and Quaternary palaeoecology. In D. Walker and J. C. Guppy (eds.), *Biology and Quaternary Environments*. Australian Academy of Science, Canberra, 53–68.

Weast, R. C. 1976. *CRC Handbook of Chemistry and Physics*. 57th edition, CRC Press, Cleveland, Ohio.

Webb, T. 1980. The reconstruction of climatic sequences from botanical data. *Journal of Interdisciplinary History* 10, 749–72.

Weihaupt, J. G. 1977. Morphometric definitions and classificatios of oxbow lakes, Yukon river basin, Alaska. *Water Resources Research* 13, 195–6.

Wendland, W. M. and Bryson, R. A. 1974. Dating climatic episodes of the Holocene. *Quaternary Research* 4, 9–24.

Whalen, N. B. 1971. Cochise culture sites in the central San Pedro Drainage Basin, Arizona. PhD thesis, University of Arizona.

Wharton, C. H., Kitchens, W. M., Pendleton, E. C. and Sipe, T. W. 1982. The ecology of bottomland hardwood swamps of the southeast: a community profile. In J. R. Clark and J. Benforado (eds.), *Wetlands of the Bottomland Hardwood Forests*. Elsevier, Amsterdam, 87–100.

Wheeler, A. 1972. The origin and distribution of the freshwater fishes of the British Isles. *Journal of Biogeography* 4, 1–24.

Wheeler, E. A. 1986. *Computer-Aided Wood Identification: Reference Manual*. North Carolina State University, North Carolina.

Whetton, P., Adamson, D. and Williams, M. 1990. Rainfall and riverflow variability in Africa, Australia and eastern Asia linked to El Niño – Southern Oscillation event. *Geological Society of Australia Symposium Proceedings* 1, 71–82.

Whitaker, W. 1889. The Geology of London and Part of the Thames Valley. *Memoir of the Geological Survey*, London.

White, A. 1979. *Antiquities from the River Witham.* Lincolnshire Museums Archaeology Series 11–14, Lincolnshire County Council.

White, J. 1985.The Gearagh woodland, Co. Cork, *Irish Naturalists Journal* 21, 377–424.

Williams, E. L. 1846. Account of the works constructed for improving the navigation of the river Severn with their effect in discharging the floodwaters. *Minutes of the Proceedings of the Institute of Engineers* 4, 361–71.

  1860. Account of the works recently constructed upon the river Severn, at the Upper Lode near Tewkesbury. *Minutes of the Proceedings of the Institute of Civil Engineers* 19, 527–45.

Williams, G. J. 1968. The buried channel and superficial deposits of the lower Usk and their correlation with similar features in the lower Severn. *Proceedings of the Geologists Association* 79, 325–48.

Williams, G. P. 1984. Palaeohydrologic equations for rivers: equations and methods. In J. E. Coster and P. J. Fleisher (eds.), *Developments and Applications of Geomorphology.* Springer-Verlag, Berlin, 343–69.

Williams, M. 1971. *The Draining of the Somerset Levels.* Cambridge University Press, Cambridge.

Williams, M. A. J. 1966. Age of alluvial clays in the Western Gezira, Republic of Sudan. *Nature* 211, 270–1.

Williams, M. A. J., Dunkerley, D. L., De Deckker, P., Kershaw, A. P. and Stokes, T. 1993. *Quaternary Environments.* Edward Arnold, London.

Williams, R. 1973. *The Country and the City.* Chatto and Windus, London.

Wills, L. J. 1938. The Pleistocene development of the Severn from Bridgnorth to the sea. *Quarterly Journal of the Geological Society of London* 94, 161–242.

Wittfogel, K. A. 1957. *Oriental Despotism: A Comparative Study of Total Power.* Yale University Press, New Haven.

Wolman, M. G. 1967. A cycle of sedimentation and erosion in urban river channels. *Geografiska Annaler* 49A, 385–95.

Wolman, M. G. and Leopold, L. B. 1957. River floodplains: some observations on their formation. *United States Geological Survey Professional Paper* 282C, 87–107.

Woodman, P. C. 1977. Recent excavations at Newferry, Co. Antrim. *Proceedings of the Prehistoric Society* 43, 155–99.

  1978. The chronology and economy of the Irish Mesolithic: some hypotheses. In P. Mellars (ed.), *The Early Postglacial Settlement of Northern Europe.* Duckworth, London, 18–31.

Woodward, J. (ed.) 1995. *Mediterranean Quaternary River Environments.* A. A. Balkema, Rotterdam.

Wooldridge, S. W. 1938. The glaciation of the London basin and the evolution of the Lower Thames drainage system. *Quarterly Journal of the Geological Society of London* 94, 627–67.

  1957. Some aspects of the physiography of the Thames in relation to the Ice Ages and Early Man. *Proceedings of the Prehistoric Society* 23, 1–19.

Wright, E. V. 1976. *The North Ferry Boats: A Guidebook.* National Maritime Museum, Greenwich.

Wright, H. E. 1971. Retreat of the Laurentide ice sheet from 14,000 to 9,000 years ago. *Quaternary Research* 1, 316–30.

Wright, H. E. and Frey, D. G. 1963. *The Quaternary of the United States.* Princeton University Press, Princeton.

WWF 1985. *Das Auenschutzprojekt des W.W.F.* Rettet die Auen. WWF-Auen-Institut, Rastatt.

Wymer, J. J. 1962. Excavations at the Maglemosan sites at Thatcham, Berkshire, England. *Proceedings of the Prehistoric Society* 13, 329–61.

  1968. *Lower Palaeolithic Archaeology in Britain: As Represented by the Thames Valley.* John Baker, London.

1976. The interpretation of Palaeolithic cultural and faunal material found in Pleistocene sediments. In D. A. Davidson and M. Shackley (eds.), *Geoarchaeology*. Duckworth, London.

1985. *The Palaeolithic Sites of East Anglia*. Geo Books, Norwich.

Wymer, J. J. and Dimblebey, G. W. 1959. Excavations on the Mesolithic site at Thatcham, Berks. *Berkshire Archaeological Journal* 57, 1–33.

Wymer, J. J., Jacobi, R. M. and Rose, J. 1975. Late Devensian and early Flandrian barber points from Sproughton, Suffolk. *Proceedings of the Prehistoric Society* 41, 235–41.

Yang, E. 1972. Unit stream power and sediment transport. *Journal of the Hydraulics Division, American Society of Civil Engineers* 98, 1805–26.

Young, R. W. 1983. The tempo of geomorphological change: evidence from southeastern Australia. *Journal of Geology* 91, 221–30.

Young, R. W. and Nanson, G. C. 1982. Terrace formation in the Illawarra region of New South Wales. *Australian Geographer* 15, 212–19.

Zeuner, F. E. 1945. *The Pleistocene Period: Its Climate, Chronology and Faunal Succession*. Royal Society Publications 130, London.

SUBJECT INDEX

INDEX OF RIVERS AND
ARCHAEOLOGICAL SITES